# DYLAN THOMAS

*Some passages have been revised, and new material has been added, since the original edition.*

PAUL FERRIS

# DYLAN THOMAS

## A Biography

PARAGON HOUSE
NEW YORK

First Paragon House edition, 1989

Published in the United States by
Paragon House Publishers
90 Fifth Avenue
New York, NY 10011



Originally published in Great Britain by Hodder & Stoughton, and in the United States by The Dial Press.

Library of Congress Cataloging-in-Publication Data

Ferris, Paul, 1929–
Dylan Thomas / by Paul Ferris. — 1st pbk. ed.
p cm.
Reprint. Originally published: New York : Dial Press, c1977.
Bibliography: p.
Includes index.
ISBN 1-557-78215-6
1. Thomas, Dylan, 1914–1953—Biography. 2. Poets, Welsh—20th century—Biography. I. Title.
[PR6039.H52Z637 1989]
821′.912—dc19
[B] 88-30125
CIP

Manufactured in the United States of America

*For Marjorie Moreton*

# Contents

# ILLUSTRATIONS



## Acknowledgments

1. The British Library Newspaper and *South Wales Evening Post*; 2. British Tourist Authority; 3. Gwen Watkins; 4. Nell Trick; 5. Glyn Jones; 6. Alfred Janes; 7. Nicolette Devas; 8. Radio Times Hulton Picture Library; 9. Kenneth Scowen; 10. Mark S. Murray Threipland; 11. John Brinnin; 12. Elizabeth Reitell; 13. Humanities Research Centre, the University of Texas at Austin; 14. Amos Vogel.

# *Acknowledgements*

THE Trustees for the Copyrights of Dylan Thomas have helped me considerably, both with permission to print unpublished material, and with general information and advice. All three – the late David Higham, Stuart Thomas and Wynford Vaughan-Thomas – knew Dylan Thomas, and understood the problems of trying to write about him. David Higham, who was his literary agent, also let me see the office files relating to Thomas; Dent, his publishers, were similarly helpful.

Dylan Thomas's widow, Caitlin, who read this book when it was first published, thought there was 'not enough emphasis on the booze, not only at the last but from the first: it ate up all our money and all our lives'. I'm grateful to Mrs Thomas for this and other assistance.

Dylan Thomas's daughter, Aeronwy Thomas-Ellis, has talked to me at length. So have many others. For interviews, correspondence and other assistance my thanks are due to the following:

Dannie Abse, Leo Abse, Jerome Agel, William Alfred, Gladys Laugharne-Allen, Edgar Anstey.

Mary Ellin Barrett, Lyn Bartlett, Vernon Bartlett, Eric Barton, John Bennett, Roger Bierne, Tom Blackburn, Oswell Blakeston, Thomas E. Blantz, Samuel N. Bogorad, J. McG. Bottkol, John Malcolm Brinnin, Marianne Brock, Cleanth Brooks, D. J. R. Bruckner, Louis J. Budd, Marie Burke, Gray Burr.

Max Chapman, Waldo Clarke, Douglas Cleverdon, Nest Cleverdon, Brenda Cole, Leslie Cole, Mrs B. J. Connors, Gwendolyn Courtney, Fred Cowley, Mrs Gardner Cox, Raymond Coxon, Armour Craig.

David Daiches, Elizabeth Daniels, Aneirin Talfan Davies, Mrs Emlyn Davies, J. Davies, Ken Davies, Lorraine Davies, Mary Davies, Gwevril Dawkins, Peter De Vries, Nicolette Devas, Francis Dillon, Armel Diverres, John F. Dowd.

Anne C. Edmonds, J. Griffith-Edwards, Addie Elliott, Mrs Albert Evans, Gwynfor Evans, Will Evans, Joe Everingham, Gavin Ewart.

David Farmer, Ronnie Farr, Mrs Pat Feltenstein, Charles Fisher, Constantine FitzGibbon, Roy Fuller.

K. C. Gay, Don Gifford, Brendan Gill, Sir William Glock, Mark Goulden, Malcolm Graham, Ruby Graham, W. Greville-Griffiths, Geoffrey Grigson, Bernard Gutteridge.

Leonard Hamilton, Jack Heliker, Ian Henderson, Nigel Henderson, Wyn Henderson, Bill Henry, Rayner Heppenstall, Barbara Holdridge, Irene Howell, David M. Hughes, Mr and Mrs Eric Hughes, Bruce Hunter, Noel Husbands.

Fred Janes, Mary Janes, Marjorie Jarrett, Graham Curtis Jenkins, Edgar Johnson, C. B. Jones, Evelyn Burman Jones, Francis Jones, Glyn Jones, Kitty Jones, R. M. Jones.

J. R. K. Kantor, P. J. Kavanagh, Evelyn Kirkpatrick, Seymour Klein.

James Laughlin, Theodosia Legg, Mervyn Levy, Annie Lewis, E. Glyn Lewis, Mrs Mansell Lewis, Jack Lindsay, Cordelia Locke, Harry Locke, George Long, David Lougée, T. D. Lucy, Elisabeth Lutyens.

E. F. McInerny, Charles McKelvie, Rollie McKenna, Charles W. Mann, Marianne Mantell, David Markson, Lord Marley, Arthur Calder-Marshall, William H. Matchett, Roland Mathias, Ossie Mayo, Samuel Middlebrook, Raymond Mitchell, Frank Morley, Royston Morley, Howard Moss, B. W. Murphy.

Judith Neal, Jack Nener, Geoffrey Nicholson, Gwen Nobbs.

John Ormond, Hettie Owen, Ruth Wynn Owen.

Denys Parsons, Norman Holmes Pearson, Hugh Porteus, Anthony Powell, H. A. Prescott, Cecil Price, John Prichard, Bill Pritchard, Cyril Pritchard, Doris Probert, John Pudney, Marshall Pugh.

Bill Read, Jan Read, George Reavey, Gertrude Reed, David Rees, J. R. Rees, Alastair Reid, Ben Reid, D. V. Rhydderch, Keidrych Rhys, Peggy Richards, Alan Road, Ann E. Robinson, Bill Rogers, Rutherford D. Rogers, Ethel Ross.

Jacob Schwarz, William Scott, Harvey Shapiro, Rupert Shephard, Rose Slivka, Elizabeth Smith (formerly Reitell), Janet Adam Smith, R. D. Smith, Lady Snow, Stephen Spender, Frances Steloff, Anthony Storr, Ernest A. Strathmann, John Sundell, Lola L. Szladits.

Haydn Taylor, Margaret Taylor, Saundra Taylor, David J. Thomas, Eve Thomas, Kent Thompson, Mark Murray Threipland, Molly Murray Threipland, John Thurgar, William York Tindall, Nell Trick, Ronald Tritton.

Barry Ulanov.

Edward Vasta, Vernon Venable, Peter Viereck, Amos Vogel.

Sybil Walters, Armitage Watkins, Gwen Watkins, Ray B. West, Jr, Antonia White, Emlyn Williams, Emrys Williams, Gordon Williams, J. Morgan Williams, Mary Ann Williams, Oscar Williams, Tudor Williams, W. G. Willis, Dorothy Wilson, Garff B. Wilson, T. R. Wiseman, Ralph Wishart, Basil Wright.

Stan Yonge.

A few names have been deliberately omitted to avoid embarrassment. I am sorry if anyone has been left out by mistake.

For permission to see and make use of material, I am grateful to the Humanities Research Centre of the University of Texas at Austin; the Lockwood Memorial Library, State University of New York, Buffalo; the Houghton Library of Harvard University; the New York Public Library; the Lilly Library, Indiana University; the National Library of Wales; the British Museum; the B.B.C. Written Archives Centre; Swansea University College; Swansea Public Library (as it used to be called), and Llanelli Public Library. The University of London Library let me use their facilities for borrowing and reading microfilm. The head of the *Observer* Research Department, Valerie Ferguson, dealt patiently with some odd inquiries.

The author and publisher are grateful to the following for permission to use copyright material:

The Trustees for the Copyrights of the late Dylan Thomas for extracts from unpublished poems and prose;

J. M. Dent and Sons Ltd, and the Trustees for the Copyrights of the late Dylan Thomas for extracts from *The Life of Dylan Thomas* by Constantine FitzGibbon, *Selected Letters of Dylan Thomas*, ed. Constantine FitzGibbon, Thomas's *Collected Poems*, *Dylan Thomas: The Poems*, ed. Daniel Jones, *Dylan Thomas: Early Prose Writings*, ed. Walford Davies, and *Poet in the Making*, ed. Ralph Maud;

J. M. Dent and Sons Ltd, Faber and Faber Ltd and the Trustees for the Copyrights of the late Dylan Thomas for extracts from *Letters to Vernon Watkins*, ed. Vernon Watkins;

Dr Daniel Jones for extracts from unpublished poems written jointly with Dylan Thomas;

Mrs Gwen Watkins for extracts from 'Notes on Dylan Thomas' by Vernon Watkins.

The following books have also been quoted:

*Dylan Thomas in America* by John Malcolm Brinnin (Dent, 1956),

*Closing Times* by Dan Davin (O.U.P., 1975), *Two Flamboyant Fathers* by Nicolette Devas (Collins, 1966), *The Magical Dilemma of Victor Neuberg* by Jean Overton Fuller (W. H. Allen, 1965), *Here at the New Yorker* by Brendan Gill (Random House, 1976), *The Party's Over Now. Reminiscences of the Fifties* by John Gruen (Viking Press), *Four Absentees* by Rayner Heppenstall (Barrie & Rockliff), *Augustus John.* Vol. II: *The Years of Experience* by Michael Holroyd (Heinemann, 1975), *Important to Me. Personalia* by Pamela Hansford Johnson (Macmillan, 1974), *The Dragon Has Two Tongues* by Glyn Jones (Dent, 1968), *Meetings with Poets* by Jack Lindsay (Muller, 1968), *A Goldfish Bowl* by Elisabeth Lutyens (Cassell, 1972), *Memoirs of the Forties* by J. Maclaren-Ross (Alan Ross, 1965), *The Days of Dylan Thomas* by Bill Read (Weidenfeld, 1964), *Selected Letters* by Edith Sitwell (Macmillan, 1970), *Dylan Thomas: The Legend and the Poet*, ed. E. W. Tedlock (Heinemann, 1960), *Leftover Life to Kill* (Putnam, 1957), and *Not Quite Posthumous Letters to My Daughter* (Putnam, 1963) by Caitlin Thomas, *A Reader's Guide to Dylan Thomas* by William York Tindall (Thames & Hudson, 1962), *Dylan Thomas: 'Dog among the Fairies'* by Henry Treece (Lindsay Drummond, 1949).

Material has also been used from the following:
The *South Wales Evening Post*, the *Western Mail*, *The Reporter* (Mary Ellin Barrett) and Caedmon Records.

# *Introduction*

I HAVE tried to understand Dylan Thomas as a figure who, despite an air of fraudulence at times, was truly obsessed with his vocation as a poet: a tormented, exaggerated man, often his own worst enemy, in whom others may recognize their own experiences both of happiness and of defeat. My private reason for wanting to write about him is that I was born in a suburb of Swansea, fifteen years after Thomas and a mile from his house. The fence of the newly-built lunatic asylum that 'leers down the valley like a fool' in one of his notebook poems was at the end of the garden, its hooked nails pointing both ways, and I would wake, terrified, at the voices of madmen in my dreams. I was twelve before I heard of Dylan Thomas, when I read 'The Peaches' in a wartime paperback. But in the Grammar School we soon became Thomas fans and imagined some lingering presence in the place.

When I came to look for fresh material about his life, I found far more than I could reasonably have expected. Much of it – in Texas, Indiana and other archives, mainly American – has not been referred to by anyone, let alone incorporated in a narrative. Extensive B.B.C. archive material has also become available. As far as completed stories and poems by Thomas are concerned, the barrel has been fairly thoroughly scraped. But for a biographer there was an untapped hoard of worksheets, doggerel verse, lecture notes and miscellaneous jottings in notebooks and on scraps of paper. There are many unpublished letters. Some were available for the *Selected Letters* but for various reasons were not used. Others have come to light since. Not all this material is yet in the hands of collectors; letters and fragments can still be unearthed.

So much has been written about Thomas in the last quarter of a century that any claim to have produced fresh material needs to be as specific as possible. The sources of information are listed, page by page, in the Notes (which also contain material that for one reason or another – usually because it was too detailed – is not in the main narrative). Where the Notes identify the source of papers as a manuscript collection (e.g. Texas or B.B.C. Archives), or an individual, it means that the material is hitherto unpublished. In this category come, for example, Thomas's letters (reproduced in part or in full) to: Sundry radio and TV producers, pp. 172, 183/381, 233–4, 244, 280, 285, 408; Richard Church, p. 146; Clement Davenport, pp. 184–5; John Davenport, pp. 167, 173–4, 176, 235, 245, 249, 279; Pennar Davies, p. 171/378; J. M. Dent & Co., p. 214; T. S. Eliot, p. 285; 'Ellen', p. 309; Charles Fisher, p. 224; 'Francis', p. 388; C. Gordon Glover, pp. 19, 236–7; Geoffrey Grigson, pp. 136–7; David Higham, pp. 231, 234; Marged Howard-Stepney, p. 291; Daniel Jones, pp. 51–3, 131–2; Mimi K. Josephson, p. 322; James Laughlin, p. 222; Peter Lunn Ltd, p. 207; 'Mr Miles', p. 116; John Ormond (Thomas), pp. 238, 389; Ruth Wynn Owen, pp. 196, 384; Laurence Pollinger, p. 179; George Reavey, p. 167; Keidrych Rhys, p. 177; Edith Sitwell, pp. 137–8, 372; Stephen Spender, pp. 179, 180; Donald Taylor, p. 386; Haydn and Nancy Taylor, pp. 135, 159–60; Margaret Taylor, pp. 222, 224, 225, 245, 249, 259, 275, 293; D. J. Thomas and Florence Thomas, pp. 156–8, 176–7; Llewelyn Thomas, p. 320; Oscar Williams, pp. 292, 315; Ruth Witt-Diamant, pp. 269, 293. There is also a letter to Vernon Watkins (pp. 206–7) which has been reproduced only in a Welsh magazine.

Among the other unpublished ms and documentary material, it may be worth mentioning that it includes a fair amount of verse by Thomas – ranging from scraps of doggerel and scatological limericks, to juvenilia, a shaky translation from the German, and even some mature work. As a quick guide, this extremely mixed bag can be found on pp. 3, 38, 39, 48–9, 94, 139, 189, 204–5, 290, 291–2, 323, 324, 349, 350, 366, 368, 370, 372–3, 384. Brief extracts from film scripts by Thomas are on pp. 191 and 192.

A group of letters written by his sister Nancy to her fiancé,

Haydn Taylor, in 1932 and 1933, which Mr Taylor came across in 1976, casts light on the quarrelsome Thomas household in Cwmdonkin Drive: the domestic backcloth to *18 Poems.* Among other papers used for the first time are medical documents relating to Thomas's death in New York: a death he probably wished upon himself, although it is likely that the tragedy was finally set in train by an ill-advised drug injection.

Interviews with about two hundred people have produced much information (as with the written material, it can usually be identified as such by reference to the Notes). If he had lived, Dylan Thomas would have been sixty-four in October 1978. Many of his contemporaries are thus still available; although his fondness for those older than himself tends to shorten the odds among close friends. The fact that Thomas was notorious from an early age has advantages and disadvantages. People had reason to remember things about him (and to keep his letters); but stories change in the telling, and because he was a chronic liar himself, there is an ample supply of tall tales. I have cross-checked where possible and either weeded out the less probable stories or printed them with reservations.

*Swansea and London* PAUL FERRIS
*1974–7*

'I am man's reply to every question,
His aim and destination.'

'Deary me I'd rather be a poet anyday and live on guile and beer.'

DYLAN THOMAS

CHAPTER ONE

# *Names from the Past*

THE Boat House at Laugharne on the South Wales coast is built into the side of a cliff, and seems a suitable property for a poet. In Dylan Thomas's time the wooden verandah that juts over the rocks and shelly mud of the estuary was patched with tin. Now it has been repaired for the summer tourists. An educational trust that runs a private school in Swansea, forty miles away by road, bought the house from the poet's widow in 1974, paying eight times what it cost in 1949, when Mrs Margaret Taylor, Thomas's most consistent benefactor, obtained it for the family. She rented it to them; they didn't own it in Thomas's lifetime. They owned remarkably little – a minimal amount of cheap furniture, an old bicycle or two, enough clothes to be decent. Poets are not supposed to be breadwinners, as Thomas had already decided when he was a schoolboy. The ravens would feed them–'soft, white silly ravens', he used to say. The method worked, after a fashion. Dylan Thomas made begging into a cottage industry in the last years of his life, despite not inconsiderable earnings. Few if any contemporary British poets were as prosperous on paper, although at the same time he managed to be perpetually poor. Drink helped to make the money go, but his poverty was more complicated than that. The Thomases spent money on ordinary, bourgeois things. They had a son at boarding school in England. Thomas belonged to a gentlemen's West End club. He liked a good cigar and went to a private dentist. Taxis were his normal way of moving about London. In Laugharne the Williams family, who ran the local transport (and much else), did a brisk trade in hired cars as the poet came and went.

Things in real life were not quite as the legend has them. But then, the Thomas legend has acquired a reality of its own. An age that ignores poets as popular figures discovered Dylan Thomas and made him into a cult, perhaps because his poetry and his life went to extremes in a way that people could recognize. He was an answer to the machine; his poems contain few images drawn from the twentieth century. The legend made him a token figure. It was encouraged, indeed it was originally created, by Thomas, with its trappings of poverty and wickedness; and no one could say that a lifetime of wanting a persona so badly was not real enough. In the end, the poet who was determined from adolescence to act like a poet, even if it killed him, had the last laugh: he did write boldly, he did make readers and listeners catch their breath. He was taken at his own valuation.

At high tide the sea comes up close to the Boat House, and the estuary, a complicated affair of sands and channels where three rivers meet, becomes part of Carmarthen Bay. Fifteen miles away to the south-east is the flat sea-serpent line of Worms Head, a promontory at the tip of Gower, the oblong peninsula that breaks the coast between Carmarthen Bay and industrial Wales to the east. Laugharne has no industry, apart from farming, fishing and Dylan Thomas, but busloads of men go to work daily at a Government testing ground for rockets and shells just along the coast. The fishing boats and occasional yachts that slide up and down the long forks of water keep clear of the sandy point to the south that marks the end of the range. Thuds like thick doors being slammed occur at intervals. Thomas would have heard them from his desk. But the juxtaposition of herons on the mudflats and weaponry on the sand-dunes didn't appeal to him as material for poems.

He lived in Laugharne for four and a half years before his death in November 1953, writing only six complete poems in that time. Sea-birds and sea-vistas creep into some of them. His subject was still himself, as it had always been, but in those last years he filled the background with scenes and creatures from nature, celebrating the world but seeing death in the living – 'Now curlew cry me down to kiss the mouths of their dust'. One of his vantage points was the window of his work-hut behind the house, higher up the cliffs. It had once been a bicycle shed.

Much of his radio play, *Under Milk Wood*, was written there, too, although it was pressure from the Americans, who wanted it for stage performance first, that made him finish it, not long before he died among them. He was not a happy man by that time. He was drunk less often and less extravagantly in Laugharne than in London and New York, but life plagued him wherever he went. His wife Caitlin said he was rehashing his adolescence, one of her many accurate barbs. He had gout and trouble with income tax. Time slipped through his fingers; he never seemed to get to grips with anything. He must have spent long hours in the shed not doing very much, not always sober, in between the times when he was painfully assembling 'Lament' and 'Poem on his birthday'. Some of his worksheets that were scooped from floors or out of cupboards after his death, and later sold for good money to American collectors,[1] are covered with doggerel verses and lists of debts ('Milk £25, Butcher £25, Post Office £67 ...'). There are some self-pitying verses that begin as a letter to 'Dear Marged', a rich Welshwoman who was another of his benefactors:

> And Money is the dunghill King
> And his royal nark is the dun . . .

The back of the work-hut opens on to the cliff walk, and visitors see it before they reach the path leading down to the Boat House. A plaque on the door says in olde-worlde script: 'In this building Dylan Thomas wrote many of his famous works, seeking inspiration from the panoramic view of the estuary.' There is a grain of truth in the suggestion that a view helped him to write. Much of Thomas's real work was done on high ground, looking down on things: usually the sea, usually in Wales.

The places he lived in during a restless life would make the

1. The bulk of Thomas's manuscripts are at the Humanities Research Centre of the University of Texas at Austin, which has acquired material both piecemeal and in quantity from private collectors. The index of the Thomas collection covers more than six hundred file cards; the material, in boxes and bound volumes, occupies many shelves. It is referred to throughout as 'Texas'.

bones of a thesis for a scholar who wants a change from interpreting the more obscure Thomas poems. He never owned a house or a flat: they were all rented, borrowed or camped in. Before the Boat House, Thomas and family were in an Oxfordshire village, South Leigh, for a year and a half. Before that they lived in a damp summerhouse at the end of a garden in Oxford as the guests of A. J. P. Taylor, the historian, and his wife Margaret. (It was she who bought the house in South Leigh, and after it the Boat House.) This post-war period was barren; in three years he wrote only one poem, during a visit to Italy. He was in the wrong places. Like many writers he drew energy from a location, even though he scorned it at times; West Wales, imprinted on him as a child, was the place that consistently provoked him to write, and his rude remarks about it were irrelevant to what he felt at a different level. This is not to say that absence from Wales was the root of his problems. But it is a fact that nearly all his poems were written there. The last period in which he wrote intensively over a short period, faintly echoing the frenzy of his adolescence, was the year from mid-1944 to mid-1945. He was based in Wales all that time, with intermittent trips to London. At first he stayed in another part of Carmarthenshire, at a place called Blaen Cwm ('the end of the valley'), a pair of stone cottages by a stream running down to the River Towy, owned by his mother's family, who can still be found living on the small farms and buried in the big churchyards of the district. Fernhill, the farm where he used to go for summer holidays as a child, was only a mile away, although the aunt who lived there had died years before.

Thomas had been writing poems at Blaen Cwm since he was a teenager, when he thought it was dismally wet and Welsh. ('I can smell the river and hear the beastly little brook that goes gingle-gingle past this room,' he wrote to Pamela Hansford Johnson when he was nineteen.) At least one of his early published poems, 'My hero bares his nerves', was written there when he was eighteen. Some authorities think it a poem about masturbation. (Its last line, 'He pulls the chain, the cistern moves', presents difficulties to scholars who are reluctant to admit they are reading about a lavatory.) Eleven years later, at

Blaen Cwm again in 1944, he made the simpler statements of 'Poem in October' –

> It was my thirtieth year to heaven
> Woke to my hearing from harbour and neighbour wood

– and provided anthologists with one of their favourite pieces of straightforward Thomas.

From Blaen Cwm the family moved in the autumn of 1944 to New Quay, on the Cardiganshire coast, and lived in a bungalow on the cliffs, rented from a doctor. This was the site of a shooting incident, when the bungalow with Thomas in it was machine-gunned late one night by a drunken Army officer. Television researchers call there occasionally, when someone is making a programme about Thomas, and look in vain for bullet scars in the walls. The lawn ends abruptly; steps go down to the beach below. The steep-streeted village of New Quay is a mile away across the water, and the broad eye of Cardigan Bay fills the scene, with the Snowdon range of mountains sitting like clouds on the horizon to the north. On the grounds of output, the bungalow deserves a plaque of its own. Among the poems written there were 'The Conversation of Prayer', 'A Winter's Tale' and 'A Refusal to Mourn the Death, by Fire, of a Child in London'. In all, that year supplied eleven of the ninety poems in *Collected Poems*. The last of them was 'Fern Hill' (Thomas wrote it as two words), which drew the loudest applause from his American audiences a few years later – a poem about lost childhoods that ended a phase of his life.

Going back in time, the middle years of the war, when Thomas lived mainly in and around London, produced no serious verse at all. Early in the war he wrote eight or nine poems, most of them in Wales, either at Laugharne – not in the Boat House – or at a house on the outskirts of Swansea where his parents were living. The only time in his life when he performed steadily as a poet without having a Welsh view from the window was between his marriage in 1937 and the first year of the war, 1940, when he and his wife spent long periods at her mother's house in the South of England because they could not afford to go elsewhere. Over three years, ten or eleven of the

*Collected Poems* were written there. During those years he was busy cannibalizing his notebooks of adolescent poems, and several of the ten or eleven owe something to earlier versions.

Most important of all is the period before Thomas left Swansea in 1934, aged twenty, for 'smoky London paved with poems'. It was not a sharp break, since from 1934 until the next turning point, his marriage, he was out of London more than he was in it, as often as not back in Swansea: the gritty seaside town where he felt safe. More than thirty, probably more than forty, of the ninety *Collected Poems* in their final or near-final versions, as well as others that provided skeletons to go back to later, come from this enclosed world of adolescence that was an end in itself; he never wrote like that again.

The house where he lived with his parents is semi-detached, which means there is room to squeeze past one side of it into a square of back garden. A plaque on the front wall, provided by the city council, gives the name and dates, 1914–1953, for pilgrims who trudge up the hill via the lower reaches of the suburb, the Uplands. A tall man standing in the garden can see the humps of the Mumbles Head, enclosing Swansea Bay on the west, and a strip of sea between the chimney-pots of the street below. From bedroom windows at front and back upstairs, there are views of docks, sea and untidy town, and, in one direction, distant trees and commonland where the suburbs dissolve into Gower. Dylan Thomas's bedroom was small and poorly lit. A hot-water tank rumbled inside a cupboard. Presumably he did some of his writing there, and some of it downstairs in his father's study, a schoolmaster's den full of books; the door has an ancient piece of stained glass in it that may have been there since the house was built in 1914, just before Thomas was born.

In some ways the places are immaterial. His poems of adolescence, or of the last bitter days of his maturity, read no better as poems because of a connection with a provincial villa or a cliff in Laugharne. But a place helps to fix a poem in the mind. No. 5, Cwmdonkin Drive, Swansea, with its over-fond mother and disappointed father, seems just the place for a raw-nerved boy like Thomas to incubate his private germs.

In an autobiographical story written after he left Swansea, 'The Fight', Thomas described his 'bedroom by the boiler', and left a clue for the observant. He wrote: 'A poem I had had printed in the "Wales Day by Day" column of the *Western Mail* was pasted on the mirror to make me blush, but the shame of the poem had died. Across the poem I had written, with a stolen quill and in flourishes: "Homer Nods".' Under the title of 'His Requiem', it was his second poem to appear in print (a previous piece was published in the school magazine), and the first to earn money.

The date was January 1927; he was twelve years old, and the *Western Mail*, a Cardiff paper on sale throughout Wales, was a natural target for an ambitious schoolboy. The poem he sent them was the kind that newspapers used to print in more genteel days. It was about a man who died unmourned, except for a linnet he once fed:

> Nobody cared a bit, folks said,
> When the wicked old man at the gate lay dead . . .

Thomas's delighted parents kept the ten-shilling cheque without cashing it, as a souvenir. Years after Thomas was dead, someone discovered that 'His Requiem' wasn't Thomas's at all: he had copied it from an issue of the *Boy's Own Paper* of four years earlier. It was the poem that was stolen, not the quill. Whatever lesson one draws from that, and from a further attempt at plagiarism a couple of years later in the school magazine, it suggests how badly Dylan Thomas wanted to be a poet, and how uncertain he was of his talent.

The Thomas family was the result of a common enough process, people growing away from a rural background into the life of cities. In Wales, which is a country that the twentieth century has done its best to turn into a region of Britain, the process was often more complicated and more painful, because it meant shifting from the Welsh language to English, and exchanging one culture for another. A century ago, before the onset of modern Welsh nationalism, this was not generally regarded as a betrayal: rather, it was commonsense.

Dylan Thomas's father, David John Thomas, was part of this flight from the national past. He came from a rural family, first identifiable in the shape of William and Ann Thomas, who were married and living at Brechfa, in North Carmarthenshire, by the early 1830s. Among their children was Evan. By the 1870s Evan was married (to another Ann), with his home at Johnstown, then a village on the edge of Carmarthen town. Among Evan's children was David John, the father of Dylan, who was born at Johnstown in 1876.

Even for Evan Thomas's generation, the drift to new ways had begun. Evan worked for the Great Western Railway, and was known locally as 'Thomas the Guard'. A job on the railway, for a villager who was steady and reliable enough to find one, was a way of bettering oneself without leaving the district. Anglicized Swansea, thirty miles away down the line, where the red furnace-light shone on the clouds at night, was a different world; people who went there to live didn't come back. Carmarthen was a market town, with a deep hinterland of dairy farms, sheep-walks and smallholdings to the north, south and west. The railway passed through the countryside, Welsh-speaking and chapel-going, without changing it.

Evan Thomas the Guard had a brother, William ('Gwilym' in the Welsh form), who was a clergyman and a poet; he was a figure of some importance, although to have a poet in the family was nothing unusual at that time and place. Poetry was nearer the surface than in a comparable English community. The 'Celtic imagination', a tired phrase but a useful one to describe a streak of temperament with its roots in prehistory, makes much of ghosts, gods, dreams and the natural scene – rocks and forest, birds and horses, the weather and the sea. Is there meaning behind these things? It is the child's question, greeted in silence. But at least the things become more real and more accessible when they are seen through a poet's eye, and are treated accordingly. Words, it seems, are more important than deeds. The Welsh are not men of action. When they are caricatured – as they have been, often enough, by the English and by the Welsh themselves – they appear as over-excited people with sing-song voices who wave their arms about and never stop talking except to burst into a hymn. They have, in the contemptuous phrase of practical men, the gift of the gab. The Welsh have also a lingering reputation for being sly and devious, perhaps because of their earlier status as a conquered people, defeated centuries ago but never absorbed: inbred, suspicious, living on their wits, whiling away the time with private songs and memories behind the stone wall of their language. Altogether an odd collection, with poets on all sides – a farm labourer or a miner or a quarryman, writing verses in fearsome metrical patterns for a knowledgeable audience that expects him to be a craftsman, chiselling away at the language. In the correct idiom, a writer who composes an englyn, a complex verse-form, is said to 'chip' it, as a sculptor chips a stone. What the poet says may be less important than the way he says it.

In Evan Thomas's generation – that is, the generation before D. J. Thomas, who was to be Dylan's father – brother William or Gwilym was a figure of importance. He was born in 1834, and brought up by an aunt and uncle in a strict religious atmosphere in a Carmarthenshire village. In his youth he was a cobbler. He went to the theological college in Carmarthen, then on to Glasgow University, and returned home in 1860 as a Unitarian minister. He also kept a school, and wrote extensively as a radical, advocating social reform. His poetry is said to be mystical rather than religious, though not particularly distinguished. The *Dictionary of Welsh Biography* (which lists about twenty William Thomases, several of them poets) describes him as 'minister, social reformer, writer and schoolmaster', in that order. But he had a 'bardic' name, which is something between a pseudonym and a courtesy title, calling himself Gwilym Marles after a stream, the Marlais, that ran out of the hills near his birthplace. His reputation (and the reason that biographical details survive for him and not for Evan and a third brother) is largely due to his rôle as an activist on behalf of tenants against landowners. He and his congregation were evicted from their chapel by the local landowner, and he enjoyed brief fame as a preacher-politician, dying at the age of forty-five, in 1879. He was the family's claim to distinction. D. J. Thomas, his nephew, was to give Gwilym's bardic name to Dylan and Dylan's sister,

Nancy. Gwilym's life and character sound remote from those of Dylan Thomas. But his presence may have reached through to his great-nephew via D. J. Thomas, who cared deeply about the poet's vocation and was proud of the ancestral bard.

Meanwhile, Gwilym's brother, Evan the Guard, and his wife Ann were bringing up their family. The son who was to be Dylan Thomas's father was born in 1876, three years before his Uncle Gwilym died. He was one of at least four children, with two brothers and a sister. His forenames, David John, were (and still are) a favourite combination in Wales, which has thousands of David John Thomases. He grew up as 'Jack' Thomas, a poor boy with brains, he used to say later. He was ambitious, though it's not clear for what; he had a clever tongue, took care of his appearance and held a good opinion of himself. His character was aloof and fastidious, and in later years many people called him a snob, though not to his face; his temper was respected. It must have been this backbone of angry dignity that his son grieved to see breaking long after, when he wrote 'Do not go gentle into that good night'. In the draft notes for another poem to his father, the 'Elegy' that he left unfinished, Dylan Thomas wrote: 'His mother said that as a baby he never cried; nor did he, as an old man.'

Whatever feelings of pride he carried in himself, Jack Thomas was unable, as a boy with brains but no money, to avoid doing the inevitable thing for someone of his talents and background. Thomas the Guard was determined his son should be a schoolmaster. He resisted at first, but succumbed in the end, probably by easy stages. For a year, in Carmarthen, he was a pupil-teacher. Welsh was still regarded as no language to use when educating young Victorians of the British Empire, although a movement to reinstate it began in the 1880s. 'Welsh Wales' is still a world that many ambitious boys want to escape from; when D. J. Thomas was a teenager, it was more circumscribed than it is now. He took the natural course, escaping from the language, at least, by going to the University College of Wales at Aberystwyth, and specializing in English, history and education. Given his talents, he might have escaped altogether. He was able to go to Aberystwyth, in 1895, because he won a scholarship; four years later he graduated with a first-class honours degree in English. According to Florence, his wife, he was offered a travelling fellowship. If this was his chance, he missed it. He became a schoolmaster in South Wales, and grew to be an unhappy man. Mrs Thomas, elaborating her tale, said he declined the fellowship because he was 'tired'. She was not always a reliable witness; and the university has no record of offering D. J. Thomas any award. Perhaps she was reflecting some other disappointment when she said that 'he was sorry afterwards, of course'. He was undoubtedly a man with regrets. They put an edge on his tongue. He despised many of his colleagues, resented the fact that important academic appointments in Swansea went to those he considered his inferiors, and left behind the memory of a sardonic provincial schoolmaster who was his own worst enemy. There are stories that he had written poetry (presumably in English) as a young man, even that it was published in local papers; Dylan Thomas once told this to the poet Ruthven Todd, adding that D.J. was bitterly disappointed at its reception. D.J. cultivated the air of a man who deserved better things. Some of those who knew the family are still half convinced that he graduated from Oxford University; or that, having gone to Oxford, he had to leave because his parents could not afford to keep him there. In these local memories there survives a trace of D.J.'s regrets.

There are local memories of another matter, closely related. It seems that D. J. Thomas, the young schoolmaster with prospects, was forced to marry in a hurry. Perhaps this is why he was 'sorry afterwards'. Mrs Addie Elliott, who worked for the family as a girl, and who came from St Thomas, the same working-class district of Swansea as Florence, says that 'they definitely had to get married. We all knew in St Thomas.' It is generally agreed that Jack and Florence had little in common; when their children were growing up, she could still aggravate him over the tea-table with chatter about clothes or children that he considered foolish, making him lose his temper and leave the room in an uproar, with Florence in tears. But as a young woman she was attractive: small, round-eyed and vivacious, a deacon's daughter who believed in enjoying herself.

Her family name was Williams. They, too, were from Carmarthenshire, where the family was thick on the ground between the villages of Llanybri and Llangain, four or five miles south-west of Carmarthen town. The family is difficult to trace, not least because Williams is such a common name in Wales,[2] and these particular Williamses had little to distinguish them, unlike the Thomases with their bard, Gwilym Marles. But they were a close-knit family, with (in retrospect) a slightly sinister air of inbred lives spent in primitive places, that was to creep into Dylan Thomas's childhood, perhaps into his life. His obsession with horrors in general no doubt sprang from his obsession with the horrors of the flesh – his own flesh – but they were fed and may have been shaped by the spirits of his maternal ancestors, the 'undeniably mad unpossessed peasantry of the inbred crooked county', as he once called them. Thomas's real subject was to be the tormented landscape of himself. But there is a parallel, imagined landscape of West Wales – haunted, ingrowing, ill-fated – that seeps into some of his prose, and is now and then on the edge of his poems. For this he can thank the Williamses.

Florence's mother, Anna, was a Williams, and so was her father, George. George and Anna were probably first cousins. Intermarriage was a recognized way of keeping farms and money in the family, but at the same time there was always the fear of promoting a strain of insanity. Traces of this fear among the Williamses a century ago can still be heard in conversations, and must have been heard by Dylan Thomas.

George and Anna were both born in or very close to 1840. George was a son of Waunfwlchan, a small farm near the road that runs beside the River Towy from Carmarthen to Llanstephan; it is just behind the cottages at Blaen Cwm. Anna seems to have come from a larger farm a mile away, Pen-y-Coed. Among close relatives of George and Anna (they may

2. A handful of surnames serves much of the population. Welsh society, more clannish and isolated than England's, made do with Christian names until comparatively recent times. Eventually John became Jones, William became Williams and so on. After the ubiquitous Jones, the commonest Welsh surnames are probably Thomas and Davies.

have been her siblings) were two, a man and a woman, with a reputation as heavy drinkers. The best-remembered in the area is Daniel – 'Dr Dan', because he often needed to see a doctor. Dr Dan, a bachelor, once worked in a big store in Swansea or London, or both. He is remembered for chronic chest trouble ('weak chests' were later to be an obsession with Florence), said to have been aggravated by dust produced by 'ripping the calico in the shop'. The skeleton in Dan's cupboard was drink. According to an ancient anecdote, 'The doctor told him to get a bottle of whisky and rub it in his bad leg, but he drank the whisky and rubbed the bottle in instead.'

George and Anna were to rear seven children, of whom Florence was the youngest. One of the sons, Bob, was 'not quite the round shilling', as the Welsh say, a mental defective of sorts. There are hints of another child who was mentally unstable, thus confirming the family's worst fears about inbreeding. The mystery is too distant to unravel. A gravestone at Capel Newydd, in Llanybri, where many of the Williamses are buried, records the death of an eighth child of George and Anna – David George, in 1892, aged eighteen. No one remembers anything about him, though, even in this district of long memories.

George Williams, like Evan Thomas of Johnstown, worked on the railway. But he took the plunge and went to Swansea. It was there, in St Thomas, on the east side of the town, that he and Anna brought up their family in the latter part of the nineteenth century. Their close links with Carmarthenshire remained, and were still strong a generation later when Dylan Thomas was a child. But henceforth they were urban people. Anna is still referred to on farms as 'Auntie Anna, Abertawe' – the Welsh name for Swansea.[3]

Like most districts of Swansea, St Thomas is built on a hill, in this case Kilvey, though it covers only the lower slopes. The neighbourhood was in general poor. The town was originally on the west bank of the Tawe. Castle, parish church and harbour were there, and so were the first coal and cargo docks.

3. 'Abertawe' means 'at the mouth of the Tawe', the river on which the town stands. 'Tawe' is pronounced 'Tow-air', like 'plough-air'.

Industry spread to the north of the town, straddling the Tawe up the once-green Swansea Valley. By the last quarter of the nineteenth century, smoke had charred the edges of Kilvey, and rows of terraced houses for workmen were being built there. While middle-class suburban Swansea developed to the west, towards Gower, cheap brick boxes for dockers and tin-plate workers spread to the north and east.

The grandly named Delhi Street, where George Williams lived eventually at No. 29, was a broad avenue leading nowhere, the width of the road making the little houses look all the pokier. But it was the kind of street where front steps were scrubbed and door-knockers polished daily, lived in by families who were on their way up, not down. George rose from porter to inspector. He was made a deacon of Canaan Congregational Church, the usual square stone edifice, around the side of the hill that looks down at the Tawe. The roads peter out at this level. Wind bumps against rock outcrops and low walls chalked with *Jesus loves me*; the district is decaying now, but at the end of the last century it was part of an industrial heartland.

George and his wife shared in the new prosperity. They gave their children a respectable start. Thomas, the eldest, became a clergyman, but later married a woman with money, and was to be seen driving around in a hansom cab, arousing envy. Ann married a farmer, Jim Jones, from the same part of the countryside as her parents – when they were children, the Williamses used to spend holidays on one or other of the farms, and there were regular comings and goings between St Thomas and Carmarthenshire. Jim was a bad farmer: he drank. He and his wife began married life on a smallholding; moved to a larger property at Pentowin, which looks across the estuary to Laugharne; and came to terms with failure a few miles away at Fernhill, which Ann Jones kept going with willpower and a strong pair of hands. This is the 'Gorsehill' of Dylan Thomas's story 'The Peaches', thinly concealed on the random principle that he used in all his autobiographical fiction; Uncle Jim is there undisguised as Jim Jones, and so is Aunt Annie. She was the Ann of 'After the funeral', one of the few poems where Thomas rose to the occasion of a subject other than himself.

Polly, the next sister, was a kindly girl who didn't marry. Then there was Theodosia, or 'Dosie', who bore a favourite name in the family (there are still Theodosias on farms in South Carmarthenshire, distantly related). Dosie did well for herself by marrying a clergyman, the Rev. David Rees. She met him when he 'answered a call', in the chapel phrase, and came to be minister at Canaan, where she played the organ. Rees was a desirable husband, a man with presence, a notable preacher, something of a classical scholar: a figure cut from a favourite Welsh pattern, and someone who was sure to be pained in the unlikely event that he should ever have a nephew who drank like a fish and wrote strong poetry. A few years later he answered another call, to the church of Paraclete, in the Mumbles, then a fishing village and now a western suburb of Swansea, where Dylan Thomas went to stay with his aunt and uncle as a child, and saw religion in action, close to. 'I hate you from your dandruff to your corns,' wrote Dylan, and Uncle David was heard to say that the boy should be in a madhouse.

Some of these aunts and uncles from Florence's side of the family, as well as at least one uncle from D.J.'s side, are the figures of Thomas's Christmas reminiscences who dozed and rumbled in the front parlour at Cwmdonkin Drive while young Thomas looked at his toys and the Useful Books that told him everything about the wasp, except why. There were two further brothers in the St Thomas family, John and Bob. Both worked on the docks, which had now spread to the east bank of the river, either as stevedores or coal trimmers. Eventually John seems to have owned a small cargo-handling business and to have built up a modest capital, probably not more than a few thousand pounds, but sufficient in those days to set him apart. His house was in Bay View, better placed than Delhi Street below – 'John was the senior one, he lived higher up the mountain', they still recall in draughty Carmarthenshire farmhouses, although John has been dead for more than sixty years. Altogether he owned three houses in St Thomas, and according to his daughter – another Theodosia – he once lent a brother two thousand pounds. It was John's money and gifts in kind, going either direct or funnelled via the kind-hearted Polly, that helped sustain his sister Florence's family in Cwmdonkin Drive, on the other, more pretentious, side of town, when they were in one of their financial pickles. John made himself unpopular among the Williamses by marrying a Swansea girl when he was aged about forty. They saw the houses and bank balances fade away, and there was much bad feeling.

When John died a few years later – not long before the First World War – brother Bob inherited enough to keep him in comfort. He was the simple one, shy and slow-witted, who could be seen shuffling over the bridge from St Thomas with a shopping bag, wearing an overcoat green with age that came down to his ankles. In the end he went to earth in the cottages at Blaen Cwm with his sister Polly to look after him, where he outlived all his brothers and sisters. Relatives at a farm along the lane, Llwyn Gwyn, brought him up to the house during his last illness, and he died there. The family Bible records: 'W. R. Williams (Bob) died September 17, 1962, aged 85.' The day I was there, in 1975, an ancient wooden cradle, heavy with linen, was airing in front of an open coal fire. A daughter was due back from hospital with her new baby during the afternoon. They were going to call it Dylan.

Finally, there was Florence, the youngest child of George and Anna Williams, born in 1882, when her mother was in her early forties. She was nineteen years younger than her eldest sister, Ann. Being the baby of the family, fussed over by grown-up brothers and sisters, may have helped make her sparkle; she was livelier than the others. She attended two schools, and when she first knew D. J. Thomas, was employed as a seamstress at a local drapery store. The date of their meeting isn't known; it may have been only a short time before they were married, at the end of 1903. One Swansea story is that D.J., by this time resigned to school-mastering, saw her at the fashionable Congregational church in Castle Street, where they were later married. But this sounds like a genteel version, describing what ought to happen to a deacon's daughter, and what did happen to sister Dosie. D.J. was no chapel-goer in later years, though it's conceivable that he behaved differently when he was a young man, and chapel was a social occasion.

Florence's account to Ethel Ross, a younger friend with whom she stayed towards the end of her life, sounds the true one. They met one weekend at a fair in Johnstown, she said, and her new sweetheart asked to see her outside the shop in Swansea on Monday evening. Probably both had been spending the weekend with their respective families, Florence on one of the farms, perhaps Fernhill with sister Ann, and Jack with his parents at Poplar Cottage, where Thomas the Guard brought up his family. In a photograph taken, probably at Poplar Cottage, a few years later, D.J. is still good-looking and youthful. His thinning hair is carefully brushed over the baldness. He is clean-shaven, in contrast to his two brothers, who are heavily moustached, and his father, whose face is barely visible between the patriarchal white beard and tall-crowned hat. They all look content to belong to the old-fashioned world they live in, except D.J.

Jack and Florence were married on 30 December 1903, and the child was born some time the following year. Reputedly it was stillborn or died within a few days; at the time there was no legal obligation to register such births, and no record of it can be traced. They had set up home in Sketty, a village to the west of Swansea that was already turning into a suburb. The small terraced house in Sketty Avenue, near a pond and a junction of muddy roads, would have been as good an address as D.J. could have afforded. Perhaps, too, it was conveniently remote from prying eyes. Children conceived out of wedlock were common enough, certainly in country districts; when she was old and gossipy, Florence used to tell gleeful yarns about (significantly) incest and other goings-on in Carmarthenshire. But her parents could hardly have been indifferent.

For a few years the Thomases stayed in Sketty. There was a dairy farm just behind the house, and the shops of the old village, down the hill, weren't far away. The Grammar School, an undistinguished group of buildings on a hill in the town, was less than two miles distant, not far for a man who enjoyed walking, as D.J. did; and the new electric trams already came part of the way from Swansea. But by the time the next child was born, a girl, in 1906, they had moved into the town itself, to

Montpellier Street, close to the Grammar School. The midwife who attended Mrs Thomas said that they left Sketty Avenue because it lacked mains drainage, and Florence feared for the health of another child. The baby was christened Nancy Marles, keeping alive the name of D.J.'s poet-uncle, and promptly lived up to Florence's fears by being 'delicate'. Mrs Thomas fussed endlessly about her children's health, always making them iller than they were. Tuberculosis, still rampant at the start of the century, though already on the wane, was her bugbear. Her father died two years after her marriage, in 1905, and she used to tell people that he had T.B. (the death certificate shows pneumonia). Her uneasy regard for the disease was handed on to her son Dylan, who was able to adapt it to his own strange needs, and who fell in readily with her anxieties about wheezy chests, pale cheeks and flushed brows. On the other hand, it is true that Nancy was dead before she was fifty, Dylan before he was forty. The fussy mother may have had something to be fussy about.

Her husband, too, was something of a hypochondriac; perhaps of the kind that fears illness because it can degrade as well as harm. He couldn't bear physical crudities. Later, living in retirement in the cottages at Blaen Cwm, he would go out for the day when the council lorry was due to empty the earth closets at the back. At school, where his tongue was much feared, one of his favourite words of abuse was 'guttersnipe'. He sought perfection in the classroom in a hopeless kind of way, rapping knuckles with a ruler when a boy mispronounced Chaucer, warming to anyone who cared about the language. Stupid boys enraged him, dirty boys revolted him. A boy who was unwise enough to break wind would be told icily to control his bowels. A snigger at a poetic thigh or bosom provoked the full blast of his anger, and the class would be called little swine, unfit to receive the pearls of English literature.

Because he cared about his subject, his standard of teaching was high. He had a reputation for getting boys into Oxford and Cambridge; people still remember that he could predict which poems from the set-books would feature in the Central Welsh Board examinations. He loved to read aloud in clear, rich tones, barely flecked with an accent. It was the style on which his son came to base his own sonorous delivery, that way of reading poems and telling funny stories that some found unforgettable, others fraudulent. When a journalist was writing an article about Dylan Thomas in 1948, he sent a draft for the poet's comments. Back came a letter with a page about D.J., the lonely figure who was so important in Thomas's life. In uncharacteristically quiet style, he wrote: 'His reading aloud of Shakespeare seemed to me, and to nearly every other boy in the school, very grand indeed; all the boys who were with me at school, and who have spoken to me since, agree that it was his reading that made them, for the first time, see that there *was*, after all, *something* in Shakespeare and all this poetry . . .' But for most of the time, D.J. seems to have found it an uphill fight to advance the cause of Virtue and Good Literature, the school motto. The trouble lay in his exacting nature rather than in the school itself, which was probably better than average, in a country where education was taken seriously, and where few boys were sent away to private schools in England. For the doctor and the works manager, as for the shopkeeper and the railway clerk, the Grammar School was the natural place for a son to go.

According to Caitlin, Dylan Thomas's wife, who saw much of her father-in-law over fifteen years, he longed all his life to be the cultivated gentleman as well as the successful man of letters. Perhaps he was fighting against traits in his own nature as well as his provincial surroundings. He had what could have been regarded as weaknesses – sex, possibly, drink, definitely. It is said that he drank to excess when young. He certainly drank enough as a schoolmaster to make people smile. At school there were boys who claimed to be able to tell when he and the classics master, W. S. ('Soapy') Davies, had been to the Mountain Dew for pints of beer in the lunch-hour. 'Soapy' was his only close friend among his colleagues, supposedly because he alone had a good enough degree to win D.J.'s respect. They could be seen drinking in town on Wednesdays, the school half-day. At home, his wife and anyone who happened to be there learnt to look out for the red cheeks, the voluble manner and the flashes of temper. He didn't drink dangerously or wildly; just a little too much to go unnoticed by the neighbours.

In 1914, when Nancy was seven, Florence was pregnant again, and the Thomases decided to move to a bigger house. They chose the Uplands, a busy suburb nearer the town centre than Sketty, and already well populated with prospering citizens. It seems to have been more than the Thomases could afford. They were always short of money. When they were first married, D.J. added to his income by teaching Welsh at evening classes, which must have gone against the grain for a man whose daytime colleagues never heard him speak the language. Mrs Thomas used to pay the tradesmen in rotation: the butcher had to wait for the fishmonger, the fishmonger for the grocer. It was the price of keeping up with the bourgeoisie, a game that both the Thomases played, though his reasons were more complicated than hers. Seen from working-class districts on the other side of the town, such places as St Thomas, this was the hypocrisy of the self-important suburbs – which were not as distant in mood or income as they would have been in an English town with a deeper-rooted middle-class. It made places like Sketty and the Uplands all the more visible as targets for scorn. 'What is sex?' ran a Swansea gibe at the false accents affected by the anglicized suburbs. It was, said the answer, what Sketty people had their coal delivered in.

D.J. must have found the charitable hand-outs that came from Delhi Street painful to receive, always assuming he knew about them. Florence tried to intercept the morning mail so that he wouldn't see bills she had neglected to pay. His salary of four or five hundred pounds a year should have been sufficient, although the beer he drank and the books he accumulated in his study must have eaten into it. But Florence seems not to have been the world's best housekeeper. She was not realistic. Neither was he, for that matter. D.J. withdrew into himself as the marriage progressed. Walled up in his study, marking schoolboy essays or dreaming over Lamb and Coleridge, he didn't want to be bothered with household affairs unless they were forced on his attention. Domestic trivia he found irritating. A colleague remembers him in the staff-room on a Monday morning, complaining that he was worn out after a weekend with his family. 'My God, Williams,' he said, 'these women, they don't half chat.'

And if he was unrealistic because he wanted to shut out his failures, his wife was unrealistic in a simpler and less tormented way. She ignored unpleasantness; she was a romancer. The bills could wait. She liked to be happy. At the end of her life, when she had outlived husband, son, daughter and nearly all her brothers and sisters, the eyes would sharpen in the small face at any hint of a disagreeable inference about Dylan. She doggedly deceived herself about his drinking, his marriage and his general roguery – as most mothers do, perhaps, but on a grander scale. When necessary, she did the same for Nancy. She told Ethel Ross, her Swansea friend, that Nancy's first husband was dead, which was how she came to be married a second time. Miss Ross didn't believe her, but said nothing. Next morning Florence said, 'I told you a fib last night. He isn't dead, but I didn't want to say she'd been divorced. I've always told a white lie for Nancy's sake, and do you know, I've almost come to believe it.'

Both the children followed her in this little weakness. Gwevril Dawkins, a close friend of Nancy, in childhood and after, who remembers her with affection, says that 'like Dylan, she had an amazing imagination. She exaggerated things. Some of the reasons she gave me for leaving her husband were most improbable. I never believed them.' As for Dylan Thomas, his lack of interest in such a boring thing as the truth in everyday affairs is one of the characteristics that made him famous. His embroidered anecdotes and comical letters are one aspect; his evasiveness, duplicity and general dishonesty another. He was a marvellous liar; or, as people who resent the word insist vehemently, 'a romancer'.

The house the Thomases moved to in 1914, that was to be Dylan Thomas's observation post until he was twenty, was brand-new. Cwmdonkin Drive is a steep road, with the Uplands below, and at that time mainly farmland above. Opposite the house, on the same level of the hill, were the uneven grounds of a mansion, later a school, and beyond that again, thick with trees and sunk into a contour of the land, Cwmdonkin Park. The setting is still green and relaxing to the eye. The visitor looks over his shoulder to the smooth metal plate of the bay, bolted to the town. Far away is the north Devonshire coast, on the other side of the Bristol Channel. It remains a genteel address.

The builders were in and out of the house finishing the plastering and doing odd jobs when the Thomases moved in during the early summer. The baby was expected in September, but somebody must have miscalculated. There was time for Florence to engage a living-in maid, a sure sign of pretensions. The war had begun in August and it was not easy to find domestic help. But a friend of Polly in St Thomas had a daughter of eighteen, Addie, who was already 'in service', and she agreed to go to Cwmdonkin Drive at six shillings a week. She was there for a fortnight before the baby arrived, helping with the coal fires, the big coal oven that had to be lighted every day, and eight-year-old Nancy, who inconveniently caught measles. A washerwoman came in on Mondays and worked in the wash-house, a shed in the tiny garden, boiling clothes in the copper for two shillings and sixpence and her meals. The house had more rooms to be kept clean than appears from the outside. Downstairs, a good-sized front room looking out on Cwmdonkin Drive, used mainly on Sundays; a middle room with a separate entrance at the rear, which was D.J.'s study; and a breakfast room and kitchen at the back of the house. Upstairs were four bedrooms: one for the Thomases; one for Nancy; the big one at the front 'for best', in the Welsh way, and thus rarely occupied unless there were visitors; and the tiny boxroom where the maid slept.

The best bedroom was used for the confinement, and the baby was born on 27 October. They had difficulty in finding a name, and it was seven weeks before the birth was registered in the names of Dylan Marlais. 'Marlais' was the river from which D.J.'s uncle took his bardic title, so that both children now had a version of it in their names. 'Dylan' was an obscure figure from the *Mabinogion*, the Welsh medieval prose romances. As a noun the word means 'sea' or 'ocean'. In the *Mabinogion* Dylan makes a brief appearance when Math the son of Mathonwy challenges Aranrhod, who claims to be a virgin, to step over his magic wand. 'A fine boy-child with rich yellow hair' drops from her as she does so. Math son of Mathonwy calls him Dylan, and the child makes for the sea, his natural element.

Presumably this fragment appealed to D.J., who may have known the work in Welsh, or in Lady Charlotte Guest's version of 1849, which he could have bought in the cheap 'Everyman's Library' series from 1906. He was anglicized and yet he was a Welshman. He had opted for English literature, but he remembered the preacher-poet in the family. Was he hoping to bottle up some magic in a name? No doubt he was trying to do better for his son than the 'David John' that his parents had hung around his neck.

Florence, however, raised a practical objection. The orthodox Welsh pronunciation of Dylan is 'Dullan', which has since led to tedious arguments between the Welsh-language purists who want 'Dullan' and Dylan's friends and family who point out that he himself always said 'Dillan'. But this pronunciation, which in the end Thomas had to instruct the Welsh region of the B.B.C. to use when introducing him, came later. D.J., whose Welsh was said to be as impeccable as his English, said 'Dullan'. He must have done, because when he proposed the name (and it was virtually unknown in common use before that), Florence was afraid that people would make fun of the child: 'I didn't know if we were doing right or if they'd be calling him "dull one" before the end. Anyway, like that we left it.'[4] So, by the obscure magic that gives famous people appropriate names, he was labelled 'Dylan', where a 'John' or a 'William' would have been adequate.

4. This account was given to me by Mrs Thomas in 1955. It is only fair to say that she had another version. In an interview with Colin Edwards, recorded at the Boat House in the summer of 1958, she said flatly that the pronunciation was always 'Dillan', not 'Dullan'. But Jean Overton Fuller, who knew Thomas when he was first in London, quoted him on the subject in 1935, when he said that 'in Wales, it's pronounced Dullan', adding that English people called him 'Dillan' in their minds, 'and I think perhaps Dillan sounds more elegant than Dullan.'

CHAPTER TWO

# *His Father's Son*

THE problem for anyone who wishes to chronicle the first fifteen years of Dylan Thomas's life is that the outward episodes were essentially trivial, of the kind common to many childhoods, while inwardly the odd process of becoming a poet was in progress. To some extent this is true of all his thirty-nine years. What happened on the outside was a certain amount of sitting at desks and writing, and a great deal of fantasizing, comical story-telling, horseplay, borrowing, womanizing and drinking. If Thomas the Clown is worth anatomizing (and his official biographer[1] at first refused the invitation to write his life) he must have connections with Thomas the Poet. But Thomas's disorderly style of living makes good copy by itself. He lived, looked and sounded like the popular idea of a poet, with recognizably poetic poems to show for it; and if there were fears and empty spaces in his life, he concealed them with bizarre language and behaviour.

The interior Thomas is another matter – difficult enough to write about at any point, and especially when he was a child. For a few years at the end of his adolescence it becomes easier. From the age of fifteen until he was past nineteen, a series of notebooks preserve about two hundred poems that reflect much of what he felt and thought; and before the notebooks finished he had begun his densely-packed letters to Pamela Hansford Johnson, an autobiography in themselves. But in his earlier years he was merely a child growing up in a town by the sea,

1. Constantine FitzGibbon wrote *The Life of Dylan Thomas* at the request of the Trustees for the Copyrights of Dylan Thomas. It was published in 1965. Previously Ruthven Todd had been approached by the Trustees. Unpublished biographical manuscripts by Todd are at Texas.

about whom things are remembered and inferences can be drawn, at the observer's peril.

He was pretty, he was spoiled, he was the darling of the family. As far as love and attention go, he seems to have lacked nothing. Mrs Thomas used to say stubbornly in later years that she had spoiled both her children, and if she had her time over again, would do the same. It may be that Dylan was especially indulged. There is some evidence that the child who died or who was stillborn in 1904 was a boy. It is plausible to suggest that his mother, brought up against the background of Canaan Chapel and the Carmarthenshire Bible-belt, saw his death as a punishment for her wickedness; and the birth of another son, ten years later, as a sign that she was forgiven. Or she may simply have been a warm and affectionate mother who was instantly seduced by Dylan's angelic features and precocious ways.

All his life Dylan Thomas hankered after the warm beds and mother-love of his childhood. He liked to be looked after, and by the time he was an adult, his skill at extracting attention and sympathy was prodigious (so was his disgust with himself for doing it, sometimes, but this was no deterrent). Many of the anecdotes about his helplessness as an adult concern food and drink, making an obvious connection for psychiatrists who would define Thomas as a child, and then a man, with powerful 'oral traits'. He learned the advantages of demanding to be fed: by his mother, by his wife, by his friends, by the 'silly ravens' with money in their wallets. His mother was still removing the tops of his boiled eggs when he was seventeen. His sister-in-law, Nicolette, having breakfast at the Thomases ten years after that, was surprised to hear him ask his wife to do it. One of his harmless treats was sugared bread and milk, as given to sleepy children, served in bed by his wife when he was unwell or had a hangover. Nicolette says that Caitlin used to take it to the bedroom and lock him in with it: 'He was perfectly all right. But bread and milk is what his mother used to give him.' It even had to be cut neatly into squares, as Florence did it in Cwmdonkin Drive. Robert Pocock, a B.B.C. friend, found him in bed at Laugharne, sitting up with a woollen shawl around his shoulders, stuffing himself with his children's sweets and calling hoarsely to Caitlin for bread and milk.

The safe room with goodies for the little boy cropped up all his life. He would have himself shut up in a room, accompanied by sustenance, to encourage himself to write. Ruthven Todd saw him staying with friends in a London flat in the mid-1930s. At Thomas's request they locked him in a room with two bottles of beer between the times the pubs closed after lunch and opened again in the early evening. A few years later, at his mother-in-law's house in Hampshire, he was working in a locked room with a supply of beer and cigarettes. He is said to have produced a radio script in the same way near the end of his life, secured in the B.B.C. library overnight These stories about locked rooms for writing in were probably exaggerated by Thomas; the night in the library (as opposed to a few hours there) may have been one of his tales. But the fact that he told them showed the way his mind worked.[2]

As a child he received much physical affection. Mrs Thomas liked to kiss and cuddle. After her husband's death, when she was an old lady, she was observed in a big feather bed with one of her grandchildren, a 'naked Cupid', and two giggly country girls who slept there to keep her warm; the four of them cosily wrapped up together. Dylan's cot stood in his parents' bedroom at the back of the house, a common enough practice in families of modest means, though it can set a psychiatrist's teeth on edge. When Dylan cried, which he did often, Addie the maid would be sent for; with D.J. barking, 'Put the little bugger through the window,' she would take him into her own warm bed in the boxroom and cuddle him.

In the opinion of some psychiatrists, such experiences – especially with an imaginative child – can arouse sexual fan-

2. It is unwise to believe too many anecdotes about Thomas; equally unwise to believe none at all. Vague stories that he was locked in an hotel room to write a film script have every sign of being apocryphal. But Leigh Aman, now Lord Marley, who was production manager of *Three Weird Sisters* after the war, says categorically that Thomas spent three weeks virtually locked up on the top floor of the Royal Court Hotel in London, writing the script. Aman sometimes took him his food and limited amounts of drink.

tasies, followed by feelings of guilt and inadequacy. These may produce fears about his body and lead him to lose confidence in his sexual powers, with unfortunate results later in life.[3] That (runs the general argument) may lie behind a fear-ridden immaturity in Thomas, and his need to prove himself masculine with drink and women. His mother's over-indulgence may have had similar effects, helping to produce a passive child and a passive man. Such speculations don't 'explain' a poet but they may throw incidental light. Dylan Thomas's poems, especially the early ones, certainly contain phrases that suggest a preoccupation with subconscious sexual fears, in particular a fear of having his sex organs mutilated. These phrases revolve around images of tailors and scissors. Such images, it has been suggested, stem from *Struwwelpeter*, the illustrated book of children's stories which includes the sinister tale of 'Little Suck-a-Thumb', a child who is punished by having his thumbs sliced off by a grisly tailor with flying hair and enormous scissors, the 'great, long, red-legged scissor-man'. According to Freud, the stories, written by a Frankfurt doctor, succeed precisely because they touch on childhood complexes. Thomas knew the book when he was small, and refers to it in reminiscences of childhood. Various lines of poems – such as the 'scissors stalking, tailor age' of 'When, like a running grave' – can be cited as evidence of how his earliest fears worked their way into the open via the scissor-man. So can some of the early stories, like 'The Mouse and the Woman', which has 'a child who had cut off his double thumb with scissors'.

Women played a large part in Thomas's writing and conversation, but there is an undercurrent of failure. In several published stories they are pursued and lost. Nowhere in print does Thomas describe or even imply an ordinary, successful act of sex. Either it fails to happen or it is part of a nightmare. In another early story, 'A Prospect of the Sea' (first published in 1937), a boy meets and is sexually terrorized by a gipsy-like girl in a torn cotton frock. She has more than a touch of *Struwwel-*

3. An American psychiatrist, B. W. Murphy, has commented at length in *Creation and Destruction: Notes on Dylan Thomas*. This was written without specific knowledge of Thomas's infancy.

*peter*: 'The stain on her lips was blood, not berries; and her nails were not broken but sharpened sideways, ten black scissor-blades ready to snip off his tongue.' In real life it is likely that most of his public overtures to women – typically, at cocktail parties in America – were crude, comical lunges with small chance of success. It is said that his penis was of modest size, another cause of uneasiness. As an adolescent he was obsessed with being 'little': a little person, a little poet.

The case can be extended to explain Thomas's fears of failure as a poet. A number of the early notebook poems ask whether he dares to fly, to move away, to break out. The eventual tragedy of Thomas may have been a loss of nerve that stopped him using his powers and left him creatively impotent. This is a large speculation from a slender base of evidence. In any case, if his early experiences, whatever they were, had unfortunate effects, they were also part of a process that helped produce a poet of Thomas's uniquely morbid self-interest. The one was not available without the other. As he once wrote to the poet Henry Treece in another connection, 'My horrible self . . . would not be itself did it not possess the faults.'

Whatever the influence Florence Thomas and her family had on her son's future life, it was largely accidental. The same is not true of D.J. A clever, disappointed man, he probably hoped for a son who was a more successful edition of himself, with a double first at Oxford – he badly wanted Dylan to go to university – followed by the gilt-edged career that eluded the father. But had it been no more than that, the bond that existed between the two would hardly have been so strong, and certainly not when Dylan was still an adolescent, making a conventional show of rebellion. Dylan Thomas was critical enough, in his youthful letters, of a narrow provincial background and a chattering mother. His father, though, is never censured. To Pamela Hansford Johnson he wrote of D.J.: 'A broader-minded man I have never known.' After she had met his family, she wrote in her diary, 'That fearful D.J. is his best friend!' Dylan respected his father, perhaps because from the child's earliest years, D.J.

encouraged his natural passion for words; he was an authority on the only subject that Dylan cared about.

Thomas the Schoolmaster can hardly have thought rationally that a poet could be constructed out of his own unrealized hopes, however deep-rooted they may once have been. Nor did he take kindly to Dylan's bohemian way of life when his son became a professional poet. Yet behind the rational man, cold-lipped and overbearing, that D.J.'s colleagues at the Grammar School took him for, can be seen the shadow of an obsession. Dylan Thomas once told Ruthven Todd that his father determined his son should be more successful as a poet than he had been himself. That may be a simplified or romanticized version. But there is a story that D.J. was reading him Shakespeare before he could speak. Addie Elliott, who left the Thomases when Dylan was two years old, remembers D.J. reciting poetry to the baby, some of it his own doggerel. Her name then was Addie Drew. So

Poor Addie Drew,
She had the flu,
Then stayed in bed
Until she was dead.

Thomas used to say that the first poems he knew were nursery rhymes – which is true for most people. In written answers to a student who caught him in the right mood in 1951 he said that 'what the words stood for, symbolized, or meant, was of very secondary importance; what mattered was the *sound* of them as I heard them for the first time on the lips of the remote and incomprehensible grown-ups who seemed, for some reason, to be living in my world'. Rhetorical as ever, especially when answering questions about so important a matter as how he came to write poetry, Thomas described 'the colours the words cast on my eyes . . . and though what the words meant was, in its own way, often deliciously funny enough, so much funnier seemed to me, at that almost forgotten time, the shape and shade and size and noise of words as they hummed, strummed, jigged and galloped along. That was the time of innocence;

words burst upon me, unencumbered by trivial or portentous association; words were their springlike selves, fresh with Eden's dew, as they flew out of the air.'

Thomas added the Bible to his list of things that 'first made me love language and want to work *in* it and *for* it'. He had known its 'great stories' from his early youth; 'the great rhythms had rolled over me from the Welsh pulpits; and I read, for myself, from Job and Ecclesiastes; and the story of the New Testament is part of my life'. D. J. Thomas was agnostic, and the Thomases were not a chapel-going family. But D.J. knew his Bible; Addie used to hear him quoting from it. His mother, who visited them from Johnstown, was a strict chapel-goer. It would have been remarkable if Dylan had not been sent to chapel as a formality. Before he was five he was attending Walter Road Congregational Church, near the Uplands, where, as everywhere else at that age, he is remembered as 'looking like an angel'. Whether many sermons thundered over him from pulpits is less certain. Perhaps Uncle David Rees at Paraclete was his model; he is said to have been a popular preacher who could work up a 'hwyl', or religious fervour. But Thomas's experience of powerful sermons very likely came from the angry evangelists he would have heard on Swansea sands, standing on soap-boxes and castigating the lusts of the flesh, when he was a teenager. There are two views about Thomas and religion. One is that he was a 'religious' poet, and his life a movement towards God. The other (which seems to me the only feasible view) is that religion was a stage-prop of his poetry; he used its language and myths, which he had learnt in childhood, without ever absorbing or caring much about its central beliefs. But in either case, plenty of religion was available to him in childhood, and became seeded in his brain, along with nursery rhymes and folk tales.

Outside his home, the first place that mattered to him may have been Cwmdonkin Park, where he was taken when he was a few days old. This was an isolated place with no entrance or frontage on a main road; although it is surrounded by houses, there are people living within half a mile who have never been inside it. Originally a town reservoir was built there, half a century before; then it was turned into a lake in a hillside park. With its air of faint secretiveness, which it retains, it fits nicely into Thomas's tales of a lost, magical boyhood. Addie Elliott took him there almost daily in the pram to hear pigeons make their hollow noises and see the gulls come looking for bread in windy weather. It seems almost too appropriate, considering Thomas's later fantasies about flying, that the first word he spoke was 'bird', but that its what Mrs Elliott remembers.

In his book of more-or-less autobiographical stories, *Portrait of the Artist as a Young Dog*, Thomas wrote about an early visit to Cwmdonkin in 'Patricia, Edith and Arnold'. Edith is the 'servant girl', a successor to Addie. She takes him with her when she and her friend Patricia go to confront their mutual boy-friend, Arnold. It snows, as it frequently does in Thomas's childhood. Nothing escapes his attention, from the 'brown stains' under Edith's arms to the black hairs that show through a tear in Patricia's stocking. He is aged perhaps five or six, a clever, lovable, naughty child who relishes the thought of how spoilt he is; he seems to have shed some of his innocence already, though this may be only the way the story was written, twenty years afterwards. The park became one of Thomas's reference-points, a locked corner of childhood to brood over.

The farm at Fernhill was another place that became fixed in his imagination. About the countryside in general, Thomas always seemed in two minds. He needed to break away from urban life, but he soon tired of rural retreats. It was part of his inability ever to settle anywhere for long. But Fernhill, the green enclave, was not the ordinary countryside. He must have gone there from his earliest years. The farm is on a rise above a wooded valley, shielded from the road by fir trees; on a summer's day the plump little hills nearby are blue and green. The living quarters, slate-roofed, form three sides of a square around a small courtyard, an arrangement that makes the place a trifle more distinguished than its neighbours. It is no longer worked as a farm; electric-power lines crackle in the damp air above the barn and the remains of an orchard. Fernhill is a rare English place-name in the district. In the 1920s, when Ann and Jim Jones scraped a living from it, they kept a few cows, pigs and chickens. The premises were dirty and bedraggled. Ann, eight or nine years older than her husband, did most of the work. She made the butter, then the main produce of many Welsh smallholdings. Her husband's character is still blackened by distant relatives of Ann: 'a terrible man', they say, lazy and hard-drinking. He was known to visit Swansea to borrow money from Bob Williams, his brother-in-law, to pay the rent.

Dylan Thomas gave much the same picture in another of his *Portrait of the Artist* stories, 'The Peaches'. Uncle Jim sells a piglet when he needs money for the pub, and returns drunk after consorting with loose women in Carmarthen, staggering into the lamp-lit kitchen 'like the devil with a red face and a wet nose and trembling, hairy hands'. He still had two years to live when the book was published in 1940, and can hardly have failed to recognize himself, if anyone sent him a copy. Annie, too, is part of this earthy world, so unlike home life at Cwmdonkin Drive. Thomas presents her as warm and kindly, 'a little, brown-skinned, toothless, hunchbacked woman with a cracked, sing-song voice'. She was more than fifty years older than Dylan. In 'The Peaches' he is a Grammar School boy, aged eleven or more. But the story compresses many summer holidays into one. He made it the first story in the book, and it remained one of the two he liked best, a central memory that went on vibrating. In some disjointed manuscript notes, probably made towards the end of his life, Thomas wrote of Fernhill as 'a place with which I have come to associate all the summer of my chil . . . a lovely farm – a lonely farm – and a place with which I have come to associate all the golden – never shone a sun like that old rolling . . .'

In 'The Peaches' Jim and Annie's son Gwilym (in real life it was Idris) is 'aged nearly twenty, with a thin stick of a body and spade-shaped face'. He was born in 1897, making the year 1917, and Dylan Thomas three years old. No doubt his first memories of Idris dated from then. By the time Dylan was old enough for the Grammar School, Idris was nearer thirty. Was it then, or earlier, that Thomas, up a tree, saw his cousin, sitting on the outside lavatory? 'He was reading a book and moving his hands', a vignette that somehow slipped past the publishers in 1940.

Sex is always hovering in the background of these stories. At Fernhill it is part of the raw, exciting strangeness of the place. The run-down family countryside, still living in its past, helped to feed Thomas's love of the macabre. His childhood dreams were thick with ghosts and vampires, but he seems to have taken a perverse pleasure in frightening himself with them. 'The Peaches' includes a demon with 'wings and hooks, who clung like a bat to my hair'. When he arrives at the farm with his uncle, at night, he imagines that 'nothing lived in the hollow house at the end of the yard but two sticks with faces scooped out of turnips'. Curiously, in 'The Peaches' Thomas made scarcely any capital from the fact that, as he knew, the Carmarthen hangman was supposed to have lived in the house, as recently as the end of the nineteenth century. There seems to be some truth in the story, which is still current in the district. But the man, by the name of Evans, was only an assistant executioner, and hanged no one himself. In 'The Peaches' Thomas identifies the hangman's home as a deserted house down the road; probably he wanted to confuse local readers and stop them recognizing Fernhill too easily.

'The Peaches' was based on a true incident, the visit to the farm of a well-to-do friend called Jack Williams from Swansea. Jack's mother, stout and beringed, brings him to stay as a paying guest, arriving in a Daimler. It is for her benefit that Annie, making a pathetic attempt to be polite, brings out the tinned peaches, which, inevitably, Jack's mother declines. Mrs Williams is the epitome of suburbia, the other pole of Thomas's life. She, too, is trying to be something that she is not. Thomas painted an unkind and perhaps inaccurate picture ('she was fitted out like a mayoress or a ship') that was recognized by the original in Swansea when the story appeared. She was really Mrs Bassett, the second wife of a local man of property who at one time was mayor of the town. The family lived at Rosehill, a large house not far from Cwmdonkin Drive, higher up the slope, and Mrs Bassett and Florence Thomas were friendly. Reach-me-down clothes from the Bassett children found their way to Cwmdonkin Drive, another reason for Dylan not to like her. An acquaintance met Mrs Bassett shopping in the Uplands, and the former mayoress told her the dreadful thing that the poet who used to be their neighbour had done to her. 'He must have thought we were dull if we couldn't recognize who it was,' she said, 'but we aren't *that* dull. I shall never forgive him.'

Unfortunately writers are always greedy for material, and Thomas found his bricks and mortar where he could. Mrs Bassett fared badly. Aunt Annie might be pleasantly surprised to find herself in the anthologies as the 'sculptured Ann' who is 'seventy years of stone', in the elegiac 'After the funeral'. That poem was written, in its final form, at a time – not long before he wrote the stories in *Portrait of the Artist* – when Thomas turned briefly towards a cooler, more outward-looking view of life. He was writing compassionately about a real woman in a real place. Seven years after that, when he produced 'Fern Hill', his mood was different again, and the farm was transformed into Eden as regrets and nostalgias gnawed at him. By then aunt and uncle were dead, and Fernhill was left to its owls and nettles. It is a poem without people, occupied only by child, house, countryside and animals.

Dylan must have seen his mother's relatives often, both at Fernhill and during visits to and from the St Thomas clan. His father's family was not so close-knit. One brother, William, lived in London and seems to have been in the drapery business. Another, Arthur, lived a few miles from Swansea at Aberavon, and worked for the Great Western Railway. When Arthur's shift-working allowed, he spent weekends in Cwmdonkin Drive: a dour working-man, crossed in love and unmarried, quite unlike his brother Jack. Arthur, too, used to help the family with money from time to time. Dylan grew up amid a slightly threadbare respectability. At the age of seven he was sent to a private day-school. By this time he was accustomed to having his own way, at least where his mother was concerned. Gwevril Dawkins, who was Nancy's closest friend in Swansea, first knew him at the age of five. She and Nancy used to baby-sit when the Thomases went out. Dylan, she says, was 'an absolute tartar, an appalling boy. I remember him grabbing for oranges. He never asked.'

Mrs Thomas said it was his health that kept him away from

school for so long. She thought he was not strong enough. If it wasn't anaemia it was asthma or a weak chest, unspecific ill-health. The school he finally went to, which was surely her choice, was one of those private establishments that still cater for ambitious parents in suburbs. Jackie Bassett went there. A lady called Mrs Hole ran it at her house in Mirador Crescent, just around the corner from Cwmdonkin Drive, and charged a few pounds a term. It was no more than two rooms for general teaching, with music lessons in the drawing-room upstairs. But it went through the motions of being a school. There was a uniform: cap, tie and blazer in dark red and navy blue. Mornings began with a hymn and a prayer, and a local parson addressed the children once a term. Summoned to test the children in geography, Mr Hole would arrive red in the face and breathing heavily. Evelyn Burman Jones, who was there as a child with Dylan, says her clearest memories of the place are the piano being thumped, the metronome ticking and Mrs Hole shouting for her husband.

The dame school in Mirador Crescent provides the first glimpse from the outside of Dylan Thomas as the person that people loved to indulge. The cherubic face on a thin stalk of a body sent him off to a good start. He was teacher's pet, more often than not to be found occupying the lap of Mrs Hole's daughter, who helped with the teaching. 'Who put water in Joyce's galoshes, every morning prompt as prompt?' he asked in one of his radio reminiscences. Evelyn Jones, a friendly witness who later acted with him in amateur theatricals, says he was impregnable at Mrs Hole's. Once he seized the leg of Evelyn's chair and she flew backwards, knocking an aspidistra off a pedestal; Evelyn took the blame. She recalls that 'he always had a pain in his stomach if there was anything he didn't want to do'. Once he fell in the lane behind the school where the children played, and cut his knee on a piece of glass. He ran home saying that Evelyn had pushed him, and Mrs Thomas came down to the school to complain – 'She worshipped Dylan. They were all scared to death of her.'

Fondly, his mother sent him off each morning wrapped in thick jerseys and plenty of underclothes to keep chills and draughts at bay, even in summer; his adolescent letters often mention vests. He was all shimmering curls and mischief – that word used of attractive children, whose instant appeal is already segregating them for life from their lumpish brethren, who are liable to have it called nastiness. He was the joker; you couldn't help laughing. Term ended with a little play. One Christmas, Dylan was supposed to be a colonel, carrying a cane and reading a newspaper. He poked a hole in the paper and blew orange peel through it at the audience, then rushed about slashing the air with the cane. They brought the curtain down; Mrs Thomas loved it. No doubt people choose to remember early incidents that fit in with later legends. One of Dylan's admirers, a girl called Vera, had a friend who lived in Mirador Crescent. One day the two girls were in the lane behind the school when they were amazed and delighted to see Dylan doing something rude. 'He was shouting, "Look, I can write *God Save the King*," and peeing all over the wall. My friend and I gazed at this in astonishment. All the other little boys were trying to do it, too.' Years later when both families were living in New Quay, it was Vera's soldier husband who arrived outside the Thomas bungalow with a sub-machine gun and sprayed it with bullets, in a muddled sort of way. 'The lane was always the place to tell your secrets,' wrote Thomas, in his radio talk, 'Reminiscences of Childhood', and 'occasionally now I dream that I am turning out of school into the lane of confidences when I say to the boys of my class, "At last, I have a real secret."

' "What is it? What is it?"

' "I can fly."

'And when they do not believe me, I flap my arms and slowly leave the ground . . .'

The day he fell and cut his knee, when Evelyn Jones was blamed, he had been pretending to fly by jumping off the wall of the house. The image of flying recurs into adolescence. Where did he want to fly to? In the radio talk he crosses the docks and 'Inkerman Street, Sebastopol Street, and the street where all the women wear men's caps'. He is above St Thomas. But soon he is back over 'the trees of the everlasting park', and finally 'the yellow seashore, and the stone-chasing dogs, and the old men, and the singing sea'. Perhaps, as Kent Thompson says in his unpublished thesis on 'Dylan Thomas in Swansea', the sea that Thomas flies towards in his imagination is at once life and death. The sea was the most powerful of all symbols for Thomas, rarely absent for long from stories or poems.

To anyone who spends his childhood in that part of Swansea, the sea is inescapable. The low-lying town centre and the older working-class districts give only occasional reminders. But the hilly western suburbs and parks look down roads that point to the bay, where the town comes to a halt against six miles of tidal sands, a watery perimeter that takes in parkland, sports ground, houses, pubs, slipways, a promenade and long stretches where there is nothing but a thin layer of dunes and a stony embankment. In Thomas's day the tram-like Mumbles Railway ran the full six miles, and the tail end of a main railway line about three of them.

The foreshore was a natural place to go to throw stones, dam streams, hear hellfire preachers, mooch about in arches under the railway embankment, whistle after girls, and later lie down with them in saucers of the scrubby dunes, while passing trains threw out showers of hot cinders, and the lovers would sometimes see the silhouette of a Peeping Tom rise up slowly above the spiky marram grass. Thomas haunted the seashore. He remembers it with dogs and old men, watching oil tankers and banana boats coming out of the docks, shouting at it. He seems never to have gone *in* it, though, there or on the Gower beaches where he went with friends as soon as he was old enough. They remember him throwing stones at it, or just looking. Caitlin used to say that his hands ('small, delicate, elongated, utterly useless') were like fins. But he had no interest in swimming.

It was a happy childhood, or Thomas never suggested otherwise, although he did say to Margaret Taylor, 'There's only one thing that's worse than having an unhappy childhood, and that's having a too-happy childhood.' He was absorbed in himself, the child that parents smile at proudly behind his back and call imaginative. But he was unusually intense. In his stories of childhood he sometimes tries to photograph himself at a particular instant. In 'The Peaches', playing Indians with Jackie Bassett alias Williams, 'I felt all my young body like an excited animal ... I was aware of me myself in the exact middle of a living story, and my body was my adventure and my name.' This seems to have become a central part of Thomas's consciousness: what was going on inside his head sometimes was the thought that there he was, wondering what was going on inside his head. At a given moment he was taking part in the drama of himself. Writing to Vernon Watkins at the start of the war he said, 'I go for long bicycle rides, thinking: "Here I am on a bicycle in a war."' By that time he had learned to laugh at himself for this quirk of narcissism, but he continued to do it, adding a further layer to the joke, which underneath was not a joke, by describing the process for an audience. 'I was walking, one afternoon in August, along a river-bank,' he said in a radio talk, 'thinking the same thoughts that I always think when I walk along a river-bank in August. As I was walking, I was thinking – now it is August and I am walking along a river-bank.'

His poetry was to reflect this obsessive self-awareness by the time he was fifteen. His earliest verse shows few signs of it. The first poems which are presumed to be Thomas's are in manuscript, fair copies in a childish hand. After Dylan's death Mrs Thomas gave them to a friend, Mrs Hettie Owen; apparently she destroyed other juvenilia. Her account of how these early poems came to be written was a fond mother's view of the precocious boy, happy with pencil and paper: 'He'd come and annoy his sister. She'd say, "Write something, write a poem about an onion or the kitchen sink," and he would. I kept a lot of them for a long time and then I burnt them. But they were clever little things.' She gave the impression that some of this writing was done before he was ten. The poems are precocious. 'La Danseuse'[4] begins:

> She moved like silence swathed in light,
> Like mist in moonshine clear;
> A music that enarmoured sight
> Yet did elude the ear.

4. See Appendix.

Above 'enarmoured' another hand has written 'enamoured'. In the margin, against the word 'epitome' in the next verse, is: 'ep/i/to/me – 4 syllables'. Presumably this was D.J. at work. In another poem, 'real' and 'steel' are made to rhyme. A marginal note says firmly: 'Real is two syllables and cannot rhyme with steel.' In 'Inspirations' there is a hint of subject-matter to come. Thomas is writing about the business of writing, looking at poetry as his personal means of coming to terms with the world. This was to be a favourite area, a vein he never tired of working, poems about poetry and himself the poet: more self-awareness.

> The night is full of poetry and desire,
> And eager with unanswerable things;
> O that my beating brain could borrow wings,
> And shake the shackles of the mind's attire.
>
> For then indeed, my songs might near the touch
> More envied than the jewelled crown of kings;
> And I should be a happy heart who sings,
> Nor questions why, no[r] wonders overmuch.

Dylan may have been using a convenient formula that he had found in other people's poetry. But he soon learned to adapt it to his needs.

## CHAPTER THREE

# *A Sort of Schoolboy*

AT the age of eleven, Dylan Thomas found his first outlet for verse in the Grammar School magazine. He entered the school in the autumn of 1925, shortly before his eleventh birthday, and went into the 'A' stream, where the middle-class, anglicized boys were usually placed. It is probable that he was a fee-paying entrant, though the cost to his father would have been small. D. J. Thomas was by now resigned to a lifetime of being senior English master. In 1920 he had entertained hopes that the chair of English at the newly established Swansea University College might come his way. It went to a namesake, W. D. Thomas, whose abilities he thought inferior to his own. Colleagues say it soured him. It irked him, too, that a fellow-student at Aberystwyth, T. J. Rees, who began by teaching at a lesser school in Swansea, was now the town's well-liked Director of Education, and earning more than he was. 'My degree is better,' he would say. But even if it was, D.J.'s manner alienated people. When he was ill and away from school, as frequently happened, no one bothered to visit him. He and Florence didn't socialize with other masters and their wives. He could tell a good story with appropriate Welsh mannerisms when the mood took him, but more often he made people uneasy. A master who joined the school the year before Dylan, J. Morgan Williams, came upon D.J. unexpectedly one evening in the Bush, a public house in Sketty. He was sitting alone in the corner. He accepted the offer of a fresh pint from his young colleague and sat drinking it in silence. His tallish figure, balding and severe, was often to be seen there about nine o'clock of an evening. Local drinkers called him 'The Professor'.

As master in charge of the school magazine, which was published each term, D.J.'s approval was needed for its contents.

He can't have been troubled by his son's first effort, a harmless piece of humour about a dog whose

> greatest delight is to take a good bite
> At a calf that is plump and delicious;
> And if I indulge in a bite at a bulge,
> Let's hope you won't think me too vicious.

This was printed in December 1925, at the end of Dylan's first term. It was a year before his next effort appeared there, another piece of light verse, and soon after that he sold his first poem to the *Western Mail* in Cardiff. This was the stolen lyric, 'His Requiem'. It appeared in the 'Wales Day by Day' column on 14 January 1927, signed 'D. M. Thomas', and might have been attributed to him for ever if it had not been reprinted in 1971 in a collection entitled *Dylan Thomas: The Poems* edited by his friend, Dr Daniel Jones. The *Sunday Telegraph* printed 'His Requiem', and an observant reader wrote to say that the poem was not Thomas's: it had appeared in the *Boy's Own Paper* for November 1923, above the name of Lillian Gard. Miss Gard was a regular contributor to children's journals at the time. Thomas had not even retitled his version; he made six small changes but otherwise the poems were identical. He would hardly have taken such a risk unless he badly needed to prove – to himself, to his father, to his friends – that he could write acceptable poetry; and unless he was uncertain of his ability to do so.

It raises the question of why he wrote poetry in the first place. In some ways this is as pointless as asking why he had brown eyes and curly hair. He wrote poems because he was born with certain talents, which, given his upbringing, he made use of in an approved fashion. But students of Thomas, even friendly ones, have nagging doubts concerning the way he set about his craft. There is a feeling that he is more interested in proving himself a poet than in getting on with the business of conveying whatever it is that he wants a poem to convey. The desire to display himself to the world as an artist was very real to Thomas. He did it in his life and in his work. His poems are thick with the affectations of poetry. It is hard to avoid a suspicion that his starting point was not so much that he had 'something to say' as that he desired to be a poet: perhaps, to follow in the footsteps his father never took. Given that premise, and the streak of bravado in his nature, it is not difficult to see how he came to steal Miss Gard's little poem. It contains a concrete episode (the unloved old man, mourned by the bird) of a kind that Thomas may have found difficult to incorporate in his own verse, which was vaguer and wordier, if the juvenile manuscripts are any indication. He seized it and ran. Apparently Thomas never disclosed the deception. His most likely confidant would have been Daniel Jones, his closest friend from their Grammar School days. But if Jones knew, he would hardly have included the poem in the collection. It was removed from a subsequent edition and replaced by the verse about the dog.

A month after 'His Requiem', the *Boy's Own Paper* published 'The second best', which was light verse with an attempt at a serious message: remember life's failures. On 28 July the *Western Mail* printed 'If the Gods had but given', signed 'Dylan Morlais', a mis-spelling of 'Marlais'. It is thirty lines long; presumably this time it was Thomas's own work:

> If the Gods had but given me one long day,
> From fresh of the morning to stars at night,
> With never a glance at the clock to say
> The moments are slipping, farewell's in sight . . .

By this time the school magazine had printed a third poem, 'The Watchers', a competent parody or imitation of Sir Henry Newbolt's patriotic verse; and by 1928, when he was thirteen, Thomas's poems were appearing there regularly, as they did throughout the rest of his time at the school. Some, the least successful, were 'serious', some were 'humorous'. By 1930 he was writing poems of a different kind altogether. But for the moment these stayed in exercise books that he kept in his bedroom.

As a student, Thomas is said to have been ludicrously bad at every subject except English. The accounts may have been exaggerated to suit the legend. His father was anxious for him to go to university, and the man who was a martinet at school can't have put aside his sternness when it came to his own son. Eventually they agreed to differ with a remarkable absence of bitterness. But D.J. was still capable of being angry and disappointed at his son's exam performances when he was in the upper part of the school. It is unlikely that in his first two or three years at the Grammar School, Dylan was as undisciplined and contemptuous of the curriculum as he became in the end. As an adult he was often unhappy in the presence of clever academics. He rejected a formal education, probably with misgivings at first, and with traces of regret afterwards. Later he wrote of 'the kind of mock self-deprecating writers who always boast that they were boobs at school; that their place in the form was always black-marked bottom ... Neither particularly subtle or honest, I must say I was awful. Whether this was because of stupidity or arrogance, I am still not asking myself.' His real education, he added, consisted of 'the liberty to read whatever I cared to' among his father's books.

His progress towards schoolboy anarchy was not impeded as it might have been at a stricter school. The headmaster, Trevor Owen, was a big, genial man with a booming voice and a mild speech defect that boys would imitate, just below hearing-level. The school was permissive for those days, even lax. Owen was popular with the staff and the four hundred or so pupils. He rarely used the cane, and is said to have gone out of his way not to embarrass boys with sarcasm, unlike D. J. Thomas, whose tongue was always ready to inflict punishment. He is remembered standing at the door as the boys pour in, shouting 'Take your time!' and being swept aside. In one version of a school anecdote, he catches Dylan Thomas sneaking off the premises. 'Where are you going?' he asks. Thomas says he is taking a few hours off. 'Well, I hope you get caught,' replies Owen. In another version, the head catches him hiding in a bush in the 'Lower', a grassy sub-playground below the school.

Headmaster: 'What are you doing?'

Thomas: 'Playing truant, sir.'

Headmaster: 'Well, don't let your father catch you.'

Thomas was protected by being his father's son. J. Morgan

Williams says that 'Dylan took advantage of the fact that his father was a master. No question.' Williams taught him Latin in his first year, in Form 3A. At the beginning of a lesson he would say, 'Hands up the boys who haven't done their homework.' On one occasion he found that 'Dylan hadn't put his hand up and he hadn't done his homework either. So I gave him a clip.' He mentioned it to another master, who said, 'Look out, you'll have Jack after you.' It was months before D.J. referred to it, and then he said he wished others had done the same. But it remained a situation that Dylan could exploit, as he exploited his mother's anxiety about his health. 'I cut my knee with a penknife,' he wrote in 'The Peaches', 'and put the blood on my handkerchief and said it had come out of my ears so that I could pretend I was ill and frighten my mother.' Mrs Thomas was always ready to be frightened. She told Ethel Ross in 1954, 'Dylan used to get asthma very badly as a little boy. If one of the masters spoke sharply to him at the Grammar School he'd come home gasping in the middle of it. So they knew that if they checked him he'd be home for a week with a bad attack. In the end no one checked him and he got away with everything ... As a child he would collapse while he played with his toys. Often I'd find him lying on the rug. He suffered from acute anaemia ...'

Gwevril Dawkins, who knew the family well, says that had he been anyone else, the school would have expelled him. The trouble was not only his work or lack of it. There was a rumour of thieving. As far as Nancy was concerned it was more than a rumour. Later, when her girl friends came to the house to tea, she warned them not to leave their handbags upstairs with their coats because they were not safe from her brother. A pound note once vanished from a girl's purse. It didn't seem much of a crime to Dylan: nothing involving property ever did. 'I stole from my mother's bag; I stole from Gwyneth's bag,' he wrote in 'The Peaches', carefully listing the thefts along with the other peccadilloes, drinking his urine to see what it tasted like and looking through the keyhole with Dan Jones while the Jones's maid took a bath.

From now on there is no shortage of stories reporting minor

larceny and miscellaneous wickedness. Like many anecdotes about the famous, they can be used for laughing at or being scandalized by, depending on one's degree of sympathy with the subject. In the Uplands he is seen in Mrs Ferguson's sweet shop, waiting till she goes into the back room to get the lemonade, then plunging his hands into the box of wine gums – 'He was a bugger for wine gums,' says a friend. He can be found filing farthings to use as sixpenny bits in cigarette slot-machines – 'I wouldn't say he was alone in this, but let's say he had a better supply of filed farthings than anyone else.'[1] He impresses his neighbourhood gang by collecting for Dr Barnardo's with a box that is then broken open and the money taken for trips to the Uplands cinema, the local fleapit, where he lounges in the broken plush seats, puffing cigarettes and sometimes cigars. A school friend wrote later that 'the parents of the rest of us regarded him as a bad boy'. He was acquiring a reputation.

His bad language was noticeable, even by other boys. People who saw Cwmdonkin Drive from the inside said they knew where he got it from – his father, who swore and shouted when he lost his temper, usually as a result of something Florence said or did. He used to make fun of her less-than-perfect 'Swansea Welsh', so she didn't speak it in his presence. In later years she recalled it without apparent bitterness; she survived worse wounds than that. Mrs Dawkins remembers her as 'the hen-pecked wife of an intellectual. We'd all be sitting having tea, quite happily, but if she made some remark he considered intellectually puerile, he'd start shouting and yelling and swearing. He used to be extemely rude to Mrs Thomas, and as a result, Dylan became rude to her, and then to Nancy, and Nancy's friends.'

But Dylan continued to win people over with his charm. He could be almost excessively polite when he chose; he said such funny things; he looked so nice. Despite his frail appearance,

1. The same friend, Raymond Mitchell, says that Dylan also made money for the gang by writing 'cheap love stories' for the *Happy Mag*. Nothing signed by Thomas seems to have appeared there between 1926 and 1930, the most likely period. Lillian Gard ('His Requiem') was a contributor.

he seems to have had normal out-of-door recreations. He played cricket, a game to which he remained loyal. Cwmdonkin Park was always there for his games, organized and otherwise. In 'Return Journey', Thomas's radio script about Swansea, it is the empty park in the snow, where the park-keeper remembers the boy who used to 'climb the reservoir railings and pelt the old swans. Run like a billygoat over the grass you should keep off of.' It was another of Thomas's vanished lands. In real Swansea the park-keeper was 'old Smalley', a council employee called Smallcombe. He is the keeper of the poem "The Hunchback in the Park', with his stick for picking up leaves. Dylan took pleasure in raising his blood-pressure. Once, enraged by some horseplay, the keeper flung the spiked stick and drew blood from Dylan's ankle. Old men still remember Smallcombe, shouting through the trees.

Thomas took part in the Grammar School sports. In his first summer term, in June 1926, he won the one-mile race for under-fifteens. Because of his size he was given a handicap of a hundred yards. Local newspapers reported the event, and Thomas is said to have carried a cutting in his wallet all his life. One report headlined him as 'Smallest Competitor'. In a newspaper photograph he is thin-shouldered with skinny arms. His face is gentle and large-eyed: the child who has to prove himself against bigger boys. He ran successfully in school races and the cross-country for years.

He was always prone to do violence to himself. His nose was broken at an early age when he fell over or through the banisters at a neighbour's house while jeering at a small friend; it was never the same again. He fell over a high wall and knocked himself out, while being chased from an orchard with a gang of boys. Not long after his Sports Day victory he collided with a van while bicycling to a regatta at the Mumbles. His right wrist was broken, foreshadowing a lifetime of fractures; what Caitlin called his 'chicken bones' were always cracking. Mrs Thomas was terrified; she told neighbours that she feared for his life. Soon he was back on form, having oranges and lemonade smuggled into the hospital by other boys. (One day a concealed bottle burst under the bedclothes and cut his leg.) But, sure enough, the bones took a long time to knit, and he was there for almost a month.

Occasionally there were camping holidays in Gower. Thomas's account of camping at Rhossili, at the end of the peninsula, in the story 'Extraordinary Little Cough', is true in most of its details, down to a party of older girls in a tent near by, and the records of *No, No, Nanette* that the boys played on a clockwork gramophone. Even Brazell and Skully, the school bullies, who appear and steal the girls, were real. ('We hear great things of Brazel [*sic*] and his goal-kicking,' reported the school magazine.) Thomas is in the story as himself, but George Hooping, known as Little Cough, also has traces of his character. To prove he can do it, Little Cough runs the miles of Rhossili sands before collapsing by the camp fire – 'And when I stared round at George again he was lying on his back fast asleep in the deep grass and his hair was touching the flames.' John Bennett, who was one of the campers on those green cliffs, says that Dylan ran the length of the beach more than once. Each morning began with a walk to the post office to see if anyone's mother had sent him a postal order. Once they had only porridge left to eat all day. 'But it never rained,' says Bennett.

Dylan Thomas was never short of friends, but those he made in Swansea remained in a special category all his life. The first and most important of these was Daniel Jenkyn Jones. A professional composer who has remained in Swansea (he is a doctor of music), Daniel Jones rather than Dylan Thomas was generally thought to be the boy with the shining future. He wrote poetry as well as music, and played the piano and other instruments. His family was more broadly cultural than Thomas's; but the real importance of their meeting, which is described in the *Portrait* story 'The Fight', was that it provided Thomas with a clever, arrogant friend who could be audience, critic and collaborator. Jones was the elder by two years. Their inaugural fight took place in the 'Lower' playground, and for the next eight or nine years they were in and out of one another's houses. The Jones family lived a mile away, in Sketty, in a more comfortably bourgeois house called Warmley. There, and less frequently in Cwmdonkin Drive, they wrote joint poems and plays, organized joke concerts, played with words and generally egged one another on to be cleverer or funnier or noisier or bolder. On their first evening at Warmley, according to 'The Fight', Thomas read poems from an exercise-book while Jones, bespectacled, 'like a boy aged a hundred', listened in silence. 'Nobody had ever listened like that before ... The future spread out beyond the window, over Singleton Park crowded with lovers messing about, and into smoky London paved with poems.' Their friendship had something magical about it for Thomas, perhaps for Jones as well. It also had practical significance. The private self that Thomas was to explore in his mature poetry was territory to be entered alone, but the process of acquiring skills and trying out ideas might have been less effective and less entertaining without Jones's companionship.

For their poetry collaborations they invented a lunatic name for themselves, Walter Bram; 'bram' is Welsh for 'fart'. Many of the Bram notebooks and sheets, some of them the blank sides of gramophone price-lists, have found their way to the University of Texas. One of them has a date, 27 December 1929; Thomas was then fifteen. Jones has written that these poems, of which about two hundred survive, were 'serious play' and sometimes 'very, very beautiful; very'.[2] He wrote the odd-numbered lines, Thomas the even lines. Jones has quoted from one poem:

They had come from the place high on the coral hills
Where the light from the white sea fills the soil with ascending grace.
And the sound of their power makes motion as steep as the sky,
And the fruits of the great ground lie like leaves from a vertical flower.

2. According to Jones, introducing his edition of *The Poems*, some of the collaborations have 'created a trap into which many students of his work, including commentators and bibliographers, have fallen'. This was hardly surprising when Dr Jones (who was himself caught out by the unfortunate. 'His Requiem' in *The Poems*) remained close-lipped. Three or four of the poems printed above the initials 'D.M.T.' in the Grammar School magazines were apparently jointly written.

They had come from the place; they had come and gone again
In a season of delicate rain, in a smooth ascension of grace.

The Texas collection has many more poems, some of them no more than jingles, others achieving their effect by violent juxtaposition. Jones writes: 'Little body: long tail: animal of Heaven: frail comet!' Thomas supplies: 'I love naked women.' Some of Thomas's lines, in particular, have touches of surrealism, as if the images came unprocessed from his subconscious. One poem, with Thomas writing lines 2 and 4, reads:

A coin burns my hand, and the street is dark:
You are propped at every bending lamp, like flimsy dolls, dreaming, with rotten lips,
A robe coiled, rent and heaving:
I am dreaming, with thoughts like shining fish in a silver sea: and you, with lips and skin that will wither, and pass.

John Bennett, the Rhossili camper, who was more friendly with Jones than with Thomas, remembers the big upper-floor drawing-room at Warmley, with 'violins, violas, cellos and a beautiful piano. Sometimes I would scrape a violin, and Dylan would place one across his knees and draw the bow across the strings, producing sounds utterly beyond bearing, whereupon Danny would seize a cello, and play in a higher register, which seemed to be the criterion of excellence, as far as we were concerned.' To Bennett, 'Dylan did not appear remarkable to me for his poetry, but rather for his long-distance running. Dr Jones seemed to be (and indeed in my opinion was) a giant, intellectually, whereas Dylan seemed to be a somewhat feckless but very likeable person.' Jones had stature; Dylan was inclined to be a clown, a joker. Once Mrs Jones left some fresh figs in the room. As Thomas bit into the flesh-coloured fruit he said, 'God it's like chewing a girl's cunt.' There are still people in Swansea to whom a remark like that conjures up the 'real' Thomas they knew when young; Thomas the Poet makes them frown, as if it was something that happened behind their backs, when they weren't looking.

In Warmley, Thomas was at home. He seems to have found

much satisfaction in the fantasy-world that he and Jones created. One of their elaborate jokes when they were teenagers was the 'Warmley Broadcasting Company', using loudspeakers to transmit programmes from one room to another. They invented grotesque characters and episodes. A manuscript in Thomas's hand begins: 'W.B.C. (Warmley Broadcasting Company). Founded in November 1932 by Daniel Hautboy Jones and Dylan Moreorless Thomas, acting upon the suggestions of Tom (Tiptoes) Warner, advisory mechanician.' (Warner, another friend who became a schoolteacher, was friendly with them both.) Thomas was eighteen, already a serious and accomplished poet, though it is doubtful if anyone knew it, except perhaps Daniel Jones.

On this unique occasion [says the script] the *Very Rev. Percy*, patron and president of the W.B.C., has consented to play his most recent pianoforte composition, 'Buzzards at Dinner', which was written on the aged minister's last seal-hunting expedition. It is interesting to note that the piece was written with a piece of blubber on a block of ice. Unfortunately the ice melted beneath the rays of the midnight sun, and tonight, ladies & gentlemen, he is therefore forced to play another of his recent compositions, 'Badgers Beneath My Vest'. This piece was written by the Rev. Percy when he was in the Zoological Gardens, Old Kentucky. He scribbled the music with an old hat on the back of a passing walrus. The walrus then ran away and, owing to his great age, the rev. gentleman was unable to catch him. 'Badgers Beneath My Vest' is therefore lost to posterity. The aged gentleman will therefore play 'Salute to Admiral Beatty' . . .

Thomas and Jones, looking over Swansea from suburban windows, surveyed their future and mapped out their lives. How much their friendship, their fantasies and Swansea itself meant to Thomas is spelt out in a sad, violently sentimental letter he wrote to Jones from Ireland later still, in August 1935. It begins with the injunction that it should be read 'either late at night or when at least *half* tipsy', and says it is 'the first long letter I've ever written to you'. Thomas, whose book of *18 Poems* was already making his name, was writing the letter in memoriam for the 'WARMDANDYLANLEY-WORLD' as he calls it, with its puns and jokes and fancies. By now both were living in London

– Jones had settled at Harrow. The past was fading; Thomas couldn't bear to see it go. There is no 'Dear Dan':

I'm not much good at writing letters, I can't strike the, if I may coin a phrase, happy medium between trying to be funny, not trying to be funny, and trying not to be funny. I can't write as I talk – thank God I can't talk as I write, either – and I get highflown and fly-blown and highblown and flyfaultin if I try very consciously not to be self-conscious. Take me as I come – sounds like Onan – and remember the dear dead days that had to have a gallon or two of nonsense (often awfully good nonsense) ... I never can believe that the Warmley days are over – ('just a song at twilight when the lights Marlowe and the Flecker Beddoes Bailey Donne and Poe') – that there should be no more twittering, no more nose-on-window-pressing and howling at the streets, no more walks with vampire cries, and standing over the world, no more hold-a-writing-table for the longest, and wrong adjectives; I can't believe that Percy, who droppeth gently, can have dropped out of the world, that the 'Badger Beneath My Vest' and 'Homage to Admiral Beatty' are a song and a boat of the past; that Miguel-y-Bradshaw, Waldo Carpet, Xmas Pulpit, Paul America, Winter Vaux, Tonenbach, and Bram, all that miscellaneous colony of geniuses, our little men, can have died on us; that the one-legged grandmother – remember the panama-hat-shaped birds, from the Suez Canal, who pecked at her atlas-bone – doesn't still take photographs of Birmingham; that the queer, Swansea world, a world, thank Christ that was self-sufficient, can't stand on its bow legs in a smoky city full of snobs and quacks. I'm surer of nothing than that that world, Percy's world in Warmley, was, and still is, the only one that has any claims to permanence; I mean that this long, out-of-doored world isn't much good really, that it's only the setting, is only supposed to be the setting, for a world of your own – in our cases, a world of our own – from which we can interpret nearly everything that's worth. And the only world worth is the world of our own that has its independent people, people like Percy, so much, much more real than your father or my mother ... places and things and qualities and standards, and symbols much bigger than the exterior solidities, all of its own. Didn't we work better, weren't poems and music better, weren't we happier in being unhappy, out of that world, than in – not even out of – this unlocal, uncentral world where the pubs are bad and the people are sly and the only places to go are the places to go to? I think it is the same with you, though it's so long since I've seen you, dry months, too, that you may be, though you couldn't be, all different, all older, in your cat's lights more learnèd, even Harrowed to some sort of contentment, never regretting for one moment the almost-going of Percy's celestial circle. No, that couldn't be; that world *does* remain, in spite of London, the Academy, and a tuppenny, half-highbrow success. I never thought that localities meant so much, nor the genius of places, nor anything like that. I thought that the soul went round like a Gladstone bag, never caring a damn for any particular station-rack or hotel-cloakroom; that gestures and genius made the same gestures in Cockett and Cockfosters; didn't we look at our geniuses and say, 'We're taking you somewhere else to live, but we won't part.' I placed my hand upon my heart and said that we would never part; I wonder what I would have said had I placed it on my head. So on and on; like an unborn child in the city I want to get born and go to the outskirts. Here in Ireland I'm further away than ever from the permanent world, the one real world in a house or a room, very much peopled, with the exterior, wrong world – wrong because it's never understood out of the interior world – looking in through the windows. This sort of nostalgia isn't escapist by any means, you know that; just as the only politics for a conscientious artist – that's you and me – must be left-wing under a right-wing government, communist *under* capitalism, so the only world for that WARMDANDYLANLEY-MAN must be the WARMDANDYLANLEY-WORLD under the world-of-the-others. How could it be escapism? It's the only contact there is between yourself and yourselves, what's social in you and what isn't – though, God knows, I could shake Bram's intangible hand as seriously as the hand of Dean Inge, and with far greater sense of reality. Even surrealism, which seemed to have hopes and promise, preaches the decay of reality and the importance, and eventual dominance, (I don't like those words however much I try to look on them coldly), of unreality, as though the two could be put in two boxes: isn't Percy flesh, bone, and blood, isn't Evangeline Booth a shadow, isn't Percy a shadow, isn't Evangeline flesh, bone, & blood, isn't Percy flesh-bone-& blood-shadow, isn't Evangeline flesh-bone-and-blood-shadow, isn't Percy-Evangeline flesh bone and blood? – and so on and on. I'm not going to read this letter over afterwards to see what it reads like; let it go on, that's all; you don't mind the dashes and the hyphens and the bits of dogma and the brackets and the bits of dog-eaten self-consciousness and the sentimentality because I'm writing by candle-light all alone in a cottage facing the Atlantic. From the WARMDANDYLANLEY-WORLD I'd no more think of writing this letter than of using words like 'Proust' and 'flounce' and 'akimbo' and 'schedule' and 'urge' when talking in that W-W; I wouldn't have or need to; this is only covering old ground in words and phrases and thoughts and idioms that are all part of that world; it's only because, now, here in this terribly out-of-the way and lonely place, I feel the need for that world, the necessity for its going on, and the fear that it might be dying to you, that I'm trying to resurrect my bit of it, and make you realise again what you realise already: the importance of that world because it's the only one, the importance of us, too, and the fact that our poems and music won't and can't be anything without it. Soon I'm going out for a walk in the dark by myself; that'll make me happy as hell; I'll think of the almost-but-never-going-gone, and remember the cries of the Bulgarian scouts as I hear that damned sea rolling, and remember the first world . . . as I stand under an absurdly high hill – much too high, our world has its hills just the proper, the *nice*, length (I'm arching my index-finger & thumb and joining them tastefully) – and shout to it, 'Go on, you big shit, WARMDANDYLANLEY-WORLD has a hill twice as beautiful and with a ribbon and a bell on it, & a piece of boiled string on the top, if the WARMDANDYLANLEY-MAN wants it like that' . . . We must, when our affairs are settled, when music and poetry are arranged so that we can still live, love and drink beer, go back to Uplands or Sketty and found there, for good and for all, a permanent colony; living there until we are old gentlemen, with occasional visits to London and Paris, we shall lead the lives of small-town anti-society, and entertain any of the other members of the WARMDANDYLANLEY-WORLD who happen to visit the town . . . So Jones and Thomas, that well known firm of family provisioners, shall not move out of their town. So be it.

This letter, and the account of his friendship with Jones, has gone ahead of the story, through and beyond Thomas's adolescence in Swansea. These were the most important years of his life. During them he completed his education, such as it was, left school, worked on a newspaper, learned to drink, had (perhaps) his first sexual encounters; and wrote several hundred poems that survive, and probably several hundred more that do not. From the age of thirteen or fourteen there is an increasing amount of verse to look at. At first they are school-magazine poems. Thomas tried a variety of styles.

Her garden blooms with iris, and it seems
The moons are white flames, like the moons in dreams

he wrote in December 1928, no doubt in imitation of the Imagists who were fashionable at the time. In general his poems were straightforward, although the magazine editor once challenged a line. This was in 'Idylls of Unforgetfulness' (February 1929), which began:

To have seen countries which were glorious,
Immutable and finely dun like secret suns;
To have known them in their blue-hued valiance,
Felt their serenity of ripple-woven loveliness . . .

The editor, E. F. McInerny, said he found the second line incomprehensible. Thomas obligingly offered to change it to 'Immutable and ardurously consecrated'. This seems no clearer, but was accepted and appeared in print. Thomas was capable of writing simple but accomplished lyrics. Daniel Jones has printed six poems from manuscripts in his possession, all dated 1929. This is 'The Elm':

They are all goddesses;
Nodding like flowers,
They are further and more delicate
Than the years that dwindle;
They are deeper in darkness
Than the hours.

Celestial,
Slenderly lethal things,
Beautifully little like clouds:
Leaf driftwood that has blown.

'The Elm' is an improvement on most of his magazine verse at the time. It may be that the editors (although he was one himself by the end of 1929) had idiosyncratic ideas of what constituted a poem. His desire to please was perhaps the reason behind a second attempt at plagiarism, in 1929. McInerny received a short poem from Thomas. He found it suitable for the magazine, but his co-editor, H. M. V. Thomas, thought it sounded familiar. It was traced to Arthur Mee's *Children's Encyclopaedia*, Volume 8, page 5669, where it is one of the 'Thousand

Poems of All Times and All Countries'. The author was an American with a Welsh name, Thomas S. Jones. It is called 'Sometimes':

> Across the fields of yesterday
> He sometimes comes to me,
> A little lad just back from play,
> The lad I used to be.
>
> And yet he smiles so wistfully
> Once he has crept within;
> I wonder if he hopes to see
> The man I might have been?

Once again, it seems not to have been worth the trouble for someone who could do so much better himself. D. J. Thomas was told, and McInerny reports him as saying, 'After this, everything he writes is suspect.' McInerny said nothing to Dylan, and as far as he was concerned the matter was forgotten. At the time he assumed it to be plagiarism; Thomas didn't protest his innocence. Later McInerny thought charitably that it might have been an example of 'unconscious recall', an opinion he changed again when he heard of the *Western Mail* episode. His conclusion, a feasible one, is that Dylan was 'in an antisocial, devil-may-care mood, like a secret agent fingering a false and superfluous moustache'. It could have been one of Thomas's pointless untruths, another attempt to cover his tracks: a habit that amounted to a compulsion. He wrote in 'The Fight': 'If I lost my cap and found it in my bedroom, and my mother asked me where I had found it, I would say, "In the attic," or, "Under the hall stand." It was exciting to have to keep wary all the time in case I contradicted myself . . .' Or it could have been that other compulsion, to prove himself at all costs; in which case every little helped.

From 1930, the prime source of early Thomas is a series of four so-called notebooks – in fact they are students' exercise-books – which begins in April that year, and covers, though not entirely, the next four years. They are owned by the State University of New York at Buffalo, which bought them for a few pounds one day when Thomas was more than usually hard-up.

At least one notebook, and probably several others, no longer exist, or are being kept well concealed by their owners. At the start of the '1930 Notebook', Thomas has written 'Mainly free verse poems'. The first poem ın it is dated 27 April. It is called 'Osiris, Come to Isis', and uses Egyptian mythology to make some shaky pronouncements about love. A number of his poems that spring take love as their subject, including one that makes the familiar poetic plea for something more than sex – 'Your breasts and thighs and navel are not enough,' writes Thomas, implying that he is acquainted with such things.

He was fifteen years old, and apparently doomed to spend still more time at school. Some of these awkward, fumbling poems have a sharp sense of the uncertain boy standing still, not knowing which way to go. Can he dare to act, to move, to fly? It is the problem of what to do with his life and what to do with his poetry; each is bound up with the other. When he took this uncertainty as the subject for a poem, the writing became noticeably terse. In a poem that begins, 'No, pigeon, I'm too wise' (8 August 1930) he wrote that 'I'm not secure enough/To tell what note I could reach if I tried' and concluded:

> I'm all for ground,
> To touch what's to be touched,
> To imitate myself mechanically,
> Doing my little tricks of speech again
> With all my usual care.
> No bird for me:
> He flies too high.

Thomas seemed to be looking for a directness, a boldness, in his attitude. 'I want reality to hold within my palm,' he declared, in a poem whose first line hints at the violence that was soon to break into his writing, 'I know this vicious minute's hour' (November 1930). He was torn between the alternatives of going and staying. 'I go or die,' he concluded, none too confidently.

Anyone reading the poems at the time might have assumed that young Thomas was striking a pose when he wrote like this. Perhaps he was, to some extent. Like any intelligently precocious adolescent he was preoccupied with thoughts of girls, of death, of what, if anything, 'life' meant. He had a streak of timidity that made him afraid to fail and anxious to prove he could succeed. He also knew a good deal about the attitudes that writers in general and poets in particular take to life's problems. In his father's study, the middle room downstairs with the coloured glass in the door, he had read 'indiscriminately, and with my eyes hanging out'. He once listed the models for his early writing: 'Sir Thomas Browne, de Quincey, Henry Newbolt, the Ballads, Blake, Baroness Orczy, Marlowe, Chums, the Imagists, the Bible, Poe, Keats, Lawrence, Anon., and Shakespeare.' When he wrote about 'Your sweet inducive thighs/And raven hair', or presented himself as the unhappy lover watching a dancer –

> I, poor romantic, held her heel
> Upon the island of my palm

– he was borrowing other people's language. When it came to questioning the purpose of his life and his poems, he would have found innumerable examples in his father's books.

But in retrospect the poet's pose in that first notebook – it ends in December 1930, not long after Thomas's sixteenth birthday – can be recognized as a real concern. It is likely that by this time he was already conditioned to regard himself as a poet. He had written and thought about it for long enough. The previous year he contributed a survey of modern poetry to the school magazine that showed off a close acquaintance with names and trends. The business of poetry was serious. If he took up a poetic posture it was not because he was following other poets – or if he was, the pose was becoming the reality. At the end of the last poem in the notebook, 9 December 1930, he was once more questioning his function as a poet, but at the same time asserting his talent:

> Purpose is gone;
> I try to hold, but can't,
> Compress, inflate, grow old,
> With all the tackle of my certain magic
> Stone hard to lift.

The feeling that he had a vocation was probably both cause and effect of his failure at school. The more he thought about himself as a poet, the less attention he paid to work; the worse his prospects of passing examinations, the more attractive the prospects of being a poet. The year before, at the end of the summer term, he had sat the Central Welsh Board examination for a school-leaving certificate, with disastrous results. The normal course for a bright boy would have been to pass his 'C.W.B.' in the correct mix of subjects to satisfy university entrance requirements, then to move up to the sixth form for two years or longer, until he was old enough for university. Dylan failed altogether, allegedly floundering in every subject except English language (no records survive of pupils who didn't reach the minimum standard for a school certificate). Gwevril Dawkins was at Cwmdonkin Drive the day Dylan sat the history paper. For some of the other papers he had stayed only long enough in the examination room to know that all was lost. This time he lasted the course, and told his father that he had written twenty-two foolscap sheets. D.J. was anxious to learn what his son had had to say about Tudor England, which was in that year's syllabus. Dylan replied that he had written twenty-two pages about the French Revolution. 'D.J. was hopping mad,' says Mrs Dawkins. 'He was hitting the roof, calling Dylan a dolt and a donkey, asking what the hell he knew about the French Revolution. "I don't know anything," said Dylan. "I wrote about why it shouldn't have happened." '

It is possible that he attempted the C.W.B. the following summer, 1930. He languished in the fifth form for a second year, but it seems unlikely that D.J. gave up without a fight. Dylan probably found his health a useful defence. Mrs Thomas once spoke of a 'rather bad haemorrhage' when Dylan was fifteen, implying a chest haemorrhage. On another occasion she recalled that 'Dylan had a breakdown when he was sitting his C.W.B. at sixteen, and we had to send him down to a farm at Cardigan'. If she remembered the age correctly, this would put the breakdown in 1931.[3]

3. Mrs Thomas insisted (wrongly) in later years that Dylan was a year younger than everyone assumed – that he was born in October 1915, not 1914. She said that he added a year 'because he wanted to seem older'.

Outwardly he was leading an aimless life. For his last year at school, 1930–31, he moved into the Lower Sixth. Charles Fisher, a friend, remembers him that year 'in the prefects' room, where he would sit before a coal fire boring holes in the floor with a poker'. His mood may be echoed in the story 'Just Like Little Dogs', where he stands under a railway arch opening on to Swansea sands, and two brothers talk to him about their sexual affairs. They wear working-class caps and have the air of the unemployed. All three have nothing better to do than stand 'looking at the miles of sands, long and dirty in the early dark'. Thomas, a 'lonely night-walker and a steady stander-at-corners', tells them he is there because 'I've got nothing to do when I'm in and I don't want to go to bed'. At the end of the story he runs home; a sentence deleted from the original manuscript read, 'A clock struck one. There'd be hell to pay now', which seems to confirm that he is still a schoolboy.

In the notebooks his life was not aimless at all. They give little support, though, to the view of Thomas as the inspired boy-poet, pumping out words in a frenzy without considering what they mean. This is not to say they are easy poems. They are often difficult to follow, sometimes incomprehensible. But the difficulties arise because they are so intensely worked out. Writing verse seemed to be a hard discipline for Thomas. He was the would-be poet in search of a subject. When he found it momentarily, the language changed: the lines hardened, the words acquired an edge. That subject was himself, the secret Thomas that only Thomas knew about:

> Classic, erotic, and obscene,
> Dead and alive,
> In sleep and out of sleep,
> Tracking my sensibilities,
> Gratifying my sensualities . . .

The next poem (the one of 9 December 1930) began

> How shall the animal
> Whose way I trace
> Into the dark recesses,
> Be durable
> Under such weight as bows me down . . .

Eight years later this became the germ of a published poem, 'How shall my animal', the first notebook poem directly linked to successful publication. Soon there were other forerunners. Notebook 2, which begins in December 1930, again headed 'Mainly free verse poems', has 'Today, this hour I breathe' as its second entry, dated 18 December. Later this was to be revised, thickened and made more difficult to follow as 'Today, this insect, and the world I breathe'. The original version made at least one direct and characteristically sceptical statement:

> I have divided
> Sense into sight and trust.
> The certain is a fable.

And in 'The spire cranes' (27 January 1931), Thomas looks at the poet's situation, in a version that resembles the form in which it was eventually printed in 1938.

In some of the poems, Thomas began to use the harsher words and images that were typical of his mature verse. In the more softly romantic pieces it was still 'my golden bird the sun' or 'the rainbow's shy embrace'. But as his days as a schoolboy-poet came to an end, there was an occasional flurry of biological words: *grains*, *blood*, *seed*, *sucking*, *dust*, *wax*, *cancer*, *egg*. The effect was not sustained; on the whole they were the fragmentary poems of an adolescent trying to come to terms with his world. In a poem copied into the notebook on 6 April 1931, he snarled at love in four of its lines whose style was edging towards the 'authentic' Thomas:

> Where love is there's a crust of joy
> To hide what drags its belly from the egg,
> And, on the ground, gyrates as easily
> As though the sun were spinning up through it.

For the moment, nothing happened to these poems. They were fair copies, obviously transcribed from whatever sheets once held the original drafts, although heavily corrected in places. Once they were written they stayed in the exercise-books, except for two short pieces, dated December 1930, which were printed in the school magazine the following year as 'Two Images'. One is the poem that contains the phrase 'my golden bird the sun'; against them in the margin of the exercise-book, Thomas has written 'Ugh' and 'Ogh' to show what he thought of them later. The style of poetry he began to write in was not suitable for the school magazine, or for any other journal that he might have been bold enough to approach. London and its literary magazines must have seemed a long way off. He might have been a boy writing verses in the middle of the desert. Culture, in those days, was metropolitan, and regional Britain was not a fashionable breeding-ground for writers and painters. He was working in the dark.

Most of his writing must have been done in Cwmdonkin Drive, either in D.J.'s study or in the 'bedroom by the boiler', as he implies in the *Portrait* stories. Two years later he was telling Pamela Hansford Johnson that he wrote at the rate of two lines an hour. The first notebooks show an average of a poem a week, but companion sets of rhymed poems may have been accumulating in other notebooks. Five such poems are quoted in 'The Fight'.[4] For Thomas, writing poetry was a major activity, the most important thing he did. The notebooks show a neurotic energy accumulating; it is like a storm building up. But apart from his friendship with Jones, and possibly with one or two others, the real poems remained a private activity. In the school magazine (of which he was now sole editor) he appeared as the author of amusing verse and a de la Mare-like ghost story, as Hon. Sec. of the Debating Society ('The first subject chosen was "That the modern youth is decadent". D. M. Thomas took the affirmative') and co-founder of a Reading Circle for drama. As for his education, even a father who believed that study was the road to happiness must have realized by 1931 that Dylan was not teachable. He would leave school in the summer term. University was out of the question.

In the early summer, the note of urgent self-exploration is heard page after page. He is less plaintive, more resolute. On 1 June, in the second poem copied and perhaps written on that

4. These poems sound as if they were written when Thomas was fifteen or sixteen, rather than several years earlier, as 'The Fight' implies. They appear nowhere else. When Thomas wrote 'The Fight', about 1939, he presumably copied them from a notebook that is now lost.

date, he found his tongue, and sustained the mood throughout. The subject was himself, the poet. He slid easily into a powerful sexual image of orgasm and its aftermath, of living and dying. The poem was not interested in white necks and raven hair. It was concerned exclusively with his own sexuality, his own nervous system:

> High on a hill,
> Straddle and soak,
> Out of the way of the eyes of men,
> Out of the way,
> Straddle her wrinkled knees
> Until the day's broken –
> Christ, let me write from the heart,
> War on the heart –
> Puff till the adder is,
> Breathe till the snake is home,
> Inch on the old thigh
> Till the bird has burst his shell,
> And the carnal stem that stood
> Blowing with the blood's ebb,
> Is fallen down
> To the ground.

A few days later he was trying out what reads like a piece of automatic writing, a surrealistic babble of words. But he continued, more or less, in the same single-minded direction. On 28 July he warned his non-existent readers that

> I shall turn the strongest stomach up
> With filth I gather
> From the thousand minds, all lust and wind,
> Like a beachcomber in the time of light.

But by that time he had shut his desk and handed in his books. The magazine says that term ended on 31 July 1931. Thomas was no longer there. He had gone to work on the local newspaper.

## CHAPTER FOUR

# *Reporter, Actor, Poet*

It is doubtful whether Dylan Thomas saw himself as an ace reporter, or as any kind of reporter at all. Although the journalist's trade had certain raffish characteristics that appealed to him, he showed no great interest in being an orthodox member of the reporters' room at the *South Wales Daily Post*, the Swansea evening newspaper (its title was changed to *Evening Post* while he was there). But he can hardly have been as nonchalant as some of the accounts suggest; as in the case of the Grammar School, the legend has been at work, making him bold and comical too early. He was one of a small editorial staff. The *Post* could not afford specialist and feature writers, and reporters were expected to do a little of everything. Thomas was no exception; he was merely the latest recruit from the Grammar School, where the newspaper often found its young reporters and sub-editors. It is likely that the editor, an urbane local character called J. D. Williams, knew D. J. Thomas, and that it was his father who arranged the job, not Dylan. Mrs Thomas used to say that 'Daddy thought it would be a good opening for him'. Each morning she sent him off to work in a clean shirt and well-creased trousers.

At first he was not on the editorial staff. He began in the 'readers' room' of the printing department as a copy-holder, one of the juniors who read reporters' copy aloud in a droning voice, while their seniors, the 'correctors of the press', check and amend the proofs. Thomas was too slow; a reader he worked for said that he was 'inclined to dramatize everything'. After a couple of months he moved on to the reporters' room, and his brief career as a journalist began.[1] For a while he took

1. Thomas apparently did some writing for the paper before he was officially a reporter. He probably wrote the account of an interview with

shorthand lessons, to no purpose. From his own accounts, in the radio 'Return Journey', and a story called 'Old Garbo', he did the usual chores of a junior reporter, the 'calls' to hospital and fire-station in search of news, the visits to the mortuary, the reports of concerts and chapel bazaars. An older colleague who sub-edited his copy says it was 'appalling, with many lacunae'. Funny stories of how he reported events that never took place, or failed to report events that did, are unlikely to have been funny at the time, assuming they ever happened. Even when he was established as a 'character', licensed to be as unreliable as he chose, Thomas would sometimes kick against his reputation. 'My selfish carelessness and unpunctuality I do not try to excuse as poet's properties,' he wrote to Henry Treece in 1938. 'They are a bugbear and a humbug.' If that was the truth, then his shortcomings as a reporter must have bothered him. One story which seems to be true is that he missed the death of the matron of Swansea Hospital, in February 1932. His mother said that 'somebody rang up the *Post* to ask why her death wasn't in the paper. He should have gone to the hospital to find out if there was any news. But he didn't go there that day.' In written reminiscences, Thomas smiled at his innocence as a reporter but said nothing about incompetence. In 'Old Garbo' the worst thing anyone accuses him of is 'platitudinous verbosity' in his report of an oratorio.

He wrote a series of five articles about 'The Poets of Swansea', an historical survey, for the *Herald of Wales*, the weekly companion-paper of the *Post*. He lingered on one tragi-comic figure, Llewelyn Prichard, a nineteenth-century actor, poet and hack writer with a wax nose who drank too much and died in obscurity in Swansea when his bed caught fire. The headline was 'A Figure Lost in Lies and Legends', and the article began: 'No one can deny that the most attractive figures in literature are always those around whom a world of lies and legends has been woven, those half mythical artists whose real characters

---

Nellie Wallace, the music-hall star, which appeared in the *Daily Post* of 15 July 1931. Wynford Vaughan-Thomas remembers visiting Miss Wallace in her dressing-room at the Swansea Empire with his friend Dylan, who had 'just become a reporter on the local newspaper'.

become cloaked for ever under a veil of the bizarre.' The parallel was obvious. Thomas was already identifying himself with the likes of Prichard, cutting himself off from the local 'literary life', such as it was: 'Out of all the spinsters and thin-lipped amateurs spinning their little webs of sound, the versifiers, linking cliché to cliché with metrical perfection, the bards and the old gentlemen; out of all the poetical products of a small town, Prichard stands out flaming and aloof against the horizon. He failed to be great, but he failed with genius.' That, if necessary, was the way Thomas intended to fail.

In a sixth article Thomas devoted himself to a living poet, a Swansea schoolmaster called Howard Harris, describing him cruelly as 'a small poet with a large ambition'. Later J. D. Williams (who edited both newspapers) said that the whole series had given him 'dreadful pangs', and that it had been 'heartbreaking to give the right of way to an irreverent youth'. Thomas had to watch his step. Sent to review a chapel rendering of Longfellow's *Hiawatha* set to music, his copy damned poet, composer and performers; Williams was consulted and the sub-editors watered it down to make it fit to print. Thomas submitted a short story to the *Herald of Wales*. It ended with a head in a gas stove, hardly the thing for a weekly paper that kept reality for the news columns and liked to brighten up people's weekends with weddings and gossip. A gas stove would never have done – 'Laughingly we agreed that it would not,' wrote Williams.

The eighteen months or less that Thomas spent on the newspaper (the dates are not certain) taught him nothing he needed to know about writing but a great deal he wanted to know about growing up. At sixteen he could still look almost girlish. His thin body was crowned with curls; his eyes bulged, soft and melancholy. The dreamer with the haunted features was one of his poses in early photographs; the world-wise young sinner was to be another. With fellow reporters he developed a half-serious imitation of the American newshound, hat pulled down over his eyes and a cigarette that stayed in the mouth once it was lit; the dangling cigarette was a habit he kept all his life.

Acquaintances of the time retain bizarre images of Thomas

the Poet-and-Reporter. Gwendolyn Courtney (then Gwendolyn Bevan) was the girl-friend of another *Post* reporter, Cliff Williams. One winter's afternoon Cliff and Gwendolyn set off for Parkmill, a Gower village. Dylan, uninvited, went along too – he had seen them meet in Swansea, and walked behind them to the bus. Mrs Courtney remembers his lips, 'yellow with over-smoking'. They had a beer in the Gower Inn and walked towards the sea, Dylan still in attendance. He was morose, because, he said, a manuscript had been rejected. The day was cold and blustery. When they reached the ruins of Pennard Castle, Thomas 'stood on the rampart, if you can call it a rampart, waving his trilby and shouting, "They are rejecting me now but the day will come when the name Dylan Thomas will be echoed from shore to shore. Only I won't be alive to hear it."' Mrs Courtney thought it a ridiculous performance.

Manly drinking was another habit to be learned. The story of 'Old Garbo' concerns a drunken Saturday night out with Mr Farr, the senior reporter, followed by a remorseful Sunday afternoon in Cwmdonkin Park ('An article called "Our Lord Was a Flower-lover" moved me to tears of bewilderment and contrition'), followed by bravado in the office on Monday. Freddie Farr, who came to Swansea from another part of Wales in 1925, was a tough and skilful court reporter who also covered boxing. He was in his middle forties. In 'Old Garbo' he is a great shorthand-writer, heavy smoker, drinker of bitter beer, a humorist and a dandy gone to seed. His son says he is accurately described; he died soon after Thomas left the newspaper, despite the line near the end of 'Old Garbo', 'When I showed this story a long time later to Mr Farr . . .'

If Llewelyn Prichard fitted Thomas's stereotype of a poet, Freddie Farr fitted his ideas about a man of the world. Farr is a man who can hold his drink. Their pub crawl begins in a respectable bar, 'The Three Lamps', which was much used by professional men before wartime air raids destroyed it. Thomas half wishes his father could see him now – 'He could not fail to see that I was a boy no longer, nor fail to be angry at the angle of my fag and my hat and the threat of the clutched tankard.' Soon they move on to poorer pubs towards the docks.

Thomas is determined to keep up. He drinks rum and makes himself sick. But he has seen a slice of life. He observes (from a safe distance) a back-street tragedy, or black comedy, involving a mother, a daughter and her stillborn baby. More important, he has stood at the elbow of 'Half Hook' Farr, a man among men. He has served an apprenticeship of some kind.

Drink was to be important. Perhaps it began as a game. South Wales is a beer-drinking region where a strenuous night in male company is part of the popular culture. A youth who wants to prove his manliness, especially if he is slightly built and inwardly timid, finds a well-worn remedy in sinking pints in squalid circumstances; being sick is part of the initiation. Eventually the game became more serious. The raconteur with the bellyful of beer makes a convenient disguise for someone who is uncertain of himself, who has trouble establishing his true identity. There are ample indications that Thomas was an unsure, divided man. Drink would have been useful here. There are further possibilities. In 1932, aged seventeen, Thomas was beginning to rebel against provincialism; like others before him, it was not until he left the place that he missed it. He was outgrowing his suburban home, the nondescript town, its little poets. Getting drunk was a blow against his elders, an obvious gesture by the artist as a young dog. It was more than that, it was Sin. Beer, rather than spirits, is traditionally the drink that sends men to ruin in South Wales; it is the reeking public bar and the twelve pints of flat, soapy beer on pay-night that the chapels have inveighed against. Thomas liked to spell out his sinning in obvious ways. After beer the next wickedness was women, where he was soon to try his hand. His autobiographical stories make symbols of sinful pleasure out of actresses and dancers, once good for a delicious shudder in nonconformist Wales. His first recorded confession of sex, aged nineteen, which was very likely invented for the benefit of Pamela Hansford Johnson, was about three days of alleged love-making with a Swansea girl who had been an amateur dancer. And Caitlin Macnamara, the girl he eventually fell in love with and married, had been a professional dancer. It is hard to avoid the conclusion that he wanted to feel wicked. Miss Johnson was to observe him when they came out of pubs in Chelsea. He might have had no more than a pint of beer, but if he saw someone he knew, he pretended to be drunk. He had no difficulty in becoming genuinely drunk. The smaller the body-weight the greater the effect of alcohol. But when he grew plump he was still susceptible. Alfred Janes the painter, who says that 'Dan Jones could drink me under the bed', adds that 'I could drink Dylan under the table'.

Perhaps Thomas drank from the start for the pleasure of being rescued afterwards. It is said that some rebellious adolescents reveal their true motives by their habit of being incontinent when drunk: they behave like babies so that they can be looked after. Thomas in his cups certainly wet and soiled himself more than once. In one instance, when he was twenty-three, an older woman who mothered him had to clean him up after a drinking bout that ended in collapse. Perhaps there was an inherited tendency to drink. His father was a heavy drinker; his mother's family – the Williamses of 'Dr Dan's' generation – were susceptible.

When he was at the *Post*, his drinking attracted little attention. Nor did everyone take notice of Thomas himself. The chief reporter, a lay preacher and teetotaller called Job ('Solomon' in 'Old Garbo'), claimed later that Thomas escaped his memory altogether. The paper had other talented young men who wanted to be writers. Charles Fisher, who became a close friend of Thomas, was thought too promising to remain a reporter. Thomas was part of a widening circle of ambitious friends linked by the newspaper or amateur dramatics or simply because they lived on the same side of the town. Alfred Janes, whose parents kept a greengrocer's shop, was already at art school in London, but came back to Swansea often. He met Thomas through Daniel Jones. A lean, meticulous man who has always been loyal to him, he was later the butt of amiable Thomas jokes about his painstaking still-lifes ('One Egg, June 1936–June 1940'). Janes was something of a father-figure. Mervyn Levy, another painter who was to make his reputation in London, had already left the town, but sometimes reappeared to join the fluctuating circle of coffee-drinkers in the Kardomah

Café or pub-crawlers in the Mumbles. They were part of a Swansea network that lasted throughout Thomas's life, people he could trust and relax with. In general they don't remember him behaving badly, no doubt partly from loyalty but also because with them he was not under pressure, and so less likely to be eccentric. Wynford Vaughan-Thomas, who became the broadcaster and writer, was another member of the network; he was six years older than Thomas, and had already come down from Oxford with a degree. Jones was at the local university reading English. He was somewhat apart from the group. To Levy, he seemed 'a bit high and mighty, the great man. He didn't join our badinage and filthy jokes. But Dylan didn't come to us for help, he went to Dan. His relationship with Dan was a very serious one.' Thomas's other important Swansea friendship was to be with Vernon Watkins. When Thomas was on the *Post*, Watkins was working in a bank, as he did all his life. But he and Thomas had not yet met or begun their bemused exploration of one another's poetry.

While Thomas was being a reporter of a kind, he was dabbling in another trade that was to be more profitable in the long run. He became a member of the Little Theatre, an amateur group that staged several plays and revues each year. At the Grammar School he had acted in a couple of plays. He joined the Little Theatre soon after reviewing one of its productions for the newspaper, and in February 1932 appeared in Noël Coward's *Hay Fever* as Simon, described by a local reviewer as 'an artist with an explosive temper and untidy habits'. He seems to have flung himself into parts and achieved his effects by over-acting. 'The more fantastic the part,' says Malcolm Graham, later a professional actor, 'the better Dylan was.' For the next two or three years he appeared regularly in Little Theatre plays. His voice was already strong; soon it would thicken and begin to acquire the boom that made him as famous as his poetry. Strangely, he never refers to the amateur-acting days in his copious reminiscences about Swansea; it is the one thing he leaves out. An actor in so many things he did, he preferred not to remember himself as one.

His appearance on the street was becoming more flamboyant. He was busy escaping from his mother's well-laundered linen. In 'Return Journey' he is now 'a bombastic adolescent provincial bohemian with a thick-knotted artist's tie made out of his sister's scarf, she never knew where it had gone, and a cricket-shirt dyed bottle-green'. He fancied himself in a green pork-pie hat with a feather. D. J. Thomas was always careful of his appearance: he shaved when he was ill, wouldn't dream of going down to breakfast in a shirt without a collar, and kept his hat on whenever he could to cover his baldness. Dylan had his less orthodox brand of vanity. He may have come to look like an unmade bed, as someone once remarked, but he was never indifferent to his appearance.

His sister Nancy was a fellow member of the Little Theatre. They appeared together on the stage. Her life-story, one feels, should be important to her brother's, but it doesn't appear so. In his reminiscences Thomas wrote her out of the script, more or less. He did the same with his parents, but there are many references to them elsewhere, in letters and reports of conversations. Nancy is a blank space. When Dylan was seventeen, she was twenty-five, and still living at home; she had been there, doing nothing in particular, since she left the High School, the girls' equivalent of the Grammar School, seven or eight years before. Her chief interests seem to have been men friends, of whom she had many, and the theatre, which presented itself briefly as a possible career. She was an attractive, loquacious young woman, with the Thomas facility for mixing up fact and fiction. Her friend Gwevril Dawkins says that 'a lot of the time she burbled absolute rubbish, but she could keep a roomful of people in stitches'. On the stage she is said to have out-acted her brother, and according to Mrs Dawkins there was once talk of her going to London and joining a theatrical company. But a doctor advised against it: her health was delicate, like Dylan's, and her girlhood had been full of septic knees and attacks of asthma. So she remained in Swansea, which is probably what she would have done in any case, and spent much of her time at the Mumbles, where the Little Theatre had its headquarters. Once, helping to sew costumes, she pricked her finger and let out a stream of coarse language; the wardrobe mistress was shocked to hear such words from a girl whose family was so respectable.

By 1932, no doubt to her father's relief, she looked like settling down. Her friend was an English commercial traveller based in Swansea, Haydn Taylor. He was another of the Little Theatre set. He drove a two-seater car, earned £300 a year and planned to earn a great deal more in the near future, and saw the Thomases with a quizzical outsider's eye. 'It wasn't a naturally happy family,' he says. 'There was something unreal about it, primarily because D.J. and Florence had nothing in common. She worshipped him, waited on him hand and foot, but it wasn't a *natural* family. They never went away for holidays together.' According to Taylor, Nancy – whom he always called 'Thomas' – was afraid of her father and his sarcastic tongue. 'It was always a problem for Thomas to get money out of him if she wanted to go somewhere. He never had a bean. He used to say, "I am without money. I do not mean I don't have much money. I mean that I am *without money*." He said it in very measured tones. It was a funny family.' Taylor left the town in September 1932. An unsigned paragraph in the *Evening Post* said that 'Swansea is to lose one of its keenest dramatic exponents and followers in Mr Haydn Taylor ... who leaves this week for London, where he will take up an important business appointment'. It was written by Dylan Thomas, being nice to his future brother-in-law. By the standards of Dylan and his friends, Haydn Taylor was affluent. He was usually good for a small loan; sometimes for a quick theft. When he returned to Swansea for weekends over the next few months – he and Nancy were married the following May – Taylor stayed in Cwmdonkin Drive. He learned not to leave his wallet in the bedroom if he went to take a bath.

Nancy wrote regularly to Haydn Taylor after he had left the town, and her letters give another kind of insight into life at Cwmdonkin Drive. They don't sound as if she is embroidering the facts. She was unnerved by constant rows, which were usually about money and drink, those Thomas bugbears. As Taylor says, it was a funny family. Nancy had much affection for her father ('I have realized how terribly worried Daddy is &

how sad he is,' she wrote to Taylor in an earlier letter, of 1930), but he was enclosed in too many skins. Her mother's habit of steaming open Taylor's letters suggests the close, watchful atmosphere inside those drably wallpapered rooms. This was Nancy writing to her fiancé (they announced their engagement at Christmas 1932) on 16 January 1933:

Mother is in hellish mood because I've had letters from Mrs Bevan & Mrs Ted & have showed her neither – 'You never show me your letters as other girls do to their parents. Don't think I haven't noticed sealing wax on Haydn's letters. It's quite the rudest thing I ever heard of, you must have suggested to Haydn that I'd open them, etc. I noticed that there was no sealing wax on the letter to Aunty Polly, etc.' Your letter to Blaencwm must have been read by Mother – damn . . . Yesterday Mother said, 'Your wedding – remember Daddy won't have any money & any sort of a fuss will kill him. If you expect any sort of special fuss or clothes you ought to be ashamed of yourself . . .'

Letters in the previous months suggest hard times at home. Perhaps the atmosphere provoked Thomas as a writer, providing something to escape from, into the parallel world of poetry. Nancy's only escape was going to be marriage. D.J. may have been afraid that his daughter's love affair would come to nothing, and keep her financially dependent on him. Dylan's career as a reporter was not flourishing. Nancy wrote to Haydn on 25 September 1932:

This morning I went to town with Gwevril, returned home for lunch at 1.30. Mother & I dined in peace – at about 2.45 Pop enters – then the fun began. A very usual Saturday scene – Mother raving and in tears – I tiniest bit frightened rush upstairs dress & go out in the rain. It pours down & the wind howls . . . Question, what could I do? Nothing, I hadn't as usual, any money. I walk to Brynmill & on into the town, get grit in both eyes . . . By teatime Pop is little better. I have to sit with them all the evening – a cheerful prospect. Then I think of tomorrow – all a long Sunday sitting with the family – a family who are nervy & quarrelsome.

Then last night was Friday night – & that's the day on which Dylan gets paid – he arrived home at 12.15 (midnight). Then there was much row – nowadays, of course, I come in for Pop's nightly nay hourly grumbles . . . Thursday night – for the first time in years

– Daddy had a night out, arrived home 11.15 & smelt & looked awful ... (*Postscript, Sunday morning*) When I came to bed last night I wrote four pages to you, telling you of how Dylan arrived home past midnight, very drunk, & of all the horrible things that happened. This morning I tore the letter up ...

On 7 October 1932:

This evening Phyllis Bevan and Winnie King arrived. I made coffee for them in the kitchen, Father standing over me saying, 'This sort of thing must stop, I will not have you making food for half Swansea. If they want to eat tell them to go home. Who pays for this food I'd like to know? You must put an end to this bloody rot – if you don't tell your friends I shall.' ... It's now eleven thirty. Dylan has just come in: another row, Oh God! ... Do seal my letters carefully & put lots of wax – yesterday the wax was off – but it was sealed very firm. Do you seal it like that – or did someone open it & seal it back with gum? ...

(?) 23 October 1932:

At present I'm eating alone in the dining room. Mother grumbled at me & I asked her to shut up. Daddy heard & threw a book at me, hit me & behaved in a back street way. Finally after using language that I couldn't repeat – it was filthy – said, 'Who are you? Nobody cares what happens to you, it's a pity you're alive. All you & your beautiful brother do is to take my money from me.' To be classed with Dylan is ghastly; I now eat alone, it's better. I honestly do wish I were dead ... Last night Dylan said one day he'd strangle me ...

16 December 1932:

This lunch hour [Father] arrived home – I'd cooked a special pie & I thought he'd feel cheerful because school was over. He grumbled & grumbled & raved & swore. I like a silly gump said 'Now, Daddy' – which completely put the lid on it. 'Who the bloody hell did I think I was, etc. etc. Dictating to him, was I? He'd screw my bloody head off, etc.' Result was I had to fly upstairs for safety. I have packed my small bag & told them I'm leaving. Pop said, 'No such luck, you'll come cringing back, I know.' ...

4 January 1933:

Another thing has gone ... I left 2s 6d in my small black bag that I'd taken to the Gower Inn. On Monday the 2s 6d had gone. Mother & Daddy blamed me, said I must always carry my purse with me ...

10 January 1933:

Yesterday Eluned, Sadie & Eira came to tea. This morning Eira arrived & said that when she returned a £1 note was missing. No one was here but Dylan so he *must* have taken it . . . Tomorrow I have to go out to Eira's & take a £1 from Pop, one that he can ill afford. Dylan denies the charge & has not been home since early morn . . .

13 January 1933:

Dylan has just risen (11.30) & is in the most foul temper – rushing & raving like a tormented thing. He stays in bed most mornings & then gets up & writes. In the evening he visits Danny. *Unless* he gets any sum of money – then he goes and drinks. What will become of him Heaven knows. Last night I put a shilling in my evening bag; on arriving at the cloakroom – discovered it missing . . . I must stop; ink is wanted by raving brother . . . Mother has just been in & given me a bloody row over the ink question. 'Dylan has got up to work & now no ink, etc. Not fair for the child, etc.' . . .

By this time, the child had lost his job on the *Evening Post*, adding further to his father's worries (and accounting, no doubt, for the raids on handbags). One of his last signed articles as a reporter was a dutiful piece about Uncle David Rees, who was retiring from Paraclete Chapel. Under the headline, 'End of a Great Ministry,' he told *Herald of Wales* readers that 'Mumbles, and indeed the whole of Gower, will lose one of its best-known and best-loved inhabitants'.[2] Comic stories are told of the last straw that broke the editor's back. Mrs Thomas said that 'we saw the only thing to do was to take him from there'. Dim memories survive of the reporters' room being told on a Saturday that Thomas would not be in on Monday. This was late in 1932, probably in December (in her 16 December letter to Haydn Taylor, Nancy says that one of her father's latest problems is 'Dylan home'). But Dylan continued to write for the paper. What finally ended his career may have been an article that the *Evening Post* published on 7 January 1933. In it he mentioned a recent autobiography, Nina Hamnett's *Laughing Torso*. Miss Hamnett was a bohemian figure, once a talented

2. A notebook poem dated the following August is about 'The Reverend Crap, a pious fraud'. Above it, Thomas has added 'Rev. David Rees'.

painter who had spent many years in Paris, and was now enlightening the young in London with her stories of famous friends and lovers; Thomas was to meet her in the Fitzroy pub. Under the heading 'Genius and Madness Akin in World of Art', he trotted out a theme that he found attractive, but unwisely referred to Miss Hamnett as 'author of the banned book *Laughing Torso*'. A week later the paper carried an apology, obviously dictated by lawyers, for having suggested the book was banned – 'We are informed by Miss Hamnett it enjoys a very wide circulation'. The *Evening Post* was by now part of the Northcliffe Group, controlled from London, and the apology must have been arranged by head office.

Early in 1933, then, Thomas was a poet and writer living on his wits and his pen. His parents would have been dismayed to realize that apart from one period of three or four years in the 1940s, this state of affairs was to last for the rest of his life. Nor does it seem to have occurred to Thomas as a fully-formed intention. His letters over the next year or two talked about finding a job, before he subsided into the life of artistic poverty for which he had long been preparing himself, consciously or unconsciously. For the moment he had a home and an indulgent mother, and it was possible to have the poems without the poverty. It was under these comparatively tranquil conditions that his talents presently flared up, producing more poems in a brief period than ever before, or after.

When he first went to work for the newspaper, his output seems to have suffered. If he was copying and dating poems for the exercise-books soon after they were written, he wrote only two between December 1931 and March 1932. This was when his 'Poets of Swansea' articles were appearing. Unfortunately there is a break in the sequence of notebooks later in the year. No. 2 (the '1930–1932 Notebook') ends with a poem dated 1 July 1932, and No. 3 is headed 'This Book started 1 February 1933'. No easy line of progress can be identified in the poetry Thomas was writing, either before the missing notebook or immediately after it. The poems swerve from one style to another, striking a rhetorical attitude one day, speaking almost conversationally the next. The 'biological' language of nerves and eggs makes fleeting appearances. His themes are unremarkable for a boy of seventeen and eighteen: the fact of death, the mystery of life, the contradictions of love. A few poems reiterate his uneasiness about girls. 'Love's a descension of the drawers,' he says in one poem and in another talks of 'sawdust beneath the skirts'. Life is often empty and senseless. Man grows up only to suffer. An early version of 'The Hunchback in the Park' is dated 9 May 1932; according to Daniel Jones it was about a real hunchback who 'seemed to have nowhere else to go' and could be seen in Cwmdonkin. Another of his themes is madness. In one poem (25 June 1932) Thomas is the tormented adolescent who can't sleep and who thinks he is going mad. A lunatic asylum with a raw red tower which was then being built above Sketty is an ominous presence in this poem, where it 'leers down the valley like a fool'. It was still doing useful symbolic service a year later, when he wrote to Trevor Hughes, a Swansea friend who had left the town, to say, 'We have a new asylum. It leers down the valley like a fool, or like a snail with the two turrets of its water tower two snails' horns.' Madness was frightening but it was also exciting. No doubt Thomas was genuinely concerned about madness, but this did not prevent him taking pleasure in his fears as well. Going insane was a risk that poets took, like dying of consumption.

Trevor Hughes was an appropriate person to write to about such matters. He was a railway clerk, ten years older than Thomas – most of Thomas's early friends were older – who had sent him a short story in June 1931, after a paragraph in the *Post* announced 'a new literary publication, entitled "Prose and Verse"', from Thomas's home address. Nothing came of the magazine, but the two were soon friendly. Hughes lived with his widowed mother, who was an invalid. His brother had died of tuberculosis. In Thomas's story 'Who Do You Wish Was With Us?' he is Raymond Price, happy at first to be walking in Gower, until he begins to dwell on sick rooms and death. While Thomas was still working for the newspaper, Hughes and his mother moved to London. This led to correspondence between them, and the first letters known to have been written by Thomas.

In an undated letter, probably of January 1933, he wrote approvingly of Hughes's

solidity and perception of detail, sense of values, if you like, an at-the-root indestructibility of matter, which I haven't got. All I may eventually do is to

Astound the salons and the cliques
Of half-wits, publicists and freaks.

I was out for little else. The majority of literature is the outcome of ill men, and, though you might not know it, I am always ill.

It is never wise to rely too much on Thomas the letter-writer except for entertainment. Did he mean that the poet's perception is feverish and disoriented? Or did he see himself as romantically ill, knowing he was sure to strike a chord with his melancholy friend? Early in February he was telling Hughes:

Give me a sheet of paper and I can't help filling it in. The result, more often than not, is good and bad, serious and comic, sincere and insincere, lucid or nonsensical by the turns of my whirligig mentality, started from the wrong end, a mentality that ran before it walked, and perhaps will never walk, that wanted to fly before it had the right even to think of wings.

But Thomas took himself very seriously as a writer. The notebook poems are an attempt to make some kind of order from his experiences. The high-powered absurdities of the Warmley Broadcasting game, which date from this period, have no counterpart in the notebooks. The poems are without humour. They grind forward earnestly. Every so often the effort produces its reward for Thomas in the shape of a deeper, richer note. It is there briefly in 'Written for a personal epitaph', dated 17 October 1931:

I am man's reply to every question,
His aim and destination.

It is there again in the summer of 1932, this time more sustained. The poem is 'Out of the sighs', and it was the first to be taken from a notebook and published (in 1936) virtually unchanged. In it, Thomas rides above his uncertainties and finds comfort, of a sort, in accepting things as they are:

Out of the sighs a little comes,
But not of grief for I have vanquished that
Before the agony. The spirit grows,
Forgets, and cries.
A little comes, is tasted and found good . . .

The poem is entered in two parts, or was originally written as two poems with more than three weeks between them. The poem's sombre conclusion is not entirely clear. But it has undeniable authority:

Were this enough – bone, blood, and sinew,
The twisted brain, the fair formed loin,
Groping for matter under the dog's plate –
Man should be cured of distemper.
For all there is to give I offer:
Crumbs, barn, and halter.

With that bleak promise on 1 July 1932, the second notebook comes to an end, except for Thomas's scribbled line, 'This has taken a hell of a time'. The break in the series occurs here. When we see him at work again, in Notebook 3, it is the following February, and he is as busy as ever. One of the subjects he found was Ann Jones, the aunt at Fernhill. Early in February 1933 she was dying of cancer in Carmarthen Infirmary. Thomas wrote to Trevor Hughes, minutely inspecting his reactions, and wondering why he was 'utterly unmoved' apart from 'the pleasant death-reek at my negroid nostrils'. A telegram had summoned his mother to the death-bed. Thomas sat at home savouring the drama:

Many summer weeks I spent happily with the cancered aunt on her insanitary farm. She loved me quite inordinately, gave me sweets and money, though she could little afford it, petted, patted, and spoiled me. She writes – is it, I wonder, a past tense yet – regularly. Her postscripts are endearing. She still loves – or loved – me, though I don't know why. And now she is dying, or dead, and you will pardon the theatrical writing. Allow me my moment of drama.

Was he callous or nasty? he asked Hughes. Should he weep and feel pity? The letter shrugged its shoulders:

There must be something lacking in me. I don't feel worried, or hardly ever, about other people. It's self, self, all the time. I'm rarely interested in other people's emotions, except those of my pasteboard characters. I prefer (this is one of the thousand contradictory devils speaking) style to life, my own reactions to emotions rather than the emotions themselves.

Ann Jones died on 7 February, aged seventy. The next day Thomas wrote a first version of 'Was there a time', and informed himself that 'Time has put its maggots on my track'. Ann was buried at Llanybri, a few miles from Fernhill. Thomas, who was presumably a mourner, then wrote 'After the funeral'. Unlike the famous later version, this was not a sad celebration of her death but merely a comment on the pointlessness of dying and the hypocrisy of the mourners. Thomas may have been wrapped up in himself, but at least he was trying to be honest about it.

So far he had made no progress towards finding a publisher for his poems or for the stories that he was also writing. Whatever he thought privately about his ability as a poet, he lacked confidence in the practical nature of the product. Nor had a single distinctive style emerged. With hindsight it is easy enough to see flashes of it, but in 1933 Thomas was merely a working writer making some interesting experiments.

In the circumstances he was lucky to meet a new face, an older man from outside his circle who could offer kindly criticism and knowledgeable advice. The new friend was not a schoolmaster or a journalist, but, improbably enough, a grocer and former income-tax clerk of strong left-wing views who dabbled in literature, called Bert Trick. Again it was an older man. No doubt Thomas, with his powerful instinct for finding friends to lean on, knew what he was after when he called at the shop one evening with poems in his pocket. It stood on the corner of two residential avenues at the lower end of the Uplands, facing a park, Brynmill. Trick was about to put up the shutters. Thomas bought some cigarettes and said he had read a poem by Trick in a local newspaper. Invited into the living-room behind the shop, he soon produced his own poems, and was asked to read them. From childhood Thomas liked to read his poems aloud; to listen was to be his friend. Trick listened and said the right things. He was a hard-bitten little man in his mid-thirties, almost twice Thomas's age, who began life as an engineering apprentice in a neighbouring town, and was now active in the local Labour Party. His family had helped him buy the shop a few years earlier. Disgusted with capitalism and fascism, he looked hopefully to his brand of ideology to build a better and more spiritual future, where good literature would find its place as naturally as social benefits. Thomas seized on all this, and for a while was a muddled disciple of Trick, who regarded him fondly as a brilliant but erratic younger brother. Dylan, he said, was 'politically illiterate' to begin with, and 'found the jargon of left-wing politics quite incomprehensible'. Trick tried to educate him, without great success. The times were right for anger about social conditions. Unemployment was especially high in Wales. Swansea had ten thousand on the register, of a total population of 170,000, and more than two thousand families on the Means Test. But the workless factories and coal-mines were not very noticeable in middle-class Uplands. The dole queues were on the other side of town. Bert Trick did his best to bring them closer for Thomas.

His own poetry, which he wrote in his spare time, was likely to have Marx and Jesus in it: he was an agnostic somewhere on the fringes of belief who liked to argue about religion, far into the night. Thomas was enthusiastic about socialism because it meant rebelling against established values. He would debate injustice and decadent Western society for hours. But with minor exceptions, the poems he was writing remained impervious to political ideas. London was full of politically committed poets with a sense of social responsibility, many of whom felt guilty because their families were members of the governing class that was alleged to be doing the damage. Thomas went no further than a few references in notebook poems, not published in his lifetime, to the horrors of the post-war world. 'The Western man has lost one lung,' he wrote on 16 February, echoing a thought that Trick put in a poem of his own, about 'lungs chewed by poison gas'. The one poem with a vaguely political content that Thomas published was 'The hand that signed the paper felled a city', which could have been inspired by Hitler – in power in Germany since earlier that year – but has a flavour of far-off tyrants, perhaps from the Bible. It is dated 17 August 1933, and inscribed 'To A.E.T.', Trick's initials, in the notebook.

Their friendship was literary as well as political. Trick was introduced to word-play; the grocer's house in Glanbrydan Avenue became a plebeian version of Dan Jones's Warmley, the centre of an informal group of friends who met there to talk and play games. Trick (who died in 1968) told Kent Thompson that they used to juxtapose unlikely words and experiment with vowel changes. 'Too many cooks spoil the broth' became 'Too many cocks spoil the breath', a typical Thomas joke. He never tired of taking words to pieces, as if they were bits of machinery, to see how the letters worked. Trick noted that when it came to his poems, 'Dylan was concerned with the words, and the meaning could look after itself.' If they moved on to the interpretation of his poems, Thomas would say, 'Your meaning is as good as mine.'

He was at home with the Tricks. Bert's wife, Nell, had an infant daughter, Pamela. One night, just before sleep, Pamela asked, 'What colour is glory?' Thomas pounced on the phrase and fitted it into a poem, later transferring it to another, 'My world is pyramid', where the question survives, obscurely. He was often at the house, bringing the small ration of beer that was all he could afford, concealed in a dandelion-and-burdock bottle of brown glass, having uproarious jokes with Trick. Nell was pregnant. When the child, a boy, was born, Dylan was her first visitor. He and Bert decided a good name for it would be Kerith, presumably from George Moore's book *The Brook Kerith*, but Nell was suspicious. She thought it was one of their silly words or an anagram for something rude, and had to be convinced otherwise before she would agree to it.

Early in 1933, Thomas sent two of his poems to London. One went to the B.B.C., which had announced a poetry competition at the end of the previous year, with a closing date of 28 February. It was called 'The Romantic Isle'. This was his first attempt to have a serious poem published outside Wales. The other was a first version of 'And death shall have no dominion', later one of his best-known poems. Trick claimed that it was he who persuaded Thomas, with difficulty, to send it to a magazine, the *New English Weekly.* More than that, it was apparently thanks to Trick that it was written in the first place.

The background to the poem was Thomas's need to find a 'philosophy'. Like most adolescents he wanted a system to believe in. The notebook poems show him painfully aware of life's contrasts. He often used the image of 'black' versus 'white', and 'black' threatened to get the better of him. Thomas had a peculiarly morbid streak. A poem dated 1 February 1933, in which he contrasts day with night, is stocked with typical ingredients: maggots on dead flesh, a vulture, a 'redcheeked vampire at the neck', a skeleton, a ghost, an eaten corpse. In another poem, two months later, he declared that 'I have been frightened of the dark for years', and dredged up more night scenes, where

a skeleton
Sits back and smiles, a tiny corpse
Turns to the roof a hideous grimace,
Or mice play with an ivory tooth.

Could the 'tiny corpse' have been his mother's first child, the baby that died? Thomas knew there had been another child. Whatever its origin, the key to the poem was where he declared that

Unless I learn the night I shall go mad.
It is night's terrors I must learn to love . . .

No doubt dreams played an important part in the writing of poems all his life, and certainly during adolescence. His correspondence with Pamela reports dreams and nightmares. If the letters are to be believed, often he slept badly and lay awake for hours. Perhaps the strangeness of his early poems owes something to the words and images that rise up in the mind in those hallucinatory periods between sleep and waking.

Horrors were undeniable; Thomas had to learn to live with them. His need to reconcile living flesh with dead flesh was a permanent obsession that reached down to the roots of his nature. He was aware of his body with a glandular mixture of pleasure and fear, as his poems were soon to demonstrate. But when he was with Trick, he could see the problem of black versus white in Trick's more pedestrian terms. He could write (on 17 February) about Western man with one lung missing, about 'exsoldiers with horrors for a face' and 'the living dead left over from the war', and consider the merits of saving the world with a faith of some kind, perhaps Christian. The poem ends: 'Believe, believe and be saved, we cry, who have no faith.' It sounds as if he was being influenced by Trick, the agnostic with the old-fashioned socialist's interest in Christianity.

One day that spring, Trick suggested they each write a poem about 'immortality'. Trick's contribution, which was published in a local newspaper the following year, spoke of the soul going up like a bird to 'a living God', and had the refrain, 'For death is not the end!' Thomas wrote 'And death shall have no dominion', dated 'April' in the notebook. Persuaded by Trick, he sent it to A. R. Orage, the editor of *New English Weekly*, who published it the following month. An expert piece of rhetoric that booms like an organ, it sounds more an act of defiance than a declaration of faith: as if Thomas was willing himself to be optimistic because it was the only way of preserving his sanity. He nearly decided against republishing it in book form. Perhaps it was part of a lifelong effort to look on the bright side that finally came to nothing.

But for the moment he was making progress. Instead of the asylum leering down the valley like a fool, he changed the image in an April poem to make the moon peer down the valley like a saint. On 22 April he wrote a poem that spelt out his new state of mind. For the last five years, he said, he had found 'no hope of harmony', no way of 'bridging white and black' –

> and now this year
> Has found a cure.
> New music, from new and loud, sounds on the air.

On 18 May, 'And death shall have no dominion' appeared in print. Trick recalled Thomas's disgust when he found that Orage didn't pay for contributions. 'It won't buy me any Woodbines,' he said. But he was now a published poet. Presently he was told that 'The Romantic Isle' was one of thirty poems chosen for broadcasting by the B.B.C. competition judges, Walter de la Mare and Edward Marsh. Eleven thousand offerings had arrived at Broadcasting House, most of them, announced the B.B.C., with an 'astonishing absence of any understanding of the business of writing poetry'. Thomas's was read in the National Programme, late in the evening, at the end of June. The poem has not survived but the title suggests one of his blander pieces.

Thomas was still uncertain what style to adopt in his verse. His next published poem, in July, had an improbable origin, an open-air performance of *Electra* in the garden of Mrs Bertie Perkins, a well-to-do resident of Sketty Green. Pigeons cooed above, harp and drums played accompanying music by Daniel Jones, and 'Soapy' Davies, classics master at the Grammar School, was annoyed to see his ex-pupil, the wastrel Thomas, mooning about under the trees, not paying attention to Sophocles. He is said to have been suitably repentant a week later when the *Herald of Wales* published Thomas's 'Greek Play in a Garden'. It was well wrought without being particularly Thomas-like. Far more ambitious poems were being added to the current notebook at the rate of two or three a week. But no single style predominated. Thomas's old doubts about himself both as person and poet recurred in 'Ears in the turrets hear' (17 July) where he was undecided again, wondering what the world had to offer. The poem (later published almost unchanged) had characteristic images – he saw himself as an island with 'a thin sea of flesh' and 'a bone coast' – but its tone was quiet, even self-pitying.

It was not until the poems he began to write late in the summer, which peered morbidly into his adolescent anatomy, that the density and violence of the 'real' Thomas began to take over. The end of August 1933 marked a turning point. Up to that date, when he was still only eighteen, Thomas had written, mainly since he left the *Evening Post*, twelve of his ninety *Collected Poems* in a form close to their final version. (He had written a further eleven of his final output that were to be more substantially revised or entirely rewritten before they appeared in print.) The twelve poems are straightforward; most can be understood at a first reading; there is little scope for critics to contradict one another about the meaning. Had Thomas been satisfied with this style, in poems like 'Ears in the turrets hear' and 'Why east wind chills', the literary establishment would have greeted him with interest but hardly such excitement as they were to show. This group was to be the backbone of the *second* book he published, in 1936, *Twenty-five Poems*, which disappointed some critics because it lacked the intense self-absorption of its 1934 predecessor, *18 Poems*. They wondered which way young Thomas was going. In fact, he had already gone. The violently introspective poems that went into the first book were mostly written after August 1933, that is, later than the 'straightforward' group that went into the second. It was these later poems, pumped out in the year from September 1933, that were quickly assembled for *18 Poems* and made him famous.

This is an over-simplified version of what was happening. Thomas was producing poems, not material for theses. There are no precise categories. The break between styles was not absolute – he wrote some straightforward, non-anatomical poems after the end of August. But a shift is apparent. After much hesitation he settled for a particular style, probably without realizing it at first. The act was part of the process of resolving his uncertainties. It went with the change of mood that had enabled him to subdue his nightmares, or at least to accept that black and white must coexist. A knot of nervous energy waited to be released. He had often felt sorry for himself, the poet who hung back, afraid to risk failure by trying too hard. 'No bird for me: /He flies too high', he wrote in 1930. In July 1933, 'Ears in the turrets hear' was equally apprehensive; its original title for publication was 'Dare I?'. Now he was to answer his questions and resolve his doubts with a surge of energy.

CHAPTER FIVE

# *A Case of Cancer*

THERE are obvious dangers in looking too enthusiastically for connections between Thomas's poetry and his everyday life in the crucial closing months of 1933. The interplay between the nature he was born with and the surroundings he was born into may have done its work when he was a child. In that case his talent was ticking away like a piece of sealed clockwork, unconnected with events at Cwmdonkin Drive or anywhere else. But it is possible that the mechanism could be, and was, modified by events.

In August he went tc London for what was probably his first visit, and furthered his career, so he hoped, by meeting some editors. Two of Thomas's friends (Trevor Hughes and the writer George Reavey) have said they met him in London in 1932, but no other evidence of such a visit has come to light. In 1933 he stayed at least some of the time with his sister and her husband, Haydn Taylor. They had married by special licence (because neither was living in the parish) in a Gower village at the end of May, and had gone to live in a houseboat on the Thames near Chertsey, on the south-west edge of London. This made a good jumping-off point for Thomas. During his visit he is said to have seen Orage of *New English Weekly* and Sir Richard Rees, who edited the monthly *Adelphi* from a flat near Albert Bridge; next month Rees published a poem by Thomas, 'No Man Believes'. It seems to have been a quiet visit; either there were no London anecdotes of the fiery boy worth telling, or, if there were, no one was yet collecting them. There is one story, but it concerns something that almost certainly never happened. Thomas is supposed to have stolen his sister's engagement ring from the houseboat. Fiction abounds in Thomas's life, and makes the business of biography even more hazardous than usual. He lied for fun or profit, and so did his sister. It was she who told the story to Gwevril Dawkins, when Mrs Dawkins (then unmarried) stayed on the houseboat in the summer of 1933. Nancy described to her what had happened the previous weekend. The Taylors had been to a party on the Saturday evening. They were late returning, but about half past five on Sunday morning they were awakened by the sound of someone leaving the boat. Haydn Taylor's loose change had gone from the chest of drawers. So had Nancy's engagement ring, a square-cut emerald set in diamonds, valued (according to Nancy) at eight hundred pounds. Taylor drove to Reading, where trains for Swansea call, caught up with Thomas, who had hitch-hiked there, and took back the ring. Mrs Dawkins believed the story for forty years. But Haydn Taylor says it is a fabrication. He could not have afforded a ring costing more than twenty or thirty pounds. It was never stolen. There was no dawn departure. The obvious conclusion is that Nancy invented the story to impress her friend with her brother's awfulness.

At home again, Thomas sent poems to Geoffrey Grigson for the magazine *New Verse* that he had started in January that year. *New Verse* had a tiny circulation, never much more than a thousand copies. But Grigson, then in his late twenties, soon made it influential. A parson's son from Cornwall, he was a clever man, a poet himself, who soon knew his way around literary London, and was to flourish as an editor with a sharp tongue and a sharper pen. The well-connected Cyril Connolly, another writer and editor, called him, 'one of the shrewdest operators on the kerb-market of contemporary letters'. Thomas picked him out as a target and accompanied his poems with a country-boy's apologia: '. . . I have developed, intellectually at least, in the smug darkness of a provincial town, and have only on rare occasions shown any of my work to any critics, generally uninterested or incompetent . . Grinding out poetry, whether good or bad, in such an atmosphere as surrounds me, is depressing and disheartening.' For the moment, Wales had a sharply diminishing appeal. The last poem in Notebook 3, dated 16 August, is the jingle about 'The Reverend Crap'.

Grigson sent the poems back. Thomas was luckier in another

direction. In April the *Sunday Referee* had announced a feature called 'The Poets' Corner' and invited contributions ('We care nothing who holds the stylus'), with predictable results. Poems poured in. The newspaper was edited by Mark Goulden, later a successful publisher, who was trying to interest a level of readership between the heavier Sunday journals, the *Observer* and *Sunday Times*, and the sex-and-crime papers farther down the market. Goulden commissioned writers like Bernard Shaw and Compton Mackenzie; it was a time when 'good writing' was still an adequate weapon for a circulation war. In charge of the Poets' Corner was a literary journalist called Victor Neuberg. Neuberg, then in middle-age, was a highly strung bisexual of peculiar habits who for years was under the spell, literally, of Aleister Crowley, the deranged magician. Together, according to Crowley, they materialized spirits and practised assorted magic. Neuberg had parted from the magician (and been ritually cursed, which gave him a nervous breakdown) twenty years before he joined the *Sunday Referee*.

At the end of July 1933, Daniel Jones comes briefly into the story. He was at a literary gathering in the cottage at Steyning, in Sussex, where Neuberg spent much of his time. So was a young London woman whose poetry had already been published in the *Referee*, Pamela Hansford Johnson. Jones was not impressed with his afternoon under the Downs, but he talked about it to Thomas, who presently sent a poem to Neuberg. It began, 'That sanity be kept I sit at open windows', and had a strong flavour of T. S. Eliot. Neuberg printed it on 3 September, describing it as 'perhaps the best modernist poem that as yet I've received'.

But by the time the poem appeared, Thomas had other things to think about. On or about 27 August, his father had visited a dentist in the Uplands. The dentist noticed an ulcer on the floor of his mouth, below the tongue, and suggested he see a doctor. D.J. was always careful of his health. His wife said that in his teaching career, there was only a single term in which he was never absent through illness. This time it was not hypochondria or a cold. He saw his family doctor, who called in a specialist, who diagnosed cancer. He was fifty-seven years old, and Haydn Taylor, who hurried to Swansea with Nancy, was given a gloomy prognosis. His chances of being alive in five years were small. The Taylors took him by car to London, where he was admitted to University College Hospital on 10 September. Next morning a painful week of treatment with radium needles began.

Over the following months he made a number of journeys between Swansea and London. In October he was treated with radium again, this time for more than two weeks. For a while his voice was affected. Haydn Taylor, collecting him from hospital to return him to Swansea, found his temper unchanged. The car was late arriving and D.J. was furious. They stopped at a pub for him to have a Guinness. By early in 1934 the malignant ulcer was fading, and near-by glands were seen to be unaffected. D.J. was lucky, a good advertisement for early diagnosis. But it was another year or so before the family could breathe again. Dylan, who regarded cancer with special awe, and used the word often in his early poems, wrung the last drop of agony from the situation. He told Trevor Hughes (January 1934) that his father had been 'operated upon for cancer of the throat', and this is the version of the illness that most people remember. (Knowing that D.J. lived for nearly twenty years more, and how Dylan loved to dramatize, sceptical friends of the family have gone to the other extreme and concluded that D.J. didn't have cancer at all.)

What effect, if any, did his father's illness have on Dylan Thomas's poetry? One or two direct references can be traced. A poem in Notebook 4 (the final poetry notebook, begun on 23 August) with the date 12 September, two days after his father entered hospital, has the opening line, 'Take the needles and the knives'. On 17 October, the day his father was readmitted to hospital, the poem later published as 'From love's first fever to her plague' has the line, 'The root of tongues ends in a spentout cancer'. But these are only curiosities. More significant is the fact that the first complete, full-blooded 'anatomical' poem is also the first poem to follow the news of his father's cancer, if, as is almost certain, the illness had been diagnosed by 6 September, the date in the notebook. The poem is

'Before I knocked', where he sees himself as (among other things) an unborn child:

> My throat knew thirst before the structure
> Of skin and vein around the well
> Where words and water make a mixture
> Unfailing till the blood runs foul;
> My heart knew love, my belly hunger;
> I smelt the maggot in my stool.

As Ralph Maud, who edited the poetry notebooks, commented, 'The stage is set for Thomas's distinctive organic imagery.' His concern with death, his morbid self-awareness, had been in the background for a long time. He had (for the moment) come to terms with his neurotic fears, if the evidence of the notebooks is to be believed. Now came the knowledge that his father had cancer and was likely to die. Thus, while he had become more sure of himself as a poet, his father's illness gave his imagination something near and frightening to bite on. It was not a distant episode like the cancered aunt on her insanitary farm; a contemporary remembers Thomas as deeply upset in the autumn of 1933. The effect on his writing can only be guessed at. But the dates of poems and illness connect. After 6 September, poems of the new kind begin to appear regularly in the notebooks, among them 'My hero bares his nerves' (17 September). On 12 October he composed, or copied out, 'The force that through the green fuse drives the flower'. Recognizing a good thing when he wrote it, Thomas sent it to Victor Neuberg, who printed it on 29 October. Poets' Corner was typographically cramped that weekend, and the text, which told perceptive readers that here was something beyond the usual run of *Referee* verse, was unceremoniously split in the middle and continued in the next column. The poem had no doubt of its own importance; apart from puns, there are no jokes in Thomas's early poems, and very few in later ones. Thomas identifies himself with natural phenomena – flowers, rocks, water, wind – as he was to do elsewhere. (Disguises were part of his basic repertoire. He might be the landscape or the weather; he could be the foetus or the egg; he took on the rôle of The Poet or Man or Christ, separately or at the same time.) Neuberg described it as 'cosmic in outlook'; he was the first to use such language about Dylan Thomas. This did not stop Thomas being contemptuous of Neuberg and his coterie.

'The force that through the green fuse' was one of the early poems that Dylan Thomas still liked, when he came to look back on them. But he preferred not to look back at all. His early poems haunted him. He spoke later of their 'vehement beat-pounding black and green rhythms like those of a very young policeman exploding', and said he had forgotten why he wrote them, no doubt because they represented an achievement in a short space of time that was never repeated. Five days after 'The force that through the green fuse' (and ten days before his nineteenth birthday) he completed 'From love's first fever to her plague', where he is the embryo, the child, the poet:

> I learnt the verbs of will and had my secret;
> The code of night tapped on my tongue.

November produced three more of the *Collected Poems*, all in his 'cosmic' style, including the mysterious 'Light breaks where no sun shines' that did more than any other single poem to draw attention to Thomas when the B.B.C.'s journal, the *Listener*, published it the following spring. Everything was packed tight in these poems. 'I like things that are difficult to write and difficult to understand,' he wrote to Charles Fisher a year or so later. '. . . I like contradicting my images, saying two things at once in one word, four in two and one in six.' Poetry, added Thomas in one of his infrequent bursts of explanation, should be 'as orgiastic and organic as copulation ... Poetry is a medium, not a stigmata on paper. Men should be two-tooled, and a poet's middle leg is his pencil.'

The early poems steam with sexual energy. Their death-symbols, the maggots and ghosts, are entwined with sex-images – the 'rainy hammer' of his father's penis against the womb, or the boy who masturbates, 'rehearsing heat upon a raw-edged nerve'. The act of masturbation is implicit in several poems, reflecting Thomas's sexual experience at the time. The style in which he was writing may have been contrived for maximum effect, but there is no doubt that he is describing what he feels, what he *is*. He was trying to encompass (in powerful 'poetic' language as befitted his vocation) what it meant to be his particular man or boy at the age of nineteen.

It is not at all certain that he had slept with a girl at the time of his nineteenth birthday, in October 1933. At that time and place, to be a male virgin at nineteen would have been unexceptional (as it still was a generation later). Conditions were not conducive; girls were apprehensive; there was nowhere to go. Mervyn Levy, a few months older than Thomas, discussed sex with him when they were sub-adolescents, and they shared a book with reproductions of nude paintings. 'We were bred in the masturbatory era,' says Levy, 'and I think Dylan carried it with him all his life.' Aged eleven or twelve, they spied on the Levys' maid and saw her washing her breasts in a handbasin.[1] Levy was sexually precocious, but he didn't sleep with a girl until he went to London, aged seventeen. On the other hand, Thomas used to claim that he was sexually experienced at fifteen. In the last weeks of his life, when *Time* magazine was having him shadowed by a private detective in New York, he was heard to say he first had sexual relations at that age. No doubt he could have been heard to say it in various places over the years. 'I should be ashamed,' he said in a lecture, 'had not shame been lost to me in the back of a lorry in, I think, nineteen hundred and thirty.'

If his claim was true, and he had sexual intercourse at a tender age, it was presumably with a girl he picked up from outside his circle. The traditional place to find a willing girl of one's own age was on the 'prom', the path along a stretch of seafront, beside the railway and the dunes. All-girl and all-boy groups would march from end to end on summer evenings, past the pallid war memorial in the middle, colliding with one another and occasionally, very occasionally, pairing off. One of Thomas's Swansea friends told Kent Thompson of an incident with a girl they took into the sand-dunes. They sat on either

1. In 'The Peaches' Thomas wrote, 'I looked with Dan Jones through the keyhole while his maid had a bath.' Perhaps there was a lot of it going on.

side and attempted to fondle her, without much success. Their ages are not given. It is said that Thomas went to the Strand, then a slum district near the docks, to look for girls, presumably prostitutes. This is the area that Thomas the Reporter visits on his pub-crawl with Freddie Farr in 'Old Garbo'.

In the last of his *Portrait of the Artist* stories, 'One Warm Saturday', Thomas describes an encounter with a girl in roughly this category, except that she is supposed to combine sex with romantic love. Thomas sees himself as a clumsy but dogged lone wolf, in search of excitement on a summer evening. The story, like others in *Portrait*, is full of details that those who know the town can recognize. Probably it reflects an amalgam of incidents, as in 'The Peaches'. Aged perhaps eighteen or nineteen, he first sees the girl in a little park by the seafront, reading a novel. She is sitting 'opposite the white-tiled urinal', no doubt an intentional detail; she is 'innocent' and demurely dressed, but at the same time 'her smile confessed her body bare and spotless and willing and warm under the cotton'. Later he sees her with friends in a pub. She is called Lou and is instantly attracted to him. Eventually he accompanies the party to a tenement block beyond the docks, for what he and the girl expect to be a night together. The story is heavy with sexual frustration. When he first sees the girl, and is afraid to speak to her, Thomas thinks, 'She could drive my guilt out; she could smooth away my shame.' When he sees her again in the pub, he is tempted to go home to dream about her – 'But only a sick boy with tossed blood would run from his proper love into a dream, lie down in a bedroom that was full of his shames, and sob against the feathery, fat breast and face of the damp pillow. He remembered his age and poems, and would not move.' In other words he resists the temptation to do as he usually does, and enjoy himself with masturbatory fantasies in his bedroom. But as the story progresses, his attempt to be grown-up comes to nothing. He leaves her in the tenement – to find a lavatory – and loses his way in the decaying block. There is no night of love. He ends as he began, by himself, on a patch of waste ground with the remains of houses, 'where the small and hardly known and never-to-be-forgotten people of the dirty town had lived and loved and died and, always, lost'. This is Thomas's compassion operating through his own sense of loss and defeat. Perhaps he did meet a Lou in Swansea, and have more success with her; certainly he took her to bed in various shapes and sizes later on. But the theme of sexual failure is apparent.

Thomas's reputation in Swansea was for amusing and occasionally outrageous behaviour; not for chasing girls. Nell Trick has no memory of seeing or hearing about a girl friend. Evelyn Jones was one of the Little Theatre group. She acted with Thomas, drank in pubs and went for walks with him. She says he made no sexual advances to her or to anyone else as far as she knew. He used to say naughty things and make the girls blush; they loved it. 'He'd say, "Let's go roistering and rude bathing," but when we got to Langland Bay he never took his socks off.' They appeared together in Congreve's *The Way of the World* in January 1934, Evelyn wearing a low-cut dress. Thomas delighted in referring to her as 'Tess of the two big villes'. She played Mincing. He kept enticing her, in her bosomy dress, into the pub that adjoined the theatre. 'He'd say, "Come on Mincing, let's mince off." I could never not go. I used to die of embarrassment, but I liked it so much.' He was a joker, a card. On the Little Theatre programmes he wrote 'C.B.' against the names of girls who were supposed to be sexually unwilling; 'C.B.' stood for 'chastity belt'. On Evelyn's twenty-first birthday Thomas sent her a letter from London to be read at her dance. It went something like –

> Sorry I cannot pavane at the tavern.
> I'm off to galliard with a Spaniard.
> Here's a toast from me to thee:
> A pox upon your chastity.

With the verse came an 'outrageous drawing' of Evelyn in a chastity belt which was being unfastened by a man labelled 'Pox'.

Thomas's first serious girl friend was almost certainly Pamela Hansford Johnson, later a novelist and the wife of a novelist, Lord (C. P.) Snow. In 1933, Pamela lived with her mother in Battersea. Her recollection is that when Thomas's Eliotflavoured poem, 'That sanity be kept', appeared there at the start of September, she wrote to say she admired it – presumably she had already heard about him from Daniel Jones when they met at Steyning. This began a short but intense correspondence and a love affair; all her letters to him have vanished, but about twenty-five of his survive. As though a door has suddenly blown open, Dylan Thomas is revealed in action. These are the most explicit letters he ever wrote. Later, his letters to others became more contrived, and, after the 1930s, increasingly concerned with absurdities, arrangements and crises, mainly over money. When he wrote to Pamela, he was giving her a running commentary on his life and thoughts.

The full correspondence totals more than fifty thousand words, and has to be read entire to do it justice. About half the surviving letters were written before they met, in February 1934. Thomas presents himself as an unhealthy little poet with a sense of humour, struggling to write in unhelpful surroundings. The word 'little' occurs time and again. He watches his little vest blowing on the line on washday and sees his little body in the armchair. 'I'm an odd little person ... a thin, curly little person, smoking too many cigarettes, with a crocked lung, and writing his vague verses in the back room of a provincial villa ... little with no health at all ... I hardly weigh anything at all ... I look about fourteen, and I have a large, round nose; nature gave it to me, but fate, and a weak banister, broke it ... lonely little person ... nice little soul ... little Welsh ear ... little feet ... little poet.' In fact (as he said in one letter) his height was about five feet six inches and he weighed eight stone ten; he was not big, certainly, but the extreme littleness, the feeling of frailty, seem to have been largely in his mind. He made a virtue of it. Perhaps to be small (or to be a mouse or a pig, both affectionate epithets he gave himself in letters to others) was to be safe and baby-like again.

Associated with his size was his health. 'Cough! cough! cough!' he writes, 'my death is marching on.' He made jokes about it. Behind the jokes is a real melancholy, but behind that again there may be a further layer of jokiness, and so on, layer by layer, making it impossible to be sure when the 'real' Dylan is reached, if ever. 'A misanthropic doctor, who apparently did not like the way I did my eyebrows, has given me four years to live,' he wrote in early November. 'May I borrow that foul expression of yours – it isn't yours really – and whisper Sez You into his ear.' A few days later he implies he has consumption. He writes: 'Four years, my sweet. 1340 days and nights. And thank you for the optimistic remarks. I don't believe it either, but then it would be very odd if I did. You should hear me cough, though.' He adds that 'your belief in my power to write' is one of the things that make him deny what the doctor said. But all this has been deflated in advance by a side-heading in the letter: *Pathos.*

Miss Johnson became worried. When they met, and there was talk of them getting married, she begged him to see another doctor. He promised, and later told her he had done as she asked. 'But it was a lie,' says Lady Snow. She came to see his tuberculosis as something he wanted, not something he had. He found the disease romantically appealing. When Thomas was first in London, the writer Rayner Heppenstall was told that Thomas's lungs would kill him within months unless he lived quietly. Thomas lived noisily and thrived. It is doubtful if any doctor delivered a four-year warning, or whether he suffered from anything worse than a tendency to be 'weak-chested' and asthmatic, aggravated by a large intake of cigarette smoke from the age of eleven. A gargantuan smoker's cough was one of his trademarks. Towards the end of his life he suffered from breathlessness. But the post-mortem found no trace of scars from old tuberculosis. There is a parallel with his liver, another organ that was unkindly treated. Thomas liked to say that he had cirrhosis of the liver, a later version of the story that he had T.B. Again, although the post-mortem showed that his liver was fatty and in bad shape, it reported no cirrhosis. Thomas was a man in search of ailments to suit the poet's personality.

If his health was a bad joke in his letters to Pamela, so was his situation. 'Swansea is a dingy hell, and my mother is a vulgar humbug,' he wrote. After a bus journey to Carmarthenshire, to stay at the Blaen Cwm cottages, he described what he had seen in the small towns they passed through, the women 'all breast and bottom', the colliers 'diseased in mind and body as only the Welsh can be . . . It's impossible for me to tell you how much I want to get out of it all, out of narrowness and dirtiness, out of the eternal ugliness of the Welsh people, and all that belongs to them, out of the pettiness of a mother I don't care for and the giggling batch of relatives.'

That was written some time in the autumn, when his father's cancer was still causing maximum distress. He makes only one or two direct references to D.J. Under the heading, 'My life. A Touching Autobiography in One Paragraph', in a letter written the week after 'The force that through the green fuse' was published, he told Pamela, 'I first saw the light of day in a Glamorgan villa, and, amid the terrors of the Welsh accent and the smoke of the tinplate stacks,[2] grew up to be a sweet baby, a precocious child, a rebellious boy, and a morbid youth. My father was a schoolmaster: a broader-minded man I have never known.' Early in 1934 he was describing how his father had spent 'the last three months . . . undergoing treatment for cancer of the throat. He is home now, partially cured and exceedingly despondent. His time limit is even shorter than mine (!). Ours is a nice 'ouse. There is one unintelligent dog, too, with the highly original name of Spot.'

Fantasy is ingrained in the letters, modifying and shaping his experiences for Pamela. In an undated letter of late 1933 he felt 'like a dead man exulting in the company of his beetles, incarnadining the monstrous earth – words, words, words – with the blood of the worms (yes, worms again, my dear) that he breaks – as a housemaid crushes a flea – between the tips of his nails. Sometimes I am very nice, but today I'm awful; I'm caught in my complexes, and they're giving me immense, if unholy, joy.' They are often very 'literary' letters, apparently heartfelt but carefully contrived. At least some (he told Pamela) were first written as notes, then copied out later. Perhaps they are most revealing when they deal, as they often do, with his poetry. Thomas was then writing about something, probably the only thing, that was of absolute importance to him. 'I do

2. The Uplands is comfortably distant from smoking chimneys.

not want to express only what other people have felt,' he wrote. 'I want to rip something away and show what they have never seen.'

He admonished Pamela for not being sufficiently personal in her poetry, as he was: 'Everything comes out of yourself, and darkness, despite what you say, has infinitely more possibilities than day.' Reproving her for calling his poetry ugly – she jibbed at his worms and cancers, until she grew accustomed to them – he pointed out that it was 'nothing but the strong stressing of the physical', with its images drawn from

> my solid and fluid world of flesh and blood ... The greatest description I know of our own 'earthiness' is to be found in John Donne's 'Devotions', where he describes man as earth of the earth, his body earth, his hair a wild shrub growing out of the land. All thoughts and actions emanate from the body. Therefore the description of a thought or action – however abstruse it may be – can be beaten home by bringing it onto a physical level. Every idea, intuitive or intellectual, can be imaged and translated in terms of the body, its flesh, skin, blood, sinews, veins, glands, organs, cells, or senses. Through my small, bonebound island I have learnt all I know, experienced all, and sensed all.

He liked to think he was in control of his material: the idea that the poems erupted from unconscious levels upset him. Sir Richard Rees of the *Adelphi* wrote to ask for more poems. Thomas sent them off, only to be told by the puzzled editor that they had 'an unsubstantiality, a dream-like quality' that reminded him of automatic writing. In that case, Thomas wrote to Pamela, 'I am nothing but a literary oddity, a little freak of nature whose madness runs into print rather than into ravings and illusions ... But he is wrong, I swear it. My facility, as he calls it, is, in reality, tremendously hard work. I write at the speed of two lines an hour. I have written hundreds of poems, & each one has taken me a great many painful, brain-racking and sweaty hours.'

His letters were pessimistic about his future as a poet. This is hardly surprising. He was writing unfashionable poems in a provincial town. No one in London (or in Wales for that matter) was clamouring for them, apart from Victor Neuberg, 'the

Vicky Bird', and Thomas regarded him with disdain from the start. Pamela had been chosen (before she and Dylan began to correspond) to begin what the *Referee* saw as a long line of prize poets, whose first book of verse would be sponsored by the newspaper. Neuberg had gushingly called her 'one of the few exquisite word-artists of our day'. Thomas did his best to criticize her poems without being too cruel; in any case she soon realized that poetry was not her vocation. But his own success was just as limited. The low-powered *Referee* was still his best hope, and by the beginning of February 1934, even the *Referee* had printed only three poems.

Thomas's situation at home had grown more precarious since his father's illness, although at the hospital in January 1934 there was no sign of malignancy, and even the patient admitted he was feeling better. He began to teach again; according to a colleague, no one from the school had visited him while he was ill. A mellowing is said to have been noticeable soon after; his sarcasm was not so sharp; he was a changed man. Dylan was under pressure to find work and earn money. His writer's day, as described to Pamela, was not encouraging for anxious parents: breakfast in bed at a quarter to ten, a leisurely morning with newspapers and books, a lunchtime pint at the Uplands Hotel, an afternoon of reading, writing or walking in Gower, an evening of pubs or Little Theatre, and finally more writing. 'Not a very British day,' as he remarked.

He was now drinking steadily, or at least he gave that impression. At the Little Theatre he went too far one night and was removed from a major part at the last minute. The play, their February production, was *Martine* by Jean-Jacques Bernard. Ethel Ross, a member of the company, says it was because he went for a drink during the dress-rehearsal, after a final warning from the producer. Malcolm Graham, who took over the part (of a journalist) from Thomas, says it was because he arrived at the rehearsal speechless with drink. Either way, there was a scene.

A week after this fiasco he went to London for his first meeting with Pamela and to look for work. They had already spoken on the telephone, arranging the visit. 'Such a rich fruity old port wine of a voice,' she wrote in her diary. When he arrived from Paddington Station she found him 'charming, very young-looking, with a most enchanting voice' A scrap of cigarette paper was stuck to his lower lip. His sweater was large, his trousers were baggy, and under his pork-pie hat was what Lady Snow recalled as 'the most beautiful curling hair, parted in the middle, the colour in those days – when he washed it – of dark gold'. But the bulging eyes and sonorous voice were what captured her, as they captured others. Her mother was enchanted, too. This was just as well for the young lovers. Life at the Johnsons in Battersea (and in Chelsea, where they moved later in 1934) was well regulated. Mrs Johnson, a widow, would not have been amused by coarseness. Pamela – short and pretty, with a faintly Oriental look about her eyes – worked in a bank. The Johnsons were respectable. When she turned from poems to novels, at which she was much better, she wrote a book for which Dylan suggested the risky title of *This Bed Thy Centre*, and she was temporarily ostracized by her father's side of the family when it was published in 1935. During the ten days of Thomas's visit they went for walks, talked late, saw an O'Casey play, wrote alternate-line poems in the Jones-and-Thomas manner, and drank a little beer from the local off-licence. Thomas had arrived with a quarter-bottle of brandy, but this was one of his gestures to the reputation he was groping for. There was no hard drinking as far as Pamela was concerned, although he wasn't under her eye at Battersea all the time. Any host of Thomas's in London was rarely certain what else his guest was up to. Some of the time he probably spent at the houseboat with Nancy and Haydn; some of it with Grigson in Hampstead.

Before he returned to Swansea, he told Pamela that he had sold some poems and stories, but had failed to find a job that suited him. She saw him off on the train, depressed to see him go. Three days later he wrote to say he was in love with her. At the end of March he was back again to spend Easter, and now he was 'my love Dylan'. He was a gentle and on the whole a well-behaved bohemian. One day before breakfast he was on his way out to buy cigarettes, wearing pyjamas, dressing gown and a black felt hat. Pamela's aunt told him to come back at once; he obeyed meekly. She persuaded him to go with her to the near-by store of Arding and Hobbs to have a portrait photograph taken. He wore a tie and faced the camera with a solemn expression, looking quite unlike the winking boy with a fag in his mouth. Pamela hoped to change him. 'Dylan tight, little devil,' the diary says once, indulgently.

'You are my only friend,' Thomas wrote in a mid-April letter, when he was back in Swansea. 'I say quite seriously that I have never really spoken to any other human being.' He dreamt of the two of them together – in front of the fire reading Beddoes, or living on a Mediterranean island. In the same letter he looked out on Cwmdonkin Drive (on a Sunday morning) at 'the rehearsed gestures, the correct smiles, the grey cells revolving around nothing under the godly bowlers. I see the unborn children struggling up the hill in their mothers, beating on the jailing slab of the womb, little realizing what a smugger prison they wish to leap into ...' But he could now talk about himself in a matter-of-fact way:

I've often wondered – I thought of asking you, but am always so vastly happy with you that I don't like introducing morbid & egotistic subjects – whether you think me as conceited a little young man as I often think you must do. I'm not really; profoundly the other way ... I'd hate you to think that I was all self-contented, self-centred, self-satisfied in regard to – well, only one little thing, the things I write. Because I'm not. And I'm not half as brave, dogmatic & collected in the company of Literary persons as I might have led you to believe.

His affairs seemed to be prospering. The *Referee* had printed more poems, 'A process in the weather of the heart' and 'Where once the waters of your face', both within a week of being written. The *Adelphi* had published a poem written the previous summer, 'The Woman Speaks', which brought an admiring letter from another young Welsh writer, Glyn Jones; confused by the title and the unfamiliar name 'Dylan', Jones was uncertain at first if the poet was man or woman. Most important of all, on 14 March the *Listener* had published 'Light breaks where no sun shines', with its portentous opening lines,

Light breaks where no sun shines;
Where no sea runs, the waters of the heart
Push in their tides . . .

Few critics have agreed what the poem means. Glyn Jones, who became a friend and admirer of Thomas, thought that it 'probably expresses something pretty trite and commonplace, in prose terms, about the foetus and the pre-natal state', adding that the actual machinery of the verse is so filled with energy that it arouses the same feeling in the reader as a 'great and intelligible poem'. Other critics have tried to be more specific. Does the light that breaks 'behind the eyes' indicate the moment of conception, or the start of man's consciousness? Is the poem about the universe seen through the human anatomy? Or the cycle of life and death? All these explanations have been proposed at one time or another. One critic even thinks the poem is about sexual intercourse. Sex undeniably enters into it. Certain phrases gave offence to sensitive *Listener* readers. In the second stanza 'A candle in the thighs / Warms youth and seed and burns the seeds of age' was clear enough. According to Dylan, writing to Pamela about it, a 'host' of letters came from 'smut-hounds', and consequently 'the B.B.C. have banned my poetry'. This was an exaggeration. The advertising department of the *Listener* was worried that advertisers might be offended, but the B.B.C. management supported the editor. Later in the year the magazine published another Thomas poem, 'Especially when the October wind'.

One result of 'Light breaks' was that three important figures in literary London wrote to him: T. S. Eliot, who was then editing the *Criterion*, Stephen Spender, and Geoffrey Grigson, who now became interested in the poet he had rejected the year before. The following month, April, Grigson's *New Verse* printed its first Thomas poem, the newly written 'Our eunuch dreams', which uses images from the cinema ('love on a reel') to explore the unreality of modern society. This poem caught the eye of Edith Sitwell, who didn't like it and used it as a stick to beat *New Verse* with. Miss Sitwell, already an imposing figure, was soon to change her mind and praise Thomas as the new comet in the sky. But in a book published later in 1934, she called the poem 'an appalling affair', saying little and doing it badly. Miss Sitwell's real reason was probably loyalty to her brother Sacheverell, who had been lambasted in *New Verse*. Thomas was becoming involved in the games that critics play.

Towards the end of April the *Referee* chose him as its second prize poet to have a collection of verse sponsored by the paper.[3] Compared with a year before, his prospects as a poet were much improved. But he sounded nervy and unhappy that spring. 'Monday was a dead day,' he wrote to Pamela on 15 April, 'the hole in space you talk of, such a deep-damp hole as I must have fallen into when I last left you.' The threatening hole, the emptiness that swallows up life, later occurred more than once in his writing. Much of his uneasiness concerned money, which he lacked, and London, where he hoped to live. Writing to Glyn Jones in mid-March he spoke of moving to London, 'possibly to starve', circumstances having made it necessary that he go 'out into the bleak and inhospitable world with my erotic manuscripts thrown over my shoulder in a sack'. The implication, here and elsewhere, is that his father's health was the reason. A letter to Glyn Jones in the summer said D.J. was about to retire, which meant that Thomas had to 'face the bitter world alone'. But it was another two years before D.J. left the Grammar School. It is as though Thomas was slowly building up the energy he needed to escape from Swansea. Part of the problem was doubtless Pamela. Whatever plans he had for her, she undoubtedly had plans for him. If he married her he would have to provide for her. He wrote to her on 2 May to say that he must earn money. He was trying to write a novel, which, he said, might be more profitable than poetry; but he was not optimistic. 'So what's the alternative? Six months ago I'd have suggested the docks or the oven with the greatest

3. Mark Goulden says that before he agreed to Thomas having the prize he insisted he visit London to be interviewed at the *Referee* office, because, he told Neuberg, 'I think we are the victims of a con-trick. Someone has done a brilliant job of sticking together bits of poems.' He met Thomas and was satisfied he was genuine. Later he lost interest in him 'because he became a disreputable person'.

equanimity. But now I've got to live. It's when I'm with other people more than when I'm by myself that I realize how much I want you and how very far away you are from me.' Thomas was trying to be practical about their future, but it didn't seem to suit him. The letter continued, 'I'm willing to work. I do work, but in an almost anti-mercenary direction. Which is no good at all for you or me. Something has to be done, but Christ knows what it is.' He talked vaguely about becoming an actor with 'a bad repertory company in Coventry, or some place like that', or going to Russia with 'a Welsh Communist organization'. But he knew what would happen: 'I sink back into a usual lethargy and continue to write of my uncommercial maggots.'

This was not the tone of his earlier letters to Pamela, before they met. Then, he was writing that 'there is no necessity for the artist to do anything. There is no necessity. He is a law unto himself, and his greatness or smallness rises or falls by that.' However grandiose and ill-tuned to the times he lived in, this was Thomas's true philosophy. Now that he thought himself in love with Pamela, 'nice, round Pamela', a personable, middle-class girl who wrote girlish things in her diary, he found himself thinking about practical bourgeois matters like getting a job. All his life part of him hankered for stability and an 'ordinary life'; when his wife Caitlin lost her temper she used to laugh at him for being bourgeois at heart, a charge that no one could level at her.

On 9 May he began a long, neurotic letter. 'I am ill,' he said, 'ill as hell. I have had a headache for a fortnight, and haven't slept for longer than that. I've lost all hope of ever going to sleep again. I lie in the dark and think. I think of God and Death and Triangles. I think of you a lot. But neither You nor the Triangles can make me sleep. I've drugged myself up to the eyelids.' He reported trouble with writing: 'The old fertile days are gone and now a poem is the hardest and most thankless act of creation.'

Between September 1933 and April 1934 Thomas had written thirteen of the poems that he was beginning to assemble for his *Referee* book, eventually to be called *18 Poems.* In April alone he wrote three, including 'I see the boys of summer' and

'If I were tickled by the rub of love'. The latter, with its declamatory final line, 'Man be my metaphor', concludes the fourth and final notebook on 30 April; after that it is no longer possible to date poems so accurately. In the remaining eight months of 1934, he probably wrote sixteen poems that were published in *18 Poems* and elsewhere; his output remained high. But a new kind of obscurity had set in.

It is difficult to generalize. But after April 1934, and for some years to come, Thomas seems to be working against the grain of his material, producing verse that was often impenetrable to the ordinary reader. His work in this period lacks some quality of instant recognition that makes the poems written in the winter and spring of 1933–4 acceptable even when their full meaning isn't clear. Thomas's favourite explanation for his obscurity (as he explained in a letter to Henry Treece in 1938) was that he tried to pack so much into a small space: 'Much of the obscurity is due to rigorous compression; the last thing [my poems] do is to flow; they are much rather hewn.' It may be that he regarded obscurity as fashionable; his letters suggest it is inevitable for a contemporary writer. A complementary explanation has been put forward by Glyn Jones: 'I sometimes think Dylan did not speak out more clearly, and concealed the meaning of his poems, because he was conscious of some intellectual inadequacy in them.' Arguably, then, Thomas's natural tendency to write in private parables combined with an anxiety to appear intellectually respectable, an ambition that his father must have encouraged from an early age. It was only gradually, in the 1940s, that he began to work a new vein of clarity, though obscurity dogged him to the end.

His letter to Pamela of 9 May continued:

I have written a poem since my last letter, but it is so entirely obscure that I dare not let it out even unto the eyes of such a kind and commiserating world as yours. I am getting more obscure day by day. It gives me now a physical pain to write poetry . . . I shall never be understood. I think I shall send no more poetry away, but write stories alone. All day yesterday I was working, as hard as a navvy, on six lines of a poem. I finished them, but had, in the labour of them, picked and cleaned them so much that nothing but their barbaric sounds remained. Or if I did write a line 'My dead upon the orbit of a rose,' I saw that 'dead' did not mean 'dead', 'orbit' not 'orbit' & 'rose' most certainly not 'rose'. Even 'upon' was a syllable too many, lengthened for the inhibited reason of rhythm. My lines, *all* my lines, are of the tenth intensity. They are not the words that express what I want to express; they are the only words I can find that come near to expressing a half. And that's no good. I'm a freak user of words, not a poet. That's really the truth. No self-pity there.

Thomas began this letter on Wednesday, 9 May. He was still writing it on Sunday, 13 May, after (he said) an incident on Saturday night in 'the deserted smoke-room of a seaside pub', where three 'repulsive looking young men' cornered him and made him hand over cigarettes and money. His mood on Sunday was as black as ever. Neuberg, writing about him in that morning's *Referee*, had called him an experimentalist. This led Thomas to remark, 'I found myself wondering who this sad named poet was, & whether he had any separate existence from the sadder person, of the night before, bullied out of his lawful cigarettes by three strong men & falling back, in the event of his comic cowardice, on to a stony pile of words.' He went on:

Anyway, I'm not an experimentalist & never will be. I write in the only way I can write, & my warped, crabbed and cabinned stuff is not the result of theorizing but of pure incapability to express my needless tortuities in any other way. Vicky's article was nonsense. If you see him, tell him I am not modest, not experimental, do not write of the present, and have very little command of rhythm ... Tell him too that I don't know anything about life-rhythm. Tell him I write of worms and corruption, because I like worms and corruption. Tell him I believe in the fundamental wickedness and worthlessness of man, & in the rot of life. Tell him I am all for cancers. And tell him, too, that I loathe poetry. I'd prefer to be an anatomist or the keeper of a morgue any day. Tell him I live exclusively on toenails and tumours. I sleep in a coffin too, and a wormy shroud is my summer suit ...

A week later it was Whitsun, and he was in Laugharne with his new friend, Glyn Jones, who had a car, and whose ancestors, like Thomas's, were buried at Llanybri, not far from Fernhill. Jones, who had been having his poems published for two or three years, was yet another older friend, aged twenty-eight; he was a schoolteacher in Cardiff, and had no ambition to be a sinner. Thomas described him to Pamela, with the suspicion of a sneer, as 'a nice, handsome young man with no vices'. Glyn Jones thinks it was Thomas's first visit to Laugharne for years, perhaps the first visit he ever paid to the place, which has the River Taf between it and the Fernhill area. They crossed it in the rowing-boat ferry, perhaps on Whit-Monday, 21 May, and had tea at Brown's Hotel, already owned by the ubiquitous Williams family.

In the gloomy parish church, Dylan fantasized about Black Masses and satanic rectors; he said he could feel evil 'oozing out of the walls'. His Whitsun letter to Pamela, written (probably) on the same day, has a feverish quality, as

> the eye of truth, tired of romancing, turns back with a material squint on my self, and marks the torture in my too-bony hand and the electric livingness in the bodies of the goldfish I carry in the lining of my hat . . . I am tortured today by every doubt and misgiving that an hereditarily twisted imagination, an hereditary thirst and a commercial quenching, a craving for a body not my own, a chequered education and too much egocentric poetry, and a wild, wet day in a tided town, are capable of conjuring up out of their helly deeps.

Thomas repeats the phrase, 'helly deeps', and launches into a tormented passage about words:

> There is torture in words, torture in their linking & spelling, in the snail of their course . . . In the beginning was a word I can't spell, not a reversed Dog, or a physical light, but a word as long as Glastonbury and as short as pith. Nor does it lisp like the last word, break wind like Balzac through a calligraphied window, but speaks out sharp & everlastingly with the intonations of death and doom on the magnificent syllables. I wonder whether I love your word, the word of your hair . . . the word of your voice. The word of your flesh, & the word of your presence.

In this strange passage, reminiscent of his previous musings about the poem where 'dead' didn't mean dead and 'rose' didn't mean rose, Thomas was close to his great obsession. Words had a disturbing quality for him. In the poem 'Especially when the October wind' (date unknown, but of early Swansea vintage) he seemed to enter a dream-like or nightmare-like state, shut inside 'a tower of words'. An everyday scene – park, children, trees, birds – and the words to describe it were somehow fused together, 'as though' (says one critic) 'there were no gaps between language and reality'. In an earlier, unpublished version of the poem, Thomas made words sound like a punishment. 'Chained by syllables at hand and foot', he sought to escape into an ordinary way of life, and 'be no words' prisoner'. Was he striking a pose or expressing a true dilemma? Glyn Jones remembers that one of his favourite quotations was the Biblical 'In the beginning was the word'. That day in Laugharne, Jones happened to use the word 'huddled'. Thomas kept repeating it, 'savouring it', wrote Jones, 'as though it were as outlandish as Chimborazo or Cotopaxi and not an ordinary English vocable in common use'. Once, in America, Thomas told Alastair Reid that 'when I experience anything I experience it as a thing and a word at the same time, both equally amazing'. Failure to see that an image is only an image, not the reality, may have been, for Thomas, not a failure at all, but a positive capacity that was at the root of his perception. The state of mind in which a person cannot tell the difference between saying that 'Jane is a rose' and 'Jane is like a rose' is familiar to psychiatrists. Mescaline and other substances can induce it. In one experiment, 'with loss of insight into the difference between analogy and the literally meant, the responses assumed psychotic-like forms'. These are dangerous waters for a biography; no doubt the poet and the madman may both have heightened or distorted perceptions. It is enough to say that Thomas's view of his own body, and thus the poems that made him famous, may have been influenced by the fact that he wrote in a state of mind where words and objects became, for the moment, essentially the same.

Thomas liked to say that his poems began with words, not ideas. He was telling Pamela in 1934 that every writer worked either '*out of* words' or 'in the *direction* of them', and he continued to say it all his life in letters, talks and book reviews. He was convinced that poetry should begin (as he put it to Charles

Fisher) 'with the substance of words'. This was not, for Thomas, a statement of the obvious. Reviewing Clare's poems in 1935, he complained that 'Clare worked towards them, not out of them, describing and cataloguing the objects that met his eyes. In the beginning was the object, not the word. He could not realize, and consequently his expression suffered, that the word is the object.' The idea obsessed Thomas. He rammed it home like a slogan, not arguing or elaborating the point, but stating it as a profound revelation, which for him it was, of the mystery of language.

Perhaps words were preferable to the reality of the things themselves. The physical world was always capable of giving him the horrors. They were there when he imagined goldfish squirming on his scalp. Wriggling things and small creatures, especially mice, both fascinated and repelled him. Nicolette Devas says he used to invent 'tortures'. He imagined what it would be like to eat a sandwich of honey and mouse. Worst of all was to be 'naked in a bath of white mice'. A sandwich of dried eyes was another of his fancies. Thomas, of course, made it enjoyable as well as horrific; once again there are the successive layers, the nightmare that becomes the material for the story, which genuinely frightens him, producing more sensations that he can enjoy talking about afterwards. Oswell Blakeston, a writer he met in London, says that 'Dylan's face would light up and he'd say, "How *often* have you thought of cancerous meat?"' Or he would tell elaborate anecdotes about how he poured boiling water on decaying meat, and the meat screamed. A severed lip with a moustache, lying on the pavement, first occurred in a *Portrait* story, and reappeared in anecdotes. Geoffrey Grigson remembers drawings (now destroyed) that Thomas made in his early twenties – 'people having their throats cut, bad dreams, a "world-devouring ghost creature" biting out genitals – Dylan was always inventing such creatures'. Glyn Jones remembers 'women with milk coming from them, a half-wit running through a wood – they struck me forcibly because they so obviously came out of the same imagination as his early stories'. The stories that Thomas began to write in Swansea, and produced for several years, continued to draw on this vein of shudders experienced with relish. Heads burst open, someone drinks a cup of semen and bird's blood, intestines dribble from a rabbit, madmen howl, a doctor grafts a cat's head on to a chicken. With a few exceptions, the stories manage to be both tedious and unpleasant, but they were important to Thomas at the time, and they show his morbid imagination at work without the constraints of verse.

The final horror may have been his body. Without a feeling that he was caught in the machinery of his own flesh and blood, presumably the anatomical poems would not have been written. His body was a trap. One notebook poem talks of 'man ... like a mole within his fleshy prison'; another of 'the jailing skin'. A friend in later life recalled him after a three-day drinking bout, scratching at his hands and saying, 'To be able to tear off my flesh, to get rid of this awful, horrifying skin we have, to get at the bone and then to get rid of that! What a wonderful thing!' When he became a public performer, he would stand at the lectern, rotund and grinning, and speak, as though of someone else, about 'that creature whose sad-sack body encircles me and whose fat head wakes up on my pillow every morning'. And the phrase he used to Pamela that damp Whitsun afternoon at Laugharne, 'a craving for a body not my own', hints at his fears.

His neurotic state in 1934 reached its climax with an undated letter, probably written a week after Whitsun, where he confessed or pretended that he had spent three days and four nights of drink and sex at a bungalow in Gower with 'a lank red-mouthed girl with a reputation like a hell', and asked Pamela to forgive him. The letter was written in a loose scrawl, unlike his usual rounded script, and headed 'Sunday morning. Bed'. He was 'absolutely at the point of breaking into little bits'. The confession was brief and lurid. He left Laugharne to stay at the bungalow with

> a friend of mine in the waster days of the reporter's office. On Wednesday evening ... his fiancée came down. She was tall and thin and dark with a loose red mouth and a harsh sort of laugh. Later we all went out and got drunk. She tried to make love to me all the way home. I told her to shut up because she was drunk. When we got

back she still tried to make love to me, wildly like an idiot ... She went to bed and my friend and I drank some more and then very modernly he decided to go and sleep with her. But as soon as he got in bed with her she screamed and ran into mine. I slept with her that night & for the next three nights. We were terribly drunk day and night. Now I can see all sorts of things. I think I've got them ... I'm just on the borders of D.T.s, darling.

This is Thomas the Sinner in full voice. He was to use drink as a reason for breaking with Pamela later in the year, implying that he was in its grip. Here he is both lecher and drunkard. The story sounds too good to be true. It fits Thomas's stereotype of wicked behaviour. The name Thomas gives in the letter is uncommon, and a woman of that name, who knew him at the time, still lives in Swansea. She agrees that the description fits her; she was 'lank' and she wore red lipstick. But the bungalow story, she says, or any story about a sexual relationship between her and Thomas, is nonsense. She was an attractive girl who had been an amateur dancer. By all accounts she was a most respectable young woman. But she was in a sinful category as far as he was concerned. If he wanted to tell a tall story involving sex, perhaps half hoping to put an end to his relationship with Pamela, the dancer with red lipstick was a useful ingredient for a fantasy.

Pamela replied to say it was all over, but Dylan begged for another chance, and on 6 June she was writing to forgive her 'darling'. On 7 June he was telling a tale again to Trevor Hughes, the Swansea friend who was already living in London:

Here I am getting older and no wiser, and have lately become entangled with an erotic girl with whom I indulge in unrepeatable displays of carnality. In your tight-tided little island, does the hank of bone and the curled slit play its hot, customary part? ...

Thomas adds that in marriage, perhaps, 'lies your salvation and mine, though I doubt whether I, personally, could remain sober and faithful for more than a week on end ... write soon to me, before I see you on my next visit to London, which will be in the next week or two'. He arrived a week later for a reconciliation with Pamela, and she and Hughes agreed to form a 'watch committee' to keep an eye on his drinking. This was an optimistic gesture. The summer of 1934 was the eleventh hour for any well-meaning friend who was anxious to turn Thomas into a sober citizen, ready to obey the rules that society unkindly lays down for poets as well as for clerks.

Under Bert Trick's tutelage he was still grappling with problems of the day, writing letters to the *Swansea and West Wales Guardian* (a short-lived weekly paper with radical leanings) advocating communism, compulsory sterilization and free clinics for psycho-analysis. One of his letters ('A Plea for Intellectual Revolution') indulged in some high-powered name-dropping. He had met Stephen Spender during a London visit earlier in the year. Thomas, briefly dabbling in political commitment, wrote that

> once I walked with Spender along a desolate London street, late one rainy afternoon. 'The streets of London – after the revolution', he said, and pointed to the empty shops, the bare stones, and the grey mist over them. And London, to us, was like a city of the dead. We imagined the silence and the distant noise of guns. There would be stillness and greyness, and blood in the streets. On a hill of bones we imagined the last financier counting his pennies before they shot him down . . .[4]

In July, Sir Oswald Mosley visited Swansea to address a fascist rally at the Plaza cinema. 'I have just left the Socialist Party and offered my services to the communists,' Thomas wrote to Pamela. 'I *was* in time for Mosley's meeting, and was thrown down the stairs.' There is no evidence that he ever belonged to a political party, and he was not thrown down the stairs. The meeting ended with the usual scuffles; according to Trick, he and Thomas 'scuttled out like a brace of frightened rabbits'. But already the dominant stories were more eccentric than that. They were about a comic figure, a little out of control even at this early stage, balanced unsteadily between his poems, which were closely controlled, and the rest of his life, which was be-

4. Spender says that he had asked to meet Thomas after reading his poems. He took William Plomer with him. They found Thomas painfully shy, and 'we talked above his head, I suppose'. He doesn't recall talking about the revolution; only walking in St James's Park and laughing at a statue.

coming unrestricted, as he considered a poet's ought to be, and tinged with scandal and farce. Thomas was successfully manufacturing a character for the world to be entertained by, part-poet and part-clown; the two went together.

Not everyone thought him amusing, but shrieks of laughter followed him around. At the Mermaid, a popular hotel in the Mumbles, he ran about on all fours barking like a dog and scampered out to find a lamp-post. 'We thought he was going to piddle over it,' says Ruby Graham, 'but he said he was a dog with rabies and bit it instead, and to the end of his days he had a chip out of a front tooth.' Evelyn Jones remembers a night they put on a play in Gower, when Dylan later led some of the cast up Cefn Bryn, a long ridge of commonland, for some ludicrous pretence of invoking spirits at a prehistoric monument, Arthur's Stone. It was a joke but it managed to be frightening as well. 'He said he had things – juice from the wortleberry, slime from a snail. I nearly passed out with fright.'

Pamela still had hopes of a normal courtship; perhaps Thomas had, too, in some corner of his mind. He was in London again for a month from the middle of August, and she was alternately in ecstasy and despair. One Sunday he went to tea with Geoffrey Grigson and didn't return till ten past one in the morning. 'Think we shall have to call things off,' says the diary. In a letter to Grigson, written from Pamela's house in Battersea, probably on this visit, he says that 'my world of good, dying fathers and bad, female poets is proving affectionately unstable'. He was trying to borrow money from Grigson. He began to have rows with Pamela. In mid-September he accompanied her and her mother to Swansea, where the visitors stayed at the Mermaid, and saw the Thomases every day. It rained and rained. Pamela had hysterics and went to a doctor. Soon she was back in London. In a letter written soon after, the last of his love letters to her that survives, Thomas says, in passing, 'I've always wondered why you won't come to bed with me.'

At last he was making serious plans to move to London. By the end of 1934 he would be a poet with a book to his name. *New Verse* had taken four of his poems since the spring, he was reviewing for the *Adelphi*, and publishing short stories like

'The Enemies', where instead of the dark world of his own body he looked outward to the darkness of a landscape, the 'Jarvis Valley', and (as in other early stories) put his misshapen characters into a witch's Carmarthenshire. In October he was one of the writers whose answers to a questionnaire appeared in *New Verse*, declaring that his poetry was 'the record of my individual struggle from darkness towards some measure of light'; that craftsmanship was what mattered, not inspiration; that he had been influenced by Freud ('whatever is hidden should be made naked'); and that he supported any revolutionary body that believed in fair shares for all. Thomas was on the edge of a reputation, although no doubt he was less sure of himself than his confident answers to Grigson's questionnaire suggest. Glyn Jones noted Thomas's fear, when he was still in Swansea, that another poet like himself might be at work in a provincial town: he needed to feel himself unchallenged, and since he had few worries about published writers, it was an unknown competitor that he feared. To Glyn Jones, who went on to make his own reputation but remained in Wales, Thomas was a curious phenomenon, with his fierce determination to be The Poet. He found it unhealthy. He was more used to the traditional Welsh view of a poet as someone who is part of his community, a man with a useful trade, not a man with a mission. In Glyn Jones's eyes, had Thomas taken a less romantic view of his function, he might have been happier and lived longer. Whether he would have written such striking poetry is another matter.

At Jones's suggestion they went to Aberystwyth one Saturday in his Austin 7 motor-car to see Caradoc Evans, the writer, whose novels and stories about Wales so offended his fellow-countrymen earlier in the century. They had tea with the great man, then went to drink by themselves in the cold little sea-town. They stayed the night in an hotel, and while Thomas lay on his bed smoking and absent-mindedly burning holes in the sheet, Jones told him the story of Dr William Price, the Welsh eccentric who called his illegitimate son Jesus Christ and burned his body on a hill when the child died. This bizarre episode was just right for Thomas, who turned it into a still more bizarre story called 'The Burning Baby'.

But Wales was incidental. Thomas had no intention of being regarded as a provincial poet, and there was no substitute for living in London. It was only later that the question of Thomas as a specifically 'Welsh' poet arose; and when it did arise, he decried it. In 1938, for example, in a letter to Henry Treece, he said that 'the Welshness of my poetry' was 'often being mentioned in reviews and criticisms, and I've never understood it'. In 1952, in a letter to Stephen Spender, thanking him for his review of *Collected Poems*,[5] he wrote, 'Oh, & I forgot. I'm not influenced by Welsh bardic poetry. I can't read Welsh.'

Both his remarks need qualifying. First, there is the obvious sense in which Thomas seems to be, if not Welsh, at least non-English. Many of his poems have the rich, dark melancholy and the flamboyant imagery that go with the 'Celtic' character, whatever that may be. The temperature of the language is above normal by English standards. The poems are songs about mysteries without solutions, gravely set out for his audience by the Poet, a man with a recognized function. Second, there is the narrower sense in which Thomas's poems may have been technically influenced by Welsh-language verse. Many critics have dismissed the matter. The classic devices are alien to English poetry. *Cynghanedd*, the best-known, is a complex and obligatory system of alliteraton and internal rhyme within each line. Some readers claim to find echoes of it in Thomas. Welsh-speaking critics are sceptical. One theory is that Thomas was influenced via Gerard Manley Hopkins, who taught himself Welsh and imported some features of Welsh prosody into his verse. When Treece wrote to Thomas to point out Hopkins's influence, Thomas wrote back to deny it.

What can be demonstrated is that Thomas wrote a number of poems within strict patterns of rhyme and metre. This is characteristic of classic Welsh verse, although Thomas was usually following rules that he invented for the purpose of a particular poem, not traditional rules laid down for poets in general. He liked technical virtuositv for its own sake. In 'I, in

5. Spender wrote, 'His poetry is not so much influenced by, as soaked in, childhood experiences of the Bible, and doubtless, also, Welsh bardic poetry.'

my intricate image' (1935), seventy-two of the one hundred and eight line-endings are variants on the sounds of the letter 'L'. Vernon Watkins failed to notice it when he first heard Thomas read the poem. Another friend who was a poet, Louis MacNeice, had to have the rhyme-scheme of 'Prologue' (1952) explained to him: the first line rhymes with the last (the 102nd), and so on, working from both ends towards the middle of the poem, where 'farms' meet 'arms' in lines 51 and 52. Thomas wrote to his publisher, 'Why I acrosticked myself like this, don't ask me.' But he was also heard to say,[6] 'It may be a waste of time for the reader, but not for the poet.'

The oddest piece of evidence is the draft of a letter that Thomas wrote to an editor in 1934, enclosing three poems, one of them 'I dreamed my genesis'. The rhythmic basis of the poem, as critics have pointed out, is the number of syllables in each line, not the pattern of stresses, which is more usual in English. Syllable-counting is a standard feature of traditional Welsh verse, and Thomas subsequently used it in many poems. Was there any connection? According to Thomas's 1934 letter, there was. He wrote that 'I dreamed my genesis' was 'more or less based on Welsh rhythms, and may seem superficially a bit strange at first'. Thomas may have had his tongue in his cheek, hoping to bamboozle an editor who wouldn't recognize a Welsh rhythm if he saw one. But it suggests that he was not quite as innocent about bardic techniques as he pretended.

The move to London was scheduled for November 1934. The plan was for Thomas to share a room with Fred Janes. He told Pamela they would be arriving with 'typewriters, easels, bedclothes, brassières for lady models, & plum cakes for Nelson's lions'; they didn't want to pay more than fifteen shillings a week, and he wondered if she happened to have a spare mat-

6. By Aneirin Talfan Davies, a former Welsh B.B.C. producer, who commissioned several of Thomas's radio talks. Davies suggests that 'Dylan's whole attitude is that of the medieval bards. They gave themselves tasks. He said he knew nothing about Welsh bardic poetry, but I often talked to him about it. You have to be wary of Dylan – he was always laying false trails. Is there a communal memory that a man taps? He may have been able to pick things out of the atmosphere, like a magician.'

tress, a chair and a table. Before he left he gave Swansea something to remember him by, with an address to a local literary society, the John O'London's. As he described it to Pamela, he lectured to an audience of thirty-five, most of them women, about sex and the revolution. 'At the beginning there was a frozen & horrified silence, but eventually I induced a few titters, &, at last, real, undeniable interest. A glassy look came into the eyes of the spinsters. I put in several wisecracks & ended with "Let copulation thrive".' He answered questions. How could a woman defend her honour in a communist society? Tin drawers, said Thomas. Did he believe in contraception? The day they legalized birth control and abortion would go down in history as a French Letter day, he said. Or so he told Pamela, adding that 'the more I see of Wales the more I think it's a land completely peopled by perverts. I don't exclude myself, who obtain a high & soulful pleasure from telling women, old enough to be my mother, why they dream of two-headed warthogs in a field of semen.'

A letter Thomas wrote to Trick the following year, and Trick's own account of the evening, confirm that it was not all fantasy. On their way to the meeting they stopped at a pub, and on coming out, stumbled into some road-works. Trick's boots were festooned with mud, which added to the hilarity when they reached the meeting-place, a carpeted room above an ironmonger's. Thomas sat at a card-table, clutching a silver-knobbed walking stick and the notes that Trick had been trying to persuade him to water down. The subject seems to have been pornography and the nineteenth-century novel. When Thomas looked back on it from his bed-sitter in London a few months later, he told Trick that 'I still think of that evening with a faint glow of "something attempted obscenely, something dung", and remember your muddy boots with pride'. He had turned his back on the tiresome reality of Wales, parochialism, middle-class values and the bedroom by the boiler. Or so he hoped.

## CHAPTER SIX

# *London*

THOMAS'S first address in London, the room he shared with Fred Janes, was at 5 Redcliffe Street, near the Brompton Cemetery and just south of Earls Court: a place in bedsitter-land. Here they lived (he told Trick in a letter) amid poems, butter, eggs, mashed potatoes and Janes's canvases. Janes was an artist but a clean-living one, and Dylan's parents trusted him to keep an eye on their son. He was physically fit; he practised with dumb-bells and could do things with his stomach muscles while Thomas watched in amazement. It was Janes who boiled up nourishing soup and kept the squalor in check. The room was unfurnished apart from two camp beds, a table from Pamela's mother, an oven like a biscuit tin which stood on the gas ring, and one chair that Janes appropriated as an easel. Mr and Mrs Thomas worried about their boy. Florence sent him a pound a week, and on at least one occasion they came to London and visited Redcliffe Street. Dylan's books were neatly arranged on the mantelpiece above the coal fire. D.J. sat on a camp bed because there was nowhere else; it collapsed under him. 'But I think the boys had a very happy time,' Florence used to say.

The district was a seedier adjunct to Chelsea. 'This is the quarter of the pseudo-artists,' Thomas wrote to Trick, 'of the beards, of the naughty expressions of an entirely out-moded period of artistic importance and of the most boring bohemian parties I have ever thought possible.' In his rôle of young socialist, Thomas struck a note of austerity with the serious-minded Trick. No doubt he saw through the pretensions of pseudo-artists. But from the start he found the raffish and bohemian irresistible, just as he found the academic a waste of time. 'Naughty', his word for other people's out-dated goings-on, was really the word for his own way of doing things. While Fred Janes worked slowly at his still-lifes – 'his apples carved in oil', Thomas said later, 'his sulphurously glowing lemons, his infernal kippers' – his room-mate was seeing how far he could go in shocking people, now that he was beyond the immediate grip of Swansea. Mervyn Levy occupied another room in the house. One of their favourite outings was to Friday-night hops at the Royal College of Art, where Levy was studying. They would have a beer or two, buy a half-bottle of port and take it into the college, where they gulped it down in the lavatory and then charged on to the dance floor, drunk and pretending to be drunker. 'We used to fall down on the floor screaming about mice and worms and magpies and things,' says Levy. 'It's incredible now. We especially wanted to affront members of Christian associations. We used to get dragged away and put on couches. I don't know why we thought this was wicked, except that we both had an acute sense of literature and literary figures – Wilde and Dowson, gutters and drink. We used to like to think we were in the gutter.' In quiet Chelsea streets, a London version of the Uplands, they climbed lamp-posts and shouted at passers-by.

Soon they all went round the corner to a house in Coleherne Road, where a landlady called Miss Mackenzie kept the wireless on loud and sang snatches of opera in the small hours. Thomas was there irregularly, sleeping on a mattress, or in a bed if somebody was away, attired for the night in assorted clothing, never pyjamas. Levy used to sing him to sleep with a song learnt from his father called 'I am the Bandolero'. Thomas loved a line that went, 'For I am waiting and watching, an outlaw defiant', and would ask for it over and over again. In the morning, still in bed, he breakfasted on beer, cake and apples, in between coughing, smoking and fanciful conversations. Just suppose, Mervy, he would say, if everything was covered in oil, we'd be living in an oilyverse – nobody would be able to stand up, the Pope would be His Oiliness, and instead of Christmas we'd have Oilmas. Or he and Levy would discuss how many mice were needed to pull a train from Glasgow to Euston. 'We could be involved for hours or even days on things like that,' says Levy. 'They became very real, they dominated our whole existence for a time.'

In appearance Thomas was still the cherub with the broken tooth. Levy recalls a black hat and a vast check overcoat. William Scott, another painter who lived at Coleherne Road, found him opulent, even sporty, in a thick tweed coat and a good suit. A third painter who saw him there, Will Evans, says that 'he seemed to be all overcoat – you were never aware of his body'. His mother kept an eye on his clothes from two hundred miles away. Haydn Taylor, his brother-in-law, once had a letter from Cwmdonkin Drive to ask if he could locate Dylan because Florence was afraid he didn't have enough socks. Thomas's clothes came and went; often they were other people's. He borrowed a pair of Will Evans's trousers and eventually returned them with the ends of the legs worn to shreds because they were too long for him. It was no use complaining; Dylan only pouted or giggled. He was heard giggling, one day, that he had just messed his trousers and left them in a laundry in the Fulham Road.

Thomas was the naughty boy from the provinces. It was how he depicted himself in the novel he began to write during the war and never finished, *Adventures in the Skin Trade*, a poor successor to the *Portrait of the Artist* stories, and the only piece of fiction that carries on in London where the other leaves off in Swansea. Samuel Bennet begins by smashing the best china and scribbling in his father's school books. His mother brushes his collar and makes sure he has plenty of vests. The story is funny enough before he reaches Paddington. But it runs out of steam as Samuel moves into an unreal London of picaresque adventures involving drink and women. Thomas abandoned the story, and it became a semi-derelict property on which he raised money more than once without ever having the will to complete it. London as a subject didn't stir his imagination; or if it did, it resulted in a vivid life at the time, not vivid prose about it afterwards.

Meanwhile *18 Poems* was published in December 1934, a month or so after he went to London. The *Referee* had decided to sponsor the book the previous April. But Thomas was not a commercial proposition; the newspaper had difficulty finding a publisher to share the risk, and for most of 1934, while Thomas was planning to leave Swansea, the poems languished. This left him free to keep changing his mind about which poems he wanted to include. He had hundreds to choose from, the contents of his notebooks, but the selection was made from the much smaller number of 'anatomical' poems (thirty or forty are known) written after August 1933. Writing to Pamela from Swansea in (probably) October 1934, after he had told Neuberg that he wanted his poems returned, he said they were a 'poor lot, on the whole, with many thin lines, many oafish sentiments, several pieces of twopenny Christ, several unintentional comicalities & much highfalutin nonsense expressed in a soft, a truly soft language. I've got to get nearer to the bones of words, & to a Matthew Arnold's hell with the convention of meaning & sense. . .' Soon after that, however, Neuberg found a publisher in David Archer, a saintly or foolish figure, in different eyes, who presided over the Parton Bookshop. Archer, once described as 'a left-wing Bertie Wooster', had a private income from his father, and tried hard to make his shop into an intellectual salon, and himself into a serious figure. He is kindly remembered by many writers. He agreed to publish Thomas, and supplied twenty pounds against the *Referee*'s guarantee of thirty pounds, which together was sufficient to pay for a tiny edition of two hundred and fifty copies. A very slim volume, it contained a note by Victor Neuberg to say that it was 'unaccompanied by either portrait or preface, at the author's request'. It was published about 18 December, and Thomas arrived back in Swansea to spend Christmas in Cwmdonkin Drive, taking with him a pile of presentation copies. He marched into the Kardomah Café and distributed signed copies to his friends.

The literary and social scene that received *18 Poems* has been described by Henry Treece:

Auden's first poems had been published four years ago, Spender's had been published one year ago. Surrealism was not to be explained by David Gascoyne, nor *Murder in the Cathedral* published for another year . . . The Sitwells were still written of as 'Eccentrics'; T. S. Eliot was, according to the *Listener*, 'A Major Critic and a

Minor Poet'. And any anthology one picked up would concentrate mainly on W. H. Davies, Harold Monro, Ralph Hodgson, Chesterton, Squire, and Blunden: with lots of Brooke and a little Owen . . . Generally, music-lovers still held up their hands in horror at the mention of Stravinsky; young men wore plus-fours for all outdoor occasions and girls wore Russian boots: Cab Calloway was the dance-band star; and all aircraft were expected to be biplanes; D. H. Lawrence wasn't to publish *Pornography and So On* for two years: readers of Freud still felt rather daring.

According to some accounts, *18 Poems* was ignored by the critics. It is true that reviews were slow in starting. In December, the only attention Thomas received was a comradely interview in the *Referee*. He was quoted as saying, 'Most writers today move about in gangs. They haven't the strength to stand and fight as individuals. But even as "gangsters" their machine guns are full, not of bullets, but of dried peas.' Thomas spoke of a happy childhood and a father who encouraged him to write. He added that life wasn't always easy for a poet determined to live by his work; that there were times when 'I'd give much to be a bank clerk in a safe job'; and that 'no poet ever understood everything he wrote himself'. On 1 January the *Morning Post*, where Grigson worked, reviewed him prominently under the headline, 'A New Poet'. The anonymous reviewer, probably Grigson, found fault with a monotony of rhythm and language, adding that 'a psychologist would observe Mr Thomas's constant use of images and epithets which are secretory or glandular'. But in general he was impressed by 'close, constricted, dark poems, individual but not private'. Later in January the *Swansea and West Wales Guardian* carried an anonymous notice, probably by Bert Trick, which observed that although the poems were not political, 'one knows instinctively his politics are correct'. In February a well-known critic, Desmond Hawkins, wrote enthusiastically in the weekly *Time and Tide*, 'This is not merely a book of unusual promise; it is more probably the sort of bomb that bursts not more than once in three years.' The *Listener* followed by observing that 'the essential principle of his poetry is delight, but the delight is bound to disgust in a very close and tenacious way';

it found affinities with Webster and Donne, and concluded that 'this is one of the most remarkable volumes of poetry that have appeared during the last few years'. *Spectator*, *New Verse* and *Times Literary Supplement* all published favourable reviews in the spring. It was more than enough to launch a poet.

Meanwhile Thomas was doing more drinking than writing. Still declaring intermittently that he was in love with Pamela, he now announced that drink had come between them. 'Dylan over for evening,' Pamela wrote in her diary on a Saturday early in January 1935. 'Says he loves me but can't resist Comrade Bottle.' A month earlier she heard him boasting of his 'rather revolting Bloomsbury fun and games'. Rayner Heppenstall, another arrival from the provinces, who was two or three years older than Thomas, met him at the end of 1934, and they had various drunken cutings that winter. Thomas's constitution seemed well able to stand the strain; and it was Heppenstall who was locked up for the night, after a drunk and disorderly outing. His circle of acquaintances grew quickly – literary journalists, poets, art students, advertising copywriters. He circulated in Soho, a more amiable place then, and in the contiguous district to the north of Oxford Street, 'Fitzrovia', from the Fitzroy public house. There he met Nina Hamnett and other minor celebrities. He began to brush against major figures; he was soon telling Trick that he had met Henry Moore and Wyndham Lewis, which may or may not have been true. His behaviour depended on his audience. Anthony Powell, an unbohemian young man who was beginning to make a name for himself as a novelist, met Thomas on several occasions. He recalled later that he was 'good company, amusing, intelligent, perfectly at his ease, drank no more and no less than the rest, was neither embarrassed nor showed off'.

Writing to Trick in February 1935 Thomas said that he and Wynford Vaughan-Thomas intended to 'have a peep, in our country-cousin way, at the Literary Great in the Café Royal'. He gave a low-key version of London life:

Some rude reviews of mine you'll see in the February *Adelphi* and also a review of my own book (what a thrill of pride when I put those long-wished words on paper) by Rayner Heppenstall who is a nice little Yorkshireman with an aptitude, even an obsession, for singing Yorkshire songs about the Seven Immortal Joys of the Holy Mary – or at least he sings them when he's drunk, and drunk he was when I first met him. Celebrities I meet often, and too often, they being a lousy set on the whole, or off it. Herbert Read, Grigson, Cameron, the Muirs and Heppenstall are the best. Racketeering abounds, and the only racket a comparatively honest person like myself can belong to is that of the squash racket. Squash 'em left and right, that's the motto.

Thomas went on to castigate left-wing intellectuals: an explicit statement that he was to echo in many later asides and gibes at politically-committed poets:

Since I've been in London I've come into contact on a number of occasions with intellectual communism and communists. They are: Morton, editor of the *Daily Worker*, Corbin, proprietor of the youthful *Notoriety*, Esmond Romilly, editor of the schoolboy communist monthly *Out of Bounds*, and with all the pseudo-revolutionaries who shall be unmentionable. I dislike all of them. Not so much as persons; most of them I assure you would be quite kind to dumb animals; but as revolutionaries and as communists or, born in wealthy, middle-class or upper-middle-class homes, educated at expensive prep-schools, public schools, and universities, they have no idea at all of what they priggishly call 'the class struggle', and no contact at all with either any of the real motives or the real protagonists of that class struggle. They are bogus from skull to navel; finding no subjects for their escapist poetry, they pin on a vague sense of propagating the immediate necessity of a social conscience, rather than clear sense of expressing their own un-pro or anti-social consciousnesses. The individual in the mass, and the mass and the individual, can be made poetically important only when the status and position of both mass and individual are considered by that part of the consciousness which is outside both. I shall never, I hope, be mixed up in any of the political ramifications of literary or pseudo-literary London. Honest writing does *not* mix with it. You can't be true to party and poetry – one must suffer. And historically, poetry is the social and economic creed that endures.

Early in March, Thomas was back in Swansea, telling Glyn Jones that 'the trials of life have proved too much for me'. To

Pamela he wrote his last letter, offering to help edit the typescript of a second novel she was writing, if she wasn't still angry for 'all the silly and careless things I've done'. Apology, usually in the opening sentence, was to characterize Thomas's letters; he was for ever disarming criticism in his first breath by saying how sorry he was. In Swansea he recuperated. His father was back at school, Bert Trick was at the shop, the remnants of the old gang still met at the Kardomah. It was one thing to scorn Wales as an abstraction, but another to break with the particular bits of Wales that solaced him. A poem written in the notebook two years earlier was published in the *Herald of Wales* as late as June 1935. The adolescent boy walks in Cwmdonkin Park:

> Who are his friends? The wind is his friend,
> The glow-worm lights his darkness, and
> The snail tells of coming rain.

As a poet, he was established in the capital of poetry by this time. But he still took the trouble to disinter a notebook poem for the local paper – possibly to make half a guinea, more likely out of nostalgia.

It was probably on his spring visit to the town that he met Vernon Watkins. Watkins, a stubborn Christian without guile in everyday life, was a strange friend for Thomas: an athlete, a scholar, an intellecual, and of course an older man. He first read *18 Poems* in a Swansea bookshop, not intending to buy it; he was absorbed in his own writing, and apart from Yeats he had no time for contemporary poets. He paid his three and sixpence reluctantly. Then he bumped into David Rees, the retired minister of Paraclete, whom he had known as a child, and obtained Thomas's address. They met soon after in Pennard, the village on the cliffs in Gower where Watkins lived. Soon they were close friends, reading their work aloud to one another and discussing technicalities, line by line. This was something that Thomas did rarely, if ever, with anyone else, once he was established as a poet. Even with Watkins, he may not have been always as enthusiastic as he appeared. Caitlin said she remembered him saying, 'Oh, my God, what a bore, I've got to talk poetry with Vernon.'

Oddly it was Watkins – unpublished for years after their meeting – who was touchy about criticism, and who took less kindly to suggestions. Thomas may not have cared for Watkins's poetry; Spender, who once heard him on the subject, thought so. But there is no doubt that Thomas liked him as a friend and respected him as a poet and critic. Many small details of Thomas poems are due to Watkins, usually single words or phrases like '*cloud-sopped* hands' in 'After the funeral'. Watkins, eight years older, was a bulwark of some kind ('the one happy person I know', Thomas wrote to him), a charitable, humorous man who teased out a quieter Thomas. He was at the opposite pole to the sodden evenings in London. There may have been an additional reason for their affinity: the gentle, even-tempered Watkins had had a severe breakdown a few years before, and been temporarily insane. Madness was a subject that fascinated Thomas. Whispers about the inbred Williamses and their fears of lunacy would have reached him since childhood. He referred often to insanity in early letters and poems, and in stories like 'The Mouse and the Woman', where the figure of the madman is probably Thomas himself. His clowning could be violent, which is what some people found so entertaining, and others scandalous. Once, with Antonia White the novelist, he began to rush about on all fours, barking like a dog. Miss White was recovering from a breakdown; it was assumed that Thomas was trying to see if he could unhinge her again.

Watkins had been ill in 1927. The son of a Swansea bank manager, he was educated at a public school, Repton, went to Cambridge, and left abruptly because he wanted to be a poet. His father refused to support him, he was pressed into becoming a bank clerk, and while lodging in Cardiff, withdrawn and unhappy, became manic and stormed about the house, declaring that he had conquered time and could control his destiny. A motor-cycle crashed outside and the rider was killed; Watkins thought he had willed it to happen. Next day, a Sunday, he took a train to Repton, attended chapel, then burst into the headmaster's study (it was Dr Fisher, later the Archbishop of Canterbury) and attacked him, shouting that Fisher was a destroyer of youth. Committed to a clinic, he kept the patients awake at night by reciting Blake, and attempted to jump from windows to see if angels would bear him up. He recovered slowly and came to view what had happened as a religious experience: he had been dragged back from the abyss. The bank let him return for his father's sake, and he was transferred to Swansea, where he worked in a small branch for the rest of his life.

There is no way of telling whether Thomas knew about the madness; Vernon Watkins's widow, Gwen, thinks that probably they did discuss it, 'in poetic terms, at least'. He intrigued Thomas; they intrigued one another. Gwen Watkins regards Dylan Thomas as the most important person in her husband's life. Watkins would hear no ill of him, insisting that he was a religious poet in the broad sense of the word, if not a religious man; he read many of his friend's poems as religious statements. Mrs Watkins regarded Thomas with a colder eye than her husband: 'I always felt the seeds of destruction were there, that he couldn't grow up.' But 'Vernon thought the drink and the unreliability were only incidental, that he'd go on to be an old man writing poetry, like Yeats'. He grieved deeply when Thomas died, and wrote many elegies.

In March 1935 they had time to begin their friendship before Thomas went to stay at a cottage in Derbyshire with a young historian, A. J. P. Taylor, and his Welsh wife, Margaret, who was interested in the arts. The machinery of 'looking after Dylan' was creaking into motion. Thomas met Taylor through a poet and advertising copywriter, Norman Cameron – the 'Cameron' of the letter to Trick quoted earlier – who in turn was a friend of Geoffrey Grigson. The idea that Dylan Thomas needed to be fussed over and saved from drink, women, late nights and bronchitis – that he must be mothered and kept in one piece – seems to have blossomed during his first months in London. Cameron apparently regarded Thomas with a mixture of distaste and affection. Like Grigson, he had a moralistic streak and felt it his duty to do something for the young provincial, nine years his junior. Cameron's own eating, drinking and womanizing were well organized. He lived at Chiswick, and when his guests got drunk and stayed the night, they were given lime-juice at bedtime to guard against hangovers. Grigson describes him as 'both worldly and very upright'. As well as being a good poet, he earned a comfortable living writing advertisements for J. Walter Thompson. Thomas called him 'Norman the Nagger'.

Cameron and Grigson were at the upper end of Thomas's London life. Grigson, later disenchanted with Thomas and his poetry, was at first an active patron, publishing his poems in *New Verse* ('a malignant egg', Grigson called it) and sending him thrillers to review for the *Morning Post*. The scruffy young Welshman and his fantasies made amusing company, in limited doses. 'Night custard', an imaginary product that was both magical and obscene, had a long conversational life. But to Grigson, at least in retrospect, he cut a poor figure beside poets like Spender and Cameron, 'better educated and highly sophisticated'. Intrigued at first, Grigson came to regard him as two-faced and intellectually bogus, with an equally unattractive private life. He found the drunken Thomas hard to take. No doubt Grigson saw him at his worst, showing off and determined to live down his background. It was Caitlin who later wrote of his puritanical streak, 'handed down from his father, that most unhappy of all men I have ever met'. What Grigson saw was the other side of the coin – 'He was such a physically, sexually unattractive little runt that Norman Cameron and I always wondered how he managed to get any girl to sleep with him. I remember when he came to stay with us in Hampstead in a filthy and squalid condition. My wife got his clothes off and got him into the bath, then found he was covered in a pink rash. We were worried – we had a child in the house – so we put him in a cab and took him to a doctor by the British Museum, who told us it was all right, he didn't have V.D.' Grigson, as he relates in his autobiography, had been through one or two inelegant encounters of his own when he was younger. Perhaps Thomas reminded him uncomfortably of things he had outgrown.

One of Thomas's nicknames at the time was 'Ditch'. Somebody else called him 'The Ugly Suckling'. Grigson settled for 'The Changeling' – 'without human affection, left by the underworld under a foxglove'. Others, too, noticed an absence of warmth or intimacy in Thomas. It is one of the contradictions that is difficult to resolve. To some he was the boon companion, raising their spirits, making their day. To others his ultimate self-centredness was chilling. There is a story, ten or so years later in date, of Thomas in a bar, telling an anecdote about a visit to the barber, and being interrupted by one of his audience who had been called to the telephone. Lamentably, said the man, his wife had just had a stillborn child, the third they had lost. Thomas said, 'Well, lamentably, you're a stillborn little couple, aren't you?' and went on with his monologue.[1]

One or two of Thomas's relationships in his early days in London are said to have been homosexual. His references to homosexuals in letters to Miss Johnson were scornful; they were 'sodom-hipped young men', 'willing-buttocked, celluloid-trousered degenerates'. But according to Oswell Blakeston and the painter, Max Chapman, Thomas dabbled in gay behaviour. Such stories, circulating in private, have been decried by others who were friends of Thomas at the time. Neither Blakeston nor Chapman makes extensive claims. According to Blakeston, who says Thomas stayed with him in Wimbledon on an early visit to London, 'He looked like a beautiful grubby angel in those days. Maybe the whole thing was an act to please one. That would have been much more likely. But he was in bed with me.' According to Chapman, 'My own experience is really based on one boozy evening, the first, when affectionate expression went beyond accepted bounds and physical contacts of a kind were reciprocated. All we ever did was feel under the table and do some kissing, french-kissing. You wouldn't say he was a queer, but he wasn't averse to being affectionate to his own sex if he found them in some way interesting.' Chapman suggests that Thomas at twenty was 'more just generally warm and sexual than disposed one way or another. In fact, that

1. Richard Burton, who was one of the audience at the bar, told the story when he reviewed FitzGibbon's biography. He added, 'I was nineteen at the time and I remember feeling immensely superior to ordinary human feelings and immensely cruel.'

technically his ratio of hetero to homo, if any, could not be less than 80/20 – which would thus make him accountable as "normal".'

Thomas sent some odd letters to Blakeston, perpetuating a fantasy that he was a Rat and Blakeston a Mouse. On 7 March 1936 he wrote, 'I haven't seen you for so long, not since we spent an evening in not going to the Queen's Hall, and not since I left you, outside the Café Rat, very rudely for a sillie. I'm coming back, travelling under the seat all the way, nibbling brown paper, at the beginning of next month. Will you meet me? And this time I'll promise not to be bad; I'll powder my snout and not run after hen-rats.'

The trite conclusion, possibly the true one, is that Thomas was anxious for experience, and set about acquiring it indiscriminately. This is certainly what happened with drink. His behaviour in London in 1935 had his friends rallying round. Arriving in the city in April after staying with the Taylors in Derbyshire, he was soon the worse for wear. It is never clear exactly what happened on these occasions, except that he made himself very drunk, and an object of sympathy. One of his new acquaintances about this time was Cyril Connolly, a rising young literary figure. A copy of *18 Poems* inscribed to him by Thomas was dated May 1935. Connolly entertained writers and painters at his flat in Chelsea. He gave a dinner party to help launch Thomas – disastrous, according to Connolly, who recalled a 'slight hush' when the guest of honour, asked what he would like to drink, replied, 'Anything that goes down my throat.' The anecdote tells one more about Chelsea dinner parties in 1935 than about Thomas, the young provincial. In Connolly's account,

Among the other guests were Desmond MacCarthy and Evelyn Waugh. Evelyn fled as soon as he could because, he said, Dylan was exactly like himself at that age when he came up to Oxford, and he couldn't bear to be reminded of it. I remember another awkward moment when Desmond was talking about Swinburne's novel *Lesbia Brandon*, and explained that it was about flagellation. Dylan's round-eyed childish face, with its innocent, slightly plastered gaze above the broken tooth, fixed on him and made him feel he had gone too far. 'Did you say "flagellation"?' asked Dylan, in his rusty cackle. Desmond drew on the exquisite tact which had enchanted the literary world . . . and reverted to the schoolboy language which cuts through age and class – 'Yes, he liked swishing.' There was a long, even more embarrassing silence. 'Did you say swishing? Jesus Christ.'

Grigson and Cameron decided it was time to separate Thomas from Comrade Bottle again. Grigson took him to Ireland for a summer holiday, to a makeshift studio (converted and then abandoned by an American artist, Rockwell Kent) in Donegal, facing the Atlantic. It had been a donkey shed, and belonged to a farm near by, which supplied the food. Here they spent a couple of weeks together. They fished in the lakes, listened to the farmer's tall tales, ate his wife's wholesome food, and frightened one another by standing under the mountains at dusk, shouting 'We are the dead' for the echoes to repeat. Away from London, Thomas was more agreeable than Grigson had known him: 'My nicest recollections of Dylan are in Ireland. He loved footling about there, by the lakes above the farm. Or on the edge of the sea, looking at the gannets.'

Left alone to continue his holiday when Grigson returned to his newspaper, Thomas worked on stories and poems, probably some of the difficult pieces that were to go into his next book. A long letter to Bert Trick said he was 'ten miles from the nearest human being, with the exception of the deaf farmer who gives me food. And in spite of the sea and the lakes and my papers and my books and my cigarettes (though they're darned hard to get and I've few left of them) and my increasing obsession with the things under the skin, I'm lonely as Christ sometimes and can't even speak to my father on an ethereal wavelength.' The usual fancies were there to provide thrills and shivers. In the letter to Daniel Jones dated 14 August, quoted from in Chapter 3, Thomas wrote:

. . . it was so late when I came back that I padlocked out the wild Irish night, looked through the window and saw Count Antigarlic, a strange Hungarian gentleman who has been scraping an acquaintance (take that literally) with me lately, coming down the hill in a cloak lined with spiders, and, suddenly very frightened, I hurried to bed. This is written in the cold of the next morning, the Count is nowhere to be seen, and it is only the thin mouth-print of blood on the window pane, and the dry mouse on the sill, that brings the night back. It's hard to pick up the night threads; they lead, quite impossibly, into the socket of a one-eyed woman, the rectums of crucified sparrows, the tunnels of coloured badgers reading morbid literature in the dark, and very small bulls, the size of thimbles, mooing in a clavichord . . .

Thomas saw himself and his fantasies, not Ireland. 'I find I can't see a landscape,' he told Trick, 'scenery is just scenery to me . . . little he wotted when he made the trees and the flowers how one of the Welsh chosen would pass them by, not even knowing that they were there. My own eyes, I know, squint inwards when, and if, I look at the exterior world, I see nothing or me; I should like very much to say that I see *everything* through the inner eye, but all I see is darkness, naked and not very nice.'

Thomas looked at himself with a degree of self-pity, unsure of where he stood. He described his homesickness for the Uplands, his father's study ('writing by my gas fire opposite the tall Greek nudes'), and the Sunday-night talks with Trick –

sitting by the fire until we've set the whole world straight, and the whole Welsh world is dark. But I wouldn't be at home if I were at home. Everywhere I find myself seems to be nothing but a resting place between places that become resting places between resting places themselves. This is an essential state of being, an abstraction as concrete as a horse-fly, that's always worrying the back of your neck, plaguing and worrying before it draws blood. I'm at home and the blood's spilt, but only until the pricked veins heal up again and my water and sugar turn red again, and the body and the brain, all the centres of movement, must shift or die. It may be a primary loneliness that makes me out-of-home. It may be this or that, and this and that is enough for today. Poor Dylan. Poor him. Poor me.

When the time came for Thomas to leave Donegal, he walked away and caught the bus without paying for his food and lodging. There was a row when Grigson and Cameron heard; they had to pay the farmer. This was probably the start of his estrangement from Grigson, who came to dislike Thomas over the next year. His poems, too, ceased to interest Grigson.

'My taste changed,' he says. *New Verse* was a magazine of rigorous standards that carried more prestige than any other regular outlet for English poetry in the 1930s. When it ceased to publish Thomas, he found no immediate substitute. In all, *New Verse* published nine of his poems, the last three in December 1935.[2]

Work on poems for a new collection occupied Thomas for much of 1935 and 1936. Despite the warm reception for *18 Poems*, he had difficulty in finding a publisher who would take the obscure along with the straightforward. Archer's Parton Street bookshop again played a part. A son of Lascelles Abercrombie, the poet, worked there. Abercrombie was friendly with Richard Church of the firm of Dent, and sent him a copy of *18 Poems* and some unpublished material. Church, then in his early forties, was a poet and novelist of a traditional kind; he had been a civil servant before he entered publishing. He was both impressed and alarmed by Thomas's poetry (and by Thomas, who embarrassed him by borrowing half a crown at their first meeting). He found the sexual images unwholesome, but he was a sufficiently good judge of talent to want to publish Thomas if only he could be persuaded to concentrate on poems that people, or Church, could understand. A dignified difference of opinion began between them and lasted for years, with Thomas calling Church a cold fish and worse behind his back, but remaining polite to his face, while Church, and Dent in general, kept hoping that Thomas would begin to write comprehensible poems. They also took care not to publish stories (there were several later on) that they thought indecent.

The first selection of poems for a book went off to Church early in October 1935 from Swansea, where Thomas had returned from Ireland via London. They included the first six

2. The three were all simple poems, at least two of them written early, 'I have longed to move away', 'The hand that signed the paper' and 'Should lanterns shine'. Even these were too much for Grigson a year later. Reviewing Thomas's *Twenty-five Poems* – which included the three – for *Poetry* (Chicago) in November 1936, he said that 'twenty-four twenty-fifths of them are psychopathological nonsense put down with a remarkable ineptitude in technique'.

parts, as much as he had written at the time, of the sequence of sonnets beginning 'Altarwise by owl-light', where images of birth, sex and death are so packed and squashed together that the poems, or poem, have been having their contents variously explained ever since. It took Church nearly two months to reply. He apparently regarded some of the poems, and especially the unfinished group of six, as surrealistic, a view guaranteed to upset Thomas. The idea that he was letting strange images fly straight out of his unconscious on to the page didn't appeal to him. But Church pressed home his criticisms. Surrealism in poetry was abhorrent and anti-social, and 'dissociated symbolism is a private eccentricity'. He asked for more poems like 'Ears in the turrets hear' and 'The hand that signed the paper'. Thomas resisted. Although he was willing to say on other occasions that 'the meaning can look after itself', he regarded the assembling of a poem as a conscious act. It may not have been as conscious as he liked to think, but that was his philosophy and his intention. He replied politely but firmly on 9 December to say that Church had got it wrong. He was not influenced by 'such a pernicious experiment as surrealism', nor, as Church had alleged, was he 'caught up in the delirium of intellectual fashion of the moment'. He went on, 'I think I do know what some of the main faults of my writing are: immature violence, rhythmic monotony, frequent muddleheadedness, and a very much overweighted imagery that leads too often to incoherence. But every line *is* meant to be understood; the reader *is* meant to understand every poem by thinking and feeling about it, and not by sucking it in through his pores, or whatever he is meant to do with surrealist writing.' Finally he told Church that he had plenty of 'simple' poems, though he thought them nothing like as good as the ones Church disliked.

In the next two months, until early February 1936, Thomas revised four or five more of the simple poems dating from early 1933. At the same time, he was adding to the other kind, both by writing new poems and by revising old ones. Vernon Watkins helped make the selection. He tried to persuade Thomas to leave out two newly-written poems, 'Now' and 'How soon the servant sun'. He thought that 'their obscurity really amounted to meaninglessness, at least for me, which was not true of any of the other poems', and warned Thomas what the reviewers might say. 'Give them a bone,' said Thomas, and included the manuscripts. Watkins was more successful in doing the opposite, persuading Thomas to use a poem that he wasn't happy with, 'And death shall have no dominion'. There was no shortage of poems to choose from. More than half the contents of *Twenty-five Poems* was based on notebook material. There are other notebook poems, never published in Thomas's lifetime, which would have done as well as some that were, if he had been willing to print them.

Few if any of *Twenty-five Poems* were written or revised in London. Thomas was in Swansea for his twenty-first birthday on 27 October. He wrote to his sister and brother-in-law to acknowledge their present of money:

Thank you both very much. It is nice to be remembered, especially at such an important, if I may coin a phrase, cross-road in life's journey.

The family lawyers, Paff Grabpole and Paff, have just departed: there's been a little bother, you know, over the transferring of the estate. Later on this evening I'm going down to the Marlais Head to give a formal address to the tenants. They're to present me, I believe, with a platinum walking-stick, complete with bell. Lord Hunt-Ball has given me a glass tube for holding tiny flannel shirts. Lady Utterly has presented me with a wooden leg.

Thanks again for the present. I bought a grey hat and a book of ballads. I also have a tweed suit covered in coloured spots, a new mackintosh, new shoes, a book, new trousers, a pullover, & no hope for the future.

There's no news. I'm working moderately hard and Dad has a very painful throat.

I'm coming to town for three days in the first week of November, and am already preparing my small jar of red paint.

The tenants are clamouring. I must go.

The November trip took place, but for most of the remainder of the year he was in Swansea. He was there all through January. For the moment he had reverted to being the provincial who made trips to London. If one reason was the need to get on with his poetry, another may have been his health. He may have had gonorrhoea. This is another cloudy episode, if it is an episode at all. His infection has been attributed, on uncertain evidence, to a girl he met at the Surrealist Exhibition in June of the *following* year, 1936.[3] He certainly boasted in London that he had caught 'a dose of clap'. Gonorrhoea was not unusual among his acquaintances; at least one close friend of Thomas in London says he was infected by a woman around this time. But the woman denies she ever slept with Thomas, and the friend doesn't think it likely.

The only suggestion in writing that he had gonorrhoea is in a letter to Geoffrey Grigson, sent from Cwmdonkin Drive. It is undated, but a reference to his reviews of thrillers for the *Morning Post* – which Grigson stopped sending him, temporarily, because Thomas was failing to deliver – suggests it may have been December 1935, when no reviews appeared for a month. But it could have been written earlier or later.

I'm an old twicer, aren't I? Here I lie, lily-faced between the sheets, looking like Shelley and the Three Little Pigs rolled into one, very pretty in my white pyjamas with a droshki cough. Thanks so much for your letter, dear Doctor, and I'm so glad the *Morning Post* has taken me back without a scolding. I promised to explain to you what happened and why after I left you in London, but now I try to I can't. I drank the night custard of the gods, but they must have been the wrong gods, and I woke up every morning feeling like hell in somebody else's bed-sitting room with concealed wash-basin. This morning I have battled with a venomous doctor who wanted me to go places with him and do things, but, old Terry, I won by a short lung. I have to stay indoors for six or eight weeks, during which time I feel sure I'll be able to work hard and well. So do send

3. FitzGibbon's account of the 1936 incident seems to confuse two possible candidates for the honour. One was the girl at the exhibition; FitzGibbon avoids giving her name, though she is easily identified. He adds that she had been 'involved in a notorious sex scandal', which suggests that she is someone else altogether, another of the rumoured candidates: a girl whose name was mentioned in a tragi-comic trial of the early 1930s. Further confusion arises because FitzGibbon dates his account of Thomas's gonorrhoea by a letter written to Thomas's wife-to-be, Caitlin. But he places the letter a year too early, in 1936 instead of 1937 (see p. 155 and Note). He doesn't mention the letter to Grigson quoted below.

me thrillers, and I promise the most satisfactory reviews. But, for the love of the great grey cunt of the world, don't tell the details of my present indisposition to anyone but Norman the Nagger: they might ruin my lecherous chances. No, I shan't begin dying yet. I've lived a bit quicker than lots of people, so I *can* begin five years under the scheduled time. But that gives me nearly ten years, and . . . that embryo you told me about is going to produce many strange and good things . . .

If his sickness was venereal, his parents are unlikely to have known of it. Mrs Thomas was busy mothering him and turning a blind eye. Her condensed version of events for the two or three years after 1934 was that Dylan went to London to share a flat with reliable Fred Janes; had a 'breakdown'; and returned to Cwmdonkin Drive, where he remained until he married. Nothing was too much trouble. When Dylan stayed up late, writing a last-minute book review that he took to the station to catch the overnight mail-train to London, his mother stayed up late as well, making him cups of coffee.

Early in 1936, Thomas was off to London again for another round of city life. Before he left, he heard from a new friend in high places, Edith Sitwell. As Grigson faded out, Miss Sitwell became Thomas's chief advocate. The fact that Thomas was willing to be flattered and approved of by her may have been a significant reason for Grigson's disenchantment with him. Her letter to Thomas in January 1936 foreshadowed an article that was to appear in the next month's *London Mercury*, belatedly reviewing *18 Poems* and a single poem, 'A grief ago', written the previous year and published in a small magazine. This poem had made Miss Sitwell look again; she changed her mind about Thomas. D.J. was visibly impressed when her letter came. Mrs Thomas hurried to tell her cronies. On 17 January Thomas was replying in his best-behaved manner on pages torn from an exercise-book. The 'starch-itch-trash' poem, which Thomas now disparaged for her benefit, was 'Our eunuch dreams', the one Miss Sitwell had attacked in her book two years earlier.

I wouldn't be able to thank you enough for your letter, so I won't try, but I loved it and appreciated it, and I'll owe you a lot always for your encouragement. No, of course, I don't care a damn for an audience, or for 'success', but it *is* exciting – I suppose it's the only external reward – to have things liked for the reasons one writes them, to be believed in by someone who's right outside the nasty schools and the clever things one (me) doesn't want to understand, like surrealism and Cambridge quarterlies and communism and the Pope of Rome. And yes God does permit everything, and health's only a little thing, and to the devil anyway with 'personal troubles' which *are* the devil – (mine are only the indescribably mean naggings of having absolutely no money at all, for I live on my few poems and stories and you know what that means, and a few rowdy habits, and the very insignificant melancholies of 'things not coming right' etc., and really nothing very much more). I'm a very happy sort of bird, and I don't care much. How I would like you to be able to do something about those new poems of mine, because there are quite enough to make a small book and I would like to have nothing more to do with Richard Church. I've a contract for poems with Dent's, but if Church dislikes my surrealist imitations so strongly that he'll be willing to break the contract – and I think he does hate them and will be willing – could I let you know then and would you help me? It *is* kind of you to suggest wanting to help them be published.

I don't think I should have mentioned that I was eighteen when I wrote that Welsh-starch-itch-trash poem; it sounded like an excuse, but it wasn't because I'm twenty-one and the same excuse would apply to every line I write. I know, though, that you didn't take it as an excuse – and anyway why should I talk about that silly poem? Why, by the way, Miss Sitwell, are people of my age – and I would say that when I know that age doesn't matter a bit in poetry, (does it?) – so terribly frightened, in their talk and letters, of being solemn and earnest for one moment? I know I am . . .

From then on he could do no wrong as poet or man in Miss Sitwell's eyes. Soon she was advising him to take a regular job, and he was agreeing that it was the most sensible suggestion in the world, except that he had no qualifications. This was true enough. But work, in any case, would have pinned him down, would have made him crystallize something that he preferred to keep fluid.

In London before the middle of February, he had another brief spell of city life, in and out of pubs, sleeping wherever there was a spare bed or couch, before stumbling away again, back to the west. Any attempt to chronicle these London trips in detail or even with coherence is impossible. They are one long anecdote in the collective memory of those who knew him then. Rayner Heppenstall, who kept a diary, is able to report that on the morning of 12 February 1936, while proceeding in the direction of Charlotte Street to find a pub, Thomas coughed, spat, regarded the spittle and said, 'Blood, boy! That's the stuff!' Such police-court detail is rare. John Pudney, the poet, remembers walking in Richmond Park with Thomas who was apparently in rude health but insisted there was something wrong with his eyes. They had to call at a chemist's to buy medication. 'I've got death in me,' Thomas kept repeating. But when it happened, give or take a couple of years, Pudney can't recall.

Episodes in pubs are the most difficult, for obvious reasons. It is hard to distinguish between one year and another; occasionally between decades. The stories have blurred edges; it is part of their essence that they should not be tied to anything so pedestrian as a date. It is not as if very much happened, except that beer was drunk and stories were told. Margaret Taylor says that Thomas was always 'awfully like a Welshman up for the Cup'. Many found him the funniest man they had ever heard. He provided instant entertainment. Heppenstall remembers scatological limericks from 1934 or 1935 that Thomas would recite to saloon-bar audiences who liked that sort of thing. One of them (unpunctuated, because Heppenstall never saw it written down) went:

> There was an old bugger called God
> Who put a young virgin in pod
>    This amazing behaviour
>    Produced Christ our saviour
> Who died on a cross poor old sod.[4]

When Thomas was in the mood he was a relentless performer. Nigel Henderson says that 'Dylan was a Pied Piper. The word

4. Heppenstall adds, 'I always want to alter the last three words to "the poor sod" because of the "old" in the first line, but the words are strictly as I heard them from Dylan.'

used to go round that he was in town and the call was to let it all hang out. I remember one occasion we put on a pansy act in Leicester Square, when there was some rugger celebration going on. We decided to go and take the mickey. We put a couple of enormous chrysanthemums in our buttonholes, and in we minced, into the pub where they all were. Of course they razzed us, and the more they razzed, the more we minced.' Henderson, now a painter, was an ex-public schoolboy, trying to write poetry and determined to shed his public-school background. The first time he met Thomas he was introduced to the night-custard fantasy. At first he was puzzled; soon he was laughing hysterically like everyone else. He showed Thomas his poems, and Thomas, who had (or said he had) little respect even for his famous contemporaries, looked at them for a while and said, 'Ah. Fucked-out Yeats'. Henderson was susceptible to Thomas but not too susceptible to notice the appetite for an audience. 'There were always new waves of people coming in, and Dylan seemed to have this quite sickening need to charm and enchant them. He had to win them to his side.' Glyn Jones, who went to stay with Thomas in London, had been seduced by his warmth from the start – 'he appeared at will to be able to lap his friends in a gay and loving atmosphere' – and by such tricks as his gift for mimicry, when he imitated Welshy art students in Swansea discussing one another – ' 'e's not 'alf a good shader, aye.' Jones found him sensitive to every shift of mood in a companion. But Thomas's knack of changing his opinions to suit whatever group he was with made him uneasy.

John Pudney, another friend with reservations, found him too anxious to perform. 'Meeting Dylan in a pub, he could get to be rather boring. He'd offer to bite the caps off bottles of beer with his teeth, if he could have the beer. Or he'd say, "Let's be dogs." That used to be one of his great things – he'd go behind the counter, biting people. Then he'd say, "Let's go somewhere else," and he'd want to do the same thing there. The need for an audience, that was the boring part.' The dog-on-all-fours act was also performed at Cambridge University. Thomas was there to read poems to a literary group. This was presumably the occasion that the late Professor E. M. W. Tillyard described in 1962. Tillyard was taken to an undergraduate's rooms. 'Luckily there were other people there, for meeting Thomas brought no reward. He was in the feeble, maudlin state of intoxication and spent his time crawling under the table and round the furniture, making vague animal noises. He was entirely good-natured and was kept happy by an occasional stroke of the head or pat on the back.' This foreshadowed many encounters with academic figures; they didn't bring out the best in Thomas, who (especially in America) felt an uneasy need to amuse or insult.

One common observation by friends is that he was different and on the whole nicer if he was in a small group, preferably not in London. He did not have to try so hard. But it was the trying that produced most of what there was to notice; perhaps in his poetry as well as in his saloon-bar performances. Tom Blackburn, poet, then a schoolteacher, knew him in the 1930s and after, but never to talk to away from a crowd. What he saw was a man who 'liked to be the centre of a group, to be a precipitate for laughter'. Blackburn was present when Thomas and the painter Francis Bacon were introduced. The meeting produced no exchange of brilliance. 'It was a deadly failure. They both wanted to do the same thing: talk.'

On the whole, people don't seem to have had much chance to see Thomas plain. It was not his intention that they should. He spun clouds of fantasy and deceit, making a virtue of a preference for concealment. He kept reality at arm's length with his comic monologues about the ludicrous things that happened to a funny little Welshman called Thomas who was a surrogate for somebody else, whose voice was different. Looking back at people's reminiscences of Thomas the Raconteur in action, it is possible to catch a more sinister note behind the laughter. Howard Moss of the *New Yorker*, an American friend in the 1950s, wrote that 'often, in Thomas's conversation, one could hear a tune rather different from what the words implied, orchestrating them somewhere off in the distance'. 'His reality was his poetry,' says John Pudney. 'His unreality was his way of life.' Even his poems, where he sought to make direct statements of the truth, had to be enormously contrived, the intricate mechanisms packed tight inside their shell. Writing letters or talking in bars, he described fantastic or bizarre happenings which ballooned out of trivial events, or no events at all. Glyn Jones 'once heard him describe to a ring of middle-class English bohemians the daily stripping and bathing of Welsh miners before the kitchen fire', which Thomas turned into 'a sort of unbridled sexual rout'. It is unlikely that he had ever seen a miner bathe, however innocently. But it made a good story. One monologue (which started life some years later) concerned a railway journey in wartime, when three American soldiers were in the same compartment. He had a packet of sandwiches, and a crossword puzzle to pass the time. While he ate the sandwiches he did the puzzle. Presently the pencil became blunt, and he sharpened it with a razor blade he had brought for the purpose. Then he cut himself. All the time the soldiers were watching. He tried to go on eating but he bled into his sandwich. Nobody said anything. Desperately, he put the razor blade into the bloodstained sandwich and threw it out of the window. Cordelia Locke – with her actor-husband, a post-war friend of the Thomas family – heard the story in an Oxfordshire village. It must be the same story that G. S. Fraser heard in another version, in a bar near Broadcasting House, 'about a wartime railway journey in the blackout, in a carriage crammed with large, grim, silent Canadian soldiers, and about Dylan's embarrassment in opening in front of them an untidy brown paper parcel full of sandwiches, finding that the sandwiches almost choked him under the Canadians' steady stares, and fumbling hopelessly to parcel the sandwiches up again. He made this stretch half an hour, getting funnier all the time.'

There are people in London who believe he was summoned to Buckingham Palace to read his poetry to the royal family, accompanied by his wife. He gave the Queen a piece of his mind, after which the amazing Dylan, retreating backwards from the presence, skidded on the carpet and shot out of the chamber on his bottom. There are people in London who believe that the amazing Dylan was introduced to the Queen and tried to stub out a cigarette on her hand (royalty always goaded him to an extreme verbal response among friends). The woman who tells the first royal story also records that she personally was in the bar of the Wheatsheaf one night when Thomas, standing at the counter with a crowd of people, opened his trousers and offered his penis to a girl, who screamed. Did she actually see it? No, but she knew what was happening. Arguably it matters little whether he did it or not. But it would be useful to know, with the Thomas Legend, where fantasy (both his and others') ends, the better to understand what reality meant to him.

A few years before Thomas died, Glyn Jones, who saw him only rarely by now, went to Laugharne to discuss a B.B.C. radio programme (which was never made) in a series on 'How I Write'. From the work-shed above the Boat House they could see the farmhouse across the estuary where Jones's grandfather was born. Ah, said Thomas, and that farm next to it is Pentowin, where *my* grandfather was born. It was not, as Jones heard later from old Mrs Thomas; the only family connection with Pentowin was that Annie and Jim had farmed it before they went to Fernhill. Jones saw the remark as 'another of those charming and rather childlike attempts of his at saying what would please and be of interest, and create a bond between himself and his listener'. In any case, Thomas may have thought it was true. The borderline between fact and fiction may have been blurred inside his head as well as outside it.

By the end of the winter of 1936, Thomas's London friends thought it was time they sent him off, yet again, for a holiday in the country. Thomas (according to Oswell Blakeston) was showing signs of stress; he insisted that a bus conductor said to him, 'It's a twopenny fare, but for you, Rat, it's sixpence.' Blakeston introduced him to an unshockable woman called Wyn Henderson over dinner in a Soho restaurant, an occasion master-minded by Norman Cameron, who knew that Mrs Henderson had a cottage in Cornwall, near Land's End. Mrs Henderson was the mother of Nigel Henderson; she had had three children before she was twenty-one. She was at various times a writer, a typographer and a publisher, and she knew all about the vagaries and bad habits of artists. Early in March

1936 she wrote to Thomas, who was back in Wales again, inviting him to the cottage. He replied – 'a scrubby Welshman with a three-weeks-accumulated hangover and a heart full of love and nerves full of alcohol' – to say that 'it sounds just what I want it to be, and I can write poems, and stories about vampire sextons deflowering their daughters with very tiny scythes, and draw rude little pictures of three-balled clergymen, and go to pubs and walks with you. It's all too lovely to be good; and I'd enjoy it so much.' Soon they were catching the train from Paddington. Thomas stayed with Mrs Henderson for a couple of months, first at Porthcurno, then at a house she moved to in Mousehole, a few miles away. She used to hear him working in another room, reciting poems aloud. Her brief was to look after him, so she would try to stop him slipping out for too many drinks. Once when she went to collect him from a pub he boasted that he had drunk forty pints. Farm workers helped her get him home – 'raving all the time about vampires,' says Mrs Henderson, 'telling me to be sure to shut the windows.' Thomas was incontinent on this occasion. She brought soap and water, 'washed him like a baby', and left him in clean pyjamas. His relationship with her, she says, was 'very much son to mother'. In an episode with an older woman at this time, the two drifted into bed together. The woman found him a straightforward lover who liked to be mothered. He was rather timid; inhibited and slightly furtive. 'One thought of him always as a *little* man,' she says. 'The more women who responded to him, the more secure he felt.' Wyn Henderson noted 'a curious sense of unreality about Dylan's personality. He was always building it up and reassembling it – almost as if he didn't believe in himself, not as a complete person.'

In Cornwall he was probably working on the final poems for the new book. Before leaving Swansea he had written to Richard Church with a polite ultimatum: either Dent published the 'not-so-simples' alongside the 'simples', or Thomas would take his poems elsewhere. Stories about 'vampire sextons', too, were being written around this time. The fantasies that Thomas produced in the mid-1930s were his nearest approach to surrealism, full of nightmarish scenes, hallucinations and dream-episodes.

On 20 April he wrote to Vernon Watkins to say that he was halfway through a story and had almost finished a poem. As in many of his letters to Watkins over the next ten years, he seemed to be going out of his way to make his life sound a muddle. He wished he hadn't gone to Cornwall: a suburban hill, with houses called The Elms and Rookery Nook, was more to his taste: 'I'm not a country man,' he said. He deprecated his behaviour in London ('Life No. 13: promiscuity, booze, coloured shirts, too much talk, too little work'). In Cornwall, his work stopped him being unhappy. But (he went on)

> here again I'm not free; perhaps, as you said once, I should stop writing altogether for some time; now I'm almost afraid of all the once-necessary artifices and obscurities, and can't, for the life or the death of me, get any real liberation, any diffusion or dilution or anything, into the churning bulk of the words; I seem, more than ever, to be tightly packing away everything I have and know into a mad-doctor's bag, and then locking it up: all you can see is the bag, all you can know is that it's full to the clasp, all you have to trust is that the invisible and intangible things packed away are – if they *could* only be seen and touched – worth quite a lot . . . I don't fear – we talked about it, do you remember – any sudden cessation or drying-up, any coming to the end, any (sentimentally speaking) putting out of the fires; what I do fear is an ingrowing, the impulse growing like a toenail into the artifice . . .

What Thomas feared was real enough. His adolescent burst of energy was fading into the past. By the spring or early summer of 1936 – that is, when he was still only twenty-one – he had written about half the *Collected Poems* in their final or near-final versions, and drafted early versions of another ten or so. Writing became a slower process; the words had to be dragged out. 'The impulse growing into the artifice' was a problem without an easy solution; perhaps without a solution at all. But there was some short-term consolation. Church wrote to him at Porthcurno at the end of April, 'Still I cannot understand the meaning of the poems, but in this matter I have decided to put myself aside and let you and the public face each other. I am accordingly taking steps to have the book set up in type.' The original title was to be 'Poems in Sequence'. Thomas wouldn't have this.

Writing to Church at the start of July, he said he wanted it to be 'just the number of poems there are in the book' – he didn't know how many there were, 'as I've sent the poems in batches and in such a muddly way'. The final batch had been sent nine days earlier. Counting the ten-part sonnet sequence 'Altarwise by owl-light' as one poem, there were twenty-five of them. Preparations went ahead for an edition of seven hundred copies.

By now he had left Cornwall, and was once more to-ing and fro-ing between London and Swansea. From Wales he travelled up to the Surrealist Exhibition in June, where strange exhibits and stranger people were to be seen at the New Burlington Galleries. Salvador Dali gave an inaudible lecture from inside a diver's suit, and nearly suffocated when the helmet jammed. The girl who is said, unreliably, to have given Thomas gonorrhoea was there. He read poems, with others, at an evening session to accompany the exhibition; 'I haven't discovered why,' he said in a letter to Church.

Seven or eight poems from the forthcoming book appeared in magazines during the summer, and the book itself was published on 10 September 1936. The reviews were generally favourable, but with one exception they were not as enthusiastic as they had been for *18 Poems*. The *Times Literary Supplement*, reviewing him the week after publication, was perturbed by his obscurity, and picked on one of the poems that Vernon Watkins had found meaningless, 'How soon the servant sun'. (Thomas's old editor in Swansea, J. D. Williams, picked on the other, 'Now', in a kindly but baffled notice in the *Herald of Wales*.) Desmond Hawkins, this time writing in the *Spectator*, praised Thomas's talent but found difficulty with syntax and imagery: 'On the whole he has been less successful than before in subduing his material to a communicable form.' The *New Statesman*, which managed to ignore *18 Poems* when it was published in 1934, now reviewed it (a reprint of 250 copies had been issued earlier in 1936) along with *Twenty-five Poems*, and announced that it preferred the first book – 'the record of a volcanic adolescence' – to the second, with its sharp contrast between the simpler, more ordinary pieces and the 'eerie bombast' of the rest. The review ended by observing that Thomas, a 'really original poet', was 'for the moment, perhaps, wondering which way to turn'. This was probably true. Thomas's remark to Watkins that he couldn't 'get any real liberation, any diffusion or dilution or anything, into the churning bulk of the words' was a shrewd assessment of his situation. For the first time since he was a schoolboy, he almost stopped producing poetry. After *Twenty-five Poems* he seems to have written little verse in 1936. In 1937 he produced one new poem and one notebook revision. It was not until 1938 that he was again writing with any degree of fluency.

For the moment, in 1936, the most important thing that happened to his poetry was that Edith Sitwell reviewed *Twenty-five Poems* for the *Sunday Times*. This was not a literary magazine or a weekend review, but a middle-class newspaper with a comparatively large number of readers, some of whom bought books. Edith Sitwell's name would impress people who might never have read her poetry (and would certainly not have read her eulogy of Thomas in the small-circulation *London Mercury*). Her review on 15 November was packed with phrases to delight a publisher – 'The work of this very young man (he is twenty-two years of age) is on a huge scale, both in theme and structurally ... here, alone among the poets of the younger generation ... nothing short of magnificent ... I could not name one poet of this, the youngest generation, who shows so great a promise, and even so great an achievement.' She had some reservations about 'the intense concentration of each phrase', but these were immediately softened by her remark that even when the poems were difficult, their images had 'a poignant and moving beauty'. The day the review appeared, Alfred Janes remembers going down to Pennard on the bus with Thomas to visit Vernon Watkins; the Swansea gang were still together.

No doubt as a result of Edith Sitwell's enthusiasm, *Twenty-five Poems* was reprinted the following month; the total number of copies in print was then probably 1,500. This compared favourably with most poets of the day. Dylan Thomas was finding a wider public. But it was still a tiny one by commercial standards, and there was no money to be made. It has been said that *Twenty-five Poems* reprinted three times. So it did;

but the second reprint was not until 1939, the third and last not until 1944. That printing was finally exhausted in 1950. From start to finish the book earned just fifty-eight pounds for Thomas, or a little over four pounds a year. A poet who was determined to make his living as a poet, with only a bare minimum of book-reviewing as a sideline, was not going to live very well. But Thomas, in 1936, was still determined.

CHAPTER SEVEN

# *Caitlin*

SOME time during 1936, Dylan Thomas met the person he was to marry, Caitlin Macnamara. She was a spirited woman, born in Hammersmith, in West London, of Protestant Irish parents, on 8 December 1913, and so almost a year older than Thomas. The Macnamaras were from Co. Clare, where they had property and standing. The family seat was Ennistymon House, a Georgian mansion on a hill that overlooked valley and river, and Caitlin's grandfather had been High Sheriff of the county. Her father, Francis Macnamara, was a tall, striking man who 'carried himself like a conqueror'. He could talk for hours and confidently expected to make a fortune or write an immortal book. In 1907, when he was twenty-three, he married Yvonne, the pretty daughter of a French father and an Irish mother, abandoned his law studies in London, and strove to live as a writer on an allowance of a few hundred pounds a year. A book of his poems, *Marionettes*, was published in 1909. Francis hobnobbed with writers and artists, and made a close friend of Augustus John, whom he took to Co. Clare. Meanwhile his wife produced a son and three daughters, the last of them Caitlin, who was born in Hammersmith Terrace, a row of tall, cramped houses down by the river. Shortly after, having discovered the delights of free love, Francis went off with a married woman and never came back, though he continued to be an important figure in his family's life.

Mrs Macnamara, who had little money, went from place to place with her children. For a while they came to rest at one of Augustus John's bohemian households, Alderney Manor in Dorset. In the early 1920s they settled at a modest house in Hampshire, New Inn House in the hamlet of Blashford; a few years later John and his menage arrived at near-by Fryern

Court, and the Macnamaras and the Johns mingled more than ever. Money was short at Blashford; tradesmen banged the door and thrust their bills at anyone who was unwise enough to answer. Mrs Macnamara looked down her nose at commerce. Paying bills promptly was not the way of gentlefolk; she thought it 'common', a word she used with feeling. An American author seeking information from her in 1963 was unwise enough to use the word 'colleen' in writing about Caitlin. 'Please do not use the word colleen,' replied Mrs Macnamara. 'It is common and means a girl from the bogs.'

Caitlin, by far the most fiery of the children, was a remarkable accident of styles: bold, uninhibited, delectable. Her eldest sister Nicolette Devas's accounts of their childhood are the best, indeed virtually the only, evidence of that period. Mrs Devas (who is now Mrs Shephard) suffered at the time because Caitlin and the middle sister, Brigit, took sides against her. She wrote that Caitlin was spoilt as a child. Like Dylan Thomas, she made early use of her looks. Mrs Devas described her, aged twelve, 'with Francis's bright blue eyes, thick mass of curly gold hair, her vitality and her wit that later on was to become no less than brutally cruel. As a child she was a sentimental, cuddly, chocolate-box beauty, a hard centre to Brigit's soft, sweet cream. Though determined, she was no more wild than any spirited girl with not enough to do. At this time there was no indication of the underlying savagery in her character ...' Caitlin's chief characteristic seems to have been that she did as she pleased. Once, trespassing on a near-by estate with her sisters, a gamekeeper cornered them in a fork between rivers. Nicolette was terrified. But Caitlin 'whipped down her knickers, pulled up her skirt and waded across the stream with the water waist high'. Her sisters followed; the keeper was left on the other bank, staring.

Few failed to notice Caitlin. As she grew up, the family joke, not entirely a joke, was that nothing less than a duke would do for her. She thrived on emotional scenes and 'always seemed to get away with murder'. One of her passions was dancing. Caitlin herself wrote that when she danced alone, 'no loving come ever gave her such prolonged ecstasy'. She had a striking body, and often sat for Augustus John. When she was seventeen or eighteen she went to London and found work as a chorus-girl at the Palladium; according to Mrs Devas the hours and discipline didn't appeal to her. She had the chance to go abroad when a talent-scout from Paris was in London, looking for showgirls. An offer of some kind was made to Caitlin, contingent on her guardian's permission because she was under twenty-one. Mrs Macnamara refused to give it, and Caitlin's career went no further. In a newspaper article that she wrote, or signed, in 1956, she said that when she met Dylan she was 'an ambitious Irish chorus-girl'. In fact, their meeting came several years after her Palladium appearances. But a dancer was how she liked to regard herself. Eventually she came to feel cheated of a career.

Between the Palladium and Dylan Thomas there are several years, probably two or three, to account for. For a while she danced her way through private salons in the company of an older woman, Vera Gribben, who taught and practised the 'eurhythmic' method, where bodily movements are supposed to express emotions aroused by the accompanying music. They danced for small audiences in Dublin and Paris, striking dramatic postures to Bach and Mozart. They danced in the open-air at Fryern Court, at night, under the trees; muffled laughter came unkindly out of the dark from spectators who didn't care for eurhythmics. Another venue was the Group Theatre, founded in London in 1932, where Caitlin was briefly a member. When she and Mrs Gribben danced there, T. S. Eliot was in the audience; he was seen staring at his shoes.

Little else is known of her whereabouts, except that she is said to have lived in Paris, until the first half of 1936, when she and Augustus John appear in a London pub, probably the Wheatsheaf, and John introduces her to Dylan Thomas. According to FitzGibbon, this was in the spring, shortly before Thomas made his therapeutic trip to Cornwall. In Caitlin's account, she was wearing a 'very beautiful flowery dress' that she had borrowed from one of her sisters. Dylan was 'dishevelled and looking like the parody of a poet'. He 'kind of fell all over me. Put his head on my knee and never stopped talking.' The legend, fed by Thomas, avers that they went to bed immediately. Whatever happened, John didn't knowingly hand her over to a rival, and there were undoubtedly jealousies between the men before Thomas married her. John's relationship with Caitlin was certainly sexual up to a point. FitzGibbon says that (having fallen unsuccessfully in love with one of his sons) she fell in love with John. Caitlin herself denied this in a letter to Michael Holroyd, John's biographer, where she said in effect that they slept together because that was required behaviour at Fryern Court: 'It was merely a question of a brief dutiful performance for him to keep up his reputation as a Casanova ogre.' She added that 'this lofty favour was not reserved for me alone, but one and all of his models, of whatever age and social category, suffered the identical treatment'.

If Thomas's affair with Caitlin did begin in the spring of 1936, it seems to have matured slowly. In the summer Caitlin went with Augustus John to stay at the home of Richard Hughes, the author, in Laugharne. Full-cheeked and clear-eyed, Caitlin still had the face of a schoolgirl. Thomas wrote to Hughes inviting himself and Fred Janes, and they arrived on 15 July, Janes driving his father's car. Thomas and Caitlin pretended not to know each other, or not to know each other very well. They all drove into Pembrokeshire for the afternoon, to see an exhibition of paintings at Fishguard: John and Caitlin in his powerful car, Thomas and Janes in the latter's less trustworthy vehicle. On the way back in the evening, Janes's car broke down. Thomas transferred to the other car. They stopped for refreshments in Carmarthen, and Thomas, drunk and jealous, made a scene, insisting that John take him back to Laugharne. The argument continued in the car park. Finally John punched him and drove off with Caitlin. Painter and poet had fought for her. Next morning Thomas arrived, full of rhetoric, but the episode was smoothed over. This was probably the real beginning of his affair with Caitlin.

The next reliable landmark is three months later, when Thomas sent her a postcard, franked 19 October 1936. Of the thirty-odd letters from Thomas to Caitlin[1] that survive, this is the first. The reference to his father suggests that their relationship was still at the stage of exchanging basic information. But he was apparently in love with her. The card was headed 'Sunday'.

Darling, thank you for your long lovely letter and the handkerchief which isn't a handkerchief at all but my very very favourite scarf which I wear all the time – and for the photograph. I like you when you climb,[2] but I'm awfully prejudiced, I like you when you do anything. (And that's quite separate from loving you altogether.) This squiggle is only to tell you that I've almost finished a letter for you, and a nice story, but that I won't be able to send them off until tomorrow: I have an ill father who's horribly fond of talking about death, so I sit and read to him. I love you: it's almost too wonderful (to me) to say, but I want to say it and I want to say it and I am saying it – I love you; and we'll always keep each other alive. We can never do nothing at all now but that both of us know all about it. You can do anything, & be anything, so long as it's with me. This, as you might gather Miss Macnamara, is from Dylan – & God, he must be with you soon.

The postcard ended with a long line of Xs. It must have been soon after this that he was writing to her in hospital:

Nice, lovely, faraway Caitlin, my darling, are you better, and please God aren't too miserable in the horrible hospital? Tell me everything; when you'll be out again, where you'll be at Christmas, and that you think of me and love me. And when you're in the world again, we'll both be useful if you like, trot round, do things, compromise with the They people, find a place with a bath and no bugs in Bloomsbury, and be happy there. It's that – and the *thought* of the few, simple things we want and the *knowledge* that we're going to get them in spite of you know Who and His spites and tempers – that keeps us living I think. It keeps *me* living. I don't want you for a day (though I'd sell my toes to see you now my dear, only for a minute, to kiss you once, and make a funny face at you): a day is

1. The correspondence was put up for sale at Sothebys in London by Mrs Thomas in December 1975, but was withdrawn when bidding failed to rise above £2,100.

2. Nicolette Devas has a photograph of Caitlin in a tree at Blashford, dated 1936. The Macnamaras all liked tree-climbing.

the length of a gnat's life: I want you for the lifetime of a big, mad animal, like an elephant. I've been indoors all this week, with a wicked cold, coughing and snivelling, too full of phlegm and aspirins to write to a girl in hospital, because my letter would be sad and despairing, and even the ink would carry sadness and influenza. Should I make you sad, darling, when you're in bed with rice pudding in Marlborough Ward? I want so very much to look at you again; I love you; you're weeks older now; is your hair grey? have you put your hair up, and do you look like a real adult person, not at all anymore beautiful and barmy like the proper daughters of God? You mustn't look too grown up, because you'd look older than me; and you'll never, I'll never let you, grow wise, and I'll never, you shall never let me, grow wise, and we'll always be young and unwise together . . .

Their innocence, declared Thomas, went 'awfully deep, and our discreditable secret is that we don't know anything at all, and our horrid *inner* secret is that we don't care that we don't'. He liked or needed to stress the innocence: they were not to be corrupted by the world's dirty devices. Whether or not he saw her soon after – she was at Blashford early in December – they were apart again during the first months of 1937, because she had gone to Ireland, presumably to recuperate. Ennistymon was no longer a house: Francis Macnamara, who inherited it from his father, had turned it into The Falls Hotel, and was running it with lavish hospitality and uncertain profits. He was moving steadily into failure, closely observed by Caitlin, who noted his 'thwarted bombast' and decided later on that he had passed the trait to her. His lost promise haunted her then, as she came to see similar patterns of bravado and frustration in her own life. At The Falls she was technically the barmaid. She could be seen behind the bar, 'painting water-colours most of the time and mixing little drinks'.

On 21 April she was in London with Thomas, the date spelt out in a letter to her (itself undated), the last before they were married. 21 April should have been important to Thomas because in the evening he was to make his first radio broadcast, on the B.B.C.'s West and Wales channel. For a quarter of an hour he would read poems and talk about 'Life and the Modern

Poet' from the Swansea studio. A contract (for four guineas) was sent to him at Cwmdonkin Drive in good time. When the day arrived he was in London with Caitlin, until (said the letter) 'I lost you in the morning'. A train would have taken him to Swansea in a few hours. But he left it too late. Perhaps they had quarrelled. John Pudney, who now worked for the B.B.C., rescued him by arranging that he make the broadcast from a London studio. It went out successfully, though the harassed studio assistant forgot to take Thomas's script before he left the building; the B.B.C. were never sure whose poems Thomas had read, or whether he had permission to read them, and plaintive requests followed him round for months.

Thomas's letter was written from an address in Great Ormond Street, where he had friends. He had been ill and out of touch with Caitlin. He needs her and apologizes for his shortcomings: this was to be the pattern of most of his letters, the artist in search of a strong woman.

Caitlin, Caitlin my love, I love you, I can't tell you how much, I miss you until it hurts me terribly. Can you come to London before I go to Wales again, because I think I shall have to be in Wales a long time, a couple of months almost; I've been in a nursing home with bronchitis and laryngitis or something, no voice at all, no will, all weakness and croaking and spitting and feeling hot and then feeling cold, and I'm about now but quavery and convalescent and I must see you. I haven't seen or written to you or let you know I'm alive – which, at the moment, and remembering neurasthenically my days of almost-death, I don't think I was – since Wednesday, the 21st of April when I lost you in the morning, found money, and shouted on the wireless . . .

The letter goes on[3] to beg her not to be angry for failing to write, and not to disbelieve that he loves her. This was as passionate a letter as Thomas ever wrote: they had to be together, words weren't enough, her physical absence was insupportable, and so on. If he was to be saved ('I'm dying perhaps') they had

3. Previously unpublished letters from Thomas to Caitlin cannot be included verbatim for copyright reasons. (The opening section quoted above has already been published elsewhere.) But photocopies of all the Thomas-to-Caitlin letters have found their way to Texas.

to be together in a 'haze of daftness'. Would she come with kisses and gooseberries? Or telephone? The letter ends with his name and hers in the four segments of an X, and a postscript to say he must be abstemious.

If the letter was written some time in May, the 'couple of months' in Wales didn't materialize. Probably in April his parents had left Cwmdonkin Drive. D.J. had retired at Christmas: his health remained uncertain, and he was not a happy man. Grammar School colleagues made him a presentation and expected a speech. Instead he read them Charles Lamb's essay on 'The Schoolmaster'. There was a vague feeling that he was laughing at them. He wrote to his son-in-law, Haydn Taylor, on 18 December, 'I left the Grammar School today: had a small cheque from the staff; a few books & many cheers from the boys; a letter of appreciation of my 36 years' service from the Education Committee – and that's that.' In a corner of the letter he added, 'Dylan went to London today.' There were changes ahead for all of them. D.J. and Florence moved to a smaller house in Bishopston, a Gower village just outside Swansea. Dylan, his childhood home gone, edged towards a home of his own.

In June 1937, he and Caitlin decided to get married. Perhaps the plaintive note of his sickbed letter did the trick. There was no question of marrying in secret: Thomas, as usual groping for his respectable origins when an important decision had to be taken, wrote to tell his parents what was intended. The letter, dated 10 June, came out of the blue, from Cornwall, where he and Caitlin were staying in a borrowed cottage; apparently he had not been in Swansea since the start of April. It was headed '*Important Letter*'.

Dear Mother & Dad,

There's no doubt whatever that I've been a careless, callous, and quite unreasonable person as regards letting you know about myself since I left you at the beginning of April, and, as usual, I've no excuse, and you know me well enough to realize that if I did genuinely have one I wouldn't be long in explaining and elaborating it. Since I last wrote, and that was much too long ago, I've been working hard, but not too productively, have secured a little, but not extravagantly much, money on advance for the Welsh masterpiece,[4] and have – I'm not sure how much of a shock this might be to you – during the last three days moved on to Cornwall for a little – I can't actually call it a holiday – change of sorts and of weather and of companions. I intend, things which I want to explain permitting, to stay here until the end of June, and then return home for a while – to see mother and you – before continuing the rest of this daft & postponed journey of mine. I'm staying here with Caitlin Macnamara (whose writing on the envelope mother'll probably recognize) in a cottage lent to me by a man called Sibthorp; the address isn't really Mousehole, but, as the postal system here is so bad, I've been told that a Mousehole address is far easier & quicker to write to. The cottage is in Lamorna Cove, a beautiful little place full of good fishermen and indifferent visitors. I suppose that I'm piling on the shocks and surprises in this very late letter, but I must tell you too that Caitlin and I are going to be married next week by special licence (I think that's what they call it) in the Penzance registry office. This isn't thought of – I've told mother about it many times – speedily or sillily; we've been meaning to for a long time, & think we should carry it out at once. Everything will be entirely quiet & undemonstrative, two of the villagers here will be witnesses, and neither of us, of course, has a penny apart from the three pounds which we have carefully hidden in order to pay for the licence. We'll stay on here until the end of the month, then for a time Caitlin will go home to Hampshire & I'll come back to Wales until I can make just exactly enough money to keep us going until I make just exactly enough money again. It may, & possibly does, sound a rash and mad scheme, but it satisfies us and it's all we ask for. I do hope it won't hurt you; though I know I'm a thoughtless letter-writer & (this sounds like a novelette, doesn't it?) a pretty worthless son. I want you to know now & forever that I think about you every day and night, deeply & sincerely, and that I have tried to keep myself, (& have succeeded) straight & reasonable during the time I've been away from you: a time that seems years, so much has happened. I'm completely happy at the moment, well-fed, well-washed, & well looked-after. It's a superb place – the haunt, unfortunately, of aged

4. Probably a book about a journey through Wales that Dent commissioned but never received. Thomas once told Bert Trick that he was leaving in the morning for Holyhead, thence to work his way down the west coast of Wales. But he went to London (perhaps this was the early-April trip) and spent the money there instead.

R.A.s and presidents of West Country Poets' Rambling Clubs – and a delightful cottage, and weather full of sun and breeze, and I'm so glad mother's being well again, & I send her all my love. Do you mind, but I've got to ask you to do a few things for me, simple things and, to me, very necessary ones: could you send on some clothes, my green suit, a shirt or two, one of the pairs of shoes I've left, & those dark gym-shoes. I've had to buy an extra pair of flannel trousers, but I'm still a little short of clean and changeable things. Is it too much to ask, on top of all I ask you – & on top of what so rudely I rarely acknowledge? I would be so grateful, & I mean that with all my heart. I'll write again tomorrow, because then I'll know the exact Penzance date. I'm terribly terribly without money, so can't phone or get up to Penzance to find out: Rayner Heppenstall, who's staying with his wife a few miles away, is going to lend me a few shillings tomorrow, & I can then see to the few essential things.

Please write to me quickly; I would appreciate, so very much, you sending clothes & letters; and I'll try to be much more explicit & less (I should imagine) sensationally full of Dylan-life-altering news when I write tomorrow.

All my love, apologies, & hopes,
Dylan. X

D.J. was appalled at the news. According to Florence in later years, he sent twenty pounds and his blessing. In the end he did give his blessing, but reluctantly, and not until he had done what he could – it wasn't much – to stop the 'mad scheme' of the 'young irresponsibles'. He turned to Haydn Taylor, a man of affairs, for advice; in letters and phone calls they discussed what could be done. According to Nicolette Devas, Taylor telephoned Caitlin's mother in Hampshire, and suggested that Dylan might not make an ideal son-in-law. Taylor certainly offered to go to the Cornish cottage, but D.J. concluded that it would do no good. In two letters to his son-in-law – these, and the one mentioned above, are the only surviving letters by Jack Thomas – the old schoolmaster stuck to his principles but despaired of Dylan. On 15 June he wrote to Taylor:

I said all I had to say in my letter to him, & I put things as wisely & strongly as I could. What else to do I don't know; but perhaps you can think of some way to prevent what is a disaster. The idea, if it were not so serious, would be comic. The whole thing, to any normally-minded person, is grotesque & farcical – but the farcical comedy is tragic . . .

His own marriage and his own disappointments of thirty years earlier came to mind –

I'm sure both Nancy & yourself must feel very upset over the insane idea of Dylan's marrying in his desperate financial straits. Marriage, too, as I pointed out to him, would still further damn his potential success as a writer or poet . . .

On 25 June, D.J. was writing again to Taylor, reporting that two letters and a parcel to Dylan had gone unanswered:

We don't know therefore whether he is still in Cornwall, or whether the mad marriage has taken place. So far as I can see, there is nothing we can do to 'forbid the banns'. All we know, vaguely, of 'the lady in the case' is that she is of age (approximately of Dylan's age); that she is the niece of Augustus John; that her father & mother live apart . . .

D.J.'s world of books provided no solutions. In Cornwall, meanwhile, Dylan and Caitlin were still not married, probably because they didn't have the three pounds for a licence. Thomas had heard that his brother-in-law was taking an interest in his welfare, and on 20 June he wrote to him to fend him off politely and borrow a pound or two. The letter is clumsily written; Taylor inhibited him. It may mean (it isn't very clear) that the 'lovely three-lavatoried cottage' has something to do with the decision to marry; perhaps it was there that he and Caitlin discovered the pleasures of sharing the same house. But 'home' in the letter still seems to mean Swansea. It was addressed to Nancy and Haydn, and posted without a stamp.

I heard from my late London address that you had been ringing up during the last week to try to get hold of me, and that you'd heard – from father, I suppose – of my plans for a pleasant and eccentric marriage. The people in the London address told me that they had carefully been evasive in their replies to your questions about my whereabouts as they didn't know whether or not I wished them, for whatever strange reasons I might have had, to be broadcast. Father may have told you my Cornwall address, but, in case he didn't, here it is. It's a borrowed cottage with a jungle garden and three lavatories, and is only a few miles from where I stayed last year. But I don't imagine that that's of any interest. I lead a most mysterious life, on the surface; actually, it is the almost inevitable life of any penniless drifter with a liking for odd places and odder people, very few regrets about anything and no responsibilities. You mightn't agree with 'no responsibilities' considering that I'm so very nearly married, but Caitlin is – whether that's a fortunate thing or not in the opinion of others – sufficiently like myself to care little or nothing for proprietary interests and *absolutely* nothing for the responsibilities of husbandly provision. It will not yet, of course, be possible for us to live together all the time, and we'll go away whenever we feel like it or – & this will be, until the days of our comparative prosperity, which still would mean a genuine but never-yet wretched poverty, more frequent – whenever it is, from the point of view of money or/and accommodation, essential. (I'm sorry about these tortuous phrases but I've just been reviewing, with unction, cunning & entire literary dishonesty, a book on Social Credit & the Economic War.) Incidentally, I'd like to explain about my not returning home the day after Nancy and I met at Paddington Station: the lent pound note I gave back to the original lenders, my own expected cheque did not arrive for several days, and by that time I was again in debt for almost the complete worth of the cheque. It was unfortunate in some ways, but good in others, as, had I not been in London when I should officially have been working at home, this lovely three-lavatoried cottage would never have been mine for the summer, Caitlin and I would not have come to a decision so quickly, and (perhaps, but I think it unlikely, bloodly unlikely) another social catastrophe would have been averted. So much for that. I'm sending this letter of explanation to your Laleham cottage, as I haven't had any news about your moving. I hope it reaches you. As a gesture, Christian, gentlemanly, ladylike, sisterly, in-law-brotherly, friendly, & (in face of your obvious distrust of what could be, & has, by father, been called 'this lunatic course of action') congratulatorily from a married couple of some years' standing to two younger persons about to embark on the voyage of legal matrimony, would you like to slip me a couple of quid? I'm afraid the last few words are a sorry come-down after the grandiloquence of my previous circumlocution, but I do, actually, want to buy a hell of a lot of things almost at once, &, though father's been desperately kind & sent me five pounds last week with sort of resigned wishes for my happiness, I'm still really short of the bare amount I need . . .

Early in July, Thomas was beseeching his literary agent, David Higham, who now handled his writing, to raise a few pounds from Dent. He didn't say what it was for. Wyn Henderson paid for the marriage licence. She was running a guest-house at Mousehole called the Lobster Pot, in partnership with Max Chapman. Lamorna Cove was a few miles down the coast. Soon Thomas moved to the Lobster Pot, and it was from there that he and Caitlin were married at the register office in Penzance on 11 July 1937. He wrote to tell Vernon Watkins, who hadn't met her, adding that 'she looks like the princess on the top of a Christmas tree, or like a stage Wendy; but, for God's sake, don't tell her that'.

They spent their honeymoon first at the Lobster Pot, then at a studio owned by Max Chapman, in the near-by fishing village of Newlyn. Various painters and writers were staying in the neighbourhood. Oswell Blakeston was there; he was amused when Chapman and Caitlin wandered off innocently during a pub-crawl in Penzance and Thomas had a fit of jealousy. (There was more jealousy when Augustus John arrived to take them off in his car. Thomas refused to sit at the back, and jammed himself in front with John and Caitlin.) Rayner Heppenstall was still there with his wife. As they were walking back to the Lobster Pot at night from a local inn, with the moon on the Channel, 'the splendour of the spectacle infuriated Dylan, who made savage remarks about picture-postcards and visual clichés'. There was a lot of drinking. One sunny morning Thomas and friends were in a field above Newlyn, sampling a 'champagne wine tonic' sold by a local herbalist. Thomas talked and talked, then stopped abruptly. 'Somebody's boring me,' he said. 'I think it's me.'

Nothing much was happening on the creative front in 1937. He revised 'The spire cranes' and worked on a new poem, a long piece with complex half-rhymes, originally called 'Poem (for Caitlin)' later known by its first line, 'I make this in a warring absence'. This was completed towards the end of 1937, and apparently took nearly a year to write. To read unassisted it is almost impenetrable, but it seems to have been occasioned by jealousy of Caitlin. The 'warring absence' is their separation from one another. Conceivably it reflects something of Thomas's feelings about her former relationship with Augustus John.

They were in Swansea later in the summer; then they went to stay with Caitlin's mother at New Inn House, and remained in Hampshire through the winter and most of the spring of 1938. 'This is a very lovely place,' he wrote to Watkins late in October 1937. 'Caitlin & I ride into the New Forest every day, into Bluebell Wood or onto Cuckoo Hill. There's no one else about; Caitlin's mother is away; we are quiet and small and cigarette-stained and very young.' He liked to see them as two terrible children, said Caitlin; she remembered the start of their marriage as 'our first, know-nothing, lamb-sappy days'. When her sister Nicolette stayed there she would see them going off on the bus for a lunchtime beer in Ringwood and returning an hour later with paper bags of dolly mixtures and liquorice allsorts, and bottles of fizzy children's drinks, all of them things that Thomas loved. In the afternoon they disappeared to bed with the sweets and pop; their voices could be heard reading to one another. Some days they went to the coast and collected shells to use as counters in card games. Caitlin, by all accounts, was good for him sexually. Below the surface he was uneasy with women; probably she could comfort him as mother and mistress in ways he found agreeable or even essential. She was buxom then, and he was still skinny; she claimed to have carried him across streams under one arm. Her vigour was what he liked. Years later they used to have physical fights after an evening's drinking, and Caitlin once remarked that 'I think I was a bit stronger than him, but he used to allow me to do it, somehow'. In those early days she could be quiet in company, sipping a beer or a lemonade, lost in a dream; marriage, wrote Nicolette, 'quelled Caitlin's early wildness and soothed her scratchy grudge against the world'. But she never ceased to catch the eye, with her bright-coloured skirts and the high colour in her cheeks. Sometimes she looked birdlike – a bird of prey or paradise, depending on her mood. Nigel Henderson met her in London and found her 'like the figurehead of a ship, a fantastic poet's girl, a sort of corn-goddess'.

Money was soon a problem. Thomas reviewed books spasmodically but the income was tiny. So were the fees he received for his fantastical (often surrealist) stories, about twenty of which were published during the 1930s. Royston Morley was co-editor of the short-lived *Janus*, which printed a story called 'The Horse's Ha' in 1936. Normally the magazine paid nothing at all. When Thomas insisted, Morley bought him a cheap meal at Bertorelli's and handed over half a guinea. Perceptive editors were anxious to publish him, but their funds were small. *Wales*, founded and edited by Keidrych Rhys, published five poems and four stories in the late 1930s, but was able to pay very little. There were easier ways of making money. Thomas didn't take kindly to them. But the idea of having a regular income appealed to him, in a way. From Blashford he wrote to Watkins on 21 March 1938:

> . . . I have been in London, in penury, and in doubt: In London, because money lives and breeds there; in penury, because it doesn't; and in doubt as to whether I should continue as an outlaw or take my fate for a walk in the straight and bowler-treed paths. The conceit of outlaws is a wonderful thing; they think they can join the ranks of regularly-conducted society whenever they like. You hear young artists talk glibly about, 'God, I've a good mind to chuck this perilous, unsatisfactory, moniless business of art and go into the City & make money.' But who wants them in the City? If you are a money-&-success-maker, you make it in whatever you do. And young artists are always annoyed and indignant if they hear a City-man say, 'God, I've a good mind to chuck this safe, monotonous business of money-making & go into the wilderness and make poems.'

Many of Thomas's friends regarded him as a natural bohemian, indifferent to everything but his art. It is true that he knew how to arrange his affairs so that writing poems took priority. In the spring of 1938, while they were still at Blashford, he was suddenly at work again, rewriting four notebook poems, one of them 'After the funeral', which re-emerged as a clear statement that broke away (though only temporarily) from the cloudy, awkward style that had overtaken him. But however dedicated an artist he tried to be, and indeed often succeeded in being, his background clung to him. 'I am as domestic as a slipper,' he once observed to Margaret Taylor. Gwen Watkins heard him say, 'All we want is the little semi-detached with the little regular income.' Perhaps his tongue was in his cheek. But perceptive friends noted a nervous devotion to some version of life as it was lived in Cwmdonkin Drive. Caitlin, not her husband, was the real bohemian, because she was indifferent to what people thought. 'Dylan had the proper Welsh background,' says Vera, the Swansea girl who knew him from childhood. 'The fact that he was continually misbehaving was a cross to him. He wanted people to think well of him. He was brought up like me, worrying "What will the neighbours think?" Whereas Caitlin didn't care a bugger what anyone thought. She was an aristocrat, and that was that.' Caitlin's own observations complement this: 'He just liked his warm slippers and his dish of tit-bits and pickled onions and sardines ... that he'd stuff into his mouth when he was listening to the cricket scores.'

At intervals throughout his life, it seemed to worry Thomas that he was unemployed in the sense of having no regular work. John Pudney thought he detected it in the 1930s. William Empson (who, like most poets, earned his money by teaching) wrote that Thomas told him 'how frightening it was always to have nothing to do next day: sometimes, he said, "I buy a Mars Bar, and I think tomorrow I will eat that, so then I can go to sleep because I have a plan." I did not much like this highly polished bit of tear-jerking, but there is little doubt that unemployment would have driven me to drink too.' Writing to Charles Fisher in March 1938, Thomas spoke of getting a job with the B.B.C. Later in the year he broadcast again, in a poetry-reading from Manchester,[5] after he had demanded his rail fare in advance. He had the wrong sort of attitude to be a B.B.C. employee.

From Blashford, the Thomases moved to Wales in the late spring of 1938. They went to a cottage in Laugharne, that large village with an ancient charter which insists on calling itself a town. A mildly eccentric place, its raffish air may have appealed to Thomas as much as its watery panoramas. Little or no Welsh was spoken there, although it was only a few miles from Fern-

5. 'The Modern Muse', 18 October 1938. Others taking part included Auden, Spender and Louis MacNeice.

hill and the family farms, where Welsh was the everyday tongue. The town was off the beaten track, a clannish and in-bred community with a reputation for fighting with fists and knives. The Williams family owned and operated Brown's Hotel, the local buses, the local taxis and the diesel generators that made the electricity. When there was street-fighting or a brawl on a Saturday night, Ebi Williams would throw the switches and put Laugharne in darkness. Here, for the first time, the Thomases had a home of their own. It was a poor community between the wars, and rents were cheap. The cottage they took was small and damp, on the hill running out of the bottom end of Laugharne, opposite the ruined castle – 'four rooms like stained boxes in a workman's and fisherman's row, with a garden leading down to mud and sea'. It was called Eros. There was no bathroom. Neighbours peeked through the curtains to catch glimpses of young Mrs Thomas in a flowing purple housecoat, or watch her husband, who was thought to be a writer of some kind, trotting down the hill to fetch water from the public tap, dressed in pyjamas and an overcoat. He was chubbier now; his body was filling out.

After a couple of months they moved to Sea View, a narrow, important-looking house, pink-washed and taller than its neighbours, that they rented from the Williamses. The three storeys piled three pairs of rooms side by side, like a child's idea of what a house should be. Here they lived with little money and begged or borrowed furniture, in that easy-going solitude that writers crave but are apt to grow restless with, as time goes by and nothing happens except writing. At Sea View, temporarily, the mixture was right, or it would have been, given an income of a few pounds a week. Thomas was back again in a small room in Wales, working steadily. To Henry Treece he described himself as 'small, argumentative, good-tempered, lazy, fumbling, boozy as possible, "lower-middle-class" in attitude and reaction, a dirty tongue, a silly young man'. Friends came to stay, and Caitlin took them for tiring walks across the mud-flats or over the top of Sir John's Hill. She had been pregnant since the spring. In the evening she made stews or boiled fresh cockles; the floors crackled underfoot with shells. The Williamses' electricity hadn't reached Sea View, and candles stuck in empty beer bottles lit the guests to bed. Augustus John stayed there. Treece, who admired Thomas and had decided to write a book about his poetry, came armed with questions to which Thomas gave quirky answers, or no answers at all. Vernon Watkins came down from Gower; he said afterwards that the time at Sea View was the happiest of Thomas's life.[6]

There were quarrels with Caitlin, but they evaporated quickly. She was quick-tempered yet oddly complaisant, providing, quite often, the domestic virtues that he looked for. Drinking buddies from the big city would scarcely have recognized him. John Davenport, writer and critic, was invited to Laugharne. He found that 'Dylan on his native heath was a different being from the extravagant buffoon I had met five years before in London'. In London everything was different. There, for instance, Caitlin was the poet's girl. In Laugharne she was expected to keep the house moderately clean and have meals on the table. A woman's place was at the sink or in the bed; it was how people saw things in Cwmdonkin Drive. Elisabeth Lutyens, the composer, noticed the trait in Thomas when she stayed in Laugharne ten or twelve years later. In London, where they were both working for radio after the war, they were colleagues and friends, and 'Dylan took me utterly seriously as a fellow-professional'. In Laugharne she was merely another woman around the house; Thomas infuriated her with a 'cocky, masculine, women-in-their-place attitude', and by grumbling jealously when she and Caitlin went walking or bathing together. If Caitlin herself was more accommodating than might have been expected, perhaps it was because she had been brought up in circles where the artist was licensed to lord it over the lucky females. Her father Francis once declared that a woman was a blank slate for a man to scribble on.

6. Watkins was then unmarried. Gwen Watkins, whom he married six years later, says that at the time of the 1938 visit, 'Dylan was extremely curious about Vernon's sexual life. In fact, at that time Vernon didn't have one. I think Dylan would have liked to have the three of them in bed together, to see what would happen. There was an element of cold freakishness on his part.'

For Thomas, Wales was a place and a frame of mind he settled into because it was convenient. He had the artist's instinct for self-preservation. Caitlin noted that 'he worked in a fanatically narrow groove: although there was nothing narrow about the depth and understanding of his feelings. The groove of direct hereditary descent in the land of his birth, which he never in thought, and hardly in body, moved out of. Which handed him his line of approach ready made, and his poems already matured inside him. Which gave him the snail's eye view of a blade of grass: thus imparting to his work his concentrated intensity.'

In 1938, much of his work consisted of stories, though not stories of the kind he had been writing since adolescence. Those, the fantasies and nightmares, were supposed to have been collected and published as a book by now. George Reavey was meant to be arranging it through the Europa Press, but the printers were afraid of being prosecuted for obscenity. Thomas tried to pinpoint the offensive sentences. 'The only story I can think of which might cause a few people a small and really unnecessary alarm,' he wrote to Reavey on 16 June, 'is the "Prologue to an Adventure"; this I could cut out from the book, and substitute a story about my grandfather who was a very clean old man.' On 24 August he was telling John Davenport:

> I write pathetically to George [Reavey], but he just won't answer. Publication, he has condescended to tell me on a postcard, of the stories as they stand would lead to imprisonment. What he will not tell me is the particular words, phrases, passages to which objection is taken; these my scruples will allow me to alter without hesitation; but how do I know, without being told, what words etc. the dunder printers and lawyers think objectionable: piss, breast, bottom, Love?

The list finally arrived. (One of the troublesome phrases occurred in a story about clergymen, 'The Holy Six': 'The holy life was a constant erection to these six gentlemen.') But the book never appeared. The following year the stories were still giving trouble, this time when a new book of prose and poems, *The Map of Love*, was being discussed with Dent. Church refused to print some of them, in particular the one that Thomas regarded as the best, 'A Prospect of the Sea', because it had 'unwarrantable moments of sensuality'.[7] One naughtiness did evade the safety net, in 'The Orchards', an extravagant piece about a poet called Marlais. Thomas invented a few innocent place names, LlanAsia and Aberbabel, and one that could be read backwards, Llareggub. He seems to have tried spelling most names backwards as a matter of course, to see what he could make of them. T. S. Eliot, he once remarked, was nearly 'toilets', and Llanmadog, a village in Gower, was nearly 'God man all'. Nobody noticed 'Llareggub' at the publishers. Thomas liked the joke so much that he used it again for *Under Milk Wood* (by which time the publishers had woken up, and after his death insisted on spelling it Llaregyb).

In the stories that he was writing in 1938 and 1939, later published as *Portrait of the Artist as a Young Dog*, Thomas abandoned surrealism and turned to autobiography in the shape of fiction. The original suggestion came from Church, who in 1936 proposed 'a tale of the world where your early years have been spent'. The story about the 'clean old man', 'A Visit to Grandpa's', seems to have been the first, written before he left Blashford. It is the least factual of the group, and probably the least successful.[8] 'One Warm Saturday', ostensibly about sex but really about loneliness, was written at Sea View in the summer of 1938. So was the Fernhill story, 'The Peaches', 'a long story about my true childhood'. He called them 'illuminated reporting'. He also called them 'mostly potboilers'. But they read like a true record, free from hesitations. Of the ten stories, two are about Carmarthenshire, two are set in Gower, and the remainder in Swansea. All were written by the end of 1939. A

7. The story had already appeared in the magazine *Life and Letters Today* in 1937. When Dent finally published it as the title-story of a Thomas collection in 1955, two years after his death, a reference to masturbation, 'the death from playing with yourself', was still regarded as too daring, and was omitted.

8. The story has been taken as an account of D.J.'s father, Thomas the Guard. According to Florence it was about Thomas the Guard's father – D.J.'s grandfather, William – who lived with his son and daughter-in-law at Poplar Cottage in Johnstown until he died, long before Dylan was born. D.J. told Dylan about him as a child.

manuscript version of 'Patricia, Edith and Arnold', one of the last to be completed, lists the stories already written and adds some new ideas: 'An out-of-doors story; another Dan story; a Trevor Hughes story; a little boy watching a man hang himself.' Of these, only the Hughes story, 'Who Do You Wish Was With Us?', was ever written.[9] The war interfered, or perhaps the vein was exhausted. Thomas's 'dead youth in the vanished High Street nights' was a subject he returned to often enough in radio reminiscences, but (apart from 'Return Journey') they lacked the energy of the stories. As with *18 Poems*, the mood was not sustained; another door had closed.

Thomas's mood in 1938 seems to have been confident enough. Aged twenty-three, he was already a candidate for a critical study. Henry Treece was an earnest young poet, later a leader of the so-called 'New Apocalyptic' movement. When he wrote to Thomas at Blashford, Thomas replied to say he was flattered and would be glad to help. Treece had also been in touch with Richard Church, who thought that such a study was premature. Thomas agreed, up to a point. He wrote to Treece to say that 'two small books of verse have never, to my knowledge, produced, in their writer's lifetime, a book of explanation and assessment by another writer, nor has such an adequately small reputation as mine needed an analysis of it to make it bigger. But this is not to say that I personally consider it inadvisable . . .' He dealt briskly with the unenthusiastic Church: 'A cliché-riddled humbug and pie-fingering hack, a man who has said to me, when I told him I was starving, that a genuine artist scorns monetary gain.'

In the letters that followed, Thomas told Treece a lot about himself and his poetry, though the information began to dry up after they had their not very successful meeting in the summer. (A few years later Thomas was describing him as 'a loud and brawling hypocrite'.) Writing from Blashford, Thomas spelt

9. The list is headed with another of Thomas's backward-reading jokes, 'Llaberos & Muberab in Llareggub', perhaps an alternative title for *Portrait*. Thomas told Vernon Watkins that he thought *Portrait of the Artist as a Young Dog* a 'flippant' title, and used it only for 'moneymaking reasons'.

out his solution to the poet's problem of living on air: 'I have achieved poverty with distinction, but never poverty with dignity; the best I can manage is dignity with poverty, and I would sooner smarm like a fart-licking spaniel than starve in a world of fat bones.' In June came more descriptions of poverty from the fisherman's cottage, where they were facing a week-end without cigarettes, bread or stamp for the letter – 'We wait for shillings which we have no right to expect. Bitter, cruel Laugharne; my pipe is full of butt-ends from the grate, my table crowded with the dead ends of poems, my head full of non-sense. The sun is shining on the mud; my wife is out cockling ... A little girl has called with buns; I say "no buns" though all my everlasting soul shouts for them ...' Treece obliged by sending buns and other small gifts. He was anxious to penetrate Thomas's mysteries and lay him out for critical inspection, and Thomas was forthcoming. Treece learned that most of the 'straight poems' in *Twenty-five Poems* were written before *18 Poems*; it seems to be more than Watkins was ever told. He was given an account of how Thomas wrote poetry, which has become the most widely quoted of Thomas's self-analyses. It described a process that began with an image based on the emotions, which then bred conflicting images within an intellectual framework, until finally the contradictions were resolved in 'that momentary peace which is a poem'. In other letters Thomas insisted that his poems be taken literally. This advice, not always easy to follow, was directed at, among others, Edith Sitwell, whose explanation of certain lines, he said, missed their literal meaning. Another remark to Treece that has been extensively quoted was Thomas's assertion that 'I hold a beast, an angel and a madman in me, and my inquiry is as to their working, and my problem is their subjugation and victory, downthrow and upheaval, and my effort is their self-expression'. But Thomas was equally good at rhetoric and anti-rhetoric. A year later he was writing to Treece, begging him to 'cut out that remark of mine about "I have a beast and an angel in me", or whatever it was; it makes me sick, drives me away from drink, recalls too much the worst of the fat and curly boy I know too well ...' As he grew older he became less inclined to make any serious comment on himself as a writer.

In the Treece letters he frequently expressed himself on contemporary poets. He was rude about most of them:

> Today the Brotherhood of Man – love thy neighbour and, if possible, covet his arse – seems a disappointing school-society, and I cannot accept Auden as head-prefect. I think MacNeice is thin and conventionally-minded, lacking imagination, and not sound in the ear: flop Day Lewis; and Spender, Rupert Brooke of the Depression, condemns his slight, lyrical, nostalgic talent to a clumsy and rhetorical death ...

Some of his best friends were poets, but in general he seems not to have liked them for their poetry. 'Putting little trust in most of the poetry being written today,' he told Treece, 'I put a great deal in mine.' Nor could he stomach being part of a group or movement; he was himself, someone apart. When a Welsh correspondent tried to inveigle him into a society of Welsh authors, he wrote polite letters but made his position clear: 'I don't think it does any harm to the artist to be lonely *as* an artist. (Let's all "get together", if we must, and go to the pictures.) If he feels personally unimportant, it may be that he is. Will an artistic milieu make his writing any better? I doubt it.'

As for his own writing, in 1938 he produced little but prose between the spring, in Blashford, and the autumn, when he was still in Laugharne. Then he wrote five poems, quite quickly, two of them based on notebook versions, the others newly conceived. 'A saint about to fall' was Caitlin's child, due to be born in the New Year. He was writing the poem in September, when Germany invaded Czechoslovakia and there was talk of war. 'Remember,' he told Watkins, 'this is a poem written to a child about to be born ... & telling it what a world it will see, what horrors & hells ... It's an optimistic, taking-everything poem. The two most important words are "Cry Joy".' His verse continued to be difficult, almost wilfully so, with the one exception, that autumn, of a short, disturbing poem written for his birthday at the end of October, 'Twenty-four years'. After the complicated images of the other poems the message arrived like a telegram: life means death.

His shortage of money was chronic. He was borrowing from anyone who would lend, receiving food and other hospitality from the Richard Hugheses, and running up debts in Laugharne. The B.B.C., as he had already realized, was a possible way of earning money without having to make himself into a writing hack. He could be a reading hack instead. He had a shrewd idea of his powers; in a 1939 letter, written before he had a reputation as a reader of poetry, he talks of his 'breathless boom boom boom'. Reading – it must have seemed to Thomas – would not interfere with his real work. In October he was writing to the B.B.C. in Cardiff, suggesting a radio anthology of Welsh poets, old and new, to include contemporaries 'who are now making what is really a renaissance in Welsh writing'. The producer he wrote to replied that he was looking for 'long dramatic poems in verse'. This didn't appeal to Thomas. 'I take such a long time writing anything,' he replied, 'and the result, dramatically, is too often like a man shouting under the sea ... It sounds full of dramatic possibilities, if only I was.'

He was unable or unwilling to deny himself those long stretches of time when he had to do nothing but work at a poem, or lie fallow between poems. The Thomas legend has exaggerated the extent of his poetic labours. It has made him seem an artist of abnormal dedication who habitually spent hours or days on a single line. It is true that (like many other poets) he was a craftsman who sometimes built up his poems slowly; this was especially true towards the end of his life. But most of his successful poems were written comparatively quickly. This is so of *18 Poems*, and of the 'Fern Hill' and 'Winter's Tale' group at the end of the war on which a great part of his popular reputation rests. In 1938 the revised version of 'After the funeral' was probably produced in less than a month; the second half, he told Watkins, 'came in a rush'. 'I make this in a warring absence', which took most of 1937 to write, is not his most felicitous poem. No doubt he produced poems at the rate that was natural for him, no faster and no slower. It was natural for him to let months or even years go by without producing one at all. Probably it was equally natural for him to sit in his work-room, ostensibly writing but in fact regarding the birds or calculating how much he owed the butcher and what cheques were due from editors; fragments of worksheets indicate as much; it is how most writers behave, after all. Thomas was different only in that he adopted the theatrical posture of a poet entitled by his vocation to work things out in his own time. Whether this was an indulgence or a necessary safeguard – whether it enabled him to write what he did, or interfered with a more practical and productive approach – it is impossible to say. It was simply his nature to regard himself as a special case; and to persuade others to agree.

Re-publication in America of poems and stories already published in Britain was an obvious way of earning money without extra work. Early in 1938 he was in touch with the young James Laughlin who had founded his own publishing house, New Directions. America was always a promised land for Thomas; it spelt one thing, money. He began by trying to mortgage his royalties on books to be published in America, as well as on books not yet written, in return for immediate cash. Laughlin sent him a few pounds, and made plans to bring out a first collection of Thomas's work in a small edition the following year.[10] New Directions – and Dent in London – often came in for abuse behind their backs from Thomas, but they were both loyal publishers who made little or no profit from him until the end of his life; although as it happened, they were laying up treasures for themselves. The same was true of Thomas's long-suffering literary agent, David Higham, whose ten per cents were trifling sums for many years.

Patronage seemed another good idea in 1938. An institution called the Royal Literary Fund had been known to make grants to deserving authors. Thomas roped in supporters, among them T. S. Eliot and Edith Sitwell, and presented himself as a good cause, without success. In trouble with local creditors, he wrote to John Davenport from Laugharne on 14 October:

10. *The World I Breathe*, published in December 1939 in an edition of seven hundred copies. In the five years it was in print, it earned Thomas forty-five pounds.

No grant was made me. My literary claims 'were found not strong enough for the purposes of this society'. Who *do* they give their money to? I'm an excellent and most disturbing case. Must you be a Georgian writer of belle-lettres, suffering in Surrey? Must you be in the evening of your days, with nothing to look forward to but nostalgia, borrowed copies of new books about Wilde, and inclusion in any Gawsworth anthology of the unburied dead? Or is the Royal Fund available only for successful writers having a bad year? Only *recommended* this year by the Medium Book Society! Poor chap, send him a large cheque and a luncheon invitation from a publisher's nark; let Miss Du Maurier knit him a smoking-coat, & don't forget the special, indelible inkstains. But I'm furious. And after Miss Sitwell wrote two pages to the secretary, too. You don't know, do you, any rich person I can try now? I'll dedicate my next poems to him, & write a special sponger's song. Can't I live even on the immoral earnings of my poems? No, but there must be someone, somewhere in England, who'd like to do a poet a good turn, someone who wouldn't miss just enough money to ensure me peace & comfort for a month or two to get on with the work I'm in the middle of now & which I so much want to finish. All my hopes were in that Royal set-up, & now we'll have to abscond from here, as from everywhere else I've ever lived in, leaving, this time, a house full of furniture we had the devil of a lot of cringing trouble to obtain. Thirty bloody pounds would settle everything. If you know any rich chap fond of a jingle who knows his Peters & Quennells, do let me know at once. Otherwise it'll be traipsing again, no stability at all, no home, and certainly no work. Try to think of some sap, some saint. There's no reason why I should bother you like this, but here I can't get in touch with anybody with more money than a betty with no cunt or more generosity than a fucked weazel.

They had planned to go back to Hampshire in the winter, in any case, 'to stay a little bit before our saint or monster', and they were there by the end of November – 'half-starving, worrying, and escaping from things', he told Higham, urging him to raise fifty pounds, or anything, on a projected collection of poems and stories for Dent. A few days before Christmas he was writing to Watkins:

... I've just come back from three dark days in London, city of the restless dead. It really is an insane city, & filled me with terror. Every pavement drills through your soles to your scalp, and out pops a lamp-post covered with hair. I'm not going to London again for years; its intelligentsia is so hurried in the head that nothing stays there; its glamour smells of goat; there's no difference between good and bad . . . Last year at this time Caitlin & I were doing an act in a garret. This time we're just as poor, or poorer, but the ravens – soft, white, silly ravens – will feed us.

At least three new poems were written at Blashford, including one that gave hostile readers, among them the critic James Agate in the *Daily Express*, an excuse for poking fun at what they regarded as nonsense verse. Originally called 'January 1939', the poem began:

> Because the pleasure-bird whistles after the hot wires,
> Shall the blind horse sing sweeter?

Like many Thomas phrases, it has the ring of a nursery rhyme. It refers to the practice of blinding song-birds to improve their singing. Perhaps Thomas is supposed to be the blind horse. According to Watkins, the poem originated in a dream about a blind horse which began to sing. A man in Thomas's dream said, 'He sings better now.' The poem is open to various interpretations; but in general it seems to be another version of the Poet contemplating himself, his poems and his past, the process triggered off by the dream and the New Year, perhaps on New Year's Eve. It was hardly nonsense, but it was undeniably esoteric.

Presently, resolutions forgotten, Thomas was in the insane city again, meeting Lawrence Durrell and Henry Miller. Once again it was 'shabby salons' and 'nightmare London'. A few weeks later Caitlin was in hospital at Poole, having her baby. It was a boy, born on 30 January 1939; they gave it one Welsh name, Llewelyn, and one French, Edouard. Thereafter events seemed to be repeating themselves – a few more poems, a few more debts, a few more attempts to raise money. He wrote to Bert Trick to tell him about the baby, a letter tinged with nostalgia for Swansea, and 'long filled-in Sundays with you and scrapbooks and strawberry jelly at the end . . . We're all moving away. And every single decisive action happens in a blaze of disappointment.' Neither Dylan nor Caitlin wanted to stay at

Blashford, but they still owed thirty pounds in Laugharne. In May, however, they were back at Sea View. The pattern seemingly could go on for years or a lifetime. Could Higham raise money from Dent against books to be written in future? Could patrons help? An ingenious notion occurred to Thomas: if a dozen people could be persuaded to send him five shillings a week, he would have a regular income. This idea occupied him, on and off, for months. He called it 'Thomas Flotation Limited', and talked about making people 'Thomas-minded', but it was not a joke. 'I've got to get twelve chaps,' he told John Davenport. Davenport – a generous man, who had written film scripts in Hollywood, and had a wife with money – sent him names and a cheque. Thomas perked up at once. 'No dank debtors' walls obscure us,' he wrote. 'The fawning tradesmen doff their horns. I'll draft a letter for the five bob fund & let you have it, it's grand to have your assistance. A witty letter, do you think? I'll write very soon. Or a straight-from-the-shldr? . . .' Davenport became chief organizer. The potential patrons included Edith Sitwell, Augustus John, Norman Cameron, the rich Lord Tredegar (Augustus John knew him) and the rich Peggy Guggenheim (Thomas was once introduced to her). Occasionally his letters to Davenport sound cross at people's tardiness in agreeing to help a poet in need. 'Surely there must [be] – if people can't be bothered with sending five shillings a week – some very simple method of them sending it to me monthly?' he wrote.

The scheme came to nothing. Thomas hinted to Davenport that it was his fault. But by this time it was September 1939 and the war with Germany had started at last. From Thomas's point of view, this was bad news directed personally at Dylan Thomas and family. The war was other people's concern. That was not the consensus view of the British Left, but Thomas was not adopting a political attitude. He was sulkily wishing the war would go away. In the last week of August he told Watkins he was 'messing about in the sun and pub', overcome with 'horror & terror & lassitude' as the news grew worse. To his father he wrote (thanking him for the gift of a dictionary) to say that it was 'terrible to have built, out of nothing, a complete happiness

– from no money, no possessions, no material hopes – & a way of living, & then to see the immediate possibility of its being exploded & ruined through no fault of one's own'. To others he was indignant about events in Europe. 'I think a squirrel stumbling at least of equal importance as Hitler's invasions,' he wrote to Treece in July 1938; and a year later, 'What are you doing for your country? I'm letting mine rot.' A few weeks after war was declared he was telling Bert Trick, 'My little body (though it's little no longer, I'm like a walrus) I don't intend to waste for the mysterious ends of others. If there's any profiteering to be done, I in my fashion wish to be in on it ... I can't raise up any feeling about this war at all. And the demon Hitlerism can go up its own bottom. I refuse to help it with a bayonet [or] to talk about keeping Hitlerism out of this sink of democracy ...' He tried to persuade fellow-writers to send him contributions for an article to be called 'Objection to War'. As he pointed out to D. S. Savage, this would be to the advantage of writers who intended (as Thomas did, at the time) to register as conscientious objectors. But he got little response.

The immediate effect of the war was to jeopardize his earnings. A Welsh Region broadcast had been scheduled for 6 September, a discussion with Keidrych Rhys about 'Modern Welsh Poets'.[11] It was cancelled; the B.B.C. paid part of the fee and asked for their rail ticket back. Two weeks earlier Thomas's third book, *The Map of Love*, had been published. It contained seven stories, all fanciful and some surrealist, and sixteen poems. They included 'After the funeral' and 'Twenty-four years'. But in general these poems of the 'middle period' (as it turned out to be) are less rewarding than those Thomas wrote earlier and later. The book was respectfully and sometimes warmly reviewed, with a few dissenters. Cyril Connolly – who presently

11. The discussion, which was to have been scripted in advance, worried the B.B.C. 'We *must* have this man's script before he appears in the studios,' wrote an official in disapproving blue pencil. The fears were well-grounded. When the producer, Watkin Jones, raised objections to the script, Thomas wrote to Rhys, 'It's worth agreeing with their piddling suggestions, in order to get across what we really want to. I may myself, later & with, probably, the disgust of Mr Jones, change one of my selected poems; but that can be left until the rehearsal.'

founded the magazine *Horizon*, published Thomas regularly, and praised him energetically – found the *Map of Love* poems 'difficult and baffling ... The technique remains, the inspiration gone. His being a purely Celtic writer makes his forgeries difficult to detect, but I think one can say that many of his images are nonsense, and that his hit-or-miss method is unsatisfactory, while his writing is inflated and faked.' This review, in the *New Statesman*, was one of the harshest that Thomas ever received. But Connolly, like Edith Sitwell, changed his mind.

The war was presumably the reason the book flopped as it did. Dent printed three thousand sets of sheets, and bound one thousand. Four months after publication, a colleague of David Higham wrote to say that sales were two hundred and eighty copies. 'Pretty discouraging, eh?' he added. Commercially this was worse than *Twenty-five Poems* three years earlier. Thomas had been paid seventy pounds in advances on *The Map of Love* but when it finally went out of print in 1950, his royalty-earnings were still below that figure. His fourth book did little or no better. This was the collection of stories, *Portrait of the Artist as a Young Dog*, his record of the background to the poems. An edition of 1,500 copies was published in April 1940.[12] *Time and Tide* saw it as 'a superb evocation of boyhood and adolescence'. The *Times Literary Supplement*'s reviewer found that 'the atmosphere of schoolboy smut and practical jokes and poetry is evoked with lingering accuracy but with nothing more'. Under other circumstances it might have sold well, but the times buried it.

In the early months of the war, Thomas was seeking work in a reserved occupation where he wouldn't have to do military service. He had abandoned the idea of going before a conscientious objectors' tribunal after sampling one as a spectator at the Shire Hall in Carmarthen with Keidrych Rhys. Vernon Watkins told the story at second-hand: 'As each objector came forward he was asked on what grounds he objected to military service, and in each case a mean little voice answered, "'ligious".

12. In America, Laughlin's New Directions published an edition of a thousand copies in September 1940.

Each was then asked what he was prepared to do, and each answered, in an even meaner little voice, "Nothing".' It was hardly practical, let alone decent, for Thomas to make a stand on religious grounds. A political excuse sometimes worked, and he clutched briefly at this straw. He wrote to a prominent Welsh nationalist, Gwynfor Evans, who was secretary of the Welsh Pacifists; this had twelve thousand members and was opposed to military conscription. Evans says he replied sharply and negatively to this 'unheroic' approach.

How Thomas eventually avoided military service has not been satisfactorily explained. His mother said he was unfit because of 'punctured lungs'. Vernon Watkins said it was 'scarred lungs'. Neither condition agrees with the 1953 post-mortem. He seems to have been examined at least twice. On 6 May 1940, writing to Stephen Spender from his parents' house in Bishopston, he said, 'I went, by the way, to have another army medical examination, this time in Wales, & was found to be Grade III, which will keep me out of all the main army nastiness and perhaps out of the army altogether.'[13] This implies a previous examination in England. It was possible to appear voluntarily before a military board in London, in advance of the compulsory medical interview. This may be what Thomas did, hoping to impress the examiners with his unsuitability. In a letter of 22 June to Laurence Pollinger at the David Higham agency he said that 'I'm not in the army – yet. I took Higham's advice & went before the military board who found me *3*. Whatever that will come to mean.' Higham was unable to remember what he advised. Perhaps Thomas was failed because of his recurrent asthma; or even on psychological grounds. Conceivably things

13. A week later he wrote to Spender again to say he now understood Grade III men would be called up, probably for non-combatant work. Dr Oscar Williams, chairman of the medical tribunal in Llanelli during the war, is certain that Thomas was never examined there (as several accounts say he was). Margaret Taylor heard a story that Thomas appeared for his examination in front of a doctor who had heard him read poetry the night before. 'Oh Mr Thomas, it can't be you!' said the doctor. Tudor Williams of Laugharne says Dylan was known as a 'conchie' (i.e. 'conscientious objector') early in the war, and was given 'a good hiding one night by a soldier home on leave.

were rigged in Wales by a friendly doctor. Nicolette Devas heard such a rumour.

All this time Dylan and Caitlin were shifting from place to place – Swansea for Christmas 1939, then Blashford for a few months, then back to Laugharne, then back to his parents in May 1940 with another pile of debts left behind. Watkins had been helping with money. They were buying a bed on hire-purchase at seven shillings a month, and needed a pound to stop it being taken away for non-payment. Watkins sent the money. He was forever providing little life-savers. 'TA for the great pound,' Thomas wrote on another occasion. 'I heard it singing in the envelope.' The latest flight from Laugharne was more serious than usual. Thomas appealed to Spender, telling him that books, clothes, beds, china and chairs had all been left behind at Sea View and would be sold up unless he paid his debts. This time he needed seventy pounds. Spender organized a superior whip-round – Henry Moore and Herbert Read were among the contributors – and Thomas, back in Laugharne, wrote to say that 'life's quite different now and I'm beginning to work like a small, very slow horse'. But the relief was only a postponement. Neither Dylan nor Caitlin was much good at managing money, and there was always Brown's Hotel or a fish-frail of bottled beer to take care of any surplus cash. Drink continued to play an important part in his life. When it threatened to deprive them of furniture and clothing, Caitlin rebelled and there were rows. Apparently she was a reluctant drinker then. She wrote of 'agonizing hours of unadulterated boredom I have spent in dull as ditchwater pubs with Dylan to preserve his sacred drinking myth'. He was not yet an alcoholic; perhaps was never one, in the full sense of the word, although drink was deeply woven into his life. In any case, in 1940 the disasters were still in the future.

That summer he and Caitlin stayed with John Davenport and his wife Clement at their house in the town of Marshfield, Gloucestershire. This handsome building in the main street, The Malting House, was one of Davenport's last gestures to the gracious life before his money ran out. For a while, in the early part of the war, he held open house for musicians and writers.

Lennox Berkeley the composer was there, and William Glock, then a music critic. Antonia White went there after she saw Davenport at an exhibition in London, and he told her she must come and join the fun. The house hummed with music and jokes, not to mention jealousies. Mrs Davenport was having an affair with a guest. She would sit with her husband while he played one of the grand pianos loudly in the music room, turning the pages and humouring him. Sometimes he lost his temper and threw things. He was a short, broad, clever man, inclined to be a bully when drunk, good at mimicry and general fooling about. There was a fair amount of that. Antonia White heard screams coming from upstairs. Caitlin had insisted it was time for Dylan to take a bath, and was busy with soap and water, covering the ceiling with blobs of foam. Thomas and Davenport spent much of their time writing a novel called *The Death of the King's Canary*, a not very funny satire on writers and painters of the time.[14] Half the bohemian establishment seems to be there, attending a grotesque house-party in the country. Augustus John makes a brief appearance as Hercules Jones. No doubt Yvonne Bacon is meant to be Nina Hamnett. Perhaps it has faint echoes of life at The Malting House. The verse parodies are the best part. Among them is one of Spender ('Christopher Garvin'), 'The Parachutist', apparently written by Thomas. Cyril Connolly had it set up in type for *Horizon*, but was unable to find room for it. He printed another of Thomas's *Canary* parodies, 'Request to Leda: Homage to William Empson', in 1942.

The house-party atmosphere was prolonged into the autumn. 'The summer talked itself away,' Thomas said later. In the evenings they drank the remains of Davenport's pre-war cellar and tried ineffectively to keep the black-out curtains drawn. The

14. It was eventually published in 1976, following hints that it had been 'rediscovered'. But it had been in the hands of Thomas's copyright trustees all along, and an extract appeared in book form in 1971. In general it is not clear who wrote what. A note from Davenport, at Texas, says: 'I wrote Chapter 1 and most of the parodies. Dylan did the one on Empson (Dudley) and some are collaborated on. From Chapter 1 on the book is almost exactly 50–50. Dylan finally took the manuscript away and typed it himself.'

Battle of Britain was being fought over Southern England. Europe had fallen, the air-raids were under way. His mother wrote to tell him about the first raids on Swansea. At Marshfield, a hundred miles from London, they heard war-planes from time to time. Thomas wrote to Watkins, 'Are you frightened these nights? When I wake up out of burning birdman dreams – they were frying aviators one night in a huge frying pan: it sounds whimsical now, it was appalling then – and hear the sound of bombs & gunfire only a little way away, I'm so relieved I could laugh or cry.' What frightened him, he said, was the thought of German troops marching silently up the street. Invasion seemed imminent that September, and Thomas had nightmares about it. He wrote a harsh, oblique poem about invasion, 'Deaths and Entrances', the first of a small group about the war. Cyril Connolly, liking it more than he liked *The Map of Love*, took it for *Horizon*.

In December he was in London briefly, squeezing money from the B.B.C. for a script, meeting friends, travelling back to Wales on a slow train and (he said) being asked for his identity card by Army officers because he was wearing a black hat and they thought he was a spy. He and Caitlin were back in Bishopston with his parents, squashed into little rooms. He had been writing more letters to literary persons, seeking help. Alec Waugh suggested he should write more stories and fewer letters, a joke that annoyed Thomas, who wrote crossly to Davenport, 'When I want advice from Alec Waugh I'll go to his brother.' He wrote to Davenport on 8 January 1941, 'Today the pipes burst, and Caitlin, in a man's hat, has been running all day with a mop from w.c. to flooded parlour, while I've been sitting down trying to write a poem about a man who fished with a woman for bait and caught a horrible collection.' This was the 'Ballad of the Long-legged Bait', completed in April 1941 and published in *Horizon* three months later. Connolly thought it too long (at 216 lines, it was the longest poem Thomas ever wrote), and he had it set in small type to save paper, which was rationed. Thomas was upset; according to Connolly, 'he refused to come in and correct his proofs, so that there were some appalling misprints – I remember "Jew" for "due" was one of them – for which I got all the blame.'

Thomas did hack work when he could. At Marshfield he had written two short scripts for the B.B.C.'s South American Service, one of them about Christopher Columbus. Next he was commissioned to write a programme about Czech heroes. 'Could I have a script to do without battles, d'you think?' he wrote to the producer when he sent in his draft. 'Or perhaps with only twenty or thirty?' Besides earning a few guineas, B.B.C. scripts were a means of showing that he was a writer, doing essential war work. He had escaped the Army but he was still liable to be directed into civilian employment. He corresponded hopefully with the B.B.C., writing on 6 May 1941 that 'what you said in your letter, and what you said you could say to the Ministry of Labour if necessary, I hope, will do the trick; that is, keep me for a while longer out of the factories'. To Clement Davenport he had written from Bishopston the previous month:

. . . I'm awfully busy with a long poem, and I've just borrowed this typewriter to type out the never-ending *Canary*, God moult it, and I'm helping about the house, shuffling and breaking, and I think that unless I'm careful and lucky the boys of the Government will get me making munitions. I wish I could get a real job and avoid that. Clocking in, turning a screw, winding a wheel, doing something to a cog, lunching in the canteen, every cartridge case means one less Jerry, bless all the sergeants the short and the tall, bless 'em all, blast 'em all, evenings in the factory rest centre, snooker and cocoa, then bugs in digs and then clocking in and turning and winding and hammering to help to kill another stranger, deary me I'd rather be a poet anyday and live on guile and beer . . .

This self-contained philosophy kept him afloat. The war machine left him alone. Perhaps the nearest the war came to him was earlier that winter, in February, when the Swansea town centre and parts of the working-class suburbs were destroyed in three nights of air raids. Bert Trick bumped into Dylan and Caitlin on the corner of a ruined shopping street on the morning immediately after the third and worst raid. The weather was cold; the future unpromising. It was the last time Trick was to see Thomas. He wrote, 'The air was acrid with smoke, and the hoses of the firemen snaked among the blackened entrails of what had once been Swansea Market. As we parted, Dylan said with tears in his eyes, "Our Swansea is dead".'

After these air-raids, Thomas's parents began to make plans to leave Bishopston for the family cottages in Blaen Cwm, where it would be safer and cheaper. Florence's sister Theodosia and her husband, the Rev. David Rees, had been living there, but they were dead. In the other cottage were the unmarried brother and sister from St Thomas, Bob, the recluse, and Polly, the chatterbox. D.J. was dismayed at the prospect of having his wife's relatives on the doorstep, but he was getting old and he had no option. 'Oh Gawd, here's that bitch again,' he would say when he heard Polly's voice approaching; unfortunately she was very fond of him. He told Ken and Hettie Owen, family friends from Port Talbot, that he was starved for intelligent conversation. 'There's nothing here but cows and clots,' he said. His son's visits were increasingly important; they did *The Times* crossword together. He still tried to maintain his standards, with a clean shirt every day and an upright walk. His contempt for people who spoke shoddy English or shoddy Welsh persisted. The conductor of the bus from Carmarthen to Llangain, shouting 'Stoppo!' to the driver, made him frown. On fine days he walked to Llanstephan – where his grandfather was determined to go to be buried in 'A Visit to Grandpa's' – for a quiet pint in the shadow of the castle, away from the women.

Dylan and Caitlin returned to Laugharne, to stay at the Hugheses' house alongside the ruined castle. Richard Hughes was away at the war. 'I have the romantic, dirty summerhouse looking over the marsh to write in,' he told Watkins, 'and Caitlin an almost empty, huge room to dance in. Also, we have lots of records now and we hear, quite often, another word than "ration".' To bring in some money he had decided to realize one of his few assets: the old exercise-books full of poems. In the letter to Clement Davenport quoted above he wrote:

In the pink bedroom we slept in and stored apples in and knocked about [at Marshfield], you'll find, unless they've moved, a number of, I think, red small exercisebooks full of my old poems and stories. Would it be a lot of trouble for you to send them to me? I mean, will you? I've got a chance of selling all my mss, for about the price of two large Player's after the next budget, and it's easier, and more honest too, to send the real mss rather than to copy out the copies in different coloured inks and with elaborate and ostentatiously inspired corrections . . .

FitzGibbon notes that when Thomas sold the exercise-books he was almost the same age as Keats when he died, twenty-six. Certainly he must have been aware of a break. He felt himself being separated from his past, whether it was long Sundays with strawberry jelly at the Tricks', or Swansea before the fires. Nostalgia came easily all his life; at seventeen he was already contemplating his vanished past, remarking (in a poem in one of the exercise-books now up for sale) on 'how much was happy while it lasted'; he had the Welsh weakness for backward glances. The sale was made to the Lockwood Library of the State University of New York at Buffalo via a London dealer, Bertram Rota. As well as the four poetry notebooks, Thomas sold a prose notebook and the worksheets of 'Long-legged Bait', for a total of forty-one pounds ten shillings.

The last poem to be quarried from the book was 'The Hunchback in the Park', originally written on 9 May 1932, when Thomas was on the *Evening Post*. When he revised it, on 16 July 1941, the Thomases were still at Laugharne Castle, still apparently penniless. 'Jesus, I loathe my poverty,' he wrote to Charles Fisher the day before. Watkins, who would soon be serving with the R.A.F., continued to send half-crowns and five shillings. 'See if you can squeeze another drop from your borrowed-to-death body,' wrote Thomas. 'I'm not going to tell you how grateful I am and have always been; or how vile I feel when I ask you again. Really vile. Weazels take off their hats as I stink by. No, I am sorry. I have no right. I hope I am spoiling nothing. It is just that I am useless, & have nowhere to turn.'

His publishers were reluctant to keep advancing him money for books that were either not written or failed to cover their costs. In August 1940 Laurence Pollinger, at the Higham agency, was reporting that Dent had paid a total of two hundred and twenty-six pounds under various contracts, and were refusing to pay any more; the Welsh travel book and a book of verse (perhaps an anthology) were still outstanding. Thomas then tried to oblige by writing a book that would carry on where *Portrait of the Artist* left off. This was *Adventures in the Skin Trade*, first mentioned in a letter to Watkins from Marshfield. By May 1941 Thomas was writing from Laugharne Castle, 'My prosebook's going well, but I dislike it. It's the only really dashed-off piece of work I remember doing. I've done 10,000 words already. It's indecent and trivial, sometimes funny, sometimes mawkish, and always badly written which I do not mind so much.' Soon after, 'My novel blathers on. It's a mixture of Oliver Twist, Little Dorrit, Kafka, Beachcomber, and good old three-adjectives-a-penny belly-churning Thomas, the Rimbaud of Cwmdonkin Drive.' His heart wasn't in the tale of his provincial hero, Samuel Bennet, once he had moved him from 'his parents' six-room house' to London. Dent were willing to pay twenty-five pounds for a sight of the first ten thousand words. But when they saw it they didn't like it. 'This material is not good enough', John Hadfield wrote to Laurence Pollinger in July, 'and we would like you to put this fact plainly before the author. It seems to us that Dylan Thomas has reached a crucial point in his literary career. He made a flying start, and there has been no lack of recognition of his uncommon talent ... In our view, however, he has not maintained the position which he gained by his early work. We have been very disappointed. Not a single [publisher's] reader has more to say in its favour than that it contains a number of flashes of the essential Dylan Thomas together with some music-hall laughs. At the best it is a fragment of frolicksome dirt.' Hadfield quoted phrases from the readers' reports – 'more coprolitic than ever ... his vivid but perverse and mudlarkish quality is original but it is running amuck with emphasis on the muck ... unless he pulls himself together he is going to fizzle out as an author most ignominiously.' The letter added, 'Let me make it quite clear we still retain a great interest in Thomas, and these objections to his new manuscript are not governed by prejudice against his unconventionality or experiments – indeed these are among the reasons why we have had faith in his future. It seems to us that he is now slipping into a state of literary irresponsibility ... Our urgent recommendation is that he should scrap this material and pull himself together for a much more carefully thought out and deliberately written job of work.'

Thirty years later the dirt seems non-existent. But the publishers, like Thomas himself, saw through the book. Watkins was staying with him when the letter arrived. He reported that Thomas was indignant but amused. But the rejection meant there would be no more money from his publishers. Thomas lost heart or interest soon after, and the book remained unfinished, although ultimately it was profitable to all concerned. The war, or poverty, or some growing seed of unease, or a combination of them all, was reducing Thomas's capacity to write. The only poem he wrote that summer, apart from the revision of 'Hunchback in the Park', seems to have been his second 'war' poem, a sonnet, 'Among those Killed in the Dawn Raid was a Man Aged a Hundred', where he took a detached and (for him) light-hearted view of the incident. Published in August in *Life and Letters*, it was the last poem he was to complete for a year or two. At the end of August he and Caitlin were in 'stinking, friendless London', having left Llewelyn with his grandmother at Blashford. As usual they had no money; presumably the need to earn some is what drove him to London. He wrote to Watkins, 'We've been having an awful time, and I have felt like killing myself ... I am still looking for a film job, & have been offered several scripts to do "in the near future", which might mean weeks. In the meantime, we sit in our bedroom and think with hate of the people who can go to restaurants ... We are prisoners now in a live melodrama.'

Thomas had always been interested in the cinema. (One of his school-magazine articles was a survey of 'The Films'.) Now he had contacts among directors in the expanding business of documentary films for Government and industry, most of them intended to raise morale, many of them overt propaganda. Late in 1941 he was offered regular employment as a script-writer by Donald Taylor, who ran a company called Strand Films. This removed any possibility of being drafted into uncongenial work. Thomas accepted, and went on the pay-roll at ten pounds a week. For the first time since he left the *Evening Post* he had an adequate income. But for the moment he was out of the poetry business.

CHAPTER EIGHT

# *War and 'Fern Hill'*

BETWEEN 1942 and 1945, Dylan Thomas worked on at least ten documentary films, writing scripts by himself or in collaboration, and in one or two cases acting as director. Strand had a good reputation, and his work there was well thought of. Donald Taylor took pains to point out later that Thomas was 'a technician' and 'just one of the boys'. He said he offered Thomas a job because he felt sorry for him, after hearing that he was starving and ill. But Ivan Moffat, an American writer working for Strand, who introduced Taylor to Thomas, says that 'even if I'd wanted to go to such an extreme to get Dylan a job, the robust effrontery of Dylan's pub-style must immediately have dispelled any illusions Donald may have had'. There was no question of the company carrying Thomas out of charity. Nor did he act the wild poet. When he was in London, and not working on location, he kept normal office hours, or as normal as anyone else in the film industry. Moffat says it was a lackadaisical office, with much sitting about and playing cards. Thomas was always scribbling on scraps of paper. Once Moffat did an imitation of him talking. Thomas 'took an envelope, scribbled on the back and handed it to me:

> What a pity there's nothing in Moffat
> For Moffat to imitate
> Nothing for Moffat to scoff at
> In all that juvenile spate.'

Another co-writer, Julian Maclaren-Ross, who joined Strand in August 1943, met him for the first time in the lift. Thomas wore a green pork-pie hat and a soiled raincoat, which he removed to reveal 'a very respectable dark blue suit and a white shirt with a bow tie and celluloid collar, too tight round the neck and giving the effect of someone strapped in the stocks. In these clothes he might have been a young provincial tradesman or perhaps a farmer up in London for the day on business.' His more usual office uniform was a brown check tweed jacket and grey flannels. According to Maclaren-Ross his daytime drinking was moderate, perhaps a pint of bitter at midday in the back bar of the Café Royal, the rear entrance of which was close to the Strand offices in Soho. The day they met they went drinking after work, and next morning, when they were in the office feeling seedy, Maclaren-Ross suggested they keep a bottle of whisky there to guard against future hangovers. Thomas alleged replied, 'Whisky? *In the office?*' and 'seemed absolutely appalled'. Like most Thomas anecdotes it is suggestive, not definitive; it was the response that appealed to Thomas at the time.

Donald Taylor wanted to produce feature films for the commercial cinema. His favourite idea was a film about Burke and Hare, the Scottish body-snatchers, and after the war he commissioned Thomas to write a script based on his story-line, 'The Doctor and the Devils', which was published as a book though never made into a film. In 1943, Maclaren-Ross and Thomas spent much time discussing a horror film they wanted to write. There was even talk of filming *Adventures in the Skin Trade*, which came to nothing, like most ideas in the film business. As for the documentaries, they ranged from prosaic to fanciful. 'New Towns for Old' was about town planning after the war. 'Balloon Site 568' besought women to join the anti-aircraft balloon service.[1] A more ambitious project was 'These Are the Men', a twelve-minute film using clips from the Leni Reifenstahl picture 'Triumph of the Will', which recorded the Nazi Party Rally at Nuremberg in 1934. Thomas's commentary

1. Moffat directed this film, which was made at Cardington, a Women's Auxiliary Air Force base. He recalls that 'the lady commandant, a senior W.A.A.F. officer, was on a raised platform reviewing perhaps two hundred uniformed W.A.A.F.s as they marched past. Dylan and I were both on the platform with her, improbable as that may seem now, and seemed then. Dylan turned to her in the course of this and said, "You have the most superb body, ma'am," and as she cast a look of reproof at him, added, "of women".'

superimposed his words on film of Hitler, Goebbels and the rest addressing the rally. For Hitler he wrote:

I grew into a discontented and neurotic child.
My lungs were bad. My mother spoilt me and secured my exemption from military service. Consider my triumphant path to power.
(*The crowd roars.*)
I took up art.
I gave up art because I was incompetent.
I became a bricklayer's labourer . . .

Some projects fell by the wayside. A film about the Home Guard, for which, said Maclaren-Ross, they envisaged a village 'stuffed full of eccentrics' (perhaps an early forerunner of Llareggub in *Under Milk Wood*) was cancelled by the Ministry of Information before the script was completed. 'Is Your Ernie Really Necessary?' (a parody of the wartime slogan 'Is your journey really necessary?') used light-hearted optical effects to make its points about travel. It was filmed but never released. There were problems over a film about Wales, 'Green Mountain, Black Mountain', for which Thomas wrote a lyrical script:

Morning is breaking over Wales at war. Not the long and far-away wild war of the mountain Welshman and the English kings, but the terrible near war of England and Wales and her brothers and sisters all over the earth . . .

Parts of the script had an Auden-like ring. Thomas could parody most poets when he chose. But here he was using the style for its effectiveness, not as a joke:

Remember the procession of the old-young men
From dole-queue to corner and back again,
From the pinched, packed street to the peak of slag
In the bite of the winter with a shovel and bag,
With drooping fag and turned up collar
Stamping for the cold at the ill-lit corner
Dragging through the squalor with their hearts like lead
Staring at the hunger and the shut pit-head,
Nothing in their pockets, nothing home to eat
Lagging from the slag-heap to the pinched packed street.

Remember the procession of the old-young men.
*It shall never happen again!*

The film was made for the British Council, to be shown to overseas audiences. But the Council disliked the references to unemployment, among other things, and the film was offered to the Ministry of Information. Protocol laid down that it should go to the M.O.I.'s Welsh office. For months nothing was heard. Then word came from Cardiff that the words were thought to be unsuitable. Dylan Thomas was not a *real* Welshman – he lived in London – so perhaps a certain Welsh professor might be approached to write a new script? London brushed aside the objections, and the film was issued with the commentary intact.

The most ambitious project that Thomas worked on was a fifty-minute film for the M.O.I. about wartime Britain, 'Our Country'. This had John Eldridge as the director, and music by William Alwyn. The film was much discussed at the time, although the high-flown commentary was not to everyone's taste:

Outside the kitchens and music
the laughing the loving the midnight talking the resting the sleeping
in all the blind houses
outside
the searchlighted night is at war with another darkness
and men who were late at harvest stand cold and calm and armed
on hilltops under the punishing rush of planes . . .

Perhaps Thomas's scripts were facile, but perhaps this was the quality that was needed. The work suited him. He was a poet, going through a period of uncertainty about his own writing, who had transplanted himself to a job that required facility with language but little else. He became a small part of a large propaganda machine that kept up morale and encouraged a family feeling among the British while the business of total war went ahead. He may even have welcomed an excuse not to have to write poetry for a while. Caitlin apparently regarded his film-writing as dishonest. She accused Donald Taylor of corrupting her husband. She told Jack Lindsay, the writer, how he had ripped up poems and thrown the pieces in the bin. Lindsay assumed that Caitlin had rescued them. 'It's the last thing I'd do,' she said. 'Dylan's corrupt. Corrupt right through and through. It's not for me to save him from himself. If he can't do it himself, let him rot.'[2] Lindsay wrote that 'against my will Caitlin by the force of contempt and suffering in her voice had convinced me that he was charlatan as well as marvellous boy, unscrupulous entrepreneur as well as dedicated poet'.

Thomas's film work meant periods of separation, and this may have helped turn Caitlin against Dylan as script-writer. Later in the war, presumably when he knew more about the technicalities of film, he wrote scripts without attending the office regularly, and lived mainly in the Home Counties or in Wales. But at first he was based in London; and Caitlin was not always there. Their domestic arrangements were as ill-organized as ever. At one time they lived in Hammersmith Terrace, a few doors from the house where Caitlin was born, in a studio owned by Sir Alan Herbert, whose daughter Crystal was then married to John Pudney; the Thomases had arrived on the doorstep, asking for shelter. They were often in Wales. For much of the summer of 1942, Caitlin was in the remote village of Talsarn, in Cardiganshire, in the valley of the River Aeron a few miles from the sea. This had been Thomas-country in the previous century; the little River Marlais was just to the south. Caitlin stayed there with Vera, who knew Dylan as a child in the Uplands. Vera was friendly with the Thomases in wartime London. She met and married a young Commando captain; Thomas was best man. Then her husband was posted overseas and was away for years. Some of Vera's family had moved to Talsarn to escape the bombs, and she and Caitlin stayed there. Thomas came from time to time. 'I have been here for over a week with Caitlin, with milk and mild and cheese and eggs,' he wrote to a friend in London, T. W. Earp, on 30 August 1942, 'and I feel fit as a fiddle only bigger; I watch the sun from a cool room and know

2. Ripping up manuscripts for dramatic effect was one of the games the Thomases played. Elisabeth Lutyens stayed with them at Laugharne in 1951 when Caitlin tore up a long poem, then remorsefully collected the pieces, while Dylan 'slyly remarked to me, with a chuckle, that he had dozens of copies'.

that there are trees being trees outside and that I do not have to admire them; the country's the one place you haven't got to go out in, thank Pan.' Caitlin was pregnant again by the end of the summer. The child, a girl, was born the following March in a London hospital and christened Aeron, after the river.[3] (She was also called 'Aeronwy'.)

Their home was a broken-down studio in Chelsea, in Manresa Road, one large room with a kitchen behind a curtain. The roof leaked, and Aeron's cradle had an umbrella over it. A reek of cats came from the next-door studio. A piece of dirty carpet on the floor served as an eiderdown for the bed in cold weather. But the Thomases made it a congenial place with books and a gramophone. FitzGibbon, who went there as a friend, recalled 'a rich smell of stew, and the rich sound of Dylan's voice talking or reading poems, and beer in bottles and music'. Without Caitlin to keep it in order it must have been less inviting. She was in Laugharne – perhaps because of renewed German air-raids – when Thomas wrote to her from their 'leaking studio' – amid unwashed plates, falling plaster and vermin – to say there was nothing to live for except her return to London or his next visit to Laugharne. He promises to send her money, but not much. As in the letters he was to write to his wife from America in the 1950s, Thomas, alone in London, was anxious to stress what a dreadful time he was having: alone in the big bed, hearing mice and the rain and the air-raid sirens, thinking of her far away with the new baby at her breasts. A note of pleading and apology runs through his correspondence with Caitlin. In another undated letter, written when she was staying with her mother in Hampshire, he tells her how he kisses his 'uncharitable pillow' in her absence; before explaining that he can't see her at the weekend because he has to work on a film. He talks derisively of selling his soul to the industry and says he hates film studios, film workers and films for their 'glibly naïve insincerity'. What he cares about is Caitlin, his wife and lover.

Presumably Caitlin was aware that he solaced himself with

3. Aeron was always told she had been conceived on the bank of the River Aeron.

girl friends. Keidrych Rhys saw him with a girl in the Swiss pub, in Soho, one evening. Thomas was mocking her, drinking beer from a man's shoe. Then he left to go home with her, on a bus. Rhys was on the bus, too. Caitlin and Vera boarded it, and saw Thomas with the girl. There was a scene, the girl vanished and Thomas went home with his wife. The extent of his infidelities has probably been exaggerated. Maclaren-Ross remarked that 'he would talk bawdily about sex in general but never about any woman in particular'; though Jack Lindsay found differently, when Thomas spoke of a film-producer's mistress that he claimed to have slept with. She wore leg irons. Thomas told Lindsay, 'Last week when I lay between her legs, I got a shock as the iron scraped against me. I'd forgotten it.' As in his written stories, the sexual encounter is given a twist; there is some impediment, a deformed limb or gonorrhoea or simply a failure to make love to the loved one.

One apparent affair during the war turns out not to have been an affair at all, in the sexual sense. Ruth Wynn Owen, a Welsh girl whose family came from Anglesey, was an actress in a touring company that was at Bradford in 1942. Thomas was there to make a documentary about the theatre in wartime. The unit wanted to film a rehearsal with smoking chimneys in the background. She saw 'this little man' standing in the wings as she came off the stage, and as the filming progressed, they got to know one another. He told her: 'Now that I've found you, don't go and die.' She noticed how small his hands and feet were. Soon after, he was writing to her from Strand Films, 'a ringing, clinging office with repressed women all around punishing typewriters, and queers in striped suits talking about "Cinema" and, just at this very moment, a man with a bloodhound's voice and his cheeks, I'm sure, full of Mars Bars, rehearsing out loud a radio talk on "India and the Documentary Movement". I wish I were on the Halifax moor talking to you, not to dishonest men with hangovers.'

They met, and failed to meet, in London. At the end of August, Thomas wrote from Talsarn, where he was staying with Caitlin, about a missed appointment at the stage-door:

I think I must have willed my lateness and weakness, willed it because, simply, I was ashamed of my hysterical excitement of the wet-eyed and over-protesting night before. I remembered losing my head in Piccadilly, which left very little, for my heart had gone two months ago, gone into your by-me-unkissed breast. And you'll have to forgive now, along with my tears, protestations and denials, my almost archly over-writing writing in this late, loving letter. I can be natural – my behaviour, then, in the black streets was as natural as my too-much drink and my giddiness at seeing you again allowed me – but perhaps my nature itself is over-written and complicated me out of this, you Ruth in a well. Was there something a little clinical in your attitude, or was it my windy head that blew your words about and got me dancing with love and temper among the bloody buses? . . .

Ruth was married. She fell in love with Thomas but refused to become his mistress. She found him gentle and vulnerable, inclined to boast in order to prove himself. He talked to her about his childhood. Perhaps he thought he was in love with her. But his letters are uneasy. He gave her the manuscript of a poem, and wrote her one further letter, in September 1943, from Carmarthenshire, sending her 'with all my heart, my love'. He remained very much married to his wife.

But London was still the pleasure-city. Thomas's reputation as a raconteur, a clown, a dog, a good man for a night out, had widened since the 1930s. He was still a long way from being famous, but his work for films and radio was enlarging the already long list of acquaintances who knew him and his funny ways rather better than they knew his poetry. Thomas anecdotes flourished. A streak of violence ran through many of them. He was said to have sliced off his drinking companions' ties with a razor blade. In the Café Royal he was said to have cut the lead of a dachshund, which scampered out into Regent Street and was lost. There were stories of thieving. He took shirts when he stayed with people. Rupert Shephard, the painter, and his wife Lorna loaned Thomas their flat earlier in the war; they returned to find many things missing, including a fur coat, a gramophone and the silver. Cloths and polish left lying around suggested he had cleaned the silver before taking it to the pawnbroker. The story circulated widely. In one improved-upon version, Thomas was in the act of polishing the silver when the owners returned. 'How kind, you shouldn't have bothered,' they said.

To others he was simply the good companion. He had developed his gift of absorbing those around him – those who were willing, that is – into a private world of jokes and fantasies. Vera, the Captain's wife, says simply, 'I had more fun with Dylan, and with Catty too, than with anybody else, before or since.' Elisabeth Lutyens thought him 'the funniest man in the world'. Her husband once asked her in amazement how she could have spent five hours in a pub with Thomas and cronies – 'But to me it wasn't five hours drinking in a pub, it was five hours of incredibly funny conversation.' He was not merely a passive entertainer, a trigger for laughter. He had the knack of drawing emotionally close to people. Ivan Moffat saw an 'extraordinary ability, if you had a worry, to take it over completely and make it belong to himself for a while . . . rather like a glass-blower taking a piece of hot glass, he would magnify it, produce it on an enormous, almost ludicrous scale, make it into a kind of nightmare, make it entirely his own for a while. When he handed it back to you, it was laughable. He'd made it grotesque . . .'

These were remarkable gifts; but they exacted a price, or perhaps were gifts only by virtue of a darker side that complemented them. John Davenport, who knew him better than almost anyone except one or two Swansea friends, said the ultimate tragedy of Thomas was that he lost his lyrical gift and was left with nothing but a public personality, which he despised. 'When you think of the cloudbursts of laughter,' said Davenport, 'the sheer, roaring, gorgeous seventeenth-century din of laughter which went on whenever he was around, it's difficult to believe that inside was the misery.' It was not until after the war that Thomas's doubts and fears got the better of him. But already he was moving in that direction. Hugh Porteus, a drinking companion of the thirties, met him in a pub and was 'horrified by Dylan's grossness ... he seemed stunned'. The American, William Saroyan, met him on a 'dreary day' in February 1944, with two other writers. Thomas 'seemed to be swollen by sleeplessness, nervousness, boredom, bad eating and general poor health'. He also seemed to need a bath and a change of clothing. His conversation was a monologue, 'wild, funny and grim all at once', about 'the war, the weather, art, poetry, other writers involved in the same work he was supposed to be doing ... the whole thing seemed to be some kind of rhapsodic throw-away poem'. It was the middle of the morning; all they were drinking was tea. Saroyan wondered why Thomas was knocking himself out and felt 'a little guilty, as if I were urging him on, for he was moving swiftly, towards exhaustion and collapse'.

There is little point in arguing that Thomas was 'really' someone different: to a large extent he has to remain what people took him to be. But a recollection of Gwen Watkins is pertinent. She didn't get on with Thomas, who postured and exploited her husband too much for her liking. But

> once we did make momentary contact. I reminded him of the time, many years before, when Vernon's mother was asking a group of young men what quality they would look for first in a wife. I said I had been surprised to hear that Dylan most valued seriousness. 'Why were you surprised?' he said, turning to me quickly. 'To be serious is the most important thing there is.' I told him I wasn't surprised by the proposition itself, but because he himself seemed so often to be – as Kierkegaard would say – precisely not serious. 'I am, though,' he said. 'You couldn't write my kind of poem – you couldn't write good poems *at all* – unless you were fundamentally a serious person'. And then a hanger-on touched his shoulder, and 'instant Dylan' was turned on again.

Thomas's usual behaviour was liable to be ruthless, in a way upsetting to those who saw no reason to tolerate his anarchic approach, which made normality crumble away. It is likely that he redoubled his efforts when he felt himself meeting this kind of resistance, and piled on the misbehaviour. Nicolette, Caitlin's sister, had married into a strong-minded bourgeois family, the Devases. During the war they lived in a house in Markham Square, just off the King's Road in Chelsea. The Thomases descended when least expected, requesting food, shelter and money for the taxi they always arrived in. Nicolette's husband called them 'the Visigoths from Wales'. They would arrive at dawn, like refugees, hammering the door, their possessions in a laundry basket. The Devases could never decide whether it was chance or cunning that brought them in the middle of the night, when it was impossible to turn them away. Thomas responded to the atmosphere by urinating against the living-room wall; at another relative-by-marriage's house, he defecated on the floor.

Drunkenness was habitual, but his destructive drinking seemed to come in spasms. He told Ivan Moffat that he drank to correct the imbalance between the disorder outside and the order within himself; he was drunk when he said it. Some people never saw him drunk at all, or not in a way they regarded as exceptional. He would sit in a pub with a friend and make a glass or two of beer last for hours. This was true to the end of his life, and is one reason it is difficult to tell if he was a dependent alcoholic. The hard-drinking poet was so much a part of the picture of himself that he had sought to project since adolescence, that when and if he crossed into alcoholism, the borderline was heavily obscured. Most of the evidence consists of the subjective observations of other drinkers. Jack Lindsay, a careful observer, noted three versions of Thomas during the war: sober and well-mannered; half-drunk and overflowing with humour, the boon companion; and fully drunk, gross and provoking, when he 'rapidly grew his piggish mask, heavy-lipped and snouted, with big white hands floundering, his big brown eyes growing more protuberant'. His drink was still mainly beer, but it is not true that he began to take spirits only in America. In two letters at the end of the war, five years before he went to America, he vowed to give up anything stronger than beer.[4] By 1944 or 1945, his drinking was more pronounced. It is said that ten to fifteen years of hard drinking are needed to produce changes in body organs that go with chronic alcohol-

4. To Donald Taylor, 28 October 1944: 'Have a drink for me, only make it beer, as a new resolution, now a fortnight, nearly, old, has banned all other drinks – for a long time, I trust and believe.' To David Tennant who owned the Gargoyle Club, 28 August 1945: '. . . beer only, for me, for weeks, for health . . .' Both letters were written from Wales.

ism. The post-mortem on Thomas showed such changes, in particular dilated veins in the lower part of his throat, and fatty infiltration of liver and kidneys. They are not proof of alcoholism, but they are consistent with it, and they may have been in the making since the early 1940s. There is no definitive version. Margaret Taylor, who saw him drunk and sober often enough, insists that he was not an alcoholic: 'he drank very heavily, but that is quite different'. She thinks he was more fond of his food than the true alcoholic – it was an eccentric mixture, ice-cream and nuts and sweets and shellfish, but it gave him reasonable nourishment. 'Call him a drunk,' says Mrs Taylor, 'but not an alcoholic.' Caitlin, asked on television in 1975 what effect drink had on her husband, replied, 'It ruined him, of course. He'd have been a marvellous old man now if someone had snatched the booze away from him. I don't think he was even all that keen on the booze. It was just the company and the life and the weakness.' She has no doubt that, as she puts it, 'the booze . . . ate up all our money and all our lives.'

As the war moved towards its final stages, Thomas began to detach himself from London. For a while, early in 1944, Caitlin lived in a cottage at Bosham, on the Sussex coast, and Thomas was briefly a kind of commuter. The invasion of Europe was pending; the countryside was full of soldiers. Then they moved west of London and stayed with Donald Taylor near Beaconsfield, in the cocktail belt, where (Thomas told Watkins) 'the well-off people were dry and thin and grieved over their petrolless motor-cars and played bridge like ferrets'. He rarely saw his surroundings as anything but comically disagreeable. Soon they were in Wales again, 'with my mother and father in Llangain, near Llanstephan, where everyone goes into the pubs sideways, & the dogs piss only on back-doors, and there are more unwanted babies shoved up the chimneys than there are used french letters in the offertory-boxes. It's a mean place but near Laugharne where we will go next week.' It was July. The cottage at Blaen Cwm was cramped but safe. The first of the German flying bombs, the pilotless weapon that drove more than a million people out of London, had arrived the previous month. Already there were rumours of the still more alarming rockets (which began to fall out of clear skies in September). Since Taylor raised no objection, Thomas decided he could write his scripts from afar. They failed to find rooms in Laugharne. Then in August they heard of a summer bungalow just outside the small Cardiganshire town of New Quay, thirty miles away to the north, where the coast begins the long indentation of Cardigan Bay. It was not as well-served by buses and trains as South Carmarthenshire. But cheap accommodation was scarce, and after visiting it with Thomas's parents, they took it at a rent of a pound a week, and moved there at the beginning of September.

Thomas was now writing poems again. It was as though he had disconnected himself from his recent past. One poem had been written – or completed – in the early part of the year, probably while he was still living in England. This was the thundering, exclamatory 'Ceremony After a Fire Raid', where a wartime death was again the subject. The casualty was a newborn child; Thomas was using familiar ingredients. But he seemed to be affirming life in a way he hadn't done before, raising his voice at the end with

> Glory glory glory
> The sundering ultimate kingdom of genesis' thunder.

The poem is laced with Biblical and ecclesiastical references –

> I know the legend
> Of Adam and Eve is never for a second
> Silent in my service
> Over the dead infants

– but whether Thomas was using these ingredients, and the entire poem, to make a 'religious' statement, or whether the religious symbols and associations were there because of the convenient emotional charge they contain, is open to argument.

In Wales he worked on another war-inspired poem, 'Holy Spring', and a long poem that was completed before he left Blaen Cwm, 'Vision and Prayer'. Written in stanzas of diamond and hourglass shapes, this has been cited as evidence of a crucial shift towards a Christian position. Perhaps it was a sign of the way Thomas would have liked to go, one of several poems (beginning with 'And death shall have no dominion') that groped for a solution he could believe in, but never arrived at.

The other poem completed at the Blaen Cwm cottage in the summer of 1944 (most of it was probably written there) was the ubiquitous 'Poem in October' –

> It was my thirtieth year to heaven
> Woke to my hearing from harbour and neighbour wood ...

Thomas had been writing poems at Blaen Cwm since adolescence, if not childhood. It was an appropriate place for him to produce a new style, simple and nostalgic, looking back to childhood and innocence. According to Watkins, 'Poem in October' had been 'contemplated' since 1941, when Thomas told him the first line would be 'It was my twenty-seventh year to heaven'. It was completed and sent to Watkins at the end of August, nearly two months before Thomas's thirtieth birthday. He called it 'a Laugharne poem: the first place poem I've written'. Technically it was complex, each stanza written to a strict pattern of syllable-counting in the traditional Welsh manner, with persistent vowel-rhymes within the lines. The effort seemed to have gone into the metrics, not the images, which yielded their meaning at once. Some of the language was almost trite for a poet so determined to be original. Having been criticized often enough for being too obscure, he was now criticized (though infrequently) for being too obvious. Geoffrey Grigson has detected in the poem 'a stale sentimentalism of language – "beckon", "set foot", "set forth", "pale rain", "tall tales", "marvel", "twice told", "summer noon", "heart's truth", always the inferior choice'. Grigson's view may not be the general one. But regardless of whether the plainer language betokens 'stale sentimentalism', it was not there by accident. Something had happened to Thomas. He was making direct statements, perhaps because he was more sure of himself as a poet, perhaps because he was consciously trying to rid himself of obscurity. There is another possibility. He may simply have been frightened. The war, his drinking and an uncertain future may have made it necessary for him to find firm anchorages to steady himself with. God – some sort of God – and childhood might serve. He needed safe places. The poems (it can be argued) were more direct because they were written out of pressing need, and not, as so often before, out of a desire to write arresting poetry. Watkins noted the change when he wrote about the abandoned *Adventures in the Skin Trade.* 'The pressure of the anarchy of war itself,' said Watkins, 'and the vision of distorted London took the place of his half-fictional vision and compelled his imagination forward to the "Ceremony After a Fire Raid", and to the beautiful poems evoking childhood, "It Was My Thirtieth Year to Heaven" [i.e. "Poem in October"] and "Fern Hill". He could still go back to peace, but from there he could no longer go forward.'

In the bungalow at New Quay, the Thomases settled down to a quiet winter. It was called 'Majoda', from the names of the landlord's children, Marjorie, John and David. 'I may alter the name to Catllewdylaer,' said Thomas. From the town it was a mile along the coast road, and a few hundred yards down a lane. One set of windows looked west over the sea. Thomas wrote a letter in verse to T. W. Earp:

> I sit at the open window, observing
> The salty scene and my Playered gob curving
> Down to the wild, umbrella'd, and french-lettered
> Beach, hearing rise slimy from the Welsh lechered
> Caves the cries of the parchs and their flocks. I
> Hear their laughter sly as gonococci . . .

The nearest building was another bungalow along the cliff; Vera the Commando's wife lived in it with her baby daughter. Majoda was built mainly of wood and asbestos sheets. Because it was not intended for regular occupation, living conditions were primitive. Lighting was by bottled gas and there were paraffin stoves for cooking and heating. Water came from a rain tank or a tap on the main road. Beer came from the Black Lion in New Quay. Sometimes Thomas brought a nest of flagons back in the baby's pram. Word got around that a poet lived on the cliffs. The landlord-doctor and his wife found Thomas charming, except that he tried to avoid paying the pound a week. They concluded that he heard their car coming and hid in the outside lavatory. Someone else heard about the Thomases, a cousin out of Dylan's past. She was a daughter of the John Williams who made money on Swansea docks. Another of the family Theodosias, she had married and gone to live in New Quay. Relatives warned her to say nothing in case he wanted to borrow money. So when Theodosia saw Dylan and Caitlin in the town, she kept herself to herself.

'This little bungalow is no place to work in when there's a bawling child there too,' Thomas wrote to Donald Taylor: 'the rooms are tiny, the walls bumpaper-thin, and a friend arrived with another baby with a voice like Caruso's. Now, however, I have just taken a room in a near-by house: a very quiet room where I know I can work till I bleed.' Taylor had wound up Strand but he was still in the film business, making documentaries and hoping to make features. One of his projects that Thomas worked on at Majoda was a film script from *Twenty Years A-Growing*, the book by Maurice O'Sullivan about the Blasket Islands, off the Irish coast. Nothing came of it. The Burke and Hare script was still being discussed, and Taylor seems to have raised some money on it in the autumn.

Thomas also raised a modest sum at about the same time, for an illustrated book about the streets of London for which he was to provide the text. The idea came from a firm of publishers, Peter Lunn, after he had written the captions for some photographs of London in the magazine *Lilliput* that summer. He was to be paid a hundred and fifty pounds, fifty of them more or less straight away. This was sufficient bait. Thomas turned out a three-page synopsis, headed 'A Book of Streets. Words and Pictures about Streets. Streets in London'. Its theme was to be

> Not the great thoroughfares, described, written, painted a thousand times, but the side streets, the back streets, the smaller worlds of life and death . . .
>
> And the streets of the suburbs, the smug-faced trim treed streets. And the suburban shopping street . . .
>
> And the dockside streets: the warehouse streets: the unexpected streets where one might feel a hundred miles from water and then,

> suddenly turning a corner, would see a great ship's funnel over a warehouse or a crane swinging and the voices of the sea . . .
>
> The life of streets is the life of people. And after the desolation, come:
>
> The streets one would like to see in the future. This section which is really a discussion of townplanning schemes as they exist now in this country, would make the book have, I think, a positive, and a creative end.

Apart from the gesture to 'townplanning', the streets sound more like those of Swansea than of London. In any case, the synopsis was all the publishers ever saw.

At the end of September, Thomas was in London on film business. He was also to be best man at Vernon Watkins's wedding. Watkins, now a sergeant in R.A.F. Intelligence, was to be married at the church of St Bartholomew the Great in the City on 2 October. Thomas failed to arrive on time, or at all. (One of his calls on 2 October was on Messrs Peter Lunn to collect the first ten pounds of his 'Book of Streets' money.) According to Gwen Watkins, 'Vernon was furious. He said, "Right, that's the end. The only possible excuse is that he's paralysed from the neck down, or dead." ' The excuse, when it came, was longer and weaker; but as usual, Watkins forgave him. It had taken nearly a month for Thomas to write. He enclosed a grimy letter, well-creased, explaining that he had written it on the train back to Wales, after missing the wedding, and then had forgotten to post it. Headed 'ON NOT TURNING UP TO BE BEST MAN AT THE WEDDING OF ONE'S BEST FRIEND', it explained that he had forgotten the name of the church, and 'never arrived, in black overcoat & shiny suit, rose-lapelled, breathing cachous & great good will'. The letter is scrawled in pencil and has many alterations. It pays the usual attention to style. Thomas wrote that he was jammed in the corridor of the train among soldiers 'Commando-trained to the last bayonet lunge'; then crossed out the end of the sentence and substituted 'lunge of the bayonet'. Gwen Watkins found anomalies in the letter which suggested it was not written until later. She thinks it was a fake; that Thomas 'took immense trouble to soil and crease it so that it should look as though it had lain in his overcoat pocket for weeks', and that the reason for his non-appearance at the wedding was simply that he couldn't face a formal occasion. Two months later, she and Vernon met Thomas in London, at the Café Royal. He arrived hot and morose from Waterloo Station, where he had been seeing Caitlin off to Hampshire. He had put her luggage, which included her handbag and ticket, on the wrong train, which promptly left. There had been a scene. Gwen Watkins expected him to sound apologetic about the wedding, but he didn't refer to it. Then, in February 1945, he wrote Watkins a letter that came to light only in 1972.[5] Mrs Watkins thinks that this was the real apology. Thomas was being sorry for himself again, to a friend he knew would listen. But there is a feeling of events pressing down on him. His spelling in the manuscript is worse than usual; he sounds tired or drunk, or both.

I was very glad to hear and see from you; it's been a long and complicated time since we disappointingly met, and I'm happy and relieved to think that the offence, (for my lost, preoccupied manner must really have been that) I gave when we did meet in that gabbling drink-grey crush, the worst of the town, has, if never to be forgotten utterly, lost some disfavour. (I have just been writing at length to Llewelyn, on the occasion of a fall from a tree and a split tongue, and the effort of not talking to a boy of six has made me adopt the claptrap periods of a leader-writer under gas.) I have found increasingly, as time goes on, or around, or backwards, or stays quite still as the brain races, the heart absorbs and expels, and the arteries harden, that the problems of physical life, of social contact, of daily posture and armour, of the choice between dissipations, of the abhorred needs enforced by a reluctance to 'miss anything', that old fear of death, are as insoluble to me as those of the spirit. In few and fewer poems I can despair and, at rare moments, exult with the big last, but the first force me every moment to make quick decisions and thus to plunge me into little hells and rubbishes at which I rebel with a kind of truculent acceptance. The ordinary moments of walking up village streets, opening doors or letters, speaking good-days to friends or strangers, looking out of windows, making telephone calls, are so inexplicably (to me) dangerous that I am trembling all

5. Gwen Watkins found it at the bottom of an R.A.F. kitbag. Vernon Watkins had died in 1967.

over before I get out of bed in the mornings to meet them. Waking to remember an appointment at X that coming evening is to see, before X, galleries of menacing commonplaces, chambers of errors of the day's conventions, pits of platitudes and customary gestures, all beckoning, spurning; and through, over & out of these I must somehow move before the appointment, the appointment that has now become a shining grail in a dentist's surgery, an almost impossible consummation of illegal pleasure to be achieved in a room like a big gut in a subterranean concentration-camp. And especially, of course, in London. I wish that I could have met Gwen 'properly', and glad that she wanted to; I was 'myself' in the sense that I was no one else, but I was broken on a wheel of streets and faces; equally well, I may be just as broken in the peace – what peace? of the country, hysterical in my composure, hyena-ish in my vegetabledom . . .

During the early part of 1945 he was probably busier with new poems than at any time since his youth in Swansea. This was not because everyday anxieties left him alone; on the contrary. The publishers who had been promised the 'Book of Streets' material – in the unlikely time of a few months – had to be placated. Thomas wrote from Majoda on 3 January:

. . . I'm afraid I have nothing of consecutive [*sic*] value to send you by the suggested near-date of January 6th, owing more to domestic troubles beyond my control – my wife has influenza and I am trying to combine the duties of housekeeper and children-minder along with my own work – than to the difficulty, however pleasurable, of the job itself. I suggest that we move the date forward one month: to the end of the first week of February. The plan for the book that I had started work upon I've decided to scrap, as a much better plan came to my mind . . . Roughly, my plan is this: to call the book *Twelve Hours in the Streets* and to take the life of the streets from twelve noon to twelve midnight . . . the whole might well be an imaginative, picaresque perhaps, crossection of the life of the English streets for a whole modern day . . .

This was to be eventually the formula for *Under Milk Wood*. A postscript to the letter promised that he would work on 'nothing else for the next month'. But early in February he was writing to explain that Fate or Nature had intervened again:

... I came up to London last month, with the intention of seeing you ... but almost as soon as I was up, I got caught with this annoying trouble [it was gastric flu] and was forced to travel back, through snow, in an ice-bound train ...

This tale of woe kept Messrs Peter Lunn quiet for a while.[6]

Film work, too, continued at Majoda. Early in March, two of Taylor's staff, John Eldridge and a woman assistant, went down from London to discuss a documentary. It happened that Vera's husband, the Commando captain, was home on leave. He had been dropped behind the German lines in Greece in 1943 and had served there for more than a year, training guerrillas in the mountains and helping in sabotage work. When he arrived at New Quay he found his wife on annoyingly close terms with the Thomases. She was short of money and he thought he knew where it had gone. Vera saw it differently. 'Dylan and Catty never sponged off me,' she says. 'We *shared*.' This wasn't good enough for the captain. On a Tuesday evening his wife went with the baby to her mother in another town. The captain went into New Quay and started drinking. He saw Thomas and his friends, and they cut him dead, or he thought they did. Not surprisingly, this upset him. He had spent a year living in caves with a gun in his hand. Now the clever people were laughing among themselves, showing no respect for a fighting man. Thomas, in fact, picked quarrels with more than one serviceman during the war. He had a brawl with Caitlin's brother John, who was also a Commando, and who talked about strangling Germans. This time the trouble started between the captain and Eldridge's assistant, a Jew, who thought he made an antisemitic remark. He slapped her, she scratched him, and Thomas (who claimed to have been drinking only cider) put up his fists. The captain was a big, powerful man. There was some indeter-

6. The publishers (later called John Westhouse Ltd) pursued Thomas with a writ in 1946, but were unable to track him down after he left Majoda. Finally a diligent process-server who had studied his *Radio Times* went to Broadcasting House late one evening in January 1947 and served the writ as Thomas left the studio after reading 'A Visit to Grandpa's'. Soon the solicitors reported to the publisher that 'we have since received a cheque ... for the full amount due'.

minate scuffling before they were separated. It seemed to be the end of the incident. But the captain was drunk and unhappy. Back in the empty bungalow he decided to 'put the wind up those buggers'. Like many front-line soldiers, he kept his weapons with him. At ten thirty he staggered out with a sub-machine gun and a hand grenade, and advanced on Majoda. Dylan, Caitlin and three friends were sitting around the coal fire; Aeronwy and a friend's baby were asleep in a bedroom. Suddenly they found themselves being machine-gunned. The captain meant to fire over the bungalow, but in the dark, and his condition, he mistook the elevation. He loosed off a dozen rounds, at least five of which passed through the asbestos walls of the living room. A moment later he burst into Majoda, waving gun and grenade. He wore dark glasses and there was blood on his face. Told there were babies in the house, he emptied the magazine into the ceiling and shouted, 'You're nothing but a lot of egoists.' They persuaded him to hand over the machine gun. The captain says that he then 'produced the hand-grenade, with no intention of taking out the pin, to see their reactions. They were all quite petrified except Thomas, I'll say that. He was the coolest of the lot.' Eventually the captain went away, the police were called, and he was later charged with attempted murder. At Lampeter Assizes he said he did it to frighten them. The judge told the jury there was no evidence to sustain the charge, and the fighting man was set free.[7]

Three weeks after the shooting, Thomas wrote to tell Watkins about it, adding that his previous letter 'told of my daily terrors, my everyday traps and pits, etc. I'm sure you thought I was exaggerating. At debt's and death's door I now stand with a revolving stomach . . .' The letter noted another anxiety: 'My Father is awfully ill these days, with heart disease and uncharted

7. Thomas told the court that after firing the shots, the captain had laid down his gun.

'We suggested he should go home but he refused to do so without his gun, and raising his hand with the grenade declared, "If you do not give me my gun I will throw the grenade and we will all go up together." '

Mr Justice Singleton: 'What did you do?'

Thomas: 'I gave him his gun.'

pains, and the world that was once the colour of tar is now a darker place.' With the letter came four poems: 'This Side of the Truth', 'The Conversation of Prayer', 'A Refusal to Mourn the Death, by Fire, of a Child in London' and 'A Winter's Tale'. All, presumably, had been written during the previous months, ready for a new collection to be called *Deaths and Entrances* that Dent intended to publish some time in 1945. They were to become well-known additions to the small group of Thomas's poems that identifies him for most of his readers. 'A Winter's Tale' was a fairy-tale narrative of death and rebirth. The meaning of 'The Conversation of Prayer' may have been on the lines of 'God works in a mysterious way'; or the poem may have been a secular comment on how arbitrary life is. 'This Side of the Truth' was a piece of disenchanted, almost despairing advice for his infant son about the moral indifference of the 'unminding skies', 'A Refusal to Mourn the Death' was a striking trumpet-blast from Thomas the Poet (hostile critics have seen it as pretentious) with an equivocal last line, 'After the first death, there is no other'. Read in conjunction with the other poems in the group, and taking account of the mood that his letters to Watkins reveal, it seems likely that Thomas was declaring that death was final; he was affirming the present, not the future. Or perhaps the line reflects his own uncertainties: he didn't know what to think.

Nothing about the letters that Thomas was writing suggests he was achieving any harmony with his surroundings, physical or otherwise. On the contrary, now that the war was coming to an end, and he was going to be free, like everyone else, to reorganize his life, he wanted to leave Britain altogether and go to America. When America first occurred to him as an alternative to post-war Britain is uncertain, but he was certainly thinking about it before the war in Europe ended in May 1945. On 10 February he wrote to his U.S. publisher, James Laughlin, about a volume of *Selected Writings* that Laughlin was planning. In a postscript Thomas said, 'I should like to come over to the States after the war for a few months. Any chance of getting a job to keep me while over there? Reading, talking?' By the end of the following month he was writing to Oscar

Williams, the American anthologist, to say he would 'love a little ladleful from the gravy pots over there'. Williams, who greatly admired Thomas's poems, was already selling them to magazines, acting as an unofficial literary agent.[8] But Thomas had his eye on more substantial earnings. He wrote, 'The war, they say, is all over bar the dying; and, when it is, I want to come over to America. How could I earn a living? I can read aloud, through sonorous asthma, with pomp; I can lecture on the Trend of Y or X at the Crossroads, or Z: Whither? with an assurance whose shiftiness can be seen only from the front row . . .'

On 30 July he crystallized something of what he felt about his surroundings in a long letter to Williams. The Thomases had left Majoda because the owner wanted it for the summer; they were back at Blaen Cwm – 'in a breeding-box in a cabbage valley, in a parlour with a preserved sheepdog, where mothballs fly at night, not moths, where the Bible opens itself at Revelations; and is there money still for tea?' Thomas feels a fond loathing for the place, an attitude he refined towards West Wales in the last years of his life. There is another of his obsessive references to condoms; and in 'establishing my geography' he fantasizes on the theme of his family origins.

The rainy robins tic tac at the pane. Over the hill, the hoarse noise of a train carrying holes to Hugh's Castle. Near, a grey-gulled estuary, and sheepshanks, corpses of cats, cowteeth, bottles of ether, jellyfish, french letters, indecipherable messages in jars (the secret of the *Marie Celeste*, the Number of the Beast, the name of Cain's wife, pyramid riddles, Tibetan acrostics, next year's newspapers) on the foreshore. I'm trying to establish my geography. Up the hill lane behind this house too full of Thomases, a cottage row of the undeniably mad unpossessed peasantry of the inbred crooked county, my cousins, uncles, aunts, the woman with the gooseberry birthmark who lies with dogs, the farm labourer who told me that the stream that runs by his cottage side is Jordan water and who can deny him,

8. 'Poem in October' was published in the British *Horizon* and the American *Poetry* in the same month, February 1945. 'A Winter's Tale' and 'A Refusal to Mourn' were both published in America, respectively in *Poetry* (July 1945) and *New Republic* (14 May 1945), before they appeared in Britain.

the lay preacher who believes that the war was begun only to sell newspapers which are the devil's sermon-sheets, the man who when his pony could work no longer because of old age, hanged it on an apple-tree to save a bullet, the woman who cries out 'Cancer!' as you pass her open door.

This kind of thing was part of Thomas's routine, the bizarre commentary written mainly to amuse. But behind it is something else, the hold that this particular countryside had on his imagination. He doesn't like it but he has not outgrown it; he will keep coming back to it, filling it with crooked scenes and twisted people – 'I had some beer with a man who said he was shot in the groin in the last war, and who, unable to have a woman ever since, blames it on the dirty Jews ... He told me the best way to boil lobsters, which was detailed and painful. I told him Norman Douglas's recipe for raping a dog ... He told me how he had once made a child of six drunk. It began to rain again, great wrathful drops. We parted enemies ...'

Thomas's 'vegetable background', as Caitlin called it, gave him the setting he needed to work in. It was in his blood. But in a curious way, he never came to terms with it. He needed it and hated it. Perhaps it was a trap in which he felt himself caught; and he hated to be trapped. So he continually compromised and kept moving, always coming back but always going away again. Thus, in 1945, when a year in Wales, for all its trials, had enabled him to write poems, which was the thing he cared about most, he badly wanted to escape. America was the child's land of promise. It was a long way off, glittering with goodies. He could go there and stop worrying. Money would be different in America. So he bombarded Williams with ideas. Could he work for *Time* magazine? At Harvard University? Thomas doesn't sound over-pleased at Attlee's Labour Government, which had come to power four days earlier. He could sail within three months, he says, with his wife and children – 'We would all come together because I don't want to return to this country for a long time. The rain has stopped, thank Jesus. Have the socialists-in-power-now stopped it? An income tax form flops through the window, the letterbox is choked with dockleaves. Let's get out, let's get out.'

Thomas was in London intermittently in the summer, working on films and looking for somewhere to live before they went to America. An undated letter to Caitlin has the familiar mixture of loneliness and money worries. Never has he missed or loved her more: he has wept for her through sleepless nights: he has longed for her to be around the next corner, instead of in Wales with 'two neurotics, a baby and a dog'. In London there is no house to live in and no money as yet. But he mentions the possibility of acting in 'verse plays for the Empire Service'.

So far the B.B.C. had been only a minor source of income. Thomas was developing the radio reminiscence as entertainment, but this meant taking pains over a script. It was not particularly easy money. Probably his film work as writer and narrator first led him to think seriously of radio scripts, and at the end of 1942 he wrote a fifteen-minute talk, 'Reminiscences of Childhood', for the Welsh B.B.C., which was broadcast the following February. Towards the end of 1944, when he was living at Majoda, he wrote a radio piece called 'Quite Early One Morning', which gave a fanciful account of a town whose features are those of New Quay. It reads like a sketch for *Under Milk Wood.* (That play is about Laugharne, if it is about anywhere in particular; but Thomas's fanciful West Wales was really one place made up of all the fragments, melted down in his mind.) 'Quite Early One Morning' was recorded in Wales, and the producer, Aneirin Talfan Davies, offered it to London for the national network. But London was not impressed by the 'breathless poetic voice', and the item was heard only in Wales. B.B.C. headquarters had its doubts about Celtic poets. The Welsh Children's Hour producer, Lorraine Davies, wrote to Thomas in July 1945, to suggest a talk called 'Memories of Christmas'. He thought it 'a perfectly good title to hang something on', and wrote it by the autumn, probably at Blaen Cwm. The Children's Hour Director in London (Derek McCulloch, the famous 'Uncle Mac') liked the talk but couldn't bring himself to let the 'notoriously tricky' Thomas broadcast it live, which was Children's Hour practice then. They had to pretend to Thomas, who is hardly likely to have cared anyway, that technical reasons made it necessary to record in advance. Years later he enlarged the talk for an American magazine, and in this form, as 'A Child's Christmas in Wales', made a record of it which became his most popular prose work in America.

'Memories of Christmas' is heavily nostalgic. That summer, the same mood, working on a different level, produced what is probably his most famous poem, 'Fern Hill'. It is first mentioned in a letter to Dent on 18 September 1945, when he was returning the proofs of *Deaths and Entrances*. Thomas had been dilatory over the proofs, which were originally sent to him at the end of May; the book had to be put back to 1946. The letter of 18 September shows that Thomas had been busy at Blaen Cwm. 'Unluckily for a Death', a 'marriage' poem dating from 1939, had been rewritten. Another poem (unidentified in the letter) was deleted from the proofs, and a newly-written one, the rhetorical 'In My Craft or Sullen Art', substituted. And an extra poem was added:

> I am enclosing a further poem, 'Fern Hill', not so far included in the book, which I very much *want* included as it is an *essential* part of the feeling & meaning of the book as a whole. As so much re-setting etc. will have to be done anyway, I do most earnestly hope that 'Fern Hill' can be included in the book. I myself would be very unsatisfied were it omitted. (I realize, naturally, that it should have been sent along in the first place with the others, but it was not at that time completed . . .)

The publishers added the poem at the end of the book. It is not clear how long he had been working on it. John Brinnin, the American writer, says that when he visited Laugharne in 1951, Thomas showed him 'more than two hundred separate and distinct versions of the poem'. Presumably Brinnin means there were two hundred worksheets, not an abnormal number for Thomas. The poem may have been begun at New Quay, then finished at Blaen Cwm, where the farm of Fernhill was only a mile or so away. It is nostalgic for lost beginnings. It is also a doomed poem: the poet will wake to death and 'the farm forever fled from the childless land'. It is tempting to see the machine-gunning at Majoda as an incident, both ludicrous and ugly, that drove Thomas back into himself, to levels of memory that produced the poem. Probably, though, he was responding to a more general unhappiness. He lacked certainties and he wrote accordingly. Some critics have treated it sternly, calling it sentimental or even dishonest. Others have been content to praise its singular melancholy. Thomas's mood when he wrote it is one that people can recognize without hesitation. It was a long backward glance, cunningly assembled. But it was not a poem that led anywhere, unless it was to more of the same, and Thomas did not attempt to repeat the formula. 'Fern Hill' ended an intensely creative year, the last of its kind he was to enjoy.

CHAPTER NINE

# A Voice on the Radio

FIVE years passed between the time Dylan Thomas first thought of America as a refuge, in 1945, and the time he finally arrived there, a man on the run. On the face of it they should have been good years. His book *Deaths and Entrances* confirmed his serious reputation, his voice became familiar on radio, he earned enough money to live comfortably, and Margaret Taylor made sure that he and his family were housed in Wales, by the sea. None of this had much effect on the course of his affairs, which grew steadily more confused.

About the end of September 1945, Thomas and his wife moved from Wales to London. They seem to have stayed where they could, with various friends, for the winter. America receded as Thomas came up against the problems of obtaining a visa, convincing the U.S. authorities that he was being invited by responsible people, and raising the money for the tickets. In February or March 1946 he was in St Stephen's Hospital, in London, for four days, with 'alcoholic gastritis'. He wrote to Watkins on 27 April, 'I had a little time in hospital but I'm out again now and fit as an old potato.' In general Thomas avoided doctors. Jack Lindsay was told by a doctor's wife that about 1945 Thomas visited a hospital, 'described himself as a poet, and asked to be cured of drinking obsessions'. A psychiatrist there 'treated him as something of a joke and bantered him about being a poet; he had never heard of Dylan and was mildly irritated by a patient portentously announcing himself in such terms. Dylan didn't take the raillery at all well and failed to turn up for the appointment that was made.' There is a story that he was treated at St Mary's for alcoholism about 1950. The only certain visits to hospitals were when he broke one or other of his arms. Caitlin wrote that 'he was never his proper self till there was something wrong with him; and, if ever there was a danger of him becoming "whole", which was very remote, he would crack another of his chicken bones, without delay, and wander happily round in his sling'.

After the St Stephen's episode, Thomas and family drifted out of London to the home of the A. J. P. Taylors at Oxford. For the rest of his life, Thomas was to live either free or cheaply in accommodation provided by Mrs Taylor, his staunchest patron. The original arrangement in 1946 was that the Thomases lived in a summerhouse a hundred yards from the Taylors' residence, Holywell Ford. It was a small damp building on the bank of the River Cherwell, overshadowed by poplars. A. J. P. Taylor, who became less enthusiastic about the Thomases as time went on, was still an academic historian, yet to make a popular reputation. He was a lecturer at Magdalen College, and Holywell Ford was a college property. The high wall of the Magdalen deer park ran alongside. For a year Taylor had a poet at the bottom of his garden. Caitlin would bring Aeron into the house to bath her, and the child slept there with the Taylors' two daughters. In the one-room summerhouse, conditions were not ideal. Water gurgled under the trees and the chime of Oxford bells came across the meadows, but mud, draughts, insects and general squalor prevailed. Jack Lindsay called there once, when Thomas was out. Caitlin had her sleeves rolled up, 'a lovely slattern', and Aeron was crying. A calf's-head on a dish dominated the room. 'It's beginning to stink,' said Caitlin. 'I suppose I ought to throw it away, but Dylan would be annoyed.' Thomas wrote to Watkins on 27 April, 'I want to write a poem of my own again, but it's hard here with peace and no room, spring outside the window and the gas cooker behind the back, sleep, food, loud wireless, broom and brush all in one kiosk, stunted bathing-hut or square milk bottle.'

Later Mrs Taylor provided him with a small caravan to work in. Margaret Taylor was interested in all the arts. She studied music as a girl, wrote poetry and later became a professional painter. Her mother was Irish, her father an inspector of mines from South Wales. Because she had a little money of her own, she was able to help Thomas, who took it gladly, wrote long critiques of her poems, sometimes laughed at her behind her back, as he laughed at so many of his friends, but spelt out his thanks in many letters, as well he might. Her relationship with the Thomases inevitably caused rows, in her family and in theirs (the Taylors were later divorced). At times Mrs Taylor had a possessive attitude towards Dylan that Caitlin resented. But without her, the Thomases would have found living even more difficult than they did.

*Deaths and Entrances* was published in February 1946, and widely praised. If his reputation had suffered since his first two books it was now re-established, not least because of the poems he had written between the summers of 1944 and 1945. Three thousand copies of the book were printed. A month later, Dent ordered a reprint of the same number, and bound the surplus sheets they had been storing of the three unprofitable books they had already published – *Twenty-five Poems*, *Map of Love* and *Portrait of the Artist*. In America, New Directions brought out *Selected Writings* with work from all his books, including most of the *Deaths and Entrances* poems. A new book was planned by Dent made up of published stories and the reminiscences. Thomas wanted to call it 'Top Hat and Gasworks' or 'Bob's My Uncle'. But the collection failed to mature, like other of his post-war projects.

A more reliable income was promised by radio, which helped to fill the gap left when documentary work for Donald Taylor ended in 1945 – Thomas was officially a freelance again from 6 October that year. The B.B.C. offered the best single market in the country to writers and performers. The war and social change had gone some way towards democratizing it. Two domestic channels were then in operation, the Home Service (with regional variations) and the Light Programme, as well as extensive overseas services. By the end of 1945, Thomas was a regular reader in a programme beamed to the Far East, 'Book of Verse'. John Arlott, then a talks producer, handled dozens of these readings – 'he would stand, feet apart and head thrown back, a dead cigarette frequently adhering wispily to his lower lip, curls a little tousled and eyes half-closed, barely reading the poetry by eye, but rather understanding his way through it, one arm beating out a sympathetic double rhythm as he read'. Radio suddenly discovered Thomas. He was useful should a younger-generation poet be needed for a discussion. He appeared with the poet James Stephens on the Light Programme, declaring that 'poetry, to a poet, is the most rewarding work in the world. A good poem is a contribution to reality.' He appeared with Edward Shanks, an elderly poet who didn't care much for his verse, in the North American Service. Shanks said he had shown a book of Thomas's to a friend, who called it a disaster to English poetry. Thomas retorted, 'You've rather stolen my introductory thunder – not that it was very thunderous – because I too was asking a friend whether he knew you, Shanks, and he said, "Well, of course I know his verse. Is he still alive?"'

Readings and discussions were a painless way of earning up to fifteen or twenty pounds a time. Occasionally Thomas wrote scripts, which earned more. For 'The Londoner', a thirty-minute documentary, he was paid fifty pounds for writing and taking part. An account of a day in the life of a working-class street in London, it carried faint intimations of *Milk Wood*: 'It is summer night now in Montrose Street. And the street is sleeping ...' Laurence Gilliam, the B.B.C.'s Head of Features, urged Thomas to write more like it. A documentary about a holiday outing to Margate was recorded for a New York radio station (they swapped it for a documentary about Coney Island). A particular advantage of working for radio was that in addition to a fee, Thomas was paid travelling expenses and a small 'subsistence allowance' if he had to spend a night away from home. This meant he could commute from Oxford to London several times a month at the B.B.C.'s expense. Caitlin was not greatly pleased when an afternoon's trip to a studio to spend twenty minutes reading poems developed into a drinking holiday that went on for days. When he wanted to placate her, he would take back an attempt at a peace-offering; Elisabeth Lutyens saw him setting off for Oxford with a battered music-case containing two cans of soup. Sometimes he added insult to injury by arriving in a hired car that had brought him from London, a rich man's way of travelling sixty miles.

In the autumn of 1946 the B.B.C. launched its high-culture

network, the 'Third Programme', which opened up a new market. Thomas was promptly in demand as an actor and speaker, appearing (as 'Second Brother') in Milton's 'Comus', the first drama production. He read Blake and Edith Sitwell, and talked about Walter de la Mare. He played Aristophanes in a 'panorama of Aristophanic comedy' written by Louis MacNiece, who was on the B.B.C.'s staff as a writer-producer. In November 1946 he took the part of Private Dai Evans in a radio version of David Jones's strange romance or allegory, *In Parenthesis*; a minor member of the cast (he played 'A Bombing Officer') was a young Welshman doing his conscript service in the R.A.F., Aircraftsman Second Class Richard Burton.[1] Most of the Third Programme producers who used Thomas worked for Features, a department whose rôle was never clearly defined except by the programmes they made.

Laurence Gilliam was a burly, cheerful man who had started out in concert parties and somehow found his way into broadcasting. He was not a bureaucrat; nor were his producers. Unless they were in a studio, they were as likely to be found in one of the pubs or clubs near Broadcasting House as in their offices. This suited Thomas; he found himself working among congenial people who behaved more like journalists than academics. They knew about poetry and paid him for reading it, but on the whole they didn't want to have long discussions about it.

Roy Campbell, the poet, was on the B.B.C. staff, and handled many of his Third Programme readings. Campbell found him

1. Burton wrote of this play, 'I worked with [Thomas] a few times or several, and once for instance a director said to him, we were rehearsing a radio play at the time, Dylan will you take the words Mam! Mam! and scream them for me; you understand that you are dying in No Man's Land, and when you hear the Royal Welch sing, I will give you a cue light and then scream for me woodjew there's a good chap ... and the green light flickered and Dylan, short, bandy, prime, obese and famous among the bars screamed as I have never heard, but sometimes imagined a scream, and we were all appalled, our pencils silent above the crossword puzzles, and invisible centuries-gone atavistic hair rose on our backs.' According to Burton, he screamed without taking the cigarette out of his mouth.

'the best all-round reader of verse that I ever produced', but noted that he was more effective with 'wild and woolly poets', where he could use his voice – 'it was with Blake and Manley Hopkins that Dylan became almost Superman' – and that he had difficulty with 'correct' poets like Pope and Dryden. Once (but only once, according to Campbell) Thomas arrived drunk for a live reading on the Third Programme. Campbell found him 'snoring in front of the mike with only twenty seconds left'. He slurred his first title, 'Ode on Saint Sheshilia's Day'. Later in the programme he began to wave his arms, and indicated that he didn't know how to pronounce 'Religio Laici'. Campbell said he 'had about three shots at it, bungled it, gave it up'. Next day Campbell was sent for by the Third Programme Controller, George Barnes. Thomas promised to behave himself in future; the incident was passed over.

But Thomas was never entirely acceptable to the B.B.C. management. A Third Programme memorandum of 1951, dealing with the fees paid to Thomas, said that he was not to be regarded as in the 'celebrity class', along with Eliot, Auden, C. Day Lewis and E. M. Forster. Nor would the B.B.C. ever employ Thomas in a staff job. He had hopes of this more than once. Margaret Taylor went to see a crony, a senior person at Broadcasting House, but he shook his head and said the problem was drink. Having lunch with Gilliam, Thomas drafted his perfect contract with the B.B.C.: ten pounds a week for Caitlin and a monthly trip to London for a 'piss-up'. Once, in 1950, Thomas called on the Controller of the Third Programme, seeking regular employment for a year or two. But Gilliam, who would have had to do the employing, was unwilling to take the chance.

In August 1946 Dylan and Caitlin went to Ireland with friends, Bill and Helen McAlpine, for a holiday. Thomas was also supposed to be writing about Puck Fair, held annually in Kerry, for the magazine *Picture Post*, which advanced him money for the trip; but he never did. He wrote to Margaret Taylor from Blaen Cwm, where he and Caitlin broke their journey back to Oxford:

We had breathless days in Ireland: four in Dublin – oh the steaks, the chickens, chocolate, cream, peaty porter, endless blarney of politics never later than 1922 – & the rest in Kerry, all wild sea and hills and Irish-reeling in kitchens. And a day on the Blasket: a very calm day, they said: the wind blew me about like a tissue-paper man, and dashed us against the donkeys . . . I can't tell you how much we're looking forward to being [in Oxford] again. We love it; and can never thank you both enough for having let us descend on you, you being so kind every way.

The summerhouse was still supposed to be a temporary resting place on the way to America. James Laughlin, his American publisher, was in London in the autumn, promising to look out for a suitable house. Thomas wrote on 24 November, reminding him. He made conditions: he wanted to write 'poems, stories, scripts', but not until he was in America, with his family, installed in a house in the hills, fairly near New York City, where he could earn his living by broadcasting. Also he needed money for the passage. Once there, 'All I write in America is yours for America (and I want, and mean, to write a lot), but until that is settled I have no intention of writing anything at all.' This was not a very practical ultimatum. No one was prepared to foot the bill for the uncertain rewards of shipping the Thomases to New York. Others were positively anxious to stop them going. Edith Sitwell thought that if he must go, it should be to lecture; eventually she decided it would be a disaster if he went at all. She tried hard to dissuade him. 'I was aghast when I heard he was going there,' she wrote to John Lehmann on 11 December 1946. 'I've tried *everything* – imploring, owl-like prognostications of disaster – saying that Caitlin will have a rotten time because she isn't rich. *Nothing* sways him. And his hostess at Oxford, Mrs Taylor, the wife of a don, says it is like measles – you have to have it and get over it – I mean this mania to go to America.' Edith Sitwell was worried about his drinking, but even more about the prospect of a penniless Thomas in America. She was pulling strings in literary circles to have him awarded a Society of Authors scholarship, if he must go. Alternatively he might be persuaded to try Switzerland instead. In the end he was given the money, a hundred and fifty pounds, and recommended to try Italy. Italy was a natural haven for the English man of letters in need of peace and culture; but not necessarily for Thomas, who once wrote to Lawrence Durrell that 'England is the very place for a fluent and fiery writer. The highest hymns of the sun are written in the dark . . . If I went to the sun I'd just sit in the sun.'

Perhaps in 1947 things seemed different. A bitter winter and fuel shortages disrupted Britain (even the Third Programme was suspended). In the middle of the cold spell in February, Thomas was in Swansea, gathering material for a radio feature in an occasional series called 'Return Journey'. One of Gilliam's producers, R. D. Smith, was with him. People were often surprised to find Thomas doing anything as straightforward as making notes. But he could be unexpectedly normal when it came to work. He walked about the chilly Mumbles, writing down the names of boats drawn up above the seaweed. He carried a notebook with floppy covers, rather like the ones he used for his early poems. In it he wrote the names of streets in Townhill and Mayhill, burnt out in the wartime air-raids – 'Emlyn Road badly hit. Teilo Crescent was wiped out.' He observed 'the hill which because of the houses you couldn't see before'. Nothing had been rebuilt in Swansea, the town centre was still gaunt and ruined, clocks showed the hour the bombs stopped them. The script Thomas wrote contained long lists of shops that had stood there before the war. A Swansea friend who heard the broadcast in June (it was recorded before Thomas went abroad) asked him how he could possibly have remembered them. 'Easy,' said Thomas. 'I wrote to the Borough Estate Agent.' In the script, Thomas uncovers his youth in Swansea, layer by layer; the reminiscence, at once nostalgic and comic, is more skilful than in anything he wrote except the *Portrait* stories. In the recording of the original production, which still exists, his narration is relaxed, without the exaggerated booming. Mrs Ferguson, who kept the sweet-shop in the Uplands where he used to raid the wine-gums, heard her name in the programme, and wrote to say, 'Fancy remembering the gob-stoppers.' Mrs Hole of the dame school was listening. 'I think I must be getting old,' she wrote to Thomas, 'but I don't like children very much these days.'

The Thomases went to Italy in April, taking both their children, Caitlin's sister Brigit, and Brigit's small son. 'I hope to write poems, after a year's stop,' Thomas wrote to Charles Fisher. He succeeded, but in the face of difficulties; most of the time he was in his usual state of amused belligerence about his surroundings, which might as well have been Carmarthenshire, except that it didn't rain and the red wine was cheap. He began by losing their luggage at the Italian frontier – they were travelling by train – and having to track it down in Milan, which he described to his parents, inevitably, as 'a giant, nightmare city'. They stayed a month on the Italian Riviera near Rapallo, with trips to Florence and Rome, which they seem to have enjoyed. Then they rented a house in the hills outside Florence until the end of July. Here, amid pines and olives, he worked on a poem, 'the slowest in the world', while the heat shimmered outside. 'I can smell the sun,' he wrote to Margaret Taylor. Compared with cold cottages and borrowed flats, they were living in luxury. There was a swimming pool, fresh food, beautiful vistas; Florence glittered in the distance. But Thomas was restless and uncomfortable. He wrote to John Davenport at the end of May, 'A few days ago I climbed a tree, forgetting my shape and weight, and hung this shabby barrel from a branch by my white padded mitts: they were torn neatly up the middles. Also, very slowly, I am trying to write a poem, moping over it, every afternoon in the peasant's cottage: our little spankers make so much noise I cannot work anywhere near them. God grenade them.' As the summer advanced, his letters complained increasingly of heat, insects and screaming children. By July he was telling T. W. Earp, in verse,

In a shuttered room I roast
Like a pumpkin in a serra
And the sun like buttered toast
Drips upon the classic terra,

adding, in prose, that he was 'awfully sick of it'.

1. Aunt Dosie—Theodosia, Dylan Thomas's aunt—and her husband, the Rev. David Rees. He said, "The boy should be in a madhouse."

2. The old folks at home: Dylan's paternal grandparents—"Evan Thomas the Guard," the railwayman, and his wife Ann, probably outside their cottage at Johnstown, Carmarthen.

3. The family about 1909, a few years before Dylan was born. His sister Nancy is the baby. Her parents, David John Thomas the young schoolmaster and Florence, are on the right. Evan and Ann are with Nancy, their grandchild. Extreme left is D.J.'s brother Arthur ('Uncle A. from Aberavon'). Next to him may be another brother, Tom, and his wife.

4. Dylan – angel or demon – poses in a Swansea photographer's studio with his mother (*right*), big sister Nancy and a friend of the family.

Grammar School Mile Winner.

D. M. Thomas (Mansel), who won the mile race for boys under 15 years of age, at the Swansea Grammar School sports. He is only 12 years of age.

5 & 6 This may have been the "yellowed newspaper clipping" that Thomas took from his wallet and showed John Malcolm Brinnin in America a quarter of a century later. The *Cambria Daily Leader* (June 23, 1926) got his age wrong: he was eleven. "Mansel" was his "house" at school. He is said to have run the length of the beach at Rhossili (*below*). Rhossili Bay is at the end of the Gower peninsula, west of Swansea. The camping tents of Thomas's story "Extraordinary Little Cough" were pitched on the cliffs nearby.

7a-7b Bert Trick, the socialist grocer (*above left*) who made a friend of the adolescent Thomas. "And death shall have no dominion" was written in friendly competition with Trick. Glyn Jones the writer (*right*) was another old friend who discussed poetry with him. (*Below*) With Alfred Janes, the Swansea painter, about 1935, sunbathing at the boarding house in Coleherne Road, Earls Court, London—"the quarter of the pseudo-artists," wrote Thomas.

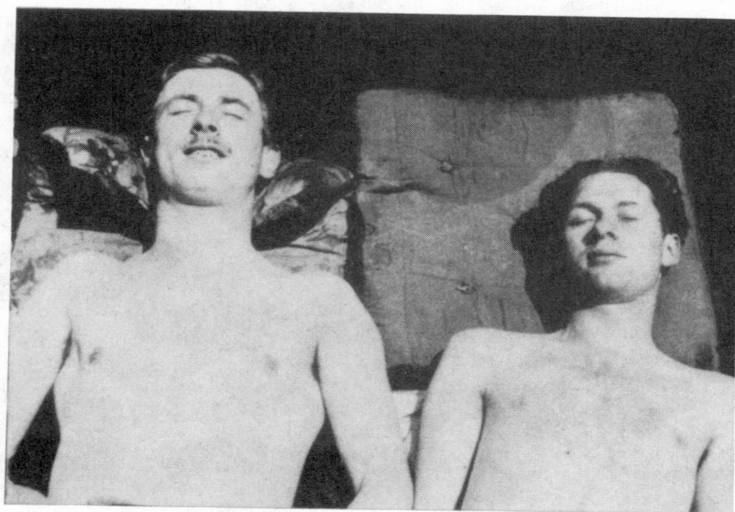

8. Dylan Thomas, aged about twenty-two, and Vernon Watkins, about thirty. Watkins remarked, 'Two of Wales's greatest poets. Don't we look soppy?'

9 & 10 (*left*) Caitlin with the Thomases' first child, Llewelyn, born January 1939. (*right*) Picknicking on the beach with Mrs. Mcnamara, Caitlin's mother, when they were living with her in Hampshire in the late 1930s.

11. Daniel Jones, Thomas's closet friend from their Grammar School days—a much later photograph (with Caitlin, Dylan's wife), when the 'Swansea gang' were spending the day at Vernon Watkin's house in Gower.

12 & 13 Thomas appeared in a one-night performance of a play by Picasso, *Desire Caught by the Tail*, in February 1950. He was in London en route to America for his first poetry-reading tour. (*Below*) Laugharne, the place he left behind. The Boat House is the distant white building on the right.

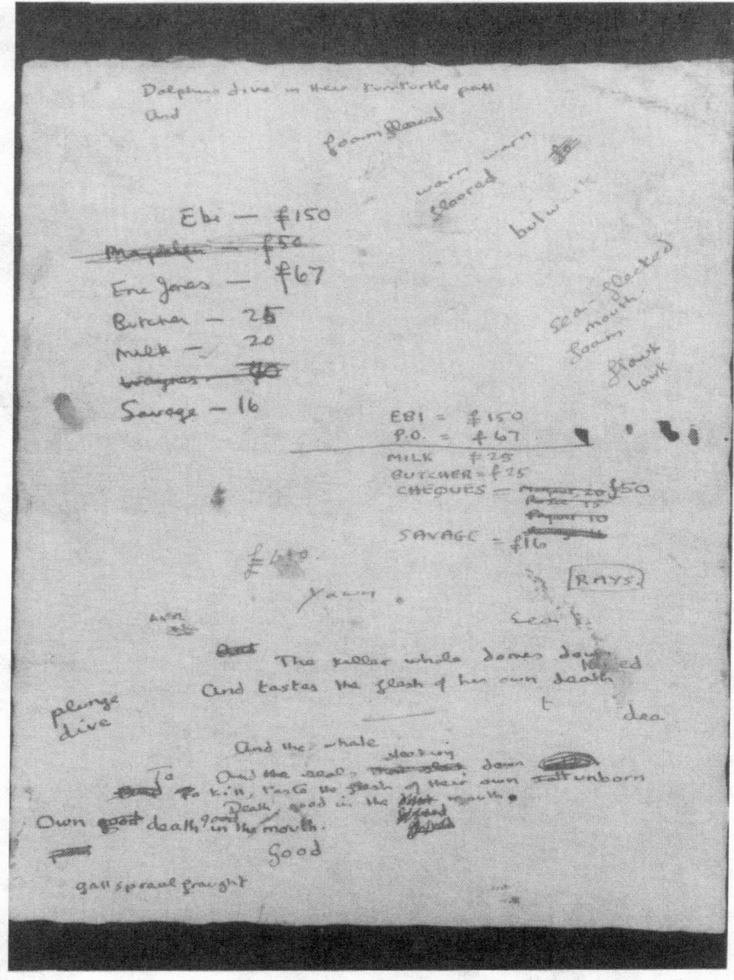

Ebi — £150
Eric Jones — £67
Butcher — 25
Milk — 20
Savage — 16

EBI = £150
P.O. = £67
MILK £25
BUTCHER = £25
CHEQUES — £50
SAVAGE = £16

RAYS

And tastes the flesh of her own death

plunge
dive

And the whale

Own death in the mouth.

Good

14. Worksheet with trial phrases from 'Poem on his birthday,' interspersed with notes about his debts. Probably from 1951, two years before he died. Thomas wrote little poetry after this.

15. Elizabeth Reitell, Brinnin's assistant at the Poetry Centre, and close friend of Thomas during his last two visits in 1953.

16. Marged Howard-Stepney, an affluent Welsh woman, who gave Thomas money from time to time.

17 & 18 (*above*) Thomas with John Brinnin, the American poet who first invited him to the United States, and arranged most of his readings there. (*below*) New York, 28 October 1953. Dylan Thomas and Arthur Miller (next to him) were among the panel of guests at a symposium on 'Poetry and the Film' organized by a group called Cinema 16. It was his last-but-one public appearance. Twelve days later he was dead.

19. The survivor: Florence Thomas at the Boat House. Husband, daughter Nancy and son Dylan all died within a year.

His social life didn't help. Florence was too close; people insisted on coming to talk about culture. 'Today we have visitors from Florence,' he wrote to Margaret Taylor on 20 June: 'a brood of translators and their wives, & one American professor. I can hear them gaggling. I haven't gone out yet. Or perhaps it is frogs and cicadas, one with an American accent.' On 11 July he wrote to her:

My social life: damp litterateurs pedal from Florence; neighbouring labouring men come in to dance; we walk, with Guido the gardener, or Eddo the tractor-driver, or others with shining hair and blue cheeks, to village cantinas. The nearest cafe, at Mosciano, is no cafe but a wine-counter in a packed, tiny, fly-black general shop. Sometimes, an Australian professor comes from Florence to shout Dinkum and Good-oh in the garden. A ... professor of Romance languages came with rimless spectacles and no lips, and was nasty ...

Sometimes he went into Florence to spend an evening in the cafés. Intellectuals gathered round. Thomas gazed into space or fell asleep. Once, visited at the villa by an Italian writer, he is reliably reported to have hidden in the wardrobe. Most of his letters show his thoughts firmly fixed on Britain. His father was chronically ill, and he wrote to Blaen Cwm regularly and solicitously. He listened to radio programmes from London, among them cricket-match commentaries by his friend John Arlott. At first the problem of where to live when they returned hung over him. America seemed to have been forgotten. But everything depended on Margaret Taylor. 'I do hope that you can help us to find a house in or near Oxford, so that we can see each other again,' he wrote to her from Rapallo, cunningly, in April. 'I want, so much, to come back to Oxford. Oh, anywhere a house. I am lost without one. I am domestic as a slipper, I want somewhere of my own, I'm old enough now, I want a house to shout, sleep, and work in. Please help; though I deserve nothing.' Mrs Taylor busied herself driving around Oxfordshire and neighbouring counties, and by the end of May she had found a house, in the small village of South Leigh. It was a grandly named cottage, The Manor House, which she bought, repaired and offered to the Thomases for a pound a week. 'How wonderful you are,' he wrote. 'Thank you with all my heart, from the depth of my teapot, from the marrow of my slippers warm before the fire, for finding a house for us . . . all I want's a new body and an alchemist's primer. Will you come often, very often? I am so happy and glad about it.' Mrs Taylor worked hard on their behalf. She organized furniture for the house. She promised to help with Llewelyn's education and spoke to the headmaster of Magdalen College School. In return he wrote her long amiable letters, and told her about the progress of his poem, 'In country sleep'. On 11 July he wrote:

> My poem, of a hundred lines, is finished, but needs a few days' work on it, especially on one verse. Then I'll send you a copy. The manuscript is thousands & thousands of foolscap pages scattered all over the place but mostly in the boiler fire. What I'll have to send you will be a fair copy. I think it's a good poem. But it has taken so long, nearly three months, to write, that it may be stilted. I hope not. I want, as soon as the last revision is made, to write, quickly, some short poems. I can't think of anything else; which isn't of course, true. I mean, when I think, I think of the poems I want to write; not of their shape but of the feeling of them, and of a few words.

Thomas said later that 'In country sleep' was to be part of a larger work called 'In country heaven'. Two further poems ('In the white giant's thigh' and 'Over Sir John's hill') were supposed to be part of the sequence, but when Thomas introduced all three on the Third Programme in September 1950, he had no idea where or how they would fit into the whole. 'In country sleep' is usually thought to be addressed to a child, presumably Aeron. It is written without complicated imagery, but it is not an easy poem to understand, despite various comments by Thomas to people in America. The critic William York Tindall told Thomas he thought it was about 'how it feels to be a father'. Thomas is said to have wept at this remark – 'but whether from vexation, beer or sentimental agreement I could not tell'. The poet is reassuring someone and warning her at the same time. She is threatened by an unidentified figure, the Thief, generally assumed to be Time or Death. Thomas told a woman who admired the poem that it was not addressed to a child at all, but to his wife, and that the Thief was jealousy. A third explanation was given in New York to a reporter. Thomas said, 'Alcohol is the thief today. But tomorrow he could be fame or success or exaggerated introspection or self-analysis. The thief is anything that robs you of your faith, of your reason for being.'

The idea that faith is being threatened runs through the poem. The year before he died he told an American student that it was started 'in cold blood', and that he 'never thought it would work'. Having been sent to Italy, Thomas may have felt he had to return with something to show for his visit. Certainly the trip achieved its aim of persuading him to write a poem again. But it was a complicated way of doing it. Nor did 'In country sleep' lead to the 'short poems' he mentioned to Margaret Taylor, or to any poems at all, that year or the next; another lengthy silence fell.

From Florence the Thomas party moved to the island of Elba for their last few weeks in the sun. This was more to Thomas's liking, with a population of fishermen and iron-ore miners, and no tourists or Florentine intellectuals. The heat still amazed him. 'It comes round corners at you like an animal with windmill arms,' he wrote to Margaret Taylor, perhaps echoing an old nightmare. 'As I enter my bedroom it stuns, thuds, throttles, spins me round by my soaking hair, lays me flat as a mat and bat-blind on my boiled and steaming bed. We keep oozing from the ice-cream counters to the chemist's. Beer is bottled God.' Nevertheless he took to Elba; so did Caitlin, who went back there after his death.

They returned to London in the middle of August, where Thomas broke his arm trying to climb in through a friend's window, stayed briefly in Wales, and so arrived at South Leigh and a roof of their own. The battered caravan was brought from Oxford and put in their unkempt garden for Thomas to work in. It was an unkempt and ancient village, in deep countryside, with no view to speak of, no local gentry, and little traffic. A few trains a day puffed along a branch railway line to the market town of Witney, five or ten minutes to the west, and Oxford, half an hour to the east. The Thomases fitted into this rustic scene. Dylan and Caitlin became local characters. They swerved about the village on muddy bicycles and played shove-ha'penny in the local pub. Limping down the lane, they were only mildly surprised to be told that she was wearing two left-foot wellingtons while he had two rights. Empty beer bottles accumulated on the path outside the house.

Sometimes Thomas went by himself to Witney on market-day and came back with a bag of shopping in the afternoon. Caitlin and the children would stand at the level-crossing as the train came in, waving. She intrigued the village. One minute she was sweeping about in garish clothes, the next she was slaving like a peasant, with a sack tied about her middle, heaving buckets of coke from the outhouse while her husband sat around apparently doing nothing. The Manor House had no hot water on tap, and heavy black kettles had to be boiled for an antiquated hip-bath; it was said that she bathed him, in front of the fire. To villagers his rôle was uncertain, except that he was a writer, and could be heard on the wireless from time to time. Once, according to Thomas, a doctor in the neighbourhood invited them to a cocktail party and introduced him to guests as Wynford Vaughan-Thomas, the famous B.B.C. war correspondent, not having heard of Dylan Thomas, the famous poet.

He continued to spread himself thin in broadcasting, always ready to use his voice. He read the part of Satan in eight episodes of *Paradise Lost* on the Third Programme (apparently as a last-minute substitute for Paul Scofield), and a potted version of W. H. Davies's *Autobiography of a Super-tramp* on fifteen consecutive Sundays for the Home Service. He introduced an edition of a long-running programme, 'Country Magazine', from the Fleece Inn at Witney, and spoke the awkwardly scripted lines that passed for jolly conversation in radio in those days. Only here and there did it sound like his style – 'I like living by the sea so much that here I am living bang in the middle of England.' But it was worth eighteen guineas plus fifteen shillings for a taxi.

He was no village drunk. South Leigh, like Wales, was a place to escape to. When he returned from exhausting visits to London, Caitlin put him to bed with bread and milk. Occasionally there were incidents at pubs. He suspected a gang of youths from a travelling fair of being too familiar with Caitlin in the bar. Outside, in the empty car-park, he confronted them, shaking but belligerent, till Caitlin arrived. She gave them a push and they drifted away. As a couple, they had acquired the married persons' quality of unsentimental closeness. Cordelia Locke watched Dylan trying to roll a cigarette, looking, she said, like a burst sausage. He produced a cigarette-rolling machine, chuckling and coughing, remarking, 'I use this and pretend ...' Mrs Locke missed the rest of the sentence. She asked Caitlin what he had said. Caitlin shook her head. 'Haven't heard a bloody word for years,' she said contentedly. Mrs Locke had known Caitlin in London when they were both teenagers. She and Harry Locke, an actor and comedian, became the Thomases' closest friends at South Leigh. She is another of those who found them incomparable – 'Just to be with them was like having a double whisky.' They were exhilarating and disturbing. Mrs Locke claims to know of a marriage that broke up because the Thomases unwittingly dragged its emotions to the surface: 'They didn't *do* anything but they had this effect on people. They were destructive in a way.' They aroused people's passions; often their admiration. A village woman who helped with cleaning and child-minding invited Caitlin to tea. Caitlin forgot and arrived a day late. The food was still ready, slightly curled at the edges. The hostess beamed. 'Ah,' she said, 'you beautiful yooman, you.' Years later Mrs Locke looked back on the Thomases at South Leigh like figures in a dream: Dylan strutting up and down the kitchen, a little pompously, declaiming a poem: Caitlin reading by an oil lamp, her features proud and haunted: Christmas decorations left hanging, months after.

Work to earn money was no problem at South Leigh, or it should not have been. Radio provided a small, reasonably steady income; films earned substantially more. Thomas's wartime work for Donald Taylor had led, as he had hoped, to better things. The Burke and Hare script, 'The Doctor and the Devils', seems to have been commissioned by Taylor himself. At some stage he sold the project to the Rank Organization, where it languished. A letter from Taylor to David Higham on 2 November 1947 said that 'the film is unlikely to be produced before 1949 because of the general decision in the Rank Organization to avoid horror and murder subjects'. But Thomas appears to have been paid three hundred and sixty-five pounds, in twelve instalments during 1947 and 1948, for his work on the script. (Later he earned more money when the script was published as a book.)

The British feature-film industry was healthy for a few years after the war. In order to conserve foreign exchange, the Government imposed a quota system which restricted the number of American films that could be shown. British studios churned out home products. Thomas was introduced to a company called British National, and collaborated on scripts for two pot-boilers, *Three Weird Sisters* and *No Room at the Inn*. Then Sydney Box of Gainsborough heard of him and signed him up to write three scripts in 1948. For these he was probably paid the best part of two thousand pounds, though none of the films was ever made. *Rebecca's Daughters*, based on material already owned by the studio, was about the nineteenth-century attacks by farmers on tollgates in the Welsh countryside. *The Beach at Falesa* was Robert Louis Stevenson's short story, set in the South Seas, and would have been a costly production. The third film, *Me and My Bike*, was to be based on an original idea, which may have been Thomas's; it was seen as a 'film operetta'. A man was to ride a succession of bicycles, ancient and modern, through his life, and finally pedal into heaven to be greeted by a chorus of bicycle-bells. The script was not written but Thomas's treatment has been published. For a year or so Thomas was a familiar figure at Gainsborough. He made irregular appearances at the studios in West London to attend script conferences, wearing a shiny blue suit and persuading colleagues to adjourn to the Shepherd's Bush Hotel at an early stage. Otherwise he sent his scripts in instalments, written in longhand, usually late, from South Leigh. There is the usual story that he had to be locked in an hotel bedroom (this time with a bottle of whisky) over a weekend to make him finish a script.

As a writer he was highly regarded by other writers at the studio. The management was less enthusiastic. His gift was for dialogue; when he had to construct a story, he was in difficulties. His idea of a plot was a straight line moving forward in time, as in *Under Milk Wood*. He might have enjoyed a career collaborating with other writers. But the Government quota was removed, the British film industry contracted, and after 1948 he was involved only in a half-hearted Gainsborough project to make a film of *Vanity Fair* with Margaret Lockwood.

His earnings during this period were those of a highly successful freelance writer. By 1948, Higham had introduced him to an accountant who handled his income-tax affairs. Thomas's tax-year ran from October (the month in which he had become self-employed after the war) to September. In 1947–8 his total earnings, as reported to the Inland Revenue, were £2,482, against which he claimed £612 for business expenses. By the time this figure was established it was the end of 1949, and Thomas, having made no provision for tax, had to find several hundred pounds out of his current earnings, which were much reduced, as well as put money aside for the following year's demand. This simple back-log of tax was the source of all the financial troubles that followed. Even then they could have been overcome in a year or two, once his American tours began. Higham took pains to deduct money from his British earnings for a 'tax fund', while leaving the family sufficient to live on. But Thomas seemed unable to help himself.

Even when he was earning the money, in 1947–8, before income-tax overtook him, he appeared to be no better off than usual. He wrote to David Higham from South Leigh on 7 October 1947:

> I've done it again. With a little money behind me, I've settled in a nice new house, bought a few things for it, behaved a little extravagantly – and now, yesterday morning, comes a letter from the bank saying that, not only am I not as well off as I imagined but that I am overdrawn and, unless something happens immediately, several cheques, made out to local tradesmen, will be returned. If they are returned, it will ruin us for ever in this village. Quite literally. It's enormously important, in a narrow tiny community like this, to keep frightfully well in with everyone, especially tradesmen, farmers, publicans, etc. And unless you can pay in for me, at once, a cheque from Dent, we will forever be *out* with the tradesmen, farmers, publicans, etc. to all of whom I have given cheques . . .

Doctors' bills for Llewelyn were burdensome. So were the expenses, later in the winter, of having his parents stay with them when Mrs Thomas had an accident. But the B.B.C. was still paying regular rail-fares to London. The house itself was costing them barely sixty pounds a year in rent and rates, if Margaret Taylor had been paid regularly, which she was not. Any attempt to discover where a person's money has gone is liable to be frustrating, let alone if it is Dylan Thomas's money. It may be argued that it is irrelevant. Those who interest themselves in the bank accounts of poets must expect to be chided for taking a worm's-eye view of the artist. But in Thomas's case it has been said repeatedly that he was hounded by tax-collectors and tradesmen – by the material world – and prevented from following his vocation. It is important to know if this was true; or if (which is more likely) he was involuntarily shaping the disagreeable circumstances himself, so that in the end, Thomas was hindering Thomas.

His friends used to wonder where the money went. There is a story that one Christmas he set off with two hundred pounds in cash to buy presents and food, and spent it in a day. Puzzled friends tried to follow his progress, shop by shop, to see where it had gone, but failed to solve the mystery. Dylan and Caitlin, staying with his parents at Bishopston, are said to have been given five pounds by Florence Thomas to buy essential clothes. They spent the day in Swansea and returned at night, penniless, with their purchases: one brassière. True or (probably) exaggerated, the stories reflect the Thomas reputation.

A psychiatrist might say that by ridding himself of money as fast as he made it, Thomas was asserting his rôle as a dependant, a man who must be looked after. Perhaps he was asserting his right to be the poet who couldn't be bothered with such trivialities. Either way he drove himself deeper into muddle and unhappiness; for in the very act of spending the money like a bohemian, he was worrying like a family man with a mortgage. Borrowing money was second nature, but now the amounts grew larger. In 1947, in Italy, he borrowed from a man in Rome; in 1950 the creditor was still trying to recover £179. If he met someone with money, Thomas was likely to ask for a loan or a subsidy – it made little difference what it was called, since it was never likely to be returned – as a matter of course. Mervyn Levy says that 'Dylan had a fair idea of his value as a person people wanted to have around': in other words, he would sometimes put a price on his company. Levy, a civilian lecturer with the Army after the war ended, had a sergeant under his command, a wealthy young man who wanted to meet Thomas. Told of this, Thomas asked Levy, 'Will he lend me a hundred pounds?' Levy thought it likely, and a meeting in a pub was arranged. Thomas asked for the money towards the end of the evening; he left with a cheque. On another occasion, Levy took him to dinner at the home of a psychiatrist in Cardiff. The doctor's wife greeted them and said her husband would be there soon. Thomas, grubby and down-at-heel, asked if he might go upstairs to wash. When he reappeared he was wearing the psychiatrist's suit, shirt, tie and socks. Levy says that no one referred to the incident all evening. Later the psychiatrist told Levy that what had really offended him was to find Thomas's filthy clothes stuffed under the bed. But if people were willing to be treated like that, Thomas had little compunction.

He was as indifferent as ever to work that didn't interest him; perhaps more indifferent. Before he went to Italy he told his parents enthusiastically that he was to write 'a full-length grand opera for William Walton'. First he was to write a synopsis. He saw it as 'a very modern tragic opera', set in a dockside slum. According to Michael Ayrton, the painter, who was a friend of Walton, Thomas's eventual contribution consisted of a postcard on which was written:

> With a sound like thunder-claps
> The little mouse comes out, perhaps.

Walton went elsewhere for his libretto.

Thomas managed to ruffle one or two radio producers. In January 1947 he was telling a lady in the department that made programmes for schools that he was 'very keen to try to put poetry over to these rather "hostile" children – or is that too harsh a word?' He was scheduled to make the broadcast in June, but they found he had gone to Italy without telling them. 'I feel that we cannot pander to his artistic temperament any further, and must give him up as a bad job,' said an irritable memorandum. Thomas had never had so many irons in the fire. At the end of 1947 he was concerned with a string of projects, apart from radio and the British National scripts. Dent planned a collection of 'Poems, 1934–1947' for the following spring; it was to include 'two long new poems'. The short-story collection was still in prospect. He wanted to write a radio play about Laugharne. He was trying to raise money to finish *Adventures in the Skin Trade*, insisting to Higham that it was not merely a 'fragment of comic romantic taradiddle without a real structure or purpose', and asking him to show the manuscript to Graham Greene with the message that 'there is a *strict* plot behind the book, that it is all planned out, and that, if he feels any interest in it, I should like very much to discuss the *rest* of the book with him'.

Domestic problems arose. His mother broke her leg; she was sixty-five. While she was in hospital at Carmarthen, Nancy went to Blaen Cwm to look after her father. Nancy's first marriage had ended in divorce; with her second husband, she was living in Devon. Thomas, visiting Blaen Cwm in the middle of the crisis, early in 1948, wrote to Caitlin that it was 'snowbound, dead, dull, damned; there's hockey-voiced Nancy being jolly over pans and primuses in the kitchen, and my father trembling and moaning all over the place, crying out sharply when the dog barks – Nancy's dog – weeping, despairing.' There had been quarrels with Caitlin before Dylan left for Wales. The letter has the familiar note of apology for bad behaviour. How can he behave so brutally to the most beautiful person on earth? Thomas spells out his distress, the journey to Wales in a freezing train, the wait at Carmarthen station in the snow for a car to take him to 'Misery Cottage', the fear that he has lost her love. Inevitably, he promises that if forgiven, he will never be a 'senseless, horrible, dulled beast' again.

The Blaen Cwm problem was worse still when Mrs Thomas left hospital. Someone had to look after the old couple, or at least be near at hand. Nancy and her husband couldn't cope; Dylan and Caitlin had to. He rented Cordelia Locke's cottage, which was temporarily empty, and his parents stayed there first, then at The Manor House. Nancy and husband helped with money, but the problem was not money so much as the new responsibility. Most of the burden fell on Caitlin. Her husband was busy with Gainsborough film scripts and B.B.C. readings. He was not busy with poems, which may be why the projected 'Poems, 1934–1947' was abandoned. Domestic life gave him excuses for avoiding serious work. An undated letter to Caitlin, temporarily away from South Leigh, reported misery at home. His father was obsessed with 'saucepans and operations'. Mrs Taylor's visits were not restful. But Thomas liked to exaggerate his troubles, the better to hide behind them. When John Davenport, now in difficulties, wrote to ask for help, Thomas replied on 26 August to say he was sorry, in detail – Llewelyn needed clothes for school next term, his parents made demands, 'Caitlin wants a pressure-cooker & a nightgown', he would have to buy a suit to read at the Edinburgh Festival, he had broken a tooth and must visit the dentist. As though to clinch the matter, 'At the bottom of the garden, a man, at three shillings an hour, is digging a new shitpit & will dig on, he says, until he reaches water. By that time I shall owe him this house, which is not mine.'

Thomas's letters were carefully adjusted to the recipient. He wrote humbly to his parents, lovingly to Caitlin, and with a determination to be clever at all costs to clever friends like Davenport. The less clever his letters, the more informative they are likely to be. He wrote, on 25 May 1948, to a journalist acquaintance, C. Gordon Glover, who had sent him the draft of an article about himself that was to appear in a magazine called *Band Wagon*. The article was of no great significance. Thomas wanted to get it right but he didn't feel the need to mock himself and life in general. This was Thomas taking a straightforward view of Thomas:

> Thanks for 'A Poet in a Pub'. The titles you boys think up!
>
> I am thirty-three, not thirty-one.
>
> I don't think I used, of my father, the words 'the finest Shakespeare reader of his day' . . .[2]

2. This is the passage already quoted on page 19.

I would not be surprised – you are quite right – if people said I was a sort of modern Villon. But my lack of surprise would be caused *not* by the fact that I think I resemble, in any way in the world, a sort of modern Villon, but because I am used to listening to balls. I am about as much a modern Villon – I cannot, incidentally, read French – as I am a modern Joanna Southcott, Raleigh, Artemus Ward or Luther.

I wasn't at Mrs Hole's kindergarten with either Dan Jones or Fred Janes (n, not m), whom I met later.

Do you think the extract, about 'Break -break break', from my autobiographical sketches,[3] is confused by mixing it up with words not in the extract? Or not? I don't, myself, think that a reader would know that this extract came from my book; or, alternatively, I think that the reader would think the whole thing, including your interpolations, came from my book. It's very tiny, anyway, & doesn't really matter. Just a little point, sir.

It is true to say that I often cover perhaps a hundred sheets of paper in the construction of one poem. But what I said was, that I often covered more than a hundred sheets of paper with drafts, revisions, rewritings, ravings, doodlings & intensely concentrated work to construct a single verse. Nor is this anything to be proud, or ashamed, of. I do not think any better of a verse because it takes weeks, and quires, to complete it. It is just that I work extremely slowly, painfully, in seclusion.

It was Aeronwy who was born in a blitz – as though it mattered! – not Llewelyn, who anticipated the war by more than six months.

Do, please, for old crimes' sake, cut out my spontaneous, and quite unbelieved-in, disparagement of village cricket. It was something I said for something to say. I'd be *awfully* pleased to see *all* references to cricket omitted. Let's leave cricket to Jack Squire; I have no ambition to join his jolly Georgian squirearchy.

Finally, as a 'Profile', your admirable article should, I think, have taken, however parenthetically, other aspects of this impermanent, oscillating, rag-bag character into consideration: aspects, I admit, of which you, with great good luck, could have little first-hand knowledge: my basic melancholy; sullen glooms and black studies; atrocious temper; protracted vegetable comas, silences and disappearances; terror of death, heights, strokes, mice; shyness and gaucheness; pompous, platitudinary, repetitive periods of bottom-raking boredom and boorishness; soulburn, heartdoubt, headspin;

3. 'The Fight', in *Portrait of the Artist*.

my all-embracing ignorance; my still only half squashed and forgotten bourgeois petty values; all my excruciating whimsicality; all my sloth; all my eye!

I enclose the article, with many thanks. What a fellow I sound! Thank God I don't have to meet myself socially, listen to myself, or, except when reluctantly shaving, see that red, blubbery circle mounted on ballooning body, that down-at-soul hick, hack, hock-loving hake which now inscribes itself, Yours ever.

Most of the time he was at South Leigh, Thomas seems to have been hankering after Wales. If Margaret Taylor could buy them a house in Oxfordshire, there was no reason why she couldn't do the same in Carmarthenshire. Wales could be seen as a practical move. It was the place where he wrote his poems; it turned an emotional key. He wrote to Richard Hughes's wife, Frances, 'Here [in South Leigh], I am too near London; I undertake all sorts of little jobs, broadcasting etc., which hinder my own work. In Laugharne if I could live there, I would work half the year on my film scripts, and half on my own poems and stories: cutting out all time-wasting broadcasts, articles, useless London visits.' He caricatured himself in a radio talk: not a very good talk, rehashing old memories, but laying out his nostalgia for inspection: 'Lost and blown about in London town, a barrel-shaped leaf, am I still the same, I said to myself, as that safe and sound loller at the corners of Wales who, to my memory, was happy as a sandman?'

He could still be rude about Wales, in the conventional expatriate manner, if he thought the audience required it. Speaking to Scottish writers in Edinburgh in 'Tributes to Hugh MacDiarmid' (the occasion for which he needed the new suit) he said, 'I am a Welshman who does not live in his own country, mainly because he still wants to eat and drink, be rigged and roofed, and no Welsh writer can hunt his bread and butter in Wales unless he pulls his forelock to the *Western Mail*, Bethesdas on Sunday, and enters public houses by the back door, and reads Caradoc Evans only when alone, and by candlelight.' No doubt he was telling a nationalist-minded audience what he thought it wanted to hear. It was an empty statement, if it meant anything more than that Thomas was regarded with suspicion by the Welsh-speaking establishment. His local standing had little effect on his earning power, especially since in 1948 he still saw film-writing as a commercial career.

If he was to return to Wales, Thomas set his heart on Laugharne. At one point he took an interest in a house in Gower, the Old Rectory at Rhossili, below the hill and near the long sands where Extraordinary Little Cough performed his feat. It was half a mile from the village, down a steep path, and was too inaccessible. Nor did Rhossili have a pub. Laugharne was convenient, yet remote in its atmosphere. It was an idiosyncratic corner of the Thomases' family country, so that he was doubly at home. He wrote to a friend at the magazine *Picture Post* offering an article about Laugharne when he would be there at Easter 1948: 'I really do know it intimately, love it beyond all places in Wales, and have longed for years to write something about it. (A radio play I am writing has Laugharne, though not by name, as its setting.)'

During the summer the Thomases went to Laugharne to see a house called Gosport. This was a comfortable place, standing alone, a short way up the hill from the cottage, Eros, where they had lived before the war. At the end of the garden the ground fell away sharply to the estuary. In the garden stood an old summerhouse; a local story said a tunnel connected it with the Castle. Thomas decided he would use it to write in. The only slight difficulty was that the occupants of Gosport, the Misses Laugharne-Allen, had no intention of selling. It was suggested to them that if they did not, posterity might have something to say. Telegrams arrived from Margaret Taylor, offering four thousand pounds on the nail. But the sisters wouldn't budge. Later in the year Mrs Taylor negotiated unsuccessfully for Richard Hughes's house, attached to the Castle. Thomas remained in the middle of England, not writing poems. He wrote to Vernon Watkins on 23 November, 'Nothing happens to me. I go to London and bluster, come back and sigh, do a little script-writing, look at an unfinished poem, go out on my bicycle in the fog, go to London & bluster.' The following month a lorry knocked him off his bicycle, breaking an arm again and cracking some ribs. It was another turgid winter, relieved, at the end of it, by a few days in Prague, where he flew as a guest of the Czech Government for the inauguration of the Czechoslovak Writers' Union. He seems to have been invited because he knew the Czech cultural attaché in London; perhaps they thought he was a communist at heart.

At last, in the spring of 1949, a suitable house at Laugharne came on the market. The Boat House stood under a sea-cliff, away from the town itself. Mrs Taylor paid two thousand five hundred pounds for it. By April or May the Thomases were living there. 'You have given me a life,' Thomas wrote to his patroness. 'And now I am going to live it.'

CHAPTER TEN

# *Laugharne and America*

THE Thomases arrived at the Boat House in the spring of 1949. Caitlin was six or seven months pregnant when they moved. Florence and D.J. had returned to Laugharne already, to a house in the main street called Pelican, which Dylan rented for them. From now on they could be visited and looked after in their own home. And for the first time, Dylan, Caitlin and their children were secure in a house in Wales that was theirs for the foreseeable future. But she was less enthusiastic. The Boat House itself was a few minutes from the main street, along an overgrown lane called Cliff Walk, which ran above the shore-line of rocks and mud. From the lane a path slanted back under the wooded cliff to the house, just above the water. In the lane itself, and overlooking the roof of the Boat House, was a bicycle shed, with a steeper set of steps coming up from below. The setting was agreeable. Across the River Taf were the chequered farm-fields around Pentowin. Beyond Laugharne in the other direction was the low ridge of Sir John's hill. Between the two, to the south-east, Laugharne's River Taf and two other rivers, the Towy and Gwendraeth, met in tidal flats and sandbanks where fishing boats were sometimes beached at low water, black specks on the backs of yellow whales. Water dominated the house. When the estuary filled at high tide, it mirrored broken light on to the walls and ceilings. In spring and autumn the end of the garden was flooded.

The shape of the coast shielded Laugharne from the worst of the south-westerly winds, but nothing kept out the drizzles and sea-mists, when the foghorn of a lightship groaned and thumped all day in the Bristol Channel. The Boat House was well placed to get more than its share of damp. It made the woodwork spongy and stained the ceilings; a verandah or balcony that ran around two sides of the house had to have its floor strengthened with squares of tin. There were six small rooms and a kitchen, confusingly organized in three storeys, with the main entrance, and the balcony, on the middle level. Until Margaret Taylor paid to have mains water brought over the cliff, the Thomases had to use a well outside the house. Rats scuttled in the outside lavatory and sometimes in the house. But Caitlin made the place snug, with big coal fires in open grates. Most of the furniture was cheap and nondescript, with rugs for the floors. On the walls were family photographs, coloured postcards and pages ripped from magazines.

For writing in, Thomas used the shed. Branches scraped the walls, ivy grew through the cracks. A fig tree partially hid the view. It could be damp and draughty, but it was peaceful, and it had the additional advantage for Thomas that he could slip away unnoticed into Laugharne. Once, Elisabeth Lutyens, staying at the Boat House, called at the Pelican to see his parents, and found him there, surreptitiously reading a thriller. His working hours, as usual, were in the afternoon. In the morning he did nothing much. He always called on his parents, and he and D. J. would sit by themselves, doing a crossword. Caitlin recalled long absences in the kitchen of Brown's Hotel, putting money on horses, listening to gossip and drinking slow pints of beer, before coming 'muzzily back to late lunch, of one of our rich fatty brews, always eaten alone, apart from the children; and I can't blame him for that ... Then, blown up with muck and somnolence, up to his humble shed, nesting high above the estuary; and bang into intensive scribbling, muttering, whispering, intoning, bellowing and juggling of words; till seven o'clock prompt.' It is said that Thomas never drank while he wrote. But he was sometimes seen going up the steps to the hut with a bottle of brown ale.

He wrote a poem immediately, to celebrate his return. This was 'Over Sir John's hill', which (Thomas said) was intended to fit somewhere into the 'In country heaven' design. It is the most topographical of his poems, firmly framed in the view from the hut. Thomas used the scene – and especially a heron at the water's edge, the songbirds, and the hawk that will strike them

– to write about mortality. The heron mourns as dusk falls; so does the poet, appearing, somewhat self-consciously, as 'I young Aesop fabling to the near night'. Birds had featured in Thomas's poems from the beginning; the heron seems to have taken on a special significance. When Caitlin's child was born, a boy, they gave it an Irish name, Colm,[1] and a Welsh name, Garan, which means heron. Florence Thomas said that when they went through Dylan's clothes after his death, they found pieces of bread in the pockets: he used to lean out of his hut and throw crumbs down to the birds. She always insisted that the herons, a common sight in the estuary, came looking for him afterwards.

'Over Sir John's hill' was cunningly filled with assonance, alliteration, onomatopoeia and every poet's trick he could think of. Watkins found it 'perhaps the most perfect poem he wrote'. With its elaborate elegiac statements, drawing heavily on natural surroundings, it is related to 'Fern Hill' and 'Poem in October', written when he last lived in Wales. But a feeling of divine or fateful judgement runs through the poem. God is invoked, but death is coming. Thomas had spoken often of dying young, as poets in fiction were supposed to do, even specifically of dying before he reached forty. Death frightened him but perhaps it also appealed to him as a solution. Caitlin wrote that 'he was never that keen on life'. It was about this time that Thomas described a dream to Leo Abse, the politician. It was soon after his return from Prague; perhaps when he was already at work on 'Sir John's hill'. A man goes from cave to cave inside a mountain, penetrating deeper into the earth. Finally he reaches a cave where a skeleton is hanging, and falls to his death. The skeleton is himself. As Abse remembers, 'The way he told it, it was a death dream – as if he was being pulled to his death, deeper and deeper into the mountain.'[2]

Before 'Over Sir John's hill' was finished, Thomas received

1. Thomas sometimes wrote it as 'Colum', the way it was pronounced.

2. The dream echoes another described by Thomas, years before – see note to p. 103. There is a further complication. Dannie Abse, the poet, has said that Thomas's 1949 dream, as described to him at second hand by his brother Leo, involved Biblical scenes, and ended, not with death, but with the Garden of Eden and a man and woman hand in hand.

the invitation he had been seeking since 1945: he was asked to go to America by someone who was willing to pay him. The offer came from John Malcolm Brinnin, who had just been made director of the Poetry Centre at the Young Men's and Young Women's Hebrew Association in New York. Brinnin was that familiar figure in America, the poet who teaches, or the academic who writes poetry. A few years younger than Thomas, he became a patron overnight, with money to spend. Brinnin had no interest in dull readings and small attendances: 'I didn't,' he says, 'want to be director of a thing with fifty people in the audience. I wanted to advertise and get subscriptions.' He admired Thomas's poetry and knew of him by hearsay. So as soon as Brinnin was appointed, he sent off an invitation for Thomas to read at the Centre for a fee of five hundred dollars, plus his air fare, and offered to sponsor him to read in other parts of the country. The letter took some time to reach Thomas and he didn't reply until 28 May, when he accepted warmly, adding that he would like to spend about three months in America, early the following year. From then on it was only a question of arranging the details.

Thomas's feelings were simple, as they always had been where America was concerned. The trip would, if properly organized, be reasonably lucrative. When he returned to Laugharne, he would be able to spend an unencumbered year writing. With American money, he told James Laughlin, 'I won't, at once, have to chase again the hack-jobs by which, dear Christ, I live, have at once to set into motion again the insignificant, wheezy little machines that sausage out crumbs and coppers for me, scriptlings, radio whinnies.' In the meantime, the hack-jobs predominated. These were causing him, and everyone else, painful problems. Before returning to Laugharne he had contracted with the B.B.C. to make a Third Programme script of William Wycherley's play *The Plain Dealer*, to include a part for himself; altogether worth a hundred guineas. Part of the fee was paid but the script failed to arrive; telegrams to the Boat House went unanswered. Then Thomas wrote at the end of May to say he had been ill – 'so perfectly bloody that I just groaned at all my obligations and put my head under the blankets'. The letter was written the same day as his letter to Brinnin, in which he said he had had influenza. But when he recovered, no script was forthcoming, then or ever. Still more bothersome was the *Peer Gynt* episode. The B.B.C. television service, moving slowly towards a national network after the war, was experimenting with classical drama. Thomas, who had never seen television at the time, was approached as early as October 1947 to see if he was interested in adapting Euripides' *The Trojan Women*. The project fell through, but a year later he was invited to try his hand at Ibsen's *Peer Gynt*. This was to be a major production in the spring of 1949. Auden is said to have been approached first, and to have refused. Thomas, laid up with a broken arm over Christmas after his bicycle accident, wrote that *Peer Gynt* was 'a great and favourite play' that he 'really would *love*' to adapt, if only they would wait longer. The B.B.C. postponed production to the autumn of 1949, and suggested a fee of two hundred and fifty guineas, by far the largest sum Thomas had been offered for anything except a film script. He cabled his agent telling him to accept and claim immediate payment of half the fee.

This was the state of affairs when the Thomases moved to the Boat House. The television producer whose job it was to prise the script from Thomas was Royston Morley. In the 1930s, Morley was the little-magazine editor who paid Thomas for a story with half a guinea and dinner at Bertorelli's. Now he had a sterner task. No script arrived on 1 July, as arranged. Perhaps Thomas had been writing 'Over Sir John's hill' instead. Pressed to deliver, he wrote angrily to his agent to say that less than half the literal translation he was to work from had arrived. In any case, he said, he was not being paid enough: Louis MacNeice had been given a year on full pay, plus a special fee, to produce a script of Goethe's *Faust*. The B.B.C., which had been threatening to ask for its money back, retreated. He was given until the autumn, then until the start of 1950, and so on until the B.B.C. abandoned hope about 1953. The half fee was never returned. The *Plain Dealer* and *Peer Gynt* episodes, together with lesser incidents, made the B.B.C. permanently suspicious of Thomas. Eventually they refused to advance money on a script until they had it in their hands. Later this had an effect on the play that Thomas wanted to write, and in the end succeeded in writing, about Laugharne. In 1949 the embryonic *Under Milk Wood* was still largely unwritten, an uncertain project somewhere between poetry and hack-job. It figured on the optimistic lists of work in hand that his agent drew up; and as an 'awful' and 'wretched' script in Thomas's letters to friends.

Colm was born on 24 July. On 30 July, following a trip to London, Thomas wrote a letter to Davenport of a kind he had managed to avoid for a year or two:

Arrived back, rather bruised, to find the financial situation here far worse than even I, in my tearful jags of the last week, could have imagined. They've stopped sending coal, & will, any moment, stop sending milk: essential things in a baby-packed, freezing house. I'm summonsed for rates. No more meat. I cannot write a cheque, of course, so that we are – for the first time for years – literally without one shilling. Four cheques have been returned from the Savage,[3] but without savage comment. And my father is dangerously ill with pneumonia; and I've had some sort of breakdown. Christ! So if you ever do come across anyone ... with a single fiver to spare, it would make a difference. Or suggest anyone to whom I could write ... I shall be forced to go to America, God help me, my breakdown, & my guts, but it's *now*, at *once*, *temporarily*, the nine quid for milk, the ten for coal, six for builder, eight for summons, without mentioning cigarettes for Cat, sweets for Aeron etc. If you do see anyone interested, *please*, old boy. For any amount. To be paid after America ... I'm on the rim ...

He may have been piling on the agony for Davenport's benefit. On 5 August he was writing calmly to Margaret Taylor, thanking her for a small loan and promising to repay 'my now almost national debt to you' in the near future – writing, he said, 'in the heaven of my hut. Wild day, big seas for Laugharne, & the boats of the Williamses lurching exactly like Williamses'.

3. Thomas was elected to membership of this gentlemen's club in March 1949, on John Davenport's proposal. Previously, and improbably, he was a member from January 1947 of the solidly bourgeois National Liberal Club. Thomas used to make himself feel better about such an eccentric choice by calling it the National Lavatory.

Yet the clamour of debts and worries grew. The logical solution was to press on with work that would earn money. But work stagnated. He made a few broadcasts, including a discussion from Swansea in October with four Welsh friends: Vernon Watkins, Alfred Janes, Daniel Jones and John Prichard. The B.B.C.'s post-war studio in the town was housed a few doors from the building that had once been the Uplands cinema. 'Though Swansea bore me,' said Thomas, and though indeed I have bored Swansea in my time, I do not now live in it. I am by nature a globe-trotter. I live in the next county.'

Nor was he writing much poetry. Nothing emerged from the garden hut. 'My table's heaped with odd lines, single words, nothing completed,' he wrote to Laughlin. He was working on a poem late in 1949, 'In the white giant's thigh', which dwelt on the countryside's past loves and dead lovers. Progress was slow. He told Watkins that the opening line, 'Through throats where many rivers meet, the curlews cry', took him three weeks to write. The poem was not completed for almost a year. In the winter of 1949, Thomas struggled unhappily. On the reverse of a worksheet of lines in mid-poem is the draft of a letter dated 24 November to a wealthy American woman, Marguerite Caetani. As 'Princess Caetani' (or Madame di Sermoneta) she edited a magazine in Rome, *Botteghe Oscure*. Thomas had met her in London on a recent visit, and persuaded her to advance him a hundred pounds against a story he was to write for her. In the draft letter he promised the story by 1 March 'if I am not, before then, stoned to death by writs'. By the time the letter was sent, the phrase was changed to read, 'if I am not, before then, popped into the cooler, peeled, pipped and sliced'. The letter was carefully put together. Thomas was trying to wear a brave smile for her benefit, while hinting at his poverty and problems. 'I do not, now, read any of my poems with much pleasure,' he wrote in the draft, 'because they tell me I should be writing other poems *now*.' He dawdled over letters: words for the sake of words. He thanked a correspondent for 'your extremely kind and helpful letter', then deleted 'kind and' and finally settled for 'your extremely nice and helpful letter'. Further down the page he apologized for the delay in writing: 'Procrastination is, like alcohol to Ben Jonson, an element in which I live.' He changed 'alcohol' to 'drink', then refined the sentence to 'Procrastination is an element in which I live.' But he was only writing to Brinnin about the American arrangements. Presumably he slaved over letters because it was more acceptable than slaving over poems.

Was he disturbed because he could not write poems, or was he not writing poems because he was disturbed? It is unlikely that Thomas himself would have known the answer. He muddled along. 'Things are appalling here,' he wrote to Davenport on 13 October. 'I owe a quarter's rent on my mother's house, Llewelyn's school fees (for last term), much to each tradesman. Yesterday I broke a tooth on a Minto. There are rats in the lavatory, tittering while you shit, and the official rat man comes every day to give them titbits before the kill. Unfortunately, for my peace of mind, the rat man has only one arm.'

He had been writing funny letters with exaggerated accounts of disasters for so long that they had become literary exercises, not to be taken too seriously. One of his well-known disaster-letters, apologizing to the Swansea branch of the British Medical Association for failing to speak at their annual dinner, must have taken almost as much energy to compose as he would have expended on the original function. Thomas was due there on 20 October, on his way back from a trip to London. By now he was beginning to speak regularly, for a fee, to clubs and societies. In his B.M.A. letter, written months later, the excuse boiled down to a car accident: a friend with a fast car drove him from London, they hit a telegraph pole near Bristol, where they spent the night, and next day, which was 20 October, friend and car had vanished, together with Thomas's suit and speech. The real journey seems to have taken longer and been more confused. But fantasy streams through all these stories of Thomas, whoever tells them. The friend with the fast car was the rich young man from whom, as a sergeant in the Army with literary inclinations, Thomas had borrowed a hundred pounds. This time Thomas and other friends hoped to take a larger sum from him to finance a new literary magazine.[4] Rich friend, Thomas and Bernard Gutteridge, a poet and advertising man, left London with champagne and cold chicken in the boot. Thomas kept insisting he must have a clean shirt for the Swansea doctors. They called at Oxford to see another friend, Dan Davin, and stayed overnight. Thomas read them poems by Hardy that he was planning to use in America. Davin, who kept a diary, says that at the end of one poem 'he burst into tears, too moved to go on'. Davin has quoted from his diary for the following day: 'Dylan is very emotional but like a good Welshman also very suspicious. Thus when he has expressed himself very warmly, in fact exposed himself, he will suddenly react violently towards a self-sneering cynicism. It imparts a curious rhythm to his talk.' Later that day (says Davin) Thomas was seen looking out of the window, complaining that the Davins' small daughter had just composed the Thomas-like lines 'I eat the wind And I drink the rain'. Eventually the party drove on to the west. Gutteridge thinks they struck another vehicle a glancing blow, and there was trouble with the police. So far it had taken them two days to travel a hundred miles. They stayed the night at Bristol, where Mervyn Levy now lived. Thomas, lying drunk and exhausted in an hotel room, asked Levy to sing him to sleep, as he did in their Earls Court days. Levy sang 'I am the Bandolero'. When he reached the line, 'For I am waiting and watching, an outlaw defiant', Thomas said, 'Oh, sing that bit again, Mervy, I'll go to sleep in a minute.' In Swansea, the doctors waited in vain.

His American plans crystallized slowly. Brinnin would act as his agent, for a percentage of the fees. Thomas asked him to help organize the official papers. 'I dare say my London Literary Agent can help a bit,' he wrote, 'but he's a stiff sod and frightens the life out of me: I believe he is always waiting for an Enormous Novel, which he won't get.' This was an ungenerous way to talk about Higham; but Thomas was quick to sneer

4. The magazine, *Circus* ('The pocket review of our time'), ran for two issues, in April and May 1950, just long enough to print a whimsical piece by Thomas in two parts, 'How To Be a Poet', which included a cruel parody of Richard Church. John Davenport was the editor.

at people behind their backs. His manner could be harsh and whining now: 'I wish I could sell my body to a rich widow,' he wrote to Laughlin; 'but it is fat now and trembles a little. I'm sick of being so damned & utterly broke, it spoils things ... I'm cold, it's raining on the sea, the herons are going home, the cormorants have packed up, I must go and play darts in the cheerless bar ...' He had decided that Caitlin shouldn't go with him to America: 'It would be difficult, expensive, and, I think, bad for her,' he told Margaret Taylor. In the same letter (dated 28 November and headed 'City of Dreadful Night') he described the latest mishap: 'On Saturday night I fell down again and cracked some ribs, how many and how badly I won't know till I'm X-rayed tomorrow ... Also I have gout in my toe, phlegm on my lungs, misery in my head ...' He joked about whether his accident was really an excuse not to work on his 'wretched script' for radio; 'I had decided, quite sternly, to finish it this week – I can do it in ten days, anyway – but conveniently, and nastily, fell down. Week after week I have put it off, pulling out a poem instead once I got into the littered, great hut ... I may, after all, break my neck as a final procrastination.'

In December, Glyn Jones was to interview him for a radio programme about 'How I Write'. Jones paid a preliminary visit to the Boat House in October, and had the usual shock of the old friend who had not seen him for years: 'His teeth, which he tried to conceal in smiling, were not good, his nose had become enormous, his face bloated and pale. He looked comical, and lovely, and terrible.' They discussed what Thomas would say in the broadcast. But when the time came, a few days before Christmas, the producer in Cardiff received a telegram from Caitlin to say that Dylan was ill with 'broken ribs'.

And then it was the New Year, and he was writing frantically to Davenport, 'You know when I was up last, at the end of my visit, I said "To hell with America, to hell with my visa," and lurched home. Well, now it's quite obvious I have to go to America, so my visa's vital. The plane ticket ... has just been sent to me.' Thus he kept up a shadowy pretence among friends that he was going against his will. He knew that a long programme of engagements at colleges and universities, arranged at his request, awaited him. He visited a 'posh dentist' in London, so he told Caitlin. They were both in London for a farewell party before he flew away on 20 February 1950, to see what America had to offer.

During the hundred days of his first visit – and for that matter, during all the time he spent in the United States – Thomas succeeded in living his own private, eccentric life without paying much attention to the country he was in. He wrote nothing about it, except for a not very funny radio talk, which was full of the broad jokes he had used on his American audiences. One of his favourites spoke of earnest crew-cut students, 'each with at least thirty-six terribly white teeth'. Sometimes he made it forty-two teeth, or described the students as 'brash, antiseptic, ardent'. But he wasn't very interested in students, or their professors, or their institutions. Even the physical geography of America was beyond him. More than one of his hosts felt he might have been on the moon, for all he knew. One place was much like another, except for San Francisco, which he loved, and New York, which is where most of his friends were. He went along with events. People bought him tickets and wrote instructions in his diary; they steered him west towards Ohio and south towards Arizona, and on the whole he arrived on time and performed as arranged. As a poet, he was quite reliable.

His chief guide and adviser was John Brinnin. Thomas seems genuinely to have liked him. Brinnin met him at Idlewild, as New York's airport was then called, and drove him into Manhattan in the cold early morning. For the next few days, Thomas went sightseeing, attended parties and drank in many bars. New York seemed to egg him on. He was asked to leave the Beekman Tower Hotel where he was staying, apparently for drunkenness. At one party, after he had made vague overtures to Katherine Anne Porter, the author, then aged fifty-nine, he suddenly seized her and lifted her up to the ceiling. People were not generally amused at these antics. It has been suggested that the guests at cocktail parties were more easily shocked in America in those days than they would have been in Britain. No doubt there is some truth in this. British social occasions take eccentricity in their stride. Many of Thomas's shock-effects in New York were achieved with remarkable ease. At a party given by Marshall W. Stearns, the critic, someone unwisely asked Thomas what the 'Ballad of the Long-legged Bait' meant. He said crisply, 'It's a description of a gigantic fuck.' This seems to have stopped the conversation. But if his audiences reacted with more alarm than they would have done in London, it is also true that in America he often behaved more extravagantly than he did in Britain. There is no record of Thomas going out of his way to shock Edith Sitwell or Cyril Connolly. In America he sometimes acted as if he wanted to shock everyone. His mood, perhaps, was a more complicated version of his mood when he moved from Wales to London in 1934. He had to prove himself as a bohemian artist. He had to conceal his fears. And the distance from home set him free, temporarily, of his inhibitions. London was an unsuccessful escape from Cwmdonkin Drive. America was an unsuccessful escape from everything. Such attempts were sure to fail because Thomas couldn't sever his connections. But the effort was bound to be both painful and entertaining.

His first engagement in America was a reading at the Poetry Centre, two days after he arrived. He was nervous and vomiting beforehand. The Young Men's and Young Women's Hebrew Association is housed in a gaunt building. 'Remember thy Creator in the days of thy youth' is chiselled in stone at the entrance. An audience of a thousand waited in the Kaufmann Auditorium. Brinnin, a dapper man, introduced their guest by saying that he came 'out of the druidical mists of Wales'. Thus Thomas was licensed to behave not only as a poet, but as a mysterious figure from a far country.[5] On that first occasion he read Yeats, Hardy, Auden and other contemporary British poets, and ended with

5. Speaking to an audience on home ground, at Llanelli, in 1952, Thomas said that outside Wales 'one is given a foreign licence to *be* a Welshman, and the odder one is the more typical is it thought to *be* of the character and behaviour of those brutal and benighted songbirds who cluster together, hymning on hilltops, in the woad and llanwigwams . . .'

some of his own work. He was loudly applauded. His rich voice overcame any problems of meaning. People frequently said that Thomas's way of reading made them understand poems for the first time; but it may be that under the influence of his voice, the literal meaning of a poem became irrelevant. Some women found the voice aphrodisiac.

To his parents Thomas wrote the kind of letters they expected to receive. 'My old duffle-coat was very helpful,' he said, describing the February cold. He had been 'gawping, like the country cousin I am, at this titanic dream world, soaring Babylon, everything monstrously rich and strange'. Caitlin, too, received a filtered version of events. There had been some parties, where the guests were 'all furiously polite and hospitable', and he had been sightseeing. Even this made him afraid of upsetting her: 'and now it must look to you, my Cat, as though I am enjoying myself here. I'm not. It's nightmare, day and night; there never was such a place ...'

Soon he was out of New York, beginning his cross-country travels. After a second reading at the Poetry Centre, he and Brinnin left the city over the weekend, driving to Westport, in Connecticut, where his host then lived. Among Brinnin's neighbours in the wooded suburbs of Westport were the novelist Peter de Vries and his wife Katinka. Brinnin and Thomas called there on Sunday evening, where, says de Vries, 'Dylan described the plot of a film he had seen, and then declaimed some *Lear*. He rather talked us into the ground. He made some remark to Katinka about talking a lot of bullshit, which she didn't contradict.' De Vries felt sympathetic and friendly towards this strange man coming in out of the night (later he wrote a novel, *Reuben, Reuben*, with Thomas as the poet). But the Thomas legend was not constructed out of such ordinary occasions. The next evening was more satisfactory from this point of view. Brinnin took Thomas to visit other friends in the neighbourhood, Stanley Edgar Hyman, who was a critic, and his wife, Shirley Jackson, who wrote novels. Brinnin's account is in low key: 'We stayed too late and drank too much and the evening ended gracelessly, with some of us out in the snow, and some of us silent before a dead television set.' Brendan Gill of the *New*

*Yorker* improved upon this. According to Gill, writing in 1975, a drunken Thomas asked a drunken Shirley Jackson if she would sleep with him, while a drunken Stanley Edgar Hyman was watching television. 'Hearing no negative in response to his question, Thomas made a pass at Shirley, who leapt to her feet and lumbered past Stanley, with Thomas in close pursuit. She mounted the front stairs, ran along the hall, stumbled down the back stairs, and again lumbered past Stanley. Shirley and Thomas made the circuit three or four times before Stanley, irritated at having his view of the ball game repeatedly interrupted by the gross beasts jogging past him, reached out and grabbed Thomas by the belt of his trousers, causing him to fall to the floor, while the winded Shirley mounted the stairs for the last time.'

Gill heard the account from Hyman, who is now dead, soon after the event; Shirley Jackson is also dead. Brinnin says it is inaccurate, but in conversation adds further details that did not appear in his own book. In this unexpurgated version, Thomas and Shirley Jackson went outside, after dark, and were 'fooling about' in the snow. There was no pursuit. Brinnin, too, went outside, because he wanted to be sick; he had drunk too much. He heard 'squeals of girlish laughter, his or hers, and then I came back into the house'. The other two were outside for only a short while. On the way home, Thomas confided to Brinnin that the cold night air had been too much for desire.

The next few weeks produced the definitive version of the legend as Thomas plunged into his reading-tour. His first stop after Westport was Yale University, along the coast at New Haven. He read there on the afternoon of 28 February and was entertained to dinner at Mory's, Yale's private dining-club. His host was Norman Holmes Pearson, a critic and scholar, who invited half a dozen colleagues, all professors. As recalled by Brinnin, who was at the dinner, the professors formed 'a brooding druidic circle apparently awaiting an oracle'. After an uncomfortable meal, Thomas 'moved to break the spell', and told dirty stories, which quickly broke up the party. Norman Pearson says that on the contrary, they were not old men who took offence (most of them were in their forties) but hosts who were trying to cope with a difficult guest. According to Pearson, it was Thomas who set the tone with his own uneasiness. 'When I met Dylan before the dinner,' he says, 'I thought he was extraordinarily tense. Then, and again during the dinner, he spent a good deal of time explaining how he could have gone to university, to Cambridge. There was a feeling – this may have been snobbishness on our part – that he was not at ease because he wasn't a university man.' He talked obscenely about the royal family. 'He became very truculent,' says Pearson. 'I can believe it became as unhappy for him as for the group.'

From New Haven and Yale he moved east to Boston and Harvard, where he gave a public reading on 1 March and recorded poems for the university's Lamont Library on the morning of 2 March. Then he was to leave for Mount Holyoke, the oldest women's college in the U.S.A., a hundred miles away at South Hadley, in the middle of Massachusetts. Brinnin had written it all down in a diary for him: 'Someone will drive you to South Hadley – you should leave Cambridge no later than noon. Your contact at Mt Holyoke is Anna J. Mill – they are planning a dinner for you before the reading which is at eight o'clock. You will stay at Mt Holyoke overnight.' Brinnin had been left behind at Westport. At Boston, Thomas was in the charge of Brinnin's friends, one of whom, Gray Burr, was to take him to South Hadley. A telegram saying they had left Boston was sent at three thirty in the afternoon. But Thomas insisted on stopping at bars and playing with pinball machines. By the time they arrived at Mt Holyoke, dinner had come and gone, and the audience was restless.

He walked unsteadily from the car, shivering and smelling of beer, asking for a lavatory. One of his hosts, Joseph McG. Bottkol of the English Department, hurriedly took him down to a men's room and filled a basin with hot water. His hands were numb and blue. When he was ready, he was taken to the hall. The reception committee was bracing itself for disaster. His speech was slurred. A teacher from a neighbouring college, Ben Reid, whose wife was at Holyoke, expected 'a painful kind of farce'. The audience waited expectantly. Thomas reached the platform and clutched the lectern. There was an absurd moment when he tried to fill a glass with water from a pitcher that someone had forgotten to fill. Thomas held it up to the light, puzzled. As he stood swaying at the lectern, a few of the girls giggled. Thomas held up his hand. 'That's right,' he said. 'Laugh at an old ham.'

After this unpromising introduction he read, as everyone agreed, 'like an angel'. Bottkol says that 'I hadn't heard anything like it before or since, and I've heard in person almost every major poet of this century except Yeats. We had a whole procession of poets at Holyoke over the years, British and American, and there's been no one like him.' Reid says that 'it seemed a sort of miracle that it could come out of a man in his condition'. On such occasions Thomas may have pretended to be drunker than he was. But there is no doubt that for many of his readings he was far from sober. In some of the recordings, his opening remarks give him away. One was made at the University of California at Los Angeles, later in the tour. Thomas begins: 'Oh, blimey (*thump*). That's the sort of thing that happens to me straigh' away. (*Laughter and pause; he seems to have knocked his water bottle over.*) Is this microphone working? It's always one of my dreads that I talk into a microphone that doesn't work. And here I am, mouthing away, and not a bloody soul can hear me (*laughter*). It's one of those Kafka dreams that occurs to everybody. You can hear? Or shall I shout? You can't hear? I KNEW. I knew it would happen, it was bound to happen one day ...' The voice is thick-tongued. But once he is reading the poetry, he seems to take hold of himself, or the poems take hold of him, and his voice thumps away with customary precision. Drink may even have improved his performance. One of his audience at Mt Holyoke, Marianne Brock, another member of the English Department, says she heard him read three years later at a neighbouring college, when he appeared sober, and his performance was not as impressive.

It was late in the evening when he was helped off the platform at Mt Holyoke. According to Brinnin, there followed a reception – it was the only incident he described at the college – where Thomas was inflamed by the bare flesh of young women. The legend-making machine seems to have been at work again.

The general outline of an outrageous Thomas, whose behaviour was promptly reported by letter and telephone to other colleges, is accurate enough. But Brinnin, who was himself anxious to discount the more extravagant portraits of Thomas as a perpetually drunken lecher, here seems to be adding his own mite to the legend. Brinnin described the reception as 'one of those occasions at which a whole harem of college girls in blue jeans and Bermuda shorts sprawl on the floor about the feet of the visiting celebrity. Within this budding grove, Dylan was bewildered, shocked by the proximity of so much bare flesh carelessly displayed, and incautious in some of his remarks. The elder ladies of the faculty, distressed and fidgety, hurried in the name of decency to bring the evening to a respectable conclusion. As I later learned, they lost no time in sending out warning signals . . .'

Soon after Brinnin's book appeared, in 1956, the Holyoke story was challenged in a University of Vermont magazine. An article quoted 'the wife of a faculty member here' who was a student at Mt Holyoke in 1950, and in the audience for Thomas's visit – 'she says that one was required to wear a skirt for dinner and for any after-dinner engagement, that "Bermuda shorts" were not yet in existence, and that when Thomas appeared – an hour and a half late – very few women (as against "a harem") were there, and those that were were soberly dressed. Whose imagination conjured up that "proximity of so much bare flesh carelessly displayed", and who was it that was "bewildered, shocked" by the fantasy?' Brinnin says now that 'I simply put that story together from what Dylan and Gray Burr told me'. Burr's recollections are hazy. Survivors of the occasion who are still at Mt Holyoke say there was no 'bare flesh'. It sounds like one of Thomas's stories that Brinnin took too literally. Bottkol remembers no reception at which students were present. Thomas went straight to a party; it was there, and mainly with older women, that he was 'outrageous, but not offensive'. Bottkol kept a diary. He wrote in it, 'Dylan Thomas here to read. Hour and a half late. Tight as an owl and the most powerful reader I've ever heard. A ludicrous party afterwards – the poet using very plain language, and making drunken love to all the lady professors of whatever age.' After the party, says Bottkol, 'I came home and did something I've never done before or since: I sat down and laughed for twenty minutes.' Marianne Brock remembers Thomas at the party 'doing a kind of total recall of female attributes. There was myself and a couple of even more dried-out old maids there, and he began on these physical attributes, starting at the feet and working systematically up to your head. We were just enchanted – it was such a delicious scene. There was no feeling that he was out of hand. But we were getting a little worried because he had a guest room in one of the student halls, and we wondered if it was wise to send him off in case he got loose among the students. But there was no problem. He fell flat on his face over the coffee table and passed out till morning.' Bottkol says he sang 'obscene little ditties', and made a remark about wanting to put his hands in a warm bosom. He also attempted to pinch a few of the ladies. That seems to have been the far edge of his lechery. After he crashed into the table, he was taken off to his lodgings and passed an uneventful night.

In the morning he was back at Bottkol's house by ten o'clock, accompanied by Peter Viereck, a poet and historian on the staff of the neighbouring Amherst College, where Thomas had his next engagement. He asked for a beer. 'He was sweet – even a little pathetic,' says Bottkol. 'He hadn't the vaguest idea where he was geographically. He might have been in New Orleans for all he knew.' There was still snow on the ground. The small town of Holyoke – red brick, white wood, trees waiting for the spring – was as quiet as a village in West Wales, but prettier. Soon Thomas was on his way to Amherst, fifteen miles away. The college here was for men only, and exclusive. Thomas was drunk when he arrived at his hotel during the afternoon, and insisted he must have a beer. The hotel bar wasn't open, so one of his hosts, Armour Craig, took him to a drug store. 'The High School kids started to come in after school, and he began to make observations about bosoms and so on in a fairly loud voice. I was scared – I thought someone would call the cops. I finally got him back to the inn and he promised he would have a nap.' His hosts had arranged an early dinner. 'He had obviously found the bar at the hotel,' says Craig. 'What was disconcerting over dinner was that his conversation wasn't sequential. He would be closed in on himself, nodding. Then he'd emerge and say something irrelevant.'

Before the reading, when Thomas was backstage, he 'suddenly sunk his head in his hands and said, "I can't go on. I miss my wife, I miss my children. I'm sure they're all dead." It was a very startling moment of hysteria.' A minute later he let himself be persuaded to walk on to the platform, where he read with customary vigour. At the party afterwards he went through his usual verbal performance with the women, and some time after midnight was persuaded to recite 'The force that through the green fuse'. He delivered it with his eyes tight shut. 'He was very drunk,' says Craig. 'It was as if he was squeezing it out of himself.'

From Amherst, Thomas returned to New York for the weekend of 4 and 5 March. Over the following weeks Brinnin had arranged engagements in Philadelphia, New York City and State, Washington D.C. and the Mid-West, followed by a long tour across the country. It is likely that Thomas found the readings less onerous than the threat of academic interrogation afterwards. American literary audiences have a tradition of making demands on their speakers. In 1950, British writing was more highly regarded in the U.S.A. than was the case twenty-five years later. A British poet could expect to be taken seriously by professionals who regarded literature as something too serious for clowning. This was not helpful to Thomas's way of doing things. Many poets are reluctant to 'explain' what their poems mean. Thomas was reluctant to talk about poetry at all. Caitlin wrote of his dislike, 'amounting to superstitious horror, of philosophy, psychology, analysis, criticism; all those vaguely termed ponderous tomes; but most of all, of the gentle art of discussing poetry'. In America his first line of defence was to say as little as possible about his own poems when he introduced them. Mt Holyoke was promised (in a last-minute cable from Brinnin) 'his own poems and selections from other British poets with commentary', but the commentary didn't materialize.

His introductory remarks, as he developed them during his

visits, were sprinkled with mild jokes and scraps of autobiography. The manner was self-deprecating. 'I am,' he would say, 'the pig that roots for unconsidered troofles in the reeky wood of his past.' His poems were 'little lyrical cripples', and he had forgotten the original impulse that produced his early work. Such material saw service in many versions, not only for lectures in Britain and America, but for B.B.C. talks. The style was becoming a parody. 'My early days!' he would tell an American audience –

> I've written so much, and talked so much, on the wireless-air and into thin air, of my dull but cramful childhood and my youth in the turbulent doldrums, that they have become to me like the childhood and youth of somebody quite else. What engulfing of young bolsters by tears in love, what salt, raw baying to the sliced dockside moon, to the inhabited stars and the whole wing-gonging Welsh sing-songing world, have I ephemerally commemorated in plush tattles and patches of near-verse prose and prose nearly verse but worse. Who, in the parks and summers, the gutters and seas, of my dead dogdays strutted and foamed and was always a wet wild and gaudily wordy whelp? Not me, O Lord. It was some other, whose hiccupping heartbeats, even, I have forgotten . . .

Thomas's reading often contained fewer of his own poems than audiences would have liked. This, too, may have been defensive. The most-read were probably 'Fern Hill', 'A Refusal to Mourn', 'This Side of the Truth', 'And death shall have no dominion', 'In My Craft' and 'Poem in October'. Those who knew the poems well or carried a text with them noted many small variants. Apart from his own work, Thomas's basic repertoire consisted of poems by modern British writers from Hardy on.[6] He made his own anthology in longhand, he told Margaret Taylor, and 'never read the same selection at more than one place . . . I used to have all the poems on my lectern, & select from them, as I went on, according to the "feel" of the

6. Thomas's list of poets, as given to Margaret Taylor, was: Hardy, Binyon, Edward Thomas, W. H. Davies, Wilfred Owen, Edwin Muir, Robert Graves, Andrew Young, T. S. Eliot, Auden, David Gascoyne, George Barker, Alun Lewis, W. R. Rodgers, Vernon Watkins, Yeats, de la Mare, Louis MacNeice, Edith Sitwell, Alex Comfort, D. H. Lawrence, John Betjeman and James Stephens.

audience'. What comments he made were usually brief and descriptive. Introducing some Hardy – whose poems, perhaps, pleased him most to read aloud – he said:

Modern readers of poetry are often put off Thomas Hardy I think by the sheer bulk of his collected works. And the small print, too. I like all his poems. I'm completely unselective about him. I think the worst thing that's going to happen to Hardy is when someone selects his work enthusiastically. I think the best thing is to read the whole damned lot. All of them. The crabbed, gnarled – I'm reading from something I've written down – the crabbed, gnarled, knotty poems, in which he seems to use language as an arthritic wrestler might grapple with a recalcitrant tree . . .

Thomas's voice, conversational when he was speaking off the cuff, acquired its boom as soon as he began to read from his notes. He was a good impromptu speaker in front of a large audience, and as he gained confidence he seems to have found the knack, as he told Mrs Taylor, of gauging its mood. Reading at the Poetry Centre on a later visit, he provoked (as far as one can judge from the tape) only hilarity when he introduced William Plomer's poem 'The Flying Bum' – 'I should explain,' he said, 'that "bum" to an Englishman does not mean what it means to an American. "Bum" means "fanny", and "fanny" does not mean to an American what it means to an Englishman (*laughter*), though geographically it's quite close' (*renewed laughter*). As Thomas gleefully told his audiences on occasion, 'I am no grey and tepid don, smelling of water-biscuits.' But having established himself during a reading as a rumbustious plain-man's poet, he had to escape before he was cross-examined on his rôle. 'You won't ask me any questions afterwards, will you?' he would say. 'I don't mind answering a bit, only I can't.' Then he would poke fun at earnest questions that probably existed only in his head: 'Are the young English intellectuals *really* psychological?' or 'Is it absolutely essential to be homosexual to write love poems to women?'

In a letter to Mrs Taylor, written during the summer, he said he had always tried to talk to students after a reading, either in their common-room or at a party, and to answer their questions informally. This may have been wishful thinking; at the time of the letter he badly wanted an academic sinecure in the U.S.A. He rarely traded serious questions and answers with students. Now and then a student newspaper sent a reporter to interview him. At Bryn Mawr, the women's college in Pennsylvania, the *College News* for 15 March printed an interview headed 'Subjective Welshman Wants to Write of Happiness'. Thomas had been there the previous week, his first engagement since Amherst. The girl reporter found it difficult to talk to him – 'unhappily and uncomfortably seated at the other end of the couch . . . His hair was dark and lustrelessly curly; his mouth small, full and deeply coloured, like a little crumpled plum . . . I had been told that he was not well; his eyes, with their hidden appeal for me to be brief, showed the effort he was making to suppress his discomfort.' She thought him kind but sad. Her first question was whether he considered a university education important to a poet. He replied, 'I wouldn't know. I never had one myself.' Should a young poet consciously imitate 'the proven great'? Thomas said he had read enormously when he was young. Was a fixed code of beliefs necessary? One's beliefs should be fluid, not dogmatic. Did he write for the eye or the ear? For the ear, said Thomas. The reporter asked him what he had been doing before he came to America. 'Well,' said Thomas, 'for the last six months I've done absolutely nothing. All I did was sit and look at the sea all day – observe it – see if it was still there.' (This response, suitably embellished, became a stock-in-trade. Two years later he was telling a representative of the Dartmouth College magazine, 'I just sit on my bottom by my house in Wales and unscientifically birdwatch, that is, I let the birds watch me. My house is right by the sea. In fact we can spit from my window into the sea, which we often do.') The last question at Bryn Mawr was about Thomas's 'future poetic plans'. He replied, 'I want to write poems of happiness. Not just poems about the little happinesses one experiences in everyday life with other human beings, but the general state of universal happiness which people could attain – if they weren't so barmy, and insane, and stupid.' Alongside the report, a bulb-nosed Thomas stares blankly at the college camera, his bow tie askew like a propeller beginning to turn.

Thomas was now earning steadily. The fees varied. Bryn Mawr paid him a hundred and fifty dollars, which seems to have been about the average for a reading. His outgoings were for rail and plane tickets, and an hotel room whenever he was in New York City. Elsewhere he was fed and accommodated by his hosts. But Brinnin soon noted that once Thomas touched money, it melted away. Whatever the reason for his lifelong flight from solvency, he was now able to indulge it on a bigger scale. Small amounts went to Caitlin. His letters record fifteen pounds on 5 April, another fifteen pounds on 7 April, and fifty dollars on 18 April. Larger amounts turned into rounds of drinks that went down other people's throats; although most of the heavy spending was probably nearer the end of the visit, when he spent several weeks in New York.

Thomas's major cross-country tour began on 14 March, when he flew to Ithaca, in New York State, for a reading at Cornell University. He was to be away from New York City for five weeks. Brinnin saw him off with tickets and instructions. At Ithaca he was met at the airport by David Daiches, who was then teaching at Cornell. Daiches found him asleep on the plane; there had been parties in New York, and Thomas said his hotel room was too hot to sleep in. He carried a jar of insomnia tablets; a doctor had prescribed them, and he had been taking them for his hangover. Daiches put him to bed for an hour or two, then took him for a bracing walk around the campus. It was a cold, sparkling day. They paused on a bridge across a gorge, discussing the merits of retiring to one's native village to write. At one point, recalls Daiches, 'he talked with utter conviction of the fact that he was finished as a poet. I can't swear he said he would die young – that may be hindsight. But he certainly talked about running out of steam.' This contrasts uneasily with his remark to the Bryn Mawr reporter a week earlier about 'poems of happiness'. As they walked through the university grounds, they passed a drinking fountain. Thomas crammed some pills into his mouth and swallowed them. 'I was starting to feel queasy,' he explained. Daiches was so alarmed that he wrote to Brinnin the next day, to say that at this rate,

Thomas was going to kill himself. He expected the worst at the poetry reading. Thomas slept through the dinner party that Daiches had arranged to precede the performance, and arrived at the hall with the usual unsteadiness and look of disarray. In an attempt to prepare the audience for disaster, Daiches gave an apologetic introduction – 'I thought I was being rather adroit. I said Britain was still suffering from post-war austerity, and that in a hospitable place like America, it was possible to kill a man with kindness. And then he made an absolute fool of me by giving a marvellous performance.'

At the Daiches' house afterwards, Thomas was amusing and well behaved. Mrs Daiches had been unable to go to the reading, so he offered to recite her favourite poem; she chose 'Poem in October'. 'There was no coyness or false modesty,' says Daiches. 'He was very quiet and gentle. The only thing that upset him was being asked for explications of his poems.'

The party ended well before midnight. Brinnin had written in the diary: 'Someone *must* drive you from Ithaca to Syracuse in time to get the twelve-thirty a.m. train to Galion, Ohio.' Daiches put him aboard and saw him safely in his sleeping berth. Thomas had forgotten the name of the man who was to meet him at Galion, three hundred miles to the south-west, and he had only a vague idea of where he was going to spend the next five weeks. 'Westward into the night,' he said. 'I feel frightened. I don't think I shall ever come back.' But Daiches suspected that he was only scaring himself with melodramas of the West.

From Kenyon College, where he had his Ohio appointment, he wrote to Caitlin that 'I never seem to sleep in a bed any more, only on planes & trains. I'm hardly living; I'm just a voice on wheels. And the damnedest thing is that quite likely I may arrive home with hardly any money at all, both the United States *and* Great Britain taxing my earnings – my earnings for us, Colum, Aeron, Llewelyn, for our house that makes me cry to think of, for the water, the heron, old sad empty Brown's . . .' He was unhappy about Caitlin, perhaps sensing her disapproval across four thousand miles. The next day he wrote to her from the Quadrangle Club, Chicago, longing to be home:

This is not, as it seems from the address above, a dive, joint, saloon, etc, but the honourable & dignified headquarters of the dons of the University of Chicago. I love you. That is all I know. But all I know, too, is that I am writing into space: the kind of dreadful, unknown space I am just going to enter. I am going to Iowa, Illinois, Idaho, Indindiana, but these, though mis-spelt, *are* on the map. You are not. Have you forgotten me? I am the man you used to say you loved . . .

The itinerary was not quite as exhausting as Thomas implied. After his reading at the University of Chicago on 16 March, he was at Notre Dame University, in Indiana, on 17 March; at the University of Illinois, Urbana, on 20 March, a Monday; and at the State University of Iowa, Iowa City, on 21 March. In all, this made seventeen performances in twenty-nine days. But he now had thirteen clear days without an engagement. He spent them at Iowa City, where his host, Ray B. West Jr, who was on the university staff, was at first disconcerted to find his house-guest would be there so long. Brinnin had written to suggest that West might find a local dentist who would make some emergency repairs. His teeth worried Thomas, probably because they damaged his appearance. Neither the Iowa dental college nor West's own dentist was willing to do anything in the time available. Thomas spent most of his days with West and his friends, in houses or bars, drinking beer, telling tall stories and doing little that was outrageous or even unusual. West's long account of the visit (published in the *San Francisco Fault* in 1972) is the best single report of Thomas as a normal human being in America. He began with the usual successful reading, having already told West that he disliked the atmosphere of universities and couldn't stand the 'bloody nitpicking' of academics. He excluded his hosts, among them the poet Robert Lowell, from this category. After the reading they took him to meet students at the local Writers' Workshop, where a girl asked him how she could earn a living if she wanted to write poetry. Thomas gave one of his ready-made answers, 'Go on the street,' and soon there were shrieks of laughter from his corner of the room. Nothing seems to have happened beyond lewd remarks. That night, when Mrs West, a plump blonde, asked Thomas if there was anything else he wanted before he retired to bed, he said, 'Yes, a nice plump blonde.' This, too, was a mechanical joke. One of his first questions to Howard Moss, the writer who became a friend in New York, was, 'Do you know a short blonde girl?'

At a later session in the Writers' Workshop building, Thomas took over one of Robert Lowell's classes, and read more verse. West (like Roy Campbell at the B.B.C.) noted that 'he was not uniformly good with all poems. He read them all the same, round-bodied, fluent, intense.' Among his choices was John Crowe Ransom's *Captain Carpenter*, a 'satiric ballad, written in mock-heroic style, so there is a temptation to give it a full, straightforward reading. I had heard Ransom read the poem, and he had stressed the irony by giving it a quiet, dry reading.' When they returned home, West played a recording of Ransom reading the ballad. Thomas listened for a few stanzas, then exclaimed, 'Sweet Jesus! The man doesn't know how to read his own poem.' This weakness of Thomas's for the full-blooded reading, no matter what the content, may have been why apparently he disliked to hear his poems read by women. Once, in a letter to a radio producer, who had asked for suggestions about readers, he replied, 'Emphatically no woman. I can't, offhand, think of one poem of mine that needs a woman's voice; any poem, indeed, that wouldn't positively be better off for not having a woman's voice.' Perhaps, too – knowing Thomas's old-fashioned views on the place of women – he felt they were unsuitable for the serious business of reading his poems.

His health, observed in Iowa in detail by West, appears unsatisfactory, though perhaps caused by nothing worse than a general reluctance to look after himself. He coughed and retched every morning, and claimed to be taking tablets prescribed for the morning-sickness of his previous host's pregnant wife. (In Oxford a year or two earlier, Dan Davin heard the pre-breakfast coughing – he said it was like a child drawing attention to its health.) Stronger American drinks must have had some effect. Hospitable measures of spirits were larger than in Britain. Thomas was an unfastidious drinker. Big chilled gins and vermouth, so cold that the strength wasn't at first apparent, were gulped down between anecdotes. In Chicago there was trouble with drink, and the word had been passed on to offer him only beer. West reports Lowell as saying that Thomas should be allowed to drink what he liked and liven up Iowa City. But for most of the visit he seems to have been happy with beer. On the two occasions he drank hard liquor, there was some mild trouble. The first time, West left him at a bar called Joe's Place in the morning. Thomas disappeared for the rest of the day, missed a dinner engagement, and arrived late in the evening, very drunk. He said a woman had taken him home and read him her bad poetry for hours while she kept refilling his glass with Scotch. The second time was a party where the hostess refused to serve only beer. Thomas, drinking martinis, fell into conversation with a doctor's wife, who tried to tell him what was wrong with the National Health Service in Britain. He called her a so-and-so bitch.

Nothing worse seems to have happened. Thomas's thirteen days in Iowa City provide little for the legend. West noticed that Thomas didn't use foul language in front of women, and was careful what he said when children were in the room. He told West's children about his own sons and daughter. 'To me,' wrote West, 'he told a different story.' He loved his daughter, he said, but his new-born son he 'detested', because he was jealous of him. Thomas's anecdotes were in his accustomed style. He said Caitlin was a ballet dancer, described a snowball fight with Russian generals in Austria (perhaps some fantasy that he spun out of his week in Czechoslovakia) and recalled how his first landlady in London gave him eggs for breakfast, which he dropped uneaten into a drawer until it was full, when he left. West was even taken to Swansea sands for 'the poignant story of an early sexual experience with a younger girl and a boy-friend of Dylan's, set on the seashore'.

The visit ended with Thomas being driven to the airport for the plane to San Francisco. He wore the faded brown tweed suit with baggy trousers that he had arrived in, and carried a blue duffle bag. West said it reminded him of the last scene of a Charlie Chaplin film.

Thomas was on the West Coast for rather less than three weeks from 4 April, and in that time gave seven readings; he also went briefly to Canada. After his first performance, at the University of California at Berkeley, he wrote to Caitlin that San Francisco was 'the best city on earth', and that he wanted to return the following spring, with her and Colm, 'when I will become, for six months, a professor in the English department of the University'. Two days later, on Good Friday, he was writing to her again from Vancouver, 'a quite handsome hell-hole', which was 'more British than Cheltenham'.

Caitlin. Just to write down your name like that. Caitlin. I don't have to say My dear, My darling, my sweetheart though I do say these words, to you in myself, all day and night. Caitlin. And all the words are in that one word, Caitlin, Caitlin, and I can see your blue eyes and your golden hair and your slow smile and your faraway voice. Your faraway voice is saying, now, at my ear, the words you said in your last letter, and thank you, dear, for the love you said and sent. I love you. Never forget that, for one single moment of the long, slow, sad Laugharne day. Never forget it in your mazed trances . . . I love you. Over this continent I take your love inside me, your love goes with me up in the aeroplaned air, into all the hotel bedrooms where momentarily I open my bag – half full, as ever, of dirty shirts – and lay down my head & do not sleep until dawn because I can hear your heart beat inside me, your voice saying my name and our love above the noise of the night-traffic, above the neon flashing, deep in my loneliness, my love . . . This afternoon I pick up my bag of soiled clothes and take a plane to Seattle. And thank God to be out of British Canada & back in the terrible United States of America. I read poems to the University there tonight. And then I have one day's rest in Seattle, & then on Sunday I fly to Montana, where the cowboys are, thousands of them, tell Ebi, and then on Monday I fly – it takes about eight hours – to Los Angeles & Hollywood: the nightmare zenith of my mad, lonely tour.

But oh, San Francisco! It is and has everything. Here in Canada, five hours away by plane, you wouldn't think that such a place as San Francisco could exist. The wonderful sunlight there, the hills, the great bridges, the Pacific at your shoes. Beautiful Chinatown. Every race in the world. The sardine fleets sailing out. The little cable-cars whizzing down the city hills. The lobsters, clams, & crabs. Oh, Cat, what food for you. Every kind of seafood there is. And all the people are open and friendly. And next year we both come to live there, you & me & Colum & maybe Aeron. This is sure. I am offered a job in two universities. When I return to San Francisco next week, after Los Angeles, for another two readings, I shall know definitely which of the jobs to take. The pay will be enough to keep us comfortably, though no more. Everyone connected with the universities is hard-up. But that doesn't matter. Seafood is cheap. Chinese food is cheaper, & lovely. Californian wine is good. The iced bock beer is good. What more? And the city is built on hills; it dances in the sun for nine months of the year; & the Pacific Ocean never runs dry . . .

You asked me about the shops. I only know that the shops in the big cities, in New York, Chicago, San Francisco, are full of everything you have ever heard of and also full of everything one has never heard of or seen. The foodshops knock you down. All the women are smart, as in magazines – I mean, the women in the main streets; behind, lie the eternal poor, beaten, robbed, humiliated, spat upon, done to death – and slick and groomed. But they are not as beautiful as you. And when you & me are in San Francisco, you will be smarter & slicker than them, and the sea & sun will make you jump over the roofs & the trees, & you will never be tired again. Oh, my lovely dear, how I love you . . .

When Thomas reached Hollywood a week or so later, he met some celebrities. Even now the air of near-innocence was there to endear him to people. Ivan Moffat, his wartime colleague at Strand Films, lived in Hollywood. Thomas told him he would like to meet a movie star. Moffat and Christopher Isherwood, another of Thomas's hosts there, introduced him to Shelley Winters at a restaurant. Moffat says he pointed at her breasts and said, 'Are they really real?' She told him he could touch if he didn't believe, and 'very tentatively, with the index finger, he touched – hardly touched. It seemed to him substantiation enough'.[7] He was invited to meet Chaplin. Isherwood took him up to the marble house in the hills where Chaplin lived. 'They were roughly the same size,' says Moffat, 'and both possessed this extremely fluid, rag-doll-like, quick emotion, striding about

7. Brinnin was told by Thomas that Miss Winters rebuffed him 'in language which was as direct as a stevedore's'. Moffat says this is not so, and that she 'liked him very much'.

the enormous drawing-room together, talking and chattering.' When Thomas said that no one in Laugharne would believe him, Chaplin sent a cable to Caitlin. But the evening ended badly, with Thomas drunk and making a fool of himself. Moffat, comparing Thomas's drinking then and in London, thought that 'in California he drank much more and it affected him in even greater proportion than before, if that is an indice of alcoholism. There was a rougher, more insensitive side to his behaviour, a disregard of other people's feelings.' He had let himself go in some way.

In San Francisco he stayed at the house of Ruth Witt-Diamant, who ran the Poetry Centre at San Francisco State College, and made a number of friends. Writing to Mrs Witt-Diamant from Laugharne a year and a half later, he said he often thought of them all,

> and, of course, of you who made my ranting holiday ridiculously happy, who showed me the exhibitionist flood-lit seals and the pansied Pacific baths and the starry city and Miller's mountain, and gave me polar beer and artichokes, and laughed with me and at me till I felt more at home than at home where it's only at [*sic*], and made me want more than anything to lurch back to the beautiful West where men are sometimes men and the bars are always exultantly open and the wind and sea and people are right and raffish and tins of fruit juice breed in the ice box . . .

He did return to San Francisco, in 1952, and took Caitlin with him. But it was not for long, and the teaching jobs in California failed to materialize. He might have been given the appointment at the University of California at Berkeley if his drinker's reputation had not stood in the way. His behaviour on campuses, though, seems to have been no worse on the West coast than it was on the East. He lost his books and notes before a reading at Pomona College, Claremont, and he kept muttering 'My God, I can't do this' as he was escorted to the stage. There was confusion over dates. At Berkeley he read without incident; but he failed to appear at a party in his honour organized by the English Department. Either then or soon after, the Department of Speech at Berkeley was considering whether to offer him an appointment to teach courses in the 'oral interpretation of literature'. A departmental committee decided without dissent that Thomas should be invited. But the Dean of the College of Letters and Science ('A conservative gentleman of the old school', according to a member of the committee) overruled the decision, on the grounds that Thomas's drinking made him unstable and a danger to students.

By 24 April he was back in New York. He was based there for the remaining five weeks of his stay, although one of the weeks was spent in a gruelling circuit that took him to New England, Michigan and Indiana. Among his short trips from New York was one to Vassar, the women's college at Poughkeepsie, where he read on the evening of 9 May. The nervous lady from the English Department who introduced him said that Mr Thomas was playing third fiddle to Eliot and Auden, both of whom they had failed to attract to Vassar. Thomas was visibly upset at this. A radiator wheezed throughout. The audience was disappointed that he had so little to say about his poems. A few days later an editorial article in the college newspaper deplored the way Thomas had been received, adding: 'It is a pity that we who are taught appreciation of the immortal of literature cannot appreciate greatness when it is in front of us.' After his Vassar reading, Thomas stayed with a staff member at the college, Vernon Venable. He and his hosts sat up half the night, talking and drinking. When he finally retired, Venable sat on the bed while Thomas launched into a drunken account of his unhappiness. According to Venable it went on for hours – 'just misery, misery, which seemed to me so pervasive that it had no source except a psychological source. That is, the man was deeply neurotic.' Venable is unable to remember details, except that part of the monologue was concerned with his love for Caitlin. In effect, says Venable, he was declaring that life was a nightmare and he couldn't stand it. Thomas, with his knack of exposing other people's emotions with his own, had a traumatic effect on Venable – 'I had had literary aspirations up to that point, but I remember thinking when he finally got through talking and I went to bed, if I were asked whether all the poetry in the world is worth that amount of suffering, that if I could press a button I'd extirpate the poetry if I could extirpate the suffering.'

In the morning Venable said goodbye to his guest, then discovered to his annoyance that Thomas had stolen his best white shirt. Friends pointed out that this put him in the select company of hosts who had been honoured to have their shirts stolen by Thomas. But Venable felt he had been cheated, not by the theft itself, but by the fact that it came only a few hours after Thomas had opened his heart. Thomas, just by being Thomas, left these minor disturbances, little quaking spots, in places he visited, where they passed into local memory, like a natural cataclysm that happened years before.

From the middle of May there was little for him to do in the way of work. He sold an essay, 'A Child's Memories of Christmas in Wales', to *Harper's Bazaar* for 300 dollars.[8] He read at the New York Poetry Centre again, this time a prose recital, on 15 May, and gave his last performance of the tour three days later, at Barnard College. It was the end of the month before he left America, in the liner *Queen Elizabeth*. Having decided not to fly more than he had to, he had difficulty (he told Caitlin) in booking a sea passage. A letter to her written on 7 May enlarged on his tiredness and loneliness. 'Pray God you love me still,' he wrote. 'Sometimes I think I shall go mad, & this time properly, thinking of you all day & night as I fly over the continent.' During his last weeks in New York, he spent much of his time in bars and at parties. He said (but not to Caitlin) that it was a 'liquid, libidinous fortnight'. John Gruen was at a party given by Oscar Williams and his wife Gene Derwood, the poet. Williams, who had been placing Thomas's material in America since 1945, seems to have been a kindly, fussy man, sometimes laughed at behind his back. Thomas is said to have tried in vain to avoid his attentions in New York. At the party, wrote Gruen, Thomas slept, then talked about Laugharne. He had his own supply of beer, four quarts. His monologue, 'magical' at first,

8. It was concocted from his 1945 B.B.C. talk, 'Memories of Christmas', and an essay he wrote for *Picture Post* in 1947, 'Conversation about Christmas'.

became 'slurred and finally incomprehensible'. A woman asked him to read from a book of his poems that she had brought with her. He fell on his knees and put his head under her skirt. Eventually he took hold of the book. Miss Derwood, meanwhile, was sitting at an easel, feverishly trying to paint him. Oscar Williams was handing round paper plates laden with a supper of mashed potato. Thomas turned the book upside down and gave a reading of 'loud mooselike bellows and nonsense syllables . . . All the while he was gesturing madly, like a Roman emperor in the throes of an epileptic seizure.' Gruen said it lasted ten minutes, before Thomas collapsed into a chair, mumbling – 'an unreachable, exhausted man on the brink of another long alcoholic sleep'.

During his weeks in New York, Thomas was occupied with one or two sexual affairs. He told Brinnin that in all, he had been involved with three women during the trip. One was a 'boyish poet', unnamed by Brinnin in his book, who is now dead. Another, 'Doris', was heavily disguised in Brinnin's account, but recognized herself. When Brinnin's book appeared she telephoned him and said, 'How could you *conceivably* think I had gone to bed with that man?' Brinnin remains uncertain whether to believe her or Thomas. The third was a journalist, clever and attractive; Brinnin and FitzGibbon call her 'Sarah'. Her real name and telephone number seem to have been the last addition to Thomas's engagements diary, and it's likely that their affair was not under way until late in the trip. He was professionally involved with her in selling an article, and this could have been how they met. Thomas's earlier campus encounters may have been largely talk. He liked to hint at bold deeds. He had been spouting verse, he told Margaret Taylor, to 'thousands of young pieces whose minds, at least, were virgin territory'. But chiefly the talk came from others, who based their anecdotes on Thomas's lewd words and gestures. The 'boyish poet' and 'Doris' may have been his lovers briefly. Only with 'Sarah', on this trip, did he have a serious encounter. They enjoyed a hotly emotional affair, and she visited Britain to meet him in secret later in 1950. Then a woman ran to Caitlin with the story. Before that happened, ending the affair, Thomas told Brinnin (in London, in September 1950) that he was in love with 'Sarah' and in love with his wife, and didn't know what to do. (Brinnin added that this was his first experience of 'seeing Dylan wrestling with a problem rather than seeking out means to circumvent it'.) In May, in New York, when the problem was in the making, Laugharne and his marriage could be kept at arm's length. The agonized tone of the letter to his wife on 7 May may be due to his relationship with 'Sarah' and the consequent emotional muddle. He told Caitlin he thought of her 'waking up alone in our beautiful bedroom ... waiting for me, for nothing, for something ... Wait for me a little longer, my own true love ... I am lonely as the grave ...'

The last entry in the engagements diary is on Thursday, 1 June, scrawled across the page in a shaky hand: 'Sail home.' It was time to go back to wife, children, herons and, hopefully, poems.

CHAPTER ELEVEN

# *No Money, Few Poems*

DYLAN THOMAS's mother once said that her son had told her, 'Wouldn't it be nice, our Mummy, if I didn't have a home to keep, so that I could keep this money and go and do my love poems!' But whenever he came back from America, said Mrs Thomas, he was greeted with bills. This was a mother's version of events. Although Thomas's 1950 visit to America earned more than he (or anyone else) expected when the original plans were made, little of the money found its way back to Laugharne. When, later on, he was assessed for British income tax on his earnings (no U.S. tax seems to have been imposed), he had nothing left to pay it with. His income from the tour was $7,680, or £2,800. He paid tax on a smaller amount than this because substantial business expenses were allowed, but the final demand must have run into hundreds of pounds. Where to turn for this money was to be part of the nightmare of the next few years.

Perhaps a few hundred dollars had been posted to Caitlin while Thomas was in America. The only large sum she received came secretly from Brinnin, who hid eight hundred dollars in a handbag that he sent with Dylan as a present. This was nearly three hundred pounds. But it melted away like the rest. As for money in the bank that would enable Thomas to write in peace, the scheme had fallen to the ground. If this was bad news for Thomas, it must have been bitter news for his wife, who had stayed at home in Laugharne, hoping for the best, only to find the familiar state of crisis resumed.

On 18 June, soon after his return, Thomas wrote to Margaret Taylor about his prospects (as he imagined they were) of a university job in America. He also hoped she could help with the British equivalent of a post as 'poet in residence'. And in the short term he simply needed money:

You wanted to know some of the details of my – sweet words – financial embarrassments, so that your ravens may help. Altho' I left Cat £10 a week – not in one sum, but to be delivered by the Bank – & also sent her several cheques from the States, [she] managed to chalk up, at the chemist's, a bill for £150. Also, I owe Llewelyn's school fees for this term, & Stanier *must* be paid the £50. And I owe Ebi for *many* taxis & for the Pelican. Say another £50. Altogether £250. And I can raise, immediately, only £50 which I cannot send Stanier as we must manage to live here. I am starting to write some U.S.A. articles for *Vogue* etc, but this will take a little time. Oh, ravens, come quick, come quick. Is there any hope? And desperately soon? . . .

The articles for *Vogue* were not written. Nor was a radio script about his visit to America that the B.B.C. wanted. So desperate was Thomas that in August, on one of his trips to London, he called on the Controller of the Third Programme, Harman Grisewood, to ask for full-time employment in broadcasting for a year or two. Grisewood thought he might help with coverage of the Festival of Britain the following year. But after discussions with Laurence Gilliam, they decided there was no job for him. He continued to make occasional broadcasts as actor or reader, leaving Caitlin in Laugharne while he travelled to London for the usual days of drinking.

Caitlin's rôle was changing as time went on. She was hardening into the discontented wife, left behind with the bills while her husband gallivanted. Thomas knew all about her unhappiness, as his letters from America make clear, with their mixture of love and apprehension. In one letter he had thanked her for her 'heartbreaking poem'. In another, he sympathized with her task as daughter-in-law, 'wailed at by old ill Thomases'. But he did nothing about it. Perhaps it was now she began to feel cheated. She must have guessed already that America had not been as he described it. Interviewed on television in 1975, she recalled that in his letters from America, Dylan was 'very careful not to tell me how much he was lionized, and about all the women and all that. He soft-pedalled that to me. He was very cunning. He always used to tell me the little things and not very much about his success. And the money he was going to bring home, and the future plans for lovely desert islands and so forth that we were going to go after. There's a lot of fantasy there.'

Laugharne's air of mouldering eccentricity didn't help. Dylan, being an unusual man, fitted in better than Caitlin, who was only an unusual woman. Women were expected to know their place in Laugharne. The small-town parochialism angered her. Thomas himself could scorn the place when the mood took him. 'This arsehole of the universe,' he wrote to American friends in July 1950, 'this hymnal blob, this pretty, sick, fond sad Wales.' But it was home for Thomas in a sense it could never be for her. 'This moist, smothering, lost boghole,' she wrote after Thomas's death, castigating the 'narrow, sly Welsh', mimicking their anxiety at 'what will the neighbours say?' 'They loved him,' says Margaret Taylor, 'but they never loved her.' To the inhabitants of Laugharne she was faintly preposterous, the handsome interloper, swimming in their sea, having ear-splitting rows with her husband under their noses, dancing and laughing and drinking when she felt like it. She belonged to an aristocratic breed of Celt, and Laugharne was inclined to disapprove. But to the end she recognized that the local rhythms were what suited her husband. Once a week they went into Carmarthen, shopped in the market, and sometimes went to a cinema, where fleas hopped in the dusty upholstery. Mrs Taylor, who bought a cottage in Laugharne, saw their life as having 'almost a Thomas Hardy rhythm'. Thomas nagged his wife to dress 'properly', which meant inconspicuously, for Carmarthen market. 'I mean it,' she wrote, 'right down to gloves, stockings, shoes; and he would have preferred a hat, but knew that was too much, even for him, to ask of me.'

Their rows were a permanent feature of life together. Caitlin told Mrs Taylor that once she didn't speak to him for a month. John Davenport, who observed matters at close range, found the domestic Dylan 'mild and even conventionally henpecked by his wife'. But when they were drunk, they fought and clawed at one another, with Caitlin taking the lead in violence. She said that 'when the drunkenness came upon us – upon me, anyhow – we had terrible physical fights, bangings and pummellings, and I think I was the violent one . . . I don't think Dylan got into many physical fights without me.' They would 'pass out in the bed and wake up in each other's arms. It was usually like that. We were very tender afterwards.' On one occasion neighbours saw her with her face swollen up, black and blue; Dylan, it was rumoured, had kicked her in the eye. 'It seems extraordinary to me now that we did not kill each other outright,' she wrote. Her jealousy over other women, especially American women, was to generate endless passion. It was his 'physical act' with someone else, she said, that she couldn't bear – that, and the loss of their romantic ideal of a faithful marriage. 'I wanted him not to betray me,' she said. 'I wanted him completely faithful to me, like he wanted me completely faithful to him.'

Between them they damaged a relationship that was many things, but always close and, in its own way, honest. 'Neither of us were lecherous bastards by nature,' Caitlin has written, 'we were both exceptionally shy people; it was purely the alcohol that made us like that, that pushed us to be what we were not. It is extraordinary but it is true – I have learnt that since. We went in for all that sex stuff because we thought it was the thing to do, we thought it made us sophisticated and smart. We tried to outsmart each other – need I tell you who won? Neither of us would ever have dared to act the way we did without the booze to egg us on.'

On another occasion, protesting bitterly about his 'weaknesses', she declared that 'I'm a very puritanical person at heart, and he just did every bloody thing he wanted to. He had no curbs on him at all. And then he became a kind of professional charm boy, and I despise that.' To Caitlin, the philandering was weakness; so was the way he let flattery and indolence subvert his poetry. Caitlin may have resented his life as an artist, seeing it as a comment on her failure to be anything more than the poet's wife. She certainly hankered after a life of her own as an artist, writing poetry in secret, still dancing when she could; an increasingly sad figure. She said later that 'I always danced, yes, even drunk! Or only drunk, eventually.' But whatever her private miseries, and public quarrels with her husband, she 'did all I could to make him work, at his own special work, and not public money-making work.'

Gwen Watkins saw them in the summer of 1950, not long after Thomas returned; they went to spend a day with her and Vernon at Pennard, at their house on the cliffs. Dan Jones and Fred Janes were there as well. It was the last visit Thomas made to the Watkinses' house. By this time Dylan and Vernon saw one another infrequently. Vernon's admiration and loyalty were undiminished. But according to Gwen Watkins, 'Dylan had less use for Vernon. You may think this unkind, but after Vernon married, Dylan concluded that he didn't have the money.' Gwen Watkins, never fond of Thomas, liked him even less that day. He boasted of what an uproarious time he had had in America, 'showing off like a small boy'. He claimed to have taken drugs for the first time; no details were given. They sat on the lawn, by the glare of the sea, eating potato crisps, and Caitlin said the only foods he could still taste were vinegar and H.P. sauce. He had drunk too much whisky and his taste buds had perished. They bickered about his taste buds and whether they were dead or just sleeping.

Soon they had something worse to quarrel over, worse even than money and suspicions about America. At the end of August, John Brinnin came to London at the start of a European holiday. A few days later Thomas's New York lover, 'Sarah', arrived. Brinnin found Thomas 'a new man' since New York: 'His clothes were new and well-matched, his shoes glinted with a high shine, his face was serene and ruddy and he was smoking a cigar.' They spent a few days in one another's company, visiting clubs and pubs, eating at Wheeler's restaurant, going to a Marx Brothers film and a revue (Thomas slept and snored on both occasions), until 'Sarah' appeared on 4 September. All three went for an outing on the river to Greenwich – this was the occasion when Thomas told Brinnin that he loved both 'Sarah' and his wife – and then the lovers left London for a brief holiday in Brighton. Thomas seems not to have taken precautions to keep his mistress concealed. Rayner Heppenstall met them in the Stag, a pub much used by Features staff at the B.B.C., on a Saturday morning. She was 'dark, with a fringe, strongly built, not small, a bit . . . arty in her clothes and manner, intelligent and full of suspicion'. In the afternoon Thomas and friend were at a wedding. They were in and out of places in London where Thomas was well known, the Café Royal, the Salisbury. It is not surprising that word got through to Laugharne, via the talkative friend. The details of what happened then are uncertain. After their London encounter, 'Sarah' crossed the Channel and sent letters to Thomas at the Savage Club. Later she told Brinnin that a woman intercepted them, and that Thomas, who by this time was ill with 'pleurisy and then pneumonia', received no word from her. Perhaps Thomas was staging a diplomatic illness. 'Sarah' returned to London but failed to see him. At one point he was staying at an hotel. Meanwhile Caitlin had the news and, apparently, the letters; this may be why Thomas was lying low. It ended the affair and opened up rifts in his marriage. Caitlin was 'mad with rage'. She realized that her husband was infatuated, although apparently he never admitted it to her; no doubt wisely, he poked fun at 'Sarah', calling her 'a stupid bitch' who was 'following me around, making a bloody nuisance'. Thus Thomas's one serious love-affair came to a sorry end. An undated letter to Davenport written from Laugharne, probably near the end of 1950, describes himself 'here in my *horribly* cosy little nest, surrounded by my detestable books, wearing my odious, warm slippers, observing the gay, reptilian play of my abominable brood, basking in the vituperations of my golden, loathing wife'. 'I remember the Thames and old "Sarah",' he wrote to Brinnin months later, carefully levelling the romance. 'I haven't heard from her since she went away.'

Thomas worked on two poems in 1950. He completed 'In the white giant's thigh', presumably after he returned from America, and read it on the Third Programme (along with 'Over Sir John's hill' and 'In country sleep') on 25 September, soon after 'Sarah's visit. He began or continued 'In country heaven', which was intended to be the title poem, or opening sequence, of the group to which the three other poems mentioned above were to belong. In it, God regards his creation with pity and tears. As Thomas described the sequence in the 25 September broadcast, it was to culminate in 'praise of what is and what could be on this lump in the skies. It is a poem about happiness.' But 'In country heaven' was never finished, and the concept (like happiness) remained wishful thinking.

Also in 1950 he seems to have made a serious start on his radio play about Laugharne. This now had the working title of 'The Town [sometimes 'The Village'] that was Mad'. The B.B.C. producer assigned to the project, Douglas Cleverdon, specialized in literary programmes. It was he who had cast Thomas as Satan in *Paradise Lost* and as the soldier who screamed in *In Parenthesis.* He was also in charge of the poetry programme on 25 September. A month later he was writing to say that the Third had 'agreed to take "The Town that was Mad" (or whatever title you prefer)'. But so far they were approving only an idea, not a script. The play was to show a town peopled by free-living eccentrics, who are declared insane by the conformists of the outside world. The citizens (led by their spokesman, Captain Cat) insist that the issue be tried in court. But when they hear the prosecution's description of the sane world, they decide to stay as they are, cordoned off. Thomas quoted sections of it to Watkins and Daniel Jones at a cricket match in Swansea in the summer of 1950. In one scene, where a mad townsman or villager confessed to lusts of the flesh, a massed male choir (representing the jury) was to chant 'Ach-y-fi!' (a Welsh expression of disgust) at each revelation. This dramatic structure was later abandoned because Thomas was unable to sustain it; as in the feature-film scripts, plots were his weakness. But in 1950 he was still trying. A letter from Cleverdon on 5 December urged him to finish 'The Village that was Mad', now that he was 'free from the distractions of this beastly cold metropolis', so that it could be scheduled for broadcasting in the middle of 1951. An undated note from Thomas to Cleverdon, sent from the Savage Club, enclosed the first thirty-nine pages of the manuscript of 'The Town that was Mad', and said he was 'very enthusiastic to finish the thing. And quickly.'

But the script slid down Thomas's list of priorities. Early in 1951 he set off on another trip, this time to Iran. The Anglo-Iranian Oil Company (later British Petroleum) had commissioned him to write a film about the benefits that British oilmen were bringing to a poor country. Paternalism was still abroad; Iranian nationalism was only just emerging. His fee was probably two hundred and fifty pounds, plus expenses. A company called Green Park was to make the film. The producer, Ralph ('Bunny') Keene, was an acquaintance of Thomas. They flew out on 8 January. Presently Thomas was writing to Caitlin from Tehran. His despair was louder than ever, presumably reflecting the 'Sarah' fiasco:

All these strange, lost days I love you, and I am lost indeed without you, my dear wife. This is so much further than America, and letters will take so much longer to travel to you and yours to me if you will ever write to me again, oh *darling* Cat. And if you do not write to me, and if you do not love me any more, I cannot go on, I cannot go on sleeplessly thinking, 'Caitlin my Cattleanchor, my dear, does not love me, O God let me die.' I can't live without you; I can't go travelling with this long, wan Bunny through this fearful, strange world unless I am sure that at the end we will be together as we are meant to be together, close & alone except for our cuckoo whom I miss very very very much, more than I could dream of. But you: I miss you more than I would miss my life although you *are* my life . . .

The letter moved on to financial matters. Green Park was to pay her ten pounds a week for the five weeks he was away ('I know it goes terribly quickly') and a cheque was on its way from Marguerite Caetani, no doubt in response to an S.O.S. Further letters begged for her love. One referred to a letter he had received from her: 'Your letter, as it was meant to, made me want to die. I did not think that, after reading it so many times till I knew every pain by heart, I could go on with these days and nights . . . But the bloody animal always does go on . . .'

Apparently Thomas found time to write at least once to 'Sarah', poking fun at the oilmen and their works. His letters to Caitlin, too, were critical of the 'horrible oilmen', and dwelt on the country's poverty. When he returned in February, either the script was never written or, if it was, the film was never made. He had barely left the country when the Iranians nationalized their oil industry. 'My job was to help pour water on troubled oil,' he wrote to Oscar Williams. In April he provided a few minutes of material for a B.B.C. radio documentary called 'Persian Oil'. This said a good deal about poverty but nothing unkind about the Anglo-Iranian Oil Company.[1] The script, highly evocative, shows how smoothly he could turn out a piece of superior hack-work when he felt like it – 'On the blue, boiled water the dhows sail out of the Bible . . . The vast tribes move, with the heat of the sun, from their winter grounds to the high green places . . . Engineers curse their dehydrated ale in the income-classed clubs. The rich are rich. Oil's oily. The poor are waiting.' In Laugharne, Caitlin awaited him; perhaps not with open arms. She was heard to complain that when she asked him to describe the rose gardens of Persia, all he could talk about were the funny stories he heard from a travelling salesman on the plane coming back. 'A typical Welshman,' she said.

That spring, Thomas activated himself to write a ribald poem, 'Lament', where the poet looks back on his sexual life from his death-bed. It has a chorus-line that Thomas thundered out in his readings – 'Sighed the old ram-rod, dying of women' (and, in succeeding stanzas, of bitches, welcome, downfall and strangers). A draft version is headed 'The Miner's Lament'. Writing to Marguerite Caetani on 20 March, when it was 'nearly finished', he described it as 'coarse and violent'. It is not difficult to detect in it Thomas's current frustrations with life. One critic sees it as an attempt by Thomas to examine in an 'honest and coherent' fashion his 'inner experience' – those fears of castration and impotence that may have been buried like landmines in his earlier poems.

Another, entirely different poem followed. 'Do not go gentle into that good night' was addressed to his father, now in chronic

1. A B.B.C. producer who proposed a more elaborate, Third Programme, script about Iran by Thomas was told by a senior colleague that 'I understand the Anglo-Iranian Oil Company has some kind of hold over what Dylan might say'.

ill-health, chiefly through heart trouble. It was written as a villanelle, rare in English verse, where two rhymes only are used in stanzas of three lines, concluding with a stanza of four lines. Thomas used this strict form to contain an exhortation to his father, a plea for him to die with anger, not humility. He sent it to Marguerite Caetani, for her to use in *Botteghe Oscure*, on 28 May, with a postscript to say that 'the only person I can't show [it] to is, of course, my father, who doesn't know he's dying'. Into it one can read Thomas's concern for the proud man with only 'frail deeds' to offer, whose word is still crucial to his son –

> And you, my father, there on the sad height,
> Curse, bless, me now with your fierce tears, I pray.

As in 'Lament', Thomas was writing plainly on a subject, in this case his father and their complex relationship, that had concerned him deeply all his life. Both these poems were written at a time of domestic unhappiness. There were quarrels with Caitlin; debts were accumulating. Yet he succeeded in writing, quite quickly, two poems that in their different ways were, for him, unusually blunt. Perhaps they were an act of boldness, an attempt, conscious or otherwise, to confront the demons and break out of whatever despair enclosed him. If so, the attempt was at least a partial success. Unfortunately it was not to be repeated.

There are two parallel strands to follow for the rest of 1951: first, what others observed of Thomas, or what he told them in his letters; second, the progress or otherwise of Thomas the Poet, shut away in his work-hut.

Outwardly he was a successful writer and broadcaster with a swashbuckling reputation. To the group of students and staff members at Swansea University College whose guest speaker he was at the end of April, he was the local boy of whom equivocal tales were told; neither was at ease with the other. His hosts were the English Society. It was no great occasion. The meeting was held in the basement table-tennis room of the Students' Union building, an old house near the Uplands. An acquaintance on the university college staff thought how unimpressive he looked as he sat through the chairman's introduction: 'His navy blue suit and jersey, full belly and balding crown made one think of a decayed seaman of the type found in small fishing villages.' Fifty or sixty people were present, not all of them from the college. It was Thomas's first appearance before an audience in his home town since his naughty lecture to the John O'London gathering seventeen years before. He began with one of his well-used openings, 'I can't manage a proper talk. I might just manage an improper one.' His remark explaining why he didn't plan to be formal, that 'I would read a lecture if I hadn't written it in invisible ink on toilet paper which I left out in the sun', was not enthusiastically received. The talk was one of his comic variants on the theme of lecturing in America, and led into the usual poetry-reading. Kingsley Amis, then a young lecturer at the college – it was another three years before his novel *Lucky Jim* appeared – described the evening in a magazine article in 1957. 'Although obviously without all charlatanry,' wrote Amis, 'he did here and there sound or behave like a charlatan.' The evening had begun at the Uplands Hotel with some unpromising exchanges. Thomas, who was drinking but not drunk, announced in his 'clear, slow, slightly haughty, cut-glass Welsh voice' that 'I've just come back from Persia, where I've been pouring water on troubled oil'. Amis, already developing a Lucky-Jim line of dialogue, made 'what was in those days my stock retort to the prepared epigram' by remarking, 'I say, I must go and write that down.' Thomas 'looked round the circle, grinning. "I have," he said.' A local acquaintance, not at the college, seems to have irritated the group by his attentions to Thomas, both before the lecture and after, when a crowd returned to the pub. Geoffrey Nicholson remembered Thomas being goaded with questions designed to make a fool of him. 'It's no good treating me as an Aunt Sally,' he said, 'because you'll get back as good as you give. I'm a fool anyway.' Amis concluded that their guest wasn't to blame for the way the evening petered out. The local acquaintance monopolized him, the students drifted away to the other end of the bar, and he was heard to complain that he had been abandoned. The mistake,

Amis decided, was to have made him an object of awe and suspicion. Given a degree of sympathy, 'I think we should have seen that his attitude was the product of nothing more self-aware or self-regarding than shyness.'

His performance for the English Society earned him a few pounds. There were many such engagements. He earned and spent, or borrowed and spent, like a man in a dream. There is no evidence that his capacity to earn money was destroyed by drink. Nor was his talent for borrowing diminished; on the contrary, he now had a range of patrons, from Margaret Taylor to Princess Caetani and Marged Howard-Stepney, a wealthy Welsh woman whose story will emerge presently. More conventional patrons were still called upon from time to time. On 28 May 1951, he wrote to T. S. Eliot:

> Very many thanks indeed for your letter & your cheque. It was extremely kind of you, and the cheque helped to ease my difficulties here. I was, as you know, very nervous in writing to you at all to ask your help; and especially since your recent reputation for wealth. It was in spite of this that I managed to write my begging letter. I was, anyway, writing to the best poet I know and not to a supposedly monied person. Thank you, again, most sincerely.

On the same day he was writing, 'tremblingly and very much in earnest', to Laurence Gilliam at the B.B.C., concerning a possible programme about the Festival of Britain. It was essential to have 'ADVANCE, IMMEDIATE . . . I owe every tradesman in town . . .' Gilliam reminded him that the rule said: No script, no money. So the feverish dance continued. It was not as though Thomas rose above everyday trivialities, scorning money as trash and pursuing his real work. His real work, as often as not, was to earn money to enable him to do more of the same work. Anxiety peers out of his letters. Caitlin said that debts kept him awake at night. When he was younger, they sometimes had to live on air. But why were his circumstances still so bad, so often? They suggest a helplessness, an eroding of confidence. He let his affairs drift into chaos because it reflected the chaos in himself.

By the spring of 1951, Thomas was already planning another

escape to America. 'I would very much like (I'd adore it) to be imported to the States next year,' he wrote to Brinnin in April, adding that this time he wanted to take Caitlin with him. In July, Brinnin and his friend Bill Read were in Europe, and spent a weekend with the Thomases in Laugharne. Caitlin soon cross-questioned Brinnin about 'Sarah', and was not pleased at his reticence. There was a disastrous outing (in a Williams-driven car) to Pembrokeshire, marked by high emotional tension. According to Billy Williams, Thomas paid for everything, which angered Caitlin still more. At the end of the day she announced, 'America is out!' Next evening she and Dylan had a fight in the dining-room. After he had fled, she harangued the Americans for an hour about her husband's failings, how American flattery went to his head, how foul women pursued him while she was left to rot with three screaming children and no money. If Caitlin was thinking about her own unhappy state, no doubt she thought about her husband's as well. America, she said once, brought out his weaknesses: 'He had no strength of character, no discipline. There was no hardness in him – he was what they call *a piece of bread* in Italy – just lovely and loved by everyone. Well, that's wrong – a man's got to have a bit of ruthlessness in his personality. He lacked that completely, and when he went to America he was just eaten alive.'

No final decision was taken about America that summer. It was among the schemes that revolved hopefully. There was a chance of film scripts from Donald Taylor. He hoped to collaborate with Ted Kavanagh, the comedy scriptwriter who wrote Tommy Handley's 'ITMA', on radio programmes. This fell through. Another scheme, that matured slowly and disagreeably through the year, was to move back to London temporarily. Thomas kept threatening or promising it. 'I'm having to sell up my house as soon as I can & move to London, which I hate,' he wrote to Oscar Williams on 28 May – untruthfully, since the house was not his to sell. Doubtless Caitlin was determined to change the system whereby she was left in Laugharne while her husband, now a certified adulterer, disappeared from sight for days on end. An undated letter to her from London, probably written about this time, talks hopelessly of finding no job (he was meeting Ted Kavanagh again that evening) and having no money. He has fallen downstairs, cutting his head and blacking his eye. A dark yellow rain is falling: London is terrible, and (he adds quickly) he knows that Laugharne, is too. The tone of the letter is sad and placatory.

In the plans for a return to London, Margaret Taylor was a prime mover. She thought that if Thomas could find sufficient bread-and-butter work in London, he would not need to return to America. This hope proved vain. Caitlin withdrew her opposition when she was persuaded, or persuaded herself, to go with her husband on his second grand tour. Nevertheless during the summer Mrs Taylor bought a house in London, in Camden Town. The address was Delancey Street; it was a worn-out district, near railway yards. The Thomases were to occupy a basement flat. But they didn't move there immediately.

Before he leaves for London, there is the matter of Thomas and his poetry that summer and autumn. During this period he wrote or completed a single poem, 'Poem on his birthday'. Thomas took his birthdays seriously; at least two earlier poems, 'Twenty-four years' and 'Poem in October', were similarly inspired. The particular significance of 'Poem on his birthday' is that with it Thomas effectively signed off his career as a poet. Only the verse 'Prologue' to his *Collected Poems* came after, and the unfinished 'Elegy'. Thomas, in 1951, can be seen as making one last attempt to find his way. In terms of output he wrote more verse than at any time since 1945; 'Poem on his birthday' was preceded by 'Lament' and 'Do not go gentle'. But whereas in the first two poems he struck out vigorously, casting a cold eye on man's (and Thomas's, and Thomas's father's) predicament, in the third poem he was waiting for death, passively hoping for the best, counting his blessings on trembling fingers. In July, when he was working on the poem, he told John Brinnin in the work-hut at Laugharne (as he had told others in America) that from now on he was determined to write only 'happy' poems. At about the same time, he gave Bill Read a manuscript summary of what 'Poem on his birthday' was to be about. The poet, it says,

celebrates, and spurns, his thirty-fifth birthday[2] . . . Birds and fishes move under and around him on their dying ways, & he, a craftsman in words, toils towards his own wounds which are waiting in ambush for him . . . Now exactly half of his three score and ten years is gone . . . he looks back at his times: his loves, his hates, all he has seen, and sees the logical progress of death in every thing he has seen & done. His death lurks for him, and for all, in the next lunatic war, and still singing, still praising the radiant earth, still loving, though remotely, the animal creation also gladly pursuing their inevitable & grievous ends, he goes towards his. Why should he praise God, and the beauty of the world as he moves to horrible death? He does not like the deep zero dark and the nearer he gets to it, *the louder he sings, the higher the salmon leaps, the shriller the birds carol.*

The poem as finally written ended on a different note. In the synopsis, Thomas saw himself singing the world's praises in a despairing attempt to hide the approach of death. In the poem he subdued the note of despair, declaring that

. . . the closer I move
To death, one man through his sundered hulks,
The louder the sun blooms
And the tusked, ramshackling sea exults;
And every wave of the way
And gale I tackle, the whole world then,
With more triumphant faith
Than ever was since the world was said,
Spins its morning of praise . . .

This was the message that Thomas would have liked to present. But in the context of his life and work in 1951 and thereafter, it has an air of forced optimism.

Many worksheets of 'Poem on his birthday' survive: Thomas had realized by now that such material was valuable to collec-

2. In the summer of 1951, Thomas was approaching his thirty-seventh birthday. His thirty-fifth birthday was in 1949. There is evidence that the poem was substantially written in 1951, though it may have been conceived and worked on earlier.

tors, and he was careful to keep the scribbled-on pages.[3] Some of the phrases suggest his mood. 'Yet, though I cry with tumbledown tongue,/Count my blessings aloud' says the published poem, at the point where it leads into the final section. Among the lines that Thomas experimented with, before he arrived at 'Yet, though I cry with tumbledown tongue', were:

> 'And then, before the downpouring rain'
>
> 'And then before the sea rage breaks and bucks'
>
> 'Let me then before the blazing night'
>
> 'And then before the tornado break'.

One worksheet has a drawing of a lighthouse on an island. The tower and the rays are blacked-in. Above it he has written: 'Darkhouse'. Occasionally lists of tradesmen's bills are mixed up with trial lines and words. Alongside 'sea-flecked mouth' is 'Ebi=£150 P.O.=£67.'

Further evidence from the work-hut can be found in manuscripts of doggerel verse. These must have survived by accident. They were not worksheets of serious poems that could be sold to American collectors in his lifetime, but anguished scribblings, left as litter, which found their way out of Laugharne when Thomas was dead. A notebook[4] containing many manuscript workings of 'Poem on his birthday' (with more of the Roget reference-numbers) and notes for the Laugharne radio play suddenly breaks into

> How can I write a poem to a human
> Being when every bloody line I write
> Is only about my loving one woman?

Presumably he meant Caitlin; the 'bloody' has been crossed out.

3. The critic David Holbrook, studying reproductions of four of these sheets, noticed numbers – '223', '161', '424' – alongside lists of synonyms, and realized that they referred to sections in Roget's *Thesaurus*. This businesslike approach dismayed Holbrook, who thought it was not at all the way to set about writing a poem.

4. Inside the front cover someone, probably Caitlin, has written in pencil: '1 June 1949. Caitlin.' Under it Thomas has written in ink: 'Laugharne. October 1951. Dylan.'

There is one rambling, incomprehensible fragment that begins

> When the promiscuous male drunkards with the floating kidney
> And the sexy, overbrimmed tankards
> Were put to timely death . . .

In another fragment Thomas wrote, obscurely but bitterly:

I do not admire them, the little thankyous:
Crying, cringing, abominable hyenas
Ashamed even of their own acknowledgment,
Who whine outside the ashbins
For another titbit.
They should be put in a sack and drowned,
Yelps, cringes, and all,
In a sea of self pity.
Why do you mingily snarl outside my window,
Despicable rodents?
Is it for me you are the self-appointed accusers?
Down with you, sulphurous ones,
My own degretation [*sic*] is enough,
Having screeched for crumbs. From the table it [illegible]
I do not need the eternal damned apologies of the hairy thankyous.
I prefer sleek, sick animals
Like Disgust:
They are always well fed.

Finally there is a poem in the form of a letter to 'Dear Marged'. Marged Howard-Stepney came from a wealthy Anglo-Welsh family, the Stepneys, who claimed descent from the Royal Tudors. Marged's mother, Catherine Stepney, inherited estates in Carmarthenshire from her father, a baronet. Catherine married another baronet, Sir Stafford Howard, and when he died she changed her name from Lady Howard to Lady Howard-Stepney. Marged, her only daughter, was born in 1913 at the family mansion in the town of Llanelli; loyal citizens subscribed to buy her a silver cradle, and called her 'Marged fach', little Marged. In 1951 she was thirty-eight, a year older than Thomas. Her two marriages had ended in divorce. She was excitable and energetic, an ice-skater and tennis-player when younger, now inclined towards eccentric friendships with the needy, who took full advantage of her generosity. Her son describes her as 'not so much genuinely interested in the arts as a saviour of lost souls'. Marged was said to suffer from 'nervous troubles'; one of her problems was drink. She was a cousin of Frances, Richard Hughes's wife, and this may have been how she came to meet Thomas. By 1951 she was giving him money, to the dismay of her advisers. Thomas's letter to her (written on the back of a 'Poem on his birthday' worksheet) begins in prose –

My dear Marged, You told me, once, upon a time, to call on you when I was beaten down, and you would try to pick me up. Maybe I should not have remembered

– then becomes verse –

> You told me, once, to call on you
> When I was beaten down . . .

A longer version, heavily corrected and smudged, reads

> Dear Marged,
> Once upon a time you told me,
> I remember in my bones,
> That when the bad world had rolled me
> Over on the scalding stones,
> Shameless, lost, as the day I came
> I should with my beggar's cup
> Howl down the wind and call your name
> And you, you would raise me up.
> The same very same time I told you,
> And swore by my heart & head,
> That I would forever hold you
> To the lovely words you said;
> I never thought so soon I'd lie
> Lonely in the whining dust;
> My one wish is to love and die,
> But life is all mustn't & must.
>
> I mustn't love, & I must die
> But only when I am told,
> And Fear sits in the mansioned sky
> And the winged Conventions scold,

And Money is the dunghill King
And his royal nark is the dun;
And dunned to death I write this jingling thing
Dunned to death in the dear sun.
This jingling thing.

Thomas was in a familiar knot. He needed money but seems to have loathed himself for going to such lengths to obtain it. His income through his literary agents in 1951 was only a few hundred pounds. The Inland Revenue was collecting its tax on the good year of 1948–9, when he earned £1,600, and would soon be demanding a share of the American takings. His plight would have been still worse but for Oscar Williams, the American anthologist, who was acting as his unofficial agent in the United States. Williams made some judicious sales, and passed money to Thomas without taking a percentage. In 1951 he sent at least $725 (about £260) to the Boat House, for 'In the white giant's thigh', the article on 'How to be a poet', some anthology rights, and, his best sale for a poem, 'Poem on his birthday'. Thomas sent this soon after he completed it, probably early in October 1951, with an undated letter in which he told Williams that

> I've spent months writing this poem, and hope you can squeeze out a real huge cheque from some moneyed illerate – it's me that's illerate, I mean illiterate – bastard for it. Months and months, and I think it's the best I've done. As always, I need money in a *terrible* hurry. Particularly urgently now, as next week we move to London. to stay in lodgings at the beginning & then to move into a house. I have gout, strained back, bronchitis, fits, and a sense of disaster, otherwise very ill. My love, and Caitlin's, to you & Gene whom we'll be seeing a lot (I hope) of in February. Please, old crazy friend, get me a lot of dough bloody, bloody *quick*. And thank you a great lot for the fifty dollars.

By the end of October, the editor of *Atlantic*, Edward Weeks, was telling Williams he was 'captivated' by the poem. He was willing to pay $200 for it. (The *Atlantic* normally paid a dollar a line for long poems; this one had 108 lines.) To pay more, said Weeks, would not be fair to Frost, Eliot and Auden.

Meanwhile Delancey Street loomed ahead. They were still

at the Boat House on 10 October, when Thomas wrote to his San Francisco friend, Ruth Witt-Diamant:

... How could I not have written, when every week of the piggish year I mean to with all my heart, that poor bloody muscle? Oh, easy, easy. The son of a sloth and a turnip, either I hang by my whiskey toes, thinking of nothing and lust, or sit bigheaded in the wet earth, thinking of turnip poems; and time snails by; and San Francisco's six thousand lamenting miles away; and Wales is dead from the eisteddfodau up; and day after day I grow lazier and fatter and sadder and older and deafer and duller; grey grizzles in my dry hairmat; gout snarls in my big toe; my children grow large and rude; I renounce my Art to make money and then make no money; I fall in love with undesirable, unloving, squat, taloned, moist unlovely women and out again like a trout; I quarrel with Caitlin and make it up in floods of salt self-pity; I fall downstairs; I frighten myself in the night, my own plump banshee; I celebrate other people's birthdays with falsely bonhomonous abandon; I daydream of Chili [*sic*] a place I never want to visit; I write poems and hide them before I can read them; and next week I shall be thirty-seven horrors old.[5] Does that, in any way, explain, dear Ruth why I haven't written? Of course it doesn't. I've no excuse, but *please* try to forgive me ... At the end of January, Caitlin and I are going to New York, financed by the Poetry Centre, Columbia, and the Museum of Modern Art in collaboration, and I should hate it if I didn't, somehow, manage to get to California and (if you could bear it) stay with you for a week ...

His woes seemed endless. The fall downstairs had happened one Saturday night. 'I fell like a barrel,' he wrote to Mrs Taylor. 'I was in bed, then, for days, with a rumpled back, and gout came too, grinding gout, and went to bed in my toe, and a summons arrived to pay a firm of plumbers for the work they did, last December, in extricating, from the w.c. pipes of a London flat we were living in, a bottle of Hammerton's Stout thrown down by Colm. And, when I could walk again, I quarrelled and fought with Caitlin over something now forgotten but which I remember in every detail ...' National Insurance officials were threatening to prosecute for unpaid contributions, his local

5. Either he was anticipating the date or the letter was written later than 10 October; Thomas's birthday was on 27 October.

debts came to fifty-four pounds, he was borrowing from his mother ('my poor mother', who would 'wait until after the grave'), and for good measure, Colm had scalded his chest.

In the middle of their domestic in-fighting, Elisabeth Lutyens arrived for a holiday at the Boat House. At first, Thomas was away. Caitlin, whose forehead was scarred, said he had left after a quarrel. He had telephoned the night before and announced, 'This is the last time you will hear my voice.' But he had reversed the charges, and she knew he had travelled only as far as Swansea. A day or two later Caitlin set off for a reconciliation. Elisabeth Lutyens went with her on the train, not looking forward to the occasion, which turned out to be even less enjoyable than she expected. There were tearful scenes – 'Dylan was on his knees, snivelling. They were both crying. They were having a whale of a time.' It took so long that they missed the last train back to Carmarthen, and had to hire a car; Miss Lutyens was the only one with enough money to pay. At home, Thomas retired to bed for several days to recover from the crisis. The Boat House larder was bare. It was difficult being a guest under these circumstances, so Miss Lutyens loaned him ten pounds, which she never saw again. Presently he was telephoning Marguerite Caetani in Rome, trying to raise money on work in progress. Miss Lutyens, who at that time had a drink problem of her own, marvelled at such goings-on. But Thomas was practising the art or craft of survival. He raised a hundred pounds from the Princess on an unfinished version of his radio play, telling her, as he told everyone, that he had to have the money in order to pay bills in order to leave Laugharne in order to start again, yet again, in London.

By the end of the autumn the Thomases were in residence in Camden Town. 'Your letter just forwarded from Laugharne to our new London house or horror on bus and nightlorry route and opposite railway bridge and shunting station,' he wrote to Brinnin on 3 December, making arrangements for the next American trip. 'No herons here.' His plans were extensive; he would try anything but settle to nothing. He took part in a quiz-show on the B.B.C. Light Programme (' "Say the Word" – half an hour of fun, and a game with words') and said he was anxious to do more. He was reading on the Third; preparing for America; making lists of the stories and poems he would write this year, next year, some time. Among titles listed in the 'Poem on his birthday' notebook are 'Poem to Caitlin', 'Poem to Colm', 'Continuation of White Giant' and 'Where Have the Old Words Got Me'. Elsewhere in the notebook, three titles of stories – 'The Album', 'Floe's Tusks' and 'The Visiting Celebrity' – are bracketed together, and against them is written: 'for the *New Yorker*'. There are further notes for one of these: 'Story begins with S. Bennet, young remittance poet, writing poem, in London bed-sitting room, about Love & the Sea. He goes out, meets Flo, falls in love, finds she has false teeth, goes home, continues his poem & writes down *Floe's tusks.*' Samuel Bennet was the hero of *Adventures in the Skin Trade*; Thomas was going back seventeen years for his material.

A single sheet of manuscript, probably of this date, has the synopsis of a story, 'Such Things Do Happen'. It sounds like an echo of the *Portrait* stories – 'Henry and Fred. Fred the egger-on, the stooge, Henry the real potential writer. Provincial 18–20. Begin with John O'London's literary meeting.' It had traces of 'Where Tawe Flows' and 'One Warm Saturday'. There was to be a girl called Lorelle de Valois. Was she a reincarnation of Lola de Kenway in 'Old Garbo'? Lola was one of the chorus girls at the Swansea Empire for a week – 'Until I died, of a wasting, painless disease, and spoke my prepared last words, they would always walk with me, recalling me to my dead youth in the vanished High Street nights . . .' But the world of *Portrait* stories, as Thomas himself had realized years before, was inaccessible. 'Such Things Do Happen', like 'Floe's Tusks', 'Poem to Caitlin' and 'Poem to Colm', was never written.

CHAPTER TWELVE

# The Knot

DYLAN and Caitlin arrived in America by sea on 20 January 1952 and left it by the same route on 16 May. They had ten days' holiday at the start, and a second holiday in the middle of the trip, which was marred by a shortage of cash because they were temporarily out of touch with Brinnin, the paymaster. The visit was tinged with farce; perhaps tragedy. Having crippled himself by earning and spending so much in 1950, Thomas went through the performance again, this time with Caitlin to double the rate at which money vanished. Before leaving Britain he had asked Brinnin if he knew anyone who would put them up, free, in New York, because 'the money I earn we want for the sights, not for board'. No doubt he was determined to give Caitlin a good time, and she was determined to have one.

She added a page or two of her own to the legend, usually by being determined to get the better of her husband. They had spectacular rows in public. He enjoyed the adulation, especially the adulation of girl students, too much for Caitlin's peace of mind. She knew he was an exceptional reader of verse, but he lacked the austerity that could have let her accept his performances with good grace. A student at Sarah Lawrence College, in New York State, asked her where she would like to sit to hear the reading. 'Sit?' she said. 'I can't tell you how many times I've heard those poems. Isn't there a bar?' She resented the whole enterprise. 'I wanted so much to be gracious,' she wrote; 'and could put on a first-class Queen Mother act on demand; that was the silly contradiction of it; but not with Dylan, not with him monopolizing every ear in the room. He had the same dislike of me receiving any attention or limelight, not that this happened so frequently.' So, 'stiff with rancour', she 'deliberately antagonized'. Between the two of them, social occasions were liable to decline. Thomas was talking to an historian friend of Brinnin when Caitlin interrupted to ask sweetly, 'Are they all stuffed shirts like yourself?' Nelson Algren, the novelist, met them at a party given in Chicago by Ellen Borden Stevenson, wife of Adlai Stevenson. When he wrote to thank his hostess, he said he liked the Thomases at first, until he began to feel sorry for them. 'I'm neither poet enough nor lush enough to appreciate him fully,' said Algren. 'You have to feel a certain desperation about everything either to write like that or to drink like that ... I really marvelled at your tolerance of our friend, when he put on his small-boy-got-to-have-his-way-or-he'll-bust act. I just don't own that sort of patience myself.'

With Caitlin at his elbow, Thomas had to negotiate even more hazards than usual. In Boston and Cambridge they were guests of honour at a party given on 9 March by the *Advocate*, Harvard's literary magazine. According to Brinnin, they left soon after Caitlin asked the company, 'Is there no man in America worthy of me?' According to Professor William Alfred, who was also there, they left because Thomas detected an attempt to provoke him sexually. Alfred says that a mischievous undergraduate 'hired a model from New York, though I think she was probably innocent. Mrs Thomas was sitting at the end of the sofa, talking to a group of undergraduates. I thought she was talking Welsh, but she had been drinking. Thomas was introduced to this model, a beautiful blonde girl, and sized up the situation immediately. Maybe somebody had warned him. He got Mrs Thomas, and they went straight out.'

As with Thomas, there was more than one side to Caitlin, and she made some straightforward friendships with Americans who penetrated the carapace. She had a soft spot for Oscar Williams and his wife Gene. 'Oscar the outrageous', as she called him, pestered her to show him the poems that he knew she wrote in secret. She liked Rollie McKenna, the photographer. But her closest friend in America was Rose Slivka, in New York. Mrs Slivka, then a sculptor's wife, had met Thomas on his first visit. He made his routine proposition, and she fended him off without difficulty. When Mrs Slivka met Caitlin, she found her 'funny and cruel and real. She was the artist's wife, and that can be a terrible place to be. People were awful to her, and she fought back. "They all hang off Dylan's pants," she used to say. She was supposed to shut up and show her devotion, but she didn't want to be buried.'

The Slivkas and the Williamses lived in Greenwich Village, that small piece of lower Manhattan where the city is on a less intimidating scale. Thomas had been there often on his first visit. He said it was 'a feebler Soho but with stronger drinks', and stayed there some of the time, at an hotel in Washington Square. In 1952 he and Caitlin, having failed to find free hospitality, settled for an hotel not far from the Village, the Chelsea, which offered cheap apartments with their own kitchenette. The Chelsea, much favoured by indigent writers, was large and faintly dilapidated. It stood on 23rd Street, a broad cross-street rattling with traffic; Caitlin was soon complaining that her movements were largely confined to it. Thomas enjoyed Village bars and company. Here he could meet former London friends who had settled in New York, like Ruthven Todd and Len Lye. His favourite bar, which he made famous by going there so often, was the White Horse Tavern in Hudson Street, run by an elderly German and his wife. Thomas's American friends thought it reminded him of London, but the immediate surroundings may have suggested Swansea. Masts and funnels of ships berthed in the Hudson River stick up at the end of streets, above buildings. Stevedores and seamen drank at the White Horse. The area still recalls a part of Swansea, between the business district and the docks, as Thomas would have known it; small bars, trees with little earth, and streets of quietly decaying houses, once genteel.

On this second visit, his reputation was growing steadily. At the end of February, New Directions published a small volume containing the six poems he had written since 1946, from 'In country sleep' to 'Poem on his birthday'. The week before it appeared, *Time* sent a reporter from its book department, Mary Ellin Barrett, to interview him. Her account eventually appeared elsewhere, and is valuable as another of those American attempts to observe Thomas in the literal manner that was considered unnecessary or tasteless in Britain. There was no Boswell in London or Laugharne; there was not even a reporter with a shorthand note. Mrs Barrett caught him at lunchtime, at the Chelsea, with a hangover ('Oh God, you are just in time for the laying out'), declaring he felt too squalid to eat in a fashionable restaurant ('I know a little Spanish restaurant around the corner where we can have a squalid, greasy little omelette'), comparing the maraschino cherry in his cocktail to a nipple. Caitlin and John Brinnin were there, a largely silent audience in Mrs Barrett's account. On the way to a steak house Thomas crept up behind a pigeon-toed old lady and imitated her walk. His lunch consisted of oysters and whisky cocktails; he spoke paranoiacally of the 'waves of hostility' from other tables because they were making a noise. Thomas confessed that he had written only six poems in six years ('It seems as if my faculties for self-criticism have grown more than my talent'), adding that he could write a poem in four or five months, 'If I'm fortunate.' Caitlin observed that she didn't know what he did with his time. As usual when someone was asking him serious questions, he gave oblique or ridiculous anwers. 'I used to write violent dreadful things,' he said. 'Now every time I see one of those unpleasant metaphors popping up, I slap it on the wrist, keep it in its place. I'm getting old. Now I write gently, quietly . . .' At this point Caitlin told him to be serious. Asked if his self-criticism might lead him to give up poetry in favour of prose, he replied with a 'lopsided smile' that 'You don't give up poetry. It may give you up, but you don't abandon it. It's always chasing you, relentlessly – a nine-foot goblin with two noses. But when you try to turn around and catch it, *pffft*! It's gone. I've never seen what a poem really looks like. But I keep trying.' He went on to say that the worst prose was written by ex-poets – 'The best prose is written about what happened, and why, to Tom, Dick and Harry, not about witches and dreams and goblins. Though possibly one might compromise – have a Tom Witch, Dick Dream and Harry Goblin.' While Brinnin consulted railway timetables and confided that he had personally to supervise the poet's movements, Thomas told Mrs Barrett that he was writing a film script of Homer's *Odyssey* and a novel called *Adventures in the Skin Trade* about 'one day in the life of a boy – a horrid little prig'. Then he said the novel was pretence. Caitlin said angrily that the novel existed. Thomas conceded that it did, but said the film script did not. A confusing lunch drew to a close. Thomas was due to give a reading at New York University. 'I suppose there is no escape,' he said.

Among Thomas's other visitors at the Chelsea in February were two young women, college graduates, who had what seemed at the time the fanciful notion that recordings of poetry could be commercially successful. The present Barbara Holdridge and Marianne Mantell were both aged twenty-two. Mrs Holdridge worked for a small publisher, Mrs Mantell for a record company. Among their ideas for records were medieval music and Shakespeare; possible backers suppressed their yawns. It occurred to them that a recording of a contemporary poet reading his own verse would add a fresh dimension to the process, not necessarily explaining what he meant, but explaining what he thought he meant. At the end of January they heard that Thomas, newly returned to America, was to read at the Poetry Centre. He had caught their attention a few months earlier when *Atlantic* published 'In the white giant's thigh' and upset some subscribers, who didn't care for 'butter fat goosegirls, bounced in a gambo bed', even if they understood that 'gambo' was a South Wales colloquialism for a farm-cart. But Mrs Holdridge and Mrs Mantell thought it a dazzling poem. They went to the Kaufmann Auditorium and heard Thomas (in Caitlin's phrase) 'booming blue thunder into the teenagers' delighted bras and briefs'. After the performance they tried to see him, but could get no further than a group of frustrated admirers, held back by ushers. They sent in a note to say they had a business proposition, writing 'B' instead of 'Barbara' and 'M' instead of 'Marianne' in case he mistook their intentions.

It was a week before they managed to meet him, for lunch at the Chelsea. Caitlin eyed them suspiciously until she concluded they were not a threat. They spent an hour or two bringing the conversation back to their proposal: five hundred dollars advance against the first thousand records, and a ten per cent royalty thereafter, for the rights to forty-five minutes of his poetry, read by himself. Thomas was easily persuaded. 'As far as Dylan was concerned,' says Mrs Mantell, 'we were just two young girls with an idea and some money.' Presently a contract was drawn up between him and Caedmon, the company they formed; no publisher was willing to back them, so the money came out of their own pockets. The recording was made on 22 February, the day after Mary Ellin Barrett interviewed him, Thomas having failed to keep an earlier date. It was a public holiday, Washington's Birthday, and there was difficulty in finding texts of the poems, which he had not brought to the studio. They agreed on 'In the white giant's thigh' and four others.[1] Thomas said he wanted to read a story: he suggested 'A Child's Christmas in Wales', and a copy of *Harper's Bazaar*, where it appeared in 1950, had to be found. Mrs Mantell thinks he was drunk when he recorded; she and Mrs Holdridge wondered afterwards if he altogether realized what he was doing. The record was issued on 2 April, and sold modestly.

As for the backbone of the second visit, another forty or so poetry readings, the pattern was much as before. Where Thomas visited a campus on more than one trip to America, local memories confuse the occasions. Perhaps his patter was more accomplished, his style a shade brassier. But events came out of the same mould. At the University of Vermont (15 February) he performed in the chapel and said he hoped the walls wouldn't crumble; next morning his hosts noted that he was taking barbiturates at breakfast. At Skidmore College, New York State (13 March), a senior girl student fell off her chair, drunk; Thomas appeared sober. At the University of California (15 April) he answered questions for the university magazine:

Q: Who do you think is writing the best poetry at present?
A: Is it a competition?
Q: Mr Thomas, do the English people read poetry?
A: A small section of them – mostly middle-aged female adolescents – read, still, a few dead poets – but not I think for the words, but for the hope and somewhat hairy desire that they may one dark

1. 'Fern Hill', 'Do not go gentle', 'Ballad of the Long-legged Bait' and 'Ceremony After a Fire Raid'.

> night meet them. Perhaps they will . . . Does poetry care if it is read by the English people, might be a question. I do know that persons (not people, which are political) prefer to read *about* poets rather than read what those bleeders write . . .

At the University of Utah (18 April) he ploughed through a long student interrogation led by a noted academic, Professor Brewster Ghiselin, where he seemed to alternate between giving modest answers and laughing at his hosts. 'I know and the birds know I'm only a fat little fool ranting on a cliff,' he said, 'but it seems that I am lots of people.'

By the end of the four months, Thomas was worn out again. Money had plagued them throughout, as he must have known it would. A note in his engagements book soon after they arrived reminded him to write to 'Marged (re money)'. In Arizona in mid-tour a brief holiday with the painters Max Ernst and Dorothea Tanning was crippled because the Thomases arrived penniless, having somehow exhausted the four hundred dollars that Brinnin had given them to last six days. A postcard to Daniel Jones from Arizona, dated 21 March, said:

> Caitlin & I are buried in the Tuzigoot stone
> on the other side of this card.
> We were killed in action, Manhattan Island, Spring, 1952,
> in a gallant battle against American generosity.
> An American called Double Rye shot Caitlin to death.
> I was scalped by a Bourbon.
> Posthumous love to you & Irene . . .

When they reached San Francisco to stay with Ruth Witt-Diamant, Thomas was greeted by a letter from his son's private school, threatening to send him home unless unpaid fees were forthcoming. Money from several engagements had to be hurriedly scraped together and sent off to Oxford to save Llewelyn from disgrace.

There are hints of another source of discomfort, perhaps more deeply rooted. At Utah, he laughed uneasily at himself as the 'fat little fool' and 'a little fat man come to make a fool of himself'. Was this the old obsession with his 'littleness', his inadequacy? To say that his achievements as a poet were ample to give him confidence is to presume that his lack of confidence was a matter of logic. At lunch with the girl from *Time* he noted the 'waves of hostility'. Permanently on the defensive, he was always vulnerable. On two occasions there were odd stories of Thomas assailed by strangers. Rose Slivka was in the White Horse when a student approached him and said, 'I want to say to you, Fuck you, Dylan Thomas.' At Sarah Lawrence College he told Alastair Reid that a man had just whispered, 'I'll tell you what, Dylan Thomas, if you hadn't written any poems, nobody would have heard of you.' It is not unusual for famous writers to be accosted. But on both occasions, Thomas seemed unduly affected. 'He kept repeating it,' says Reid. 'It had gone through him like a knife.'

His last engagement of the tour was a 'farewell performance' at the Poetry Centre on 15 May. From the platform Brinnin declared that he was the Centre's favourite son. He read poems by Yeats and an extract from Sean O'Casey's autobiography, making a slurred attempt at an Irish accent. His voice sounded heavy with fatigue. 'I'm going to read a poem of Gerard Manley Hopkins,' he said, and paused. ' "The Golden Echo and the Leaden Echo".' There was a much longer pause. Under his breath, and stumbling slightly over the words, he said, 'Thank God my s-ship goes early.' No one laughed. For once, the old ham wasn't joking.

By 1952, Thomas and his publishers had decided it was time to consolidate his reputation. Nothing substantial had been published in Britain since *Deaths and Entrances* in 1946. Two of the six poems he had written since then, 'Lament' and 'Do not go gentle', had not appeared in any form in Britain; the second, perhaps, was withheld so that Thomas's father, now seriously ill with heart trouble, would not see it. All six had appeared in American magazines, in three cases[2] following earlier publication in the Italian *Botteghe Oscure*. These were more lucrative markets, paying in hundreds of dollars where British magazines would have paid in tens of pounds. Thomas's name was widely known through his radio work. But his stand-

2. 'Over Sir John's hill', 'Lament' and 'Do not go gentle'.

ing as a poet was due for reappraisal. The only recent excuse for examining his work had been a critical study by Henry Treece, much of it written before the war, finally published in 1949 with the equivocal title *Dylan Thomas: 'Dog Among the Fairies'*. Treece, lumbered with a study that had spread itself over too many years, was not sure what to think of Thomas's future. But he saw a danger: 'It is certain that he may not persist in his self-exploration without loss to himself by stagnation and artistic atrophy, and it is more than likely that he is aware of this.'

Few journals bothered to review Treece's book, which made little impact. Poetry in general was attracting less attention than in the 1930s, when Auden and Spender were seen specifically as poets of their time. The surge of popular literacy during the war, when paperback poems and short stories flourished, was over. Paper shortages kept the literary journals thin. Nor would the reliable middle-class readership that subscribed to magazines before the war ever be quite the same. A number of the journals that printed and discussed Thomas at the start of his career had ceased publication. There was no *Life and Letters* or *Criterion* or *New English Weekly.*

The vehicle for reintroducing Thomas was to have been 'Collected Poems 1934–1950'. This was delayed, presumably until more poems had been written. By the time of Thomas's second trip to America, Dent were going ahead with production. Thomas was supposed to be providing a Preface. A telegram from Higham, sent care of Brinnin, dangled the promise of a hundred pounds from the publishers as soon as they received it. Nothing had been written when Thomas returned to Britain. The proofs awaited him, and Dent were 'howling' for them; Thomas soon had them back at Laugharne, pausing only for a party at Margaret Taylor's in Oxford, where he managed to lose a manuscript and an overcoat. The Delancey Street interlude was over. At the Boat House he eventually decided to write his preface in verse, telling Higham that he had 'no interest whatsoever' in supplying a straightforward one in prose. Work on it progressed slowly, with many interruptions to read at literary societies and earn guineas from the B.B.C. Dent howled in vain, while Thomas painfully assembled his poem, with its rhymes drawing closer together towards the middle.

According to Brinnin, Thomas said the poem began as a letter to him that was never sent. A letter from Thomas to Oscar Williams the following March, when Thomas was hoping his friend would sell the worksheets, said it was 'going to be a piece of doggerel written to someone in the States on my return from there to Wales, but soon grew involved and eventually serious'. The poem praises the natural world; again it is possible to detect a forced note. Critics have pointed out that the second half is addressed exclusively to birds, fish and animals; on the back of a manuscript draft, Thomas drew a large cat looking down at a tiny mouse. He sent proofs of the books and the manuscript of 'Prologue' to E. F. Bozman of Dent on 10 September, saying 'Why I acrosticked myself like this, don't ask me' and hoping that 'it *does* do what it sets out to do: addresses the readers, the "strangers", with a flourish, and fanfare, and makes clear, or tries to make clear, the position of one writer in a world "at poor peace".' Writing to another publisher, Charles Fry, the following February, he called it a 'tangled, sentimental poem'.

While he waited for *Collected Poems* to appear, a matter of two months or so after 'Prologue' was delivered, he tried to finish his radio play. The idea of 'the town that was mad' being put on trial had to be abandoned some time in 1951. John Davenport said he was deeply dissatisfied at this failure. But by giving up the original concept, Thomas freed himself to write the kind of loose-knit script, without a plot, where he could best use his powers as a comic writer. The play was to portray twenty-four hours in the life of a seaside town. He called it 'Llareggub', resurrecting the joke from his early stories. The characters were caricatures, the town they inhabited a fantasy – funny, sad and sentimental. At this level, which was not the level of his poetry, he was better able to keep the anguish out of his writing. By the autumn of 1951 – about the time 'Poem on his birthday' was completed – he had written half the play. He told Marguerite Caetani that he was writing it 'simply and warmly and comically with lots of movement and varieties of mood, so that ... you come to know the town as an inhabitant of it'. Eight months later, when he was back from his American tour with Caitlin, the play had made very little progress. Douglas Cleverdon, waiting patiently at Broadcasting House, tried to prod him into activity. The B.B.C. was still refusing to pay for any script by Thomas until it arrived. So he found it easier to write straightforward scripts, like his introduction to 'Spoon River Anthology', introducing poems by Edgar Lee Masters, which he wrote for Cleverdon in the summer of 1952.[3] In the end, thanks to Cleverdon's intervention, approval was given for a scheme suggested by Thomas whereby he would be paid five guineas every time he delivered a thousand words of 'Llareggub'. This was charitable but of little practical value, given the extent of Thomas's money troubles. The fee for the finished play was to be only ninety guineas. Cleverdon went down to the Boat House for a weekend in October to talk about the script. On the Monday Thomas wrote in his engagements book: 'SOLID WEEK ON LLAREGGUB, TO FINISH IT.' Then he had a realistic afterthought and changed 'WEEK' to 'SIXTEEN DAYS'. The play was not finished in that time, and by early November he was off again to give readings in London and Gloucester.

*Collected Poems 1934–1952* was published on 10 November, dedicated to Caitlin. It contained all but one poem[4] from his three previous books of verse in Britain, with the addition of the six poems written since 1946, to make a total of ninety. In a 'Note' that preceded the verse 'Prologue' Thomas said the

3. It was to write this script, according to Cleverdon, that Thomas was 'locked in the B.B.C. reference library all night'. This memory of a distant episode seems to be contradicted by Thomas's letter to Cleverdon, sending the script from Laugharne on 19 August 1952: 'I am sorry I couldn't arrange the poems better ... but I had only that one afternoon in the library with the book.'

4. The missing poem was 'Paper and Sticks', from *Deaths and Entrances*; Thomas decided it was 'awful'. It was deleted at the page-proof stage, and 'Do not go gentle', which was to have been the last-but-two poem, moved back to take its place. Perhaps Thomas, with his father in mind, felt also that 'Do not go gentle' would be less conspicuous in the middle of the book. A 1940 poem not previously published in book form, 'Once below a time', was also included.

book 'contains most of the poems I have written, and all, up to the present year, that I wish to preserve. Some of them I have revised a little, but if I went to revising everything that I now do not like in this book I should be so busy that I would have no time to try to write new poems.' Thomas is said to have been depressed when he was working on the proofs. W. R. Rodgers, a poet and B.B.C. writer, heard him say gloomily, 'I'm only a stabbed grampus,' though he 'took a sort of valedictory pride' in the poems. But the book was greeted as a major event. Philip Toynbee wrote in the *Observer* that the language Thomas had evolved was often mannered and occasionally that of a charlatan, but concluded that he was 'the greatest living poet' in English. Cyril Connolly said in the *Sunday Times* that 'at his best he is unique, for he distils an exquisite moving quality which defies analysis as supreme lyrical poetry always has'. Most reviewers quoted a phrase from the 'Note', about the poems being 'written for the love of man and in praise of God'; Thomas was one of the few poets who could make such a statement and, on the whole, get away with it. Not all the praise was uncritical, and not all the critics saw the later poems as an improvement. G. S. Fraser in the *New Statesman* said that 'one's question about some of the later poems ("In country sleep", "Over Sir John's hill") is whether he is a little too deliberately suppressing the desperately sad and forcing the joyously assertive note'. William Empson wrote after Thomas's death that 'I was disinclined to review the *Collected Poems* when it came out during his lifetime, because I would have had to say I liked the early obscure ones best, and I was afraid this would distress him'. The review that most pleased Thomas – he said he found it 'the clearest, most considered and sympathetic' – was by Spender. Thomas wrote to him to say that no other critic had ever attempted 'to set out, plainly, the difference between the writing of poetry from words and the writing of poetry towards words – though that's, of course, oversimplification'.[5]

5. Spender had said that 'the romantic characteristic of Dylan Thomas is that his poems contain the minimum material which can be translated into prose. [Words] are related to one another within the poem, like the colours of a painting, by the exercise of that sensuous word-choosing

A local reporter who interviewed Thomas early in December in Llanelli, where he had gone to read poems to the theatre club, asked him about Toynbee's phrase, 'greatest living poet'. Thomas said modestly that he must have meant somebody else. It may have been more than modesty. His confidence seemed more fragmented than ever. In one of his long, purple-prose letters to Marguerite Caetani, sent in November, he talked about giving up writing altogether.

> My need – as I imagine it – to write, may be all conceit. The bellows that fan the little flicker is nothing but wind, after all . . . Ach, my endless bleating of private woes because I am not 'allowed' to write, as though the trees would grow inward, like toenails, if I renounced this passion for self-glorification. 'Peace, let me write. Gag the tradesmen, I must write. Alms, for the love of writing.' Perhaps I should be better off pulling teeth. But even this momentary disgust I blame upon the weather. And even this disgust is 'material for writing' just as trees, and toenails, and glorification, and teeth.

As always, when he chose, Thomas summed up Thomas accurately, the writer whose reality was somehow the words on the page, not the things the words represented.

He muddled through the same old difficulties. Like a film being run again, he appealed to Spender to appeal for money. But this time the literary establishment declined to help. Marged Howard-Stepney was his best hope that winter. He had persuaded her to buy the Boat House for him, which would remove the danger that Margaret Taylor could no longer afford to let them live there for little or no rent. Marged's mother, Lady Howard-Stepney, had died earlier in the year. Marged inherited the Welsh estates, but there were difficulties in the way of her laying hands on the capital. She visited the Boat House with her advisers. Her agent did his best to curb her unwholesome obsession with wasting money on an improvident poet. The wheels turned slowly.

---

faculty of his imagination, which cares more for the feel of words than for their intellectual meanings . . . In this poetry the reader feels very close to what Keats yearned for – a "life of sensations" without opinions and thoughts.'

Family problems continued to trouble Thomas. Caitlin was steadfastly opposed to his new life as a public performer. Writing to Oscar Williams and his wife early the following year, she said that he had virtually given up writing for acting; adding that anything he sold now was either a rehash of his adolescence[6] or a promise of things to come, never to be fulfilled. No doubt she continued to be suspicious about other women. A couple of letters survive from Thomas to Ellen, a woman he had met in America, who was now in London, written in November and December. Writing from Laugharne on 9 December, after they had failed to meet in London shortly before, Thomas said that 'I was very sorry to miss you, and moped and snarled ... and was melancholy tragic and a bit sick – like an old round adolescent. But, even if my note had reached you, it would have given you very little time. As soon as I know I'm going to London next, I'll give you plenty of warning, and if you don't come I'll cut my throat on a rusty poem.' The day before was Caitlin's thirty-ninth birthday. He wrote some affectionate doggerel to tell her he loved her, beginning each of the thirteen lines with a large capital letter, so that reading from top to bottom it spelt out 'CAITLIN THOMAS'.

During the summer he had seen his sister Nancy when she visited London and Wales from India, where she now lived with her second husband, Gordon Summersby. Nancy, now forty-six years old, was unwell. Cancer was diagnosed, and she had an operation in London before returning to India in September. Dylan was more concerned about his father's health. D.J.'s illness became critical at the start of December, and it was clear that he was dying. Aneirin Talfan Davies met Thomas in Swansea. They walked to an Italian café and sat with cups of coffee. 'There he is, dying,' said Thomas, 'cursing

6. 'The Followers', a story published in *World Review* in October 1952, and probably written shortly before, reads like a conscious attempt, not very successful, to return to the *Portrait of the Artist* material. The Swansea trams hiss as they do elsewhere, the pub with notices on the wall is the one in 'Old Garbo', the barmaid is familiar. A ms fragment at Texas shows that Thomas also thought of turning it into a radio play.

the only thing he's ever believed in.' Davies took this to be another sign of religious faith. Thomas was morose and unhappy. He had never ceased to regard his father with understanding and respect, and the pattern of his life was in some measure a response to D. J. Thomas and his wishes. For the early books that Dylan Thomas read, the rhythms he absorbed, and probably for his obsession with the magic of the poet's function, he was indebted to D.J. There was something about his father, the man of letters, to which he aspired.

In the last few days of D.J.'s life, his sight and senses failed. Writing to Alfred Janes, Thomas said that 'he was in awful pain at the end and nearly blind. The day before he died, he wanted to get out of bed & go into the kitchen where [he thought] his mother was making onion soup for him. Then, a few hours afterwards, he suddenly remembered everything, & where he was, & he said, "It's full circle now".' He died on 16 December. On 29 December, Thomas wrote to Watkins to thank him for a letter of condolence. 'I miss him a great deal,' he said. 'This is only a little – after, years? – to say Happy New Year to you & Gwen & the children.'

On 5 January 1953, he wrote to Oscar Williams, looking for more dollars, to say that 'Christmas here has been so confused that I'm still ½ daft with it'. Besides his father's death, 'The children have been ill. Caitlin's pregnant again. The water pipes have burst & the house is flooded, etc. etc. And the etceteras are almost worse than the rest.' In London, David Higham had a feeling that events were edging towards real disaster. 'If there is a crisis in your general affairs that you would like to talk over with me, I'd be more than ready to do so,' he wrote. Later the same month, Thomas's affairs suffered another setback. Marged Howard-Stepney was found dead in her London house, where she lived with a woman companion. She had taken a sleeping drug; not long before, she had been under treatment in a nursing home. She was found kneeling with her head in a cushion, suffocated. The verdict at the inquest was misadventure. For the Thomases, her death came at an awkward moment, since she had not bought the Boat House in time. Later in the year he was heard in New York complaining about the 'bastards' who prevented him owning the house and the 'bloody woman' who had died.

On the surface it still seemed that his difficulties could be overcome. Margaret Taylor continued to help with money, as best she could. *Collected Poems* won the Foyle's Poetry Prize, worth two hundred and fifty pounds. Nancy's husband in India was helping to pay Mrs Thomas's rent at the Pelican. David Higham worked to rationalize Thomas's money affairs, setting aside funds for tax and bills, from an income that was now rising steadily. The B.B.C. was broadcasting more of his poems, which brought in copyright fees. *Collected Poems* was selling briskly in Britain, and, from 31 March, in America, generating royalties. Dent were planning a new collection of stories (and worrying, still, that the early ones about burning babies and lecherous clergymen were 'too raw' for publication). Thomas had signed a contract with Oxford University Press to edit a collection of Welsh fairy tales and legends. Even the Caedmon record was bringing in a little money. In the first few months of the year Thomas earned more than a thousand pounds in income that passed through his agents, and in other sums that came direct from Oscar Williams. These included a payment for additional paperback rights in *Adventures in the Skin Trade* and, probably, money for worksheets. On 3 March Thomas was sending Williams the 'Prologue' drafts to see what he could raise on them; a few months earlier, a hundred and forty-three worksheets of 'Poem on his birthday' had fetched two hundred and fifty dollars from an American collector (which was fifty dollars more than *Atlantic* paid to publish it). It is true that half of all the money that went through Higham's hands was now being deducted, with Thomas's agreement, to service debts and taxes. But this was merely a sign that his affairs were in the hands of competent advisers. There is no evidence to sustain a view of him in 1953 as the penniless poet being harassed towards the tomb. It would be more accurate to see him as the feckless poet in the process of being rescued by events – a little late in the day, but not too late.

But that view in turn is unsatisfactory. If Thomas felt desperate, he must have had his reasons. The legend of how he was cornered by debts at the end of his life was created by Thomas himself. He undoubtedly felt harassed and trapped. 'Money' was the obvious scapegoat; after all, it had caused enough trouble in the past. But whatever it may have been when he was younger and poorer, his financial muddle now was more of a symptom than a cause. What the real cause may have been is buried deep in his nature. It has been tentatively explored already; it is a matter about which it is impossible to be more than tentative. But ever since those early poems where he wonders if he 'dares', and his letters to Pamela with their reiteration of 'littleness', there is a sense in which he was always uncertain of his powers: both as man and poet. As his youth receded, and it became more difficult – as it must for any poet – to write the lyrical, egotistical verse that had intoxicated him when he was twenty, his doubts about himself may have taken hold. It is useless to suggest, as some critics have done, that Thomas's alienation from his childhood – from Fernhill and Cwmdonkin and 'the listening summertime of the dead' – could have provided a new source of energy for the poems of middle-age. What has been possible for luckier or steelier poets was not possible for him. After 'Fern Hill' he failed to find a lasting theme in his regrets for what had gone; and as the gap widened between past and present, so his energies waned. The fear of being unable to write was nearer the root of his troubles than the fear of not being able to pay the grocer. John Davenport said that in the last eighteen months of his life, he was in 'a great state of terror' – about his health, his nature, and his ability to write poetry.

Caitlin, telling Oscar Williams that all he did was rehash his adolescence, saw what had happened. Thomas's difficulty in writing extended to all manner of work. 'Llareggub' was making little or no progress. A book about America that he was supposed to be producing for the publishing firm of Allen Wingate was not being written. Money had been advanced, and the head of the firm, Charles Fry, was growing impatient. Thomas wrote to him on 17 February 1953. He spelt out his troubles: his father's death ('of cancer'), shortage of money, the fact that 'early this year my best friend in the world, a woman of my own age, died of drink and drugs' (this was Marged Howard-Stepney). Then he moved on to the real trouble. It is hard to decide how much of his letter to believe. But – allowing for the exaggerations, the laying-on of excuses, the artful efforts to keep a publisher happy – it is reasonable to see it as some indication of what was wrong. Thomas referred to 'the real reason' why the book was still unwritten –

> *that* is what you want explained. And how can I write that reason down? *That* is the thing itself: for a whole year I have been able to write nothing, nothing, nothing at all but one tangled, sentimental poem as preface to a collection of poems written years ago.
>
> Perhaps it doesn't sound and seem – that phrase, 'I have been able to write nothing' – the throttling bloody hell it's been to me for this whole waste of a twisted year. And this letter is sure to be silly and pretentious enough without my griping on about words being the light and reason of my life etcetera. [In America I read poems and] the more I used words, the more frightened I became of using them in my own work once more. Endless booming of poems didn't sour or stale words for me, but made me more conscious of my obsessive interest in them and my horror that I would never again be innocent enough to touch and use them. I came home fearful and jangled. There was my hut on a cliff, full of pencil and paper, things to stare at, room to breathe and feel and think. But I couldn't write a word. I tried then to write a poem, dreading it beforehand, a few obscure lines every dumb day, and the printed result shook and battered me in any faith in myself and workman's pride left to me.[7] I couldn't write a word after that. These are the most words I have written for a year . . .
>
> Now I can understand that one ordinary, I suppose, reaction would be to this endless jumbled dull confession: Here's somebody who read aloud and lectured too much too often and too long in a too-hospitable place and who became sated with public words and with his own exhibitionism. On his return, he couldn't get down to work; he missed the willing audience, the easy, but killing, money; as time went on, he became frightened of his failure to meet his literary commitments and now, groaning as though all disinterested heaven were lurching on to his head, conjures up, to a squeal of Welsh bagpipes, some vague psychological hoo-ha to account for his timidity and sloth.

7. Presumably this was 'Prologue'.

I know it goes deeper than that. I've lived with it a long time, or so it seems, and know it horridly well, and can't explain it. I haven't been able to write a word, of anything. Behind me, all the time, I heard, And you'll never be able to write a word again. I thought it would break me up into little self-pitying bits.

But an odd thing's happened, and only now. Or perhaps it isn't odd, and time alone has done it. Whatever the reason, since the disasters, big and midget, I mentioned some time ago, on page 93 of this letter, I've got unknotted. Now for God's sake I can't explain that; but there it is. And Higham is going to get lots of other difficulties straightened out, so that I can get down to those ogre words again without nightmares of doubt and debt, and my dear diabolic family shall be protected for a time. And I'll write that American book, or die.

Higham did, indeed, help to straighten out his affairs. But the book remained unwritten. Thomas remained as before. At the end of February he was vowing not to go ahead with a plan for a third visit to America in the spring. By the middle of March he was making the arrangements. Any escape was better than none. The knot, 'the thing itself', stayed tight.

## CHAPTER THIRTEEN

# *Running Faster*

THOMAS's health in the last year of his life was not satisfactory. But as usual, it is difficult to put a finger on the trouble. The most persistent ailments were to do with his chest. His letters refer to flu and bronchitis. A morning cough heralded the day. Margaret Taylor says he suffered from 'breathlessness" and talked of going to live in East Anglia, where the air was drier. After Thomas's death his mother told an interviewer that he had been suffering so badly with chest trouble that 'I don't wish him back'. If he walked from Boat House to Pelican, he was 'so exhausted that he couldn't speak'. As the post-mortem on Thomas was to show, his lungs were emphysematous – they had lost some of their elasticity, and so performed less efficiently. A tendency to be asthmatic, coupled with heavy smoking all his life, could have produced this condition.

Another of his ailments was gout. 'I've got gout today,' he wrote to Oscar Williams on 3 March 1953. 'God, that reads like GOAT. I mean, the one in the toe. Every time a bird flies by, I yell, thinking it might land on my toe. All I can think about is TOE.' There are stories that he was having blackouts. It is said that he 'fell like a stone as he stood by the mantelpiece of the bar in Brown's Hotel', and was unconscious for two minutes, after which he 'ordered another drink as if nothing unusual had happened'. Finally there is a rumour that he was experiencing sexual impotence. Whatever his degree of ill-health, at no time does he seem to have consulted the family doctor at St Clears who looked after Caitlin and the children; nor, as far as this doctor can tell, did Thomas go to any of his colleagues in the county.

No question of health appears to have been raised when Thomas was planning his new trip to America. The only reason for not going, once he had made up his mind, was Caitlin. She was promised 'mythical dollars', as she called them; there was talk of a winter holiday in Portugal. But she could hardly be expected to believe him any more. As he told Brinnin on 18 March, she accused him of wanting to go for 'flattery, idleness and infidelity'. (The right words, added Thomas, making a lame joke of it, were 'appreciation, dramatic work and friends'.) Presumably to appease her, he asked Brinnin to arrange a tour lasting no longer than six weeks. A month later, after furious quarrels, he was on his way to New York, in a 'hell-ship', in rough seas, writing another of his pleas for forgiveness, swearing that he hadn't wanted to leave her stuck in Laugharne, that he had been angry only with himself, that he would bring back money. The sea rocked, the engines screamed, the wind howled, and (he concluded) despair was in everything except their love.

Thomas arrived on 21 April. His programme in America included the usual campus readings. But this time the centrepiece, when he had finished it, was to be 'Llareggub' on the stage. Brinnin hoped he would be bringing the complete manuscript. Thomas disappointed him, but said there would be no difficulty in having it ready for its first performance at the Poetry Centre in New York on 14 May. At some point in the previous months the play had acquired its final title of *Under Milk Wood*. According to Brinnin, Thomas suggested it to him in a taxi, when they met briefly in London the previous autumn.[1] Urged on by Brinnin's assistant at the Poetry Centre, Elizabeth (Liz) Reitell, who was arranging for the stage production, Thomas worked at the play between engagements. He had begun this third tour with a poetry reading in Boston, performed elsewhere in New England and in New York State, then returned to Cambridge. There he read at the Poets' Theatre. At a

1. The title has never been satisfactorily explained. The wood, named as 'Milk Wood' only briefly during the play, is of no special significance. One ingenious critic has suggested a connection with milkwood trees, which secrete latex. The implication – since the wood is a haunt of courting couples – is that Thomas was making a private joke about condoms; the 'milk' could also be semen. Given his sense of humour and fondness for word-play, this is not impossible.

party afterwards given by Mrs Gardner Cox, one of the guests was Dr I. A. Richards. Thomas, ill at ease, stood talking to the distinguished literary critic. It seemed to Mrs Cox that the poet was tongue-tied. Richards embarked on a complicated question about the new play, which involved references to T. S. Eliot's *Murder in the Cathedral*. The question lasted a long time, 'and at the end of it,' says Mrs Cox, 'Dylan Thomas shuffled his feet and said, "I s'pose so." And then the silence descended for ever.' The real party came later, when the intellectuals had departed, and Thomas and a few cronies stayed on with Mrs Cox and her husband. He drank moderately but was there till dawn. She remembers only one thing he said, that giraffes had been known to copulate at eighty miles an hour.

Two days later Thomas appeared at the Poets' Theatre again, this time with a solo reading of *Milk Wood*, or as much of it as he had written. It was well received. He now had eleven days to prepare the manuscript for its first performance with a cast. It was finally put together, with some makeshift passages, less than an hour before the curtain rose in New York. Liz Reitell and Brinnin were at hand with two typists to turn Thomas's last-minute scribbles into typescripts for the cast – three men and two women, besides himself. Because *Milk Wood* had been conceived as a radio play (although the B.B.C. was still waiting for it), there were many small parts involving only a few lines. The cast shared fifty characters between them, while Thomas himself took the weight of the narrative, as 'First Voice', and played three other parts as well. There were no stage directions because it was 'a play for voices', not primarily intended for the theatre. But the only incentive to finish the play for the B.B.C. was the remainder of a ninety guinea fee. The Americans paid better, and so they had the première.

Thomas and actors sat in a row on stools, at reading desks. It was customary to tape poetry readings, and a microphone was set up, to provide the only record of Thomas performing in his own play. His opening speech – 'To begin at the beginning ...' – fell on a silent audience. The silence extended through the first jokes; perhaps no one was expecting to be made to laugh. Al Collins as Mr Mog Edwards, the draper mad with love, struck the first spark with the speech, four or five minutes into the play, where he tells his unattainable beloved, Miss Myfanwy Price who keeps the sweetshop, 'I will warm the sheets like an electric toaster.' Soon the audience realized that they were hearing a romantic comedy, and responded accordingly. Thomas was exporting a caricature, the sad and comical Welsh in their potty little village; many of the real Welsh bridled when they heard it later from the B.B.C., taking special offence at the bawdy passages. But *Milk Wood* created a world of its own. The play ends at nightfall; darkness lies ahead. The first performance received a long ovation. Brinnin said the cast took fourteen curtain calls before Thomas, 'squat and boyish in his happily flustered modesty', stepped out alone.

Thomas's American girl-friend was now Liz Reitell (earlier he had a brief re-encounter with 'Sarah' at Cambridge). Their first meeting had not been a success. Thomas was evasive about his unfinished manuscript, frivolous about its content. As Miss Reitell remembers, '*He* thought, she's one of those cold American girls. *I* thought, why all the fuss over this fool?' When they began to work together, their relationship took the obvious course. Thomas, lonely as always and anxious to be looked after, settled down comfortably with a new friend. Miss Reitell was in her early thirties. She had an expensive education at Bennington College; was a painter and a dancer; served as an officer in the Women's Army Corps, and had been married unsuccessfully. Her handsome, hawk-like face greeted callers and hangers-on who might stop him working on *Milk Wood*. Protective for his sake and jealous for hers, she joined the throng of those who were never the same again. Afterwards she concluded sadly that his vulnerability had exposed hers. At the time she found 'complete ecstasy' in his company, but failed to realize the nature and extent of his problems.

It was not the best time to fall in love with Thomas. All his solutions were temporary. His affair grew still more complicated. At the end of April his solicitor in Swansea (Stuart Thomas, a friend from Grammar School days) had issued a writ against Time-Life International, alleging libel in an article in *Time* of 6 April. The phrases objected to concerned his drinking and general unreliability.[2] Stuart Thomas says the motive for suing was outrage, not avarice. Time-Life meant to defend their remarks by saying they were true. Later, a private detective was hired to obtain evidence of Thomas's goings-on in New York.

He continued to play the part of the family man. On 23 May – when he was staying with Brinnin in his house at Cambridge before returning to New York for another reading and another *Milk Wood* at the Poetry Centre – he wrote a love-letter to Caitlin with a new version of the dream of happiness. In July they would travel to Hollywood: he was going to write an opera with Stravinsky.

> We can get a boat from London, direct but slow, to San Francisco, & then fly to Los Angeles in an hour or so. Outside Hollywood, in a huge easy house in the hills, we're to stay for the month with Stravinsky. I've seen him, just now, in Boston, and we've thought of an opera and it is – for me – so simple that the libretto can be written in the time we're there. That's not just optimistic: it *can*, & will be. In advance, I'll be given 500 pounds & our passage, first class, & then another £500 – & then royalties until we die. We'll go back from Hollywood to Laugharne, &, in the winter, we'll go to Majorca. There'll be plenty of money. This time it's working . . .

Near the end of the letter he asked if his sister was dead. Unknown to him, Nancy had died on 16 April, just as he left for America. Thomas told his wife that he had finished his 'infernally, eternally unfinished "Play" ', and that he would be flying back to Britain on 2 June, the day of Queen Elizabeth's Coronation. He should have been leaving on 26 May, but (he said) the plane had been bought out by 'rich bitches' bound for London.

Perhaps he was lingering in New York for as much 'flattery, idleness and infidelity' as possible, using the news about Stravinsky to mollify Caitlin. More likely he believed that the prospects were as good as they appeared. The proposal was firm

2. '. . . When he settles down to guzzle beer, which is most of the time, his incredible yarns tumble over each other in a wild Welsh dithyramb in which truth and fact become hopelessly smothered in boozy invention. He borrows with no thought of returning what is lent, seldom shows up on time, is a trial to his friends, and a worry to his family . . .'

enough. It came from the Opera Workshop of Boston University, who cabled Thomas on 21 May to ask if he would be willing in principle to write a libretto for Stravinsky. Assuming that poet and composer agreed, the Workshop could offer an advance of $1,500 and a similar amount on completion. This was a substantial sum. But Thomas was earning still more substantial sums by reading poetry, and they all dribbled away. In addition, he would have to produce an exacting piece of work; and he was finding it difficult to produce anything at all. For the moment he was enthusiastic. Stravinsky was in Boston, and Thomas had visited him at his hotel. The idea they discussed was a 're-creation of the world', perhaps by denizens of outer space who arrive on a devastated Earth and begin again with a new Eden. Brinnin saw him shortly afterwards, exhilarated, inventing absurd plots for operas. But no firm commission had yet been offered.

He had nine or ten days in New York before flying to London. Much of his leisure time was spent with Liz Reitell. He liked to walk around Greenwich Village with her. She became worried by his drinking. Years later she decided that he was 'terribly, clinically alcoholic. I didn't know about those things then. There was no great muse that made Dylan drink. He drank because he was an alcoholic. He had all the devils, and some of the angels, too.' He was having attacks of gout and gastritis. He fractured his arm again, falling down a flight of stairs when drunk, while on his way to the theatre with Liz and another friend. At first he didn't realize he had broken a bone. At the theatre he complained loudly that his arm hurt. The play was Arthur Miller's *The Crucible.* Thomas and the friend began swearing and jeering, and were asked to leave. The evening ended in confusion. Later, writing to his son Llewelyn about the broken arm, Thomas said it happened in his hotel bedroom when he tripped over a suitcase in the dark. 'I screamed and screamed,' he explained, 'but nobody came so I had to go back to bed.' Liz took him to her doctor, Milton Feltenstein. His arm was put in plaster, and Feltenstein treated him for his gout and gastritis. It is not known what drugs he used. He also tried to persuade his patient to drink less, and to consult a doctor when he returned home. Thomas took to Feltenstein, who seems to have given injections freely; he used to talk about the doctor's 'winking needle'.

Barbara Holdridge and Marianne Mantell were alarmed at his appearance when they saw him for a second recording session. They collected him from the Chelsea in the evening. He was leaving for London next day. His features were bloated. Besides the arm in a sling, there was a cut over his eye, and his suit was smeared with what looked like vomit. He explained the broken arm with a garbled story about an incident involving a drunken sailor. In the studio he was morose, staring into space. Mrs Holdridge and Mrs Mantell felt he was under more strain than formerly, though the recording shows no sign of this; 'And death shall have no dominion' and 'Lament' were given the usual treatment. Mrs Holdridge said he had difficulty reading 'If I were tickled by the rub of love'. One version sounded like 'the rubber's love'. Thomas swore violently at the microphone. Later Mrs Holdridge 'took the tape and passed it over the eraser head, so that it couldn't become a party piece'. 'Poem on his birthday' also caused him trouble. He failed to read the last line, 'As I sail out to die', in a way that satisfied him. With several versions on the tape, he told them to choose whichever one they liked. 'I can't,' he said. 'I'm finished.'[3] Next day he flew home. In London it was the Coronation – 'miles of cock-deep orange-peel, nibbled sandwiches, broken bottles, discarded vests, vomit and condoms, lollipops, senile fish, blood, lips, old towels, teeth, turds, soiled blowing newspapers by the unread mountain'. He found himself at a party. 'Oh, my immortal soul,' he wrote to Oscar Williams, 'and, oh, my tissues!'

In Laugharne, one of his first engagements was a visit from a journalist, Mimi Josephson. Thomas came to the door of the Boat House 'dressed in an old tweed jacket, open-necked shirt, grey flannels and a pair of plimsolls'. He talked to her about the opera, about *Milk Wood* ('prose with blood-pressure'), and about a new play he wanted to write. She was told that he was

3. The other poems recorded at this session were 'Should lanterns shine', 'There was a Saviour', 'A Refusal to Mourn the Death' and 'A Winter's Tale'.

finishing a humorous novel, *Adventures in the Skin Trade*. A photographer accompanied her, and when the article appeared in *John O'London's* later in the summer, a picture showed Thomas in his hut, his plaster-cased arm resting on manuscripts, a cigarette stuck aggressively in the corner of his mouth; the affectation had not changed in twenty years. He wrote to Mimi Josephson to thank her for making 'such a splendid rumbustious figure of this melancholy bad-natured slob mouldering away in his mud-hole by the wishy-washy water'. A draft of the letter shows that he began by writing, 'this melancholy bad-natured slob who finds it as hard to write as to squeeze blood from an old pudding'.

He was back in the rut. A few things got done. Revisions were made to *Milk Wood*. One of the new sections added after America was about an undertaker. In the original version he was 'Thomas the Death' – 'To him, the eyes of all the inhabitants are full of fear. "Not me, not me," eyes scream at him.' But he was made less forbidding and renamed Evans. The *Milk Wood* revisions dragged on through the summer. In July, Thomas went to North Wales to write about the International Eisteddfod at Llangollen for the B.B.C. Aneirin Talfan Davies, the producer, says he was in a 'bewildered haze' most of the time. He took Caitlin and Aeron with him; it was a poor substitute for California, but the opera plans were receding. Boston University was still looking for the money; Stravinsky had written from San Francisco to say he would be delighted to have Thomas as a house-guest later in the year, if he didn't mind sleeping on a sofa in the living-room. In August, Thomas made his first solo appearance on television, reading a story about a charabanc outing in a series called 'Speaking Personally'.[4] The script was not completed until after he had arrived

4. It was broadcast from a clergyman's library because the B.B.C. in Wales was short of studio facilities at the time. The Controller of TV Programmes in London sent a memo to Cardiff complaining that 'Thomas did not know his story and I thought the programme was appalling'. Cardiff rejected the criticism and quoted reviews in national newspapers calling the programme 'a joy' and 'almost a tour de force'. The story, with the title of 'A Story', was later bought by the American *Harper's Bazaar*.

for the broadcast. Thomas had not memorized all the words, and had to refer to the text. Caitlin watched him from Brown's Hotel, making sardonic remarks.

Thomas is known to have worked on one poem, 'Elegy'. It was not finished. The subject was his father's death:

> Too proud to die, broken and blind he died
> The darkest way, and did not turn away,
> A cold, kind man brave in his burning pride
> On the darkest day . . .[5]

Some bleak manuscript notes survive from this period. One page of a notebook has

> The magnificence of suffering.
> Live, Damn you, again.
> Dying in agony.
>
> His body burned until he died
> And then she [*sic*] slid into the fire.
>
> What were his eyes saying? My son, I am burning.

Other sheets have scraps of doggerel:

> Cask Bass
> Oh to bask in cask
> Bass with
> Tast.

In a letter to Daniel Jones on 24 August Thomas said:

> . . . I have to see T.V. D. J. Thomas in Swansea, *and* Aneirin [Talfan Davies], but will get that over quickly and then – Oh, to bask unasked in a Bass cask, etc!
>
> Isn't life awful? Last week I hit Caitlin with a plate of beetroot, and I'm still bleeding. I can't finish a poem, or begin a story, I chew my nails down to my shoulders, pick three-legged horses with beautiful names, take my feet for grey walks, moulder in Brown's, go to bed as though to an office, read with envy of old lonely women who swig disinfectant by the pint, think about money, dismiss it as dirt, think about dirt . . .

5. Vernon Watkins assembled the fragments and published them in tentative form. The lines quoted here are taken from the worksheets.

There are some maudlin verses about his parents, perhaps written when Thomas had been drinking; perhaps scribbled for relief as the children played on the sands beyond the house, artillery thumped on the Pendine range, and poems remained inaccessible. In the notebook:

> Come back, come back, Mother
> Oh Mother, Oh Mother, Oh Mother
> Come back to your only son
> And sorry for what he done.

On a scrap of paper:

> I am blind, too, my son.
> And father, dear mother, & father?
> Is he the only one
> Who can see the green trees blow
> And the sunshine & the snow.
> No, my son, no
> Your Father is blind as well.

On a sheet drilled through with a cigarette burn:

> A little child stood at the doorway
> With wonder in its eyes
> It cd not see the fields of may
> Or the clouds in the blue skies.

Underneath is a sentence from 'A Story' – 'And over the bridge & up the hill and under the singing wood and along the dusty road we wove, slow cows & ducks flashing by . . .'

Drafts of a letter to Marguerite Caetani, written on or around 26 August, make disturbing reading. Thomas was concocting another tale of woe, but the process was out of hand. Texas has at least eight attempts, none of them completed. Each begins, 'What can I say?' He was writing, not about his financial problems, but about the problem of why he wrote her such contorted letters. His method was to write a letter that was even more contorted than usual:

What can I say?
Why do I coil myself always into these imbecile grief-knots, sew myself blindfold & handcuffed in a sad sack, weight it with guilt

and pigiron, & then pitch me to sea, so that time & time again I must scrabble out & unravel in a panic, babbling & blowing bubbles like a puny wheezy Houdini, tangled with polyps . . .

Thomas was using his *Thesaurus* to help find the right word: one of the pages has class numbers associated with the word 'knot'. The 'Houdini' idea led to a search for the right phrase – he tried 'like a halfpenny Houdini', 'a teeny wheezy Houdini', 'a sea-slimed Houdini', 'a sea-slugged windy Houdini'. The thought that he is trapped is paramount. He must escape the 'man-trapping sea', or the 'pitfall sea', or the 'sea-clutch', or the 'claws and bars and breasts of the man-trapping seabed'. The 'freak user of words' – his self-description to Pamela in 1934 – has lost touch with outside reality. He is not so much writing a letter to a woman in Rome who will send him money, as playing uneasily with words, the things themselves, to give shapeless expression to old fears of helplessness and death:

. . . time and time again I cry to myself as I kick clear of the cling of my stuntman's sacking, 'Oh, one time the last time will come and I'll never struggle, I'll sway down here forever, handcuffed and blindfold, sliding my wound-around music, my sack trailed in the slime, with all the rest of the self-destroyed escapologists in their cages, drowned in the sorrows they drown and in my piercing own, alone and one with the coarse and cosy damned seahorsey dead, weeping my tons.' What can I tell you? . . . Why must I parable my senseless silence? my one long trick? my last dumb flourish? It is not enough that, by the wish I abominate, I savagely contrive to sink lashed and bandaged in a blind bag to those lewd affectionate raucous stinking cellars: no, I must blare my engulfment in pomp and fog, spout a nuisance of fountains like a bedwetting whale in a blanket . . .

Whatever levels of meaning can be read into Thomas's scribblings in the summer of 1953, they suggest he was in serious trouble. His course of action was inevitable: run to America again. Stravinsky wrote to say that since Boston was still finding it difficult to raise the money, he and Thomas should make a start on their own. Brinnin, in Europe at the end of the summer, went to Laugharne again in September, and sensed that for Thomas, 'almost any means of escape seemed attractive'. Brinnin tried to persuade him to stay and work in the one place where this was likely to happen. When he saw this was useless, he agreed to help arrange more performances at the Poetry Centre. Caitlin listened and said little.

Before Brinnin left, they went on a tour of south Carmarthenshire by car. Rollie McKenna was there to take photographs for the magazine *Mademoiselle*, which had bought the publication rights of *Milk Wood.* Dylan's mother went with them. They called at Fernhill; the owner let Dylan tour the rooms, the orchard and the barn. They went up the lane to Llwyn Gwyn and called at the Blaen Cwm cottages. In the evening they stopped at Llanybri to look at the family graves. Brinnin noted that Thomas had drunk only one glass of beer all day.

Among the odd jobs with which Thomas occupied himself, while he marked time before he left for New York again, was to record a radio talk, 'A Visit to America'. He filled it with material he had used on his tours. A joke about the Elgin Marbles (in which somebody, perhaps a man from the B.B.C., or a Welsh hairdresser showing off in London, speaks 'like a man with the Elgin Marbles in his mouth') had been used from Llanelli to San Francisco. On the same day, 5 October, Thomas recorded a brief contribution to a radio programme about Laugharne that was to be broadcast on 5 November: 'Off and on, up and down, high and dry, man and boy, I've been living now for fifteen years, or centuries, in this timeless, beautiful, barmy (both spellings) town ...'

Caitlin was not going to America, though she was to travel as far as London, where she and Dylan would spend a little time together. The evening before they left, they went to the cinema in Carmarthen. According to Florence Thomas, Dylan fainted during the film. The family doctor, who was at the cinema that evening, disputes this. He and his wife were sitting in front of the Thomases. Before the film began, Caitlin approached him and said she was worried about Dylan. He was having severe headaches; and in the morning they were going away. The doctor said he would pick them up in his car after the film and take them to his house in St Clears, on the way to Laugharne, so that he could examine Dylan. But when the lights came on, Dylan had vanished, probably to the Boar's Head. The doctor went home without seeing him. His mother believed he had a premonition of death; when he left next day, he came back three times to kiss her.

In London the Thomases stayed at Hammersmith with Harry and Cordelia Locke. They were there longer than expected because the plane ticket was sent to Laugharne instead of London, and they missed the original booking. Caitlin was still violently opposed to the trip; the atmosphere was strained. A few people were to recall meeting Thomas during the week or ten days he was in the city. Most of the time he seems to have been melancholy rather than drunk. Constantine FitzGibbon met him by chance outside Broadcasting House, and they drank together in a deserted bar; his future biographer found him 'subdued, even sad'. FitzGibbon wrote: 'He certainly did not seem to me to be at all suicidal in his attitude, though others who saw him during these days have told me that he talked, almost willingly, of his impending death – but then he had been doing that, in one way and another, for thirty years.' This time the circumstances were different. Thomas's existence as a poet was threatened. Nevertheless, the picture of Thomas in London during those last days is utterly different from the scenes that were to follow in New York. There was an evening with Philip Burton, when Thomas talked energetically about a new play he hoped to write. The tentative title was 'Two Streets'.[6] In a South Wales town that might have been Swansea, two children, a boy and a girl, are born in neighbouring streets. Strangers, their lives slowly come together. Thomas was vague about the details. He wanted a midwife who would attend both births. Philip Burton, as a drama producer, argued about the opening scene. 'Please,' said Thomas, 'please let me have two prodigiously pregnant women.' Burton found him equally vague about the opera. Now that the time to visit Stravinsky in California

6. Thomas telephoned Richard Burton from Philip Burton's apartment, hoping to borrow two hundred pounds 'for the education of my children'. Failing that, he offered to sell the rights to his new play, 'the story of a love affair between two streets', for the same amount. Richard Burton refused.

was approaching, he may have wondered if he would be able to write the libretto. FitzGibbon, to whom he spoke about the project, thought it frightened him. Margaret Taylor believed it would have overwhelmed him, like the *Peer Gynt* fiasco on a larger scale.

To Douglas Cleverdon's relief, the script of *Milk Wood* was delivered, after more last-minute delays, on Thursday, 15 October. Cleverdon had it typed for duplicating, and returned the original to Thomas on the Saturday. Thomas lost it over the weekend; before he left for America, he told Cleverdon he could keep it if he found it. A day or two later Cleverdon tracked it down to a Soho pub, with interesting legal consequences. In the meantime, Thomas had been given duplicated copies of the play to take with him to America.

A mixed party saw him off at the Victoria Air Terminal on 19 October. Cleverdon was there. So were Mrs Taylor and the Lockes. Thomas was sober and unhappy. Caitlin is said to have had premonitions of disaster. But it was the kind of occasion that memory distorts as people silently rearrange events, making significance out of nothing. Cordelia Locke's last glimpse of him was through the window of the coach; he was giving a thumbs-down sign.

CHAPTER FOURTEEN

# *Alcohol and Morphia*

DYLAN THOMAS's troubles had begun long before, and what happened in New York is best seen as the end of an inevitable process. It is true that there was one major element of chance in the final events that led to his collapse and death. But Thomas put himself, or let himself be put, in a position where accidents were likely to happen. A psychiatrist offers an analogy: 'A depressed, desperate middle-aged man whose marriage is in ruins, and who has failed to realize his aims, may take to driving a car in a reckless way because he does not value himself and his life. He is not actually suicidal. He doesn't care.' Margaret Taylor says that her friend died of being Dylan Thomas. Caitlin has concluded that he 'deliberately wanted to do away with himself before he was forty. He was escaping from the worst side of life. He didn't want the declining into old age, and I really can't blame him. Who does?'

Thomas arrived in New York on Monday, 19 October, and went to stay at the Chelsea. He had been expected there several days earlier, so his reservation had lapsed, and he had to make do with a small back room. He complained that it was dingy. 'The cockroaches have teeth,' he remarked to Liz Reitell, who was his close companion from the moment he arrived. He spoke of having 'escaped' from London, and upset her by referring to Caitlin as 'my widow'. When they were walking near Greenwich Village the day after his arrival, he saw a poster advertising a film about Houdini, and said that to be hopelessly trapped was the worst horror in the world; later he gave her the manuscript of his 'Houdini' letter to Marguerite Caetani. For two or three days he seems to have been abstemious. To Liz Reitell they were 'the loveliest days I had with him. He wanted to take walks. He wanted to eat. But he was also frightened.' Then he made himself ill with a heavy bout of drinking. He was nauseated and vomiting at a rehearsal of *Milk Wood*, which was to have two performances at the weekend, and told Herb Hannum, a friend of Liz Reitell, that he was too tired to sleep. In Brinnin's account,[1] he said to Hannum, 'I've seen the gates of hell tonight. Oh, but I do want to go on – for another ten years anyway. But not as a bloody invalid.'

Miss Reitell insists now that there was no question of Thomas wanting to die: 'His instinct for life was very strong. He was killed physiologically, by alcohol, not psychologically. During his last two conscious weeks he made strenuous efforts to get better.' But another conversation with Hannum the following day, as Miss Reitell reported it back to Brinnin for his book, had sinister undertones. Thomas said he would have to 'give up something'. Hannum asked if he meant life. Thomas's reply, with the original ellipses, is given as: 'No. I don't know ... I want to go on ... but I don't know. I don't know if I can. I don't feel able any more. Without my health I'm frightened. I can't explain it ...'

Towards the end of the week (probably on Friday, 23 October) Liz Reitell took him to Milton Feltenstein for a consultation. The doctor warned him about his way of living and gave him an injection of ACTH. Treatment with this substance was new and fashionable in 1953. Presumably Feltenstein was using

1. For events between 19 October, when Thomas reached New York, and 4 November, when he went into a coma, Brinnin's chief source of information was Liz Reitell; he was in New England except for the weekend of 24–25 October. She says that she wrote 'enormously long notes' for him, and that they spent two days going through her narrative. Neither Brinnin nor Miss Reitell now has the notes, or knows what became of them. Brinnin even suggests they may never have existed. This chapter is based on the account in Brinnin's book; on conversations with Liz Reitell (now Liz Smith), Jáck Heliker, David Lougée, Rose Slivka and others; on mss by Ruthven Todd at Texas; and on certain medical and other papers. Miss Reitell is the key witness in any account of Thomas's last days; her testimony to Brinnin included verbatim reports of things that he said, to her and to others, of as much as several hundred words at a time. For obvious reasons her narrative has to be viewed with caution: in 1953 and 1954 she was emotionally involved and deeply upset; in 1975 she found it difficult to rake over her past.

it to control Thomas's general symptoms of malaise, and possibly for his gout. For a while Thomas seemed better, though Brinnin was shocked to find him looking so unwell when he arrived from Boston during the final rehearsal for the Saturday *Milk Wood*. ('His face was lime-white, his lips loose and twisted, his eyes dulled, gelid, and sunk in his head.') The house-manager at the Poetry Centre noted that he was sweating, and had blotchy skin and unpleasant breath. Some of his remarks to Liz Reitell were hurtful. At a party given by Rollie McKenna that evening, Thomas was seen to be avoiding alcohol. Asked why, he said, 'It's just that I've seen the gates of hell, that's all.' The real experience, assuming it had been real, was already turned into words, into 'material'.

Over the weekend both Liz Reitell and Brinnin felt that Thomas was drawing apart from them. On Sunday there was a matinée performance of *Milk Wood*, reportedly the best of the four given in New York. At a party afterwards Thomas gulped whisky and disappeared upstairs with a woman. At a second party, he, Liz and Brinnin were reconciled in a tearful and highly emotional scene. ('Standing behind me as he held me very firmly, Dylan spoke the last words I was ever to hear him say directly to me: "John, you know, don't you? – this is for ever." ') By now Liz was aware of the dangers of entanglement with someone as demanding and destructive as Thomas, who would 'never let you go but never let you help him'. When they were returning to Greenwich Village in a taxi later that night, she stopped it near her own apartment and hurried away, leaving him to his own devices. This seems to have been as far as her attempt at self-preservation went. Next day, Monday, 26 October, he summoned her by telephone to the Algonquin Hotel, where she found him, in mid-afternoon, drinking whisky and raving about war, blood and mutilation. He implied he had taken part in wartime combat himself, that his family had been in danger, that Turkey or the Middle East had been involved. It seems likely that the Commando captain, bursting into the bungalow at New Quay with his machine-gun, was in his mind.

Outside, Thomas made faces at passers-by. He was swearing and staggering. Miss Reitell took him to a cinema and then to a bar, and although he became calmer, he continued to behave irrationally. He said repeatedly that he feared he was going mad and that 'sex' was involved in his mental state. When he saw a boy and girl with their heads together, he said, 'How filthy!' Soon he was telling his companion that he was a puritan. He recovered during the evening, but there seems no doubt that he had been temporarily deranged. Liz was shaken by the episode. Perhaps Thomas was additionally upset because the next day was his thirty-ninth birthday. A stranger approached him as they left the bar, after midnight, and asked if he was Dylan Thomas. Thomas said he was only posing as the poet. Next evening he had to leave a birthday party at the Slivkas because he was unwell. Miss Reitell took him back to the Chelsea, where he flung himself on the bed and talked of what a 'filthy, undignified creature' he was. He wept and spoke of his 'agony'.

Yet on the next two days, 28 and 29 October, he carried out two engagements without mishap. On 28 October he spoke at a symposium on 'Poetry and the Film' organized by a group called Cinema 16, playing his usual game of needling the intellectuals. A transcript of the session exists. Maya Deren, who made experimental films, was another member of the panel. When she spoke about the 'vertical' nature of poetry and contrasted it with the 'horizontal' nature of drama, Thomas was baffled, or pretended to be. He made some unfunny jokes about up-and-down movements and said that for him, poetry in the cinema 'might have been in the U.F.A. films or something that I saw as a child. Or somebody coming down some murderous dark, dark silent street, apart from the piano playing. Or it might have been a little moment when Laurel and Hardy were failing to get a piano up or down a flight of stairs. That always seemed to me the poetry.' Pressed by the chairman, he fell back on his old statement of method: 'Well, just as a poem comes out . . . one image makes another in the ordinary dialectic process (somebody left out the word "dialectic", well, I may as well bring it in, you know). So, as in a poem one image breeds another, I think, in a film, it's really the visual image that breeds another – breeds and breathes it. If it's possible to combine a verbal image to a visual image in this sort of horizontal way, I'd rather see horizontal films, myself. I like stories. You know, I like to see something going on.' (Laughter and applause.)

On 29 October, a Thursday, Thomas gave a public reading of poems at lunchtime at the City College of New York (the 'proletarian Harvard'), travelling by subway to uptown Manhattan because, he told Liz, he was conserving money so that he would have something to take back to Laugharne. After the reading he moved on to a near-by restaurant with a small party from the college; he drank beer and appeared normal. His next engagements were not until the following week. There was still no definite decision about Stravinsky and the opera, but he was to read in New England and Chicago. For the moment he was free to enjoy himself, if that is what he was doing, in New York. On Thursday and Friday he spent his time with Liz and at least one other woman, and attended parties. On Saturday night, 31 October, he was drinking heavily, according to the detective hired by *Time*.[2] At nine p.m. he arrived, drunk, at the White Horse with two friends, Dave Slivka and David Lougée; he was observed to drink lager, beer and whisky, and was said (erroneously) to have been drinking non-stop for ten days. At Toppers bar and grill on 7th Avenue he spoke of sexual impotence and said how much he loved his wife; other women were only substitutes for Caitlin. He described his first sexual relations (at the age of fifteen), and said that when he had gonorrhoea as a teenager, it took a month to cure, and had to be concealed from his family. All he wanted, he said, was to be regarded as an average human being. At two thirty a.m. he was 'seen taking Benzedrine'. It must have been a tiring night for the detective.

On Sunday morning, 1 November, Thomas spoke to Liz Reitell on the phone, and told her that he had a faint memory,

2. A small notebook used by FitzGibbon when he was preparing his biography of Thomas is among FitzGibbon's research material deposited at Texas. A page headed 'TIME DETECTIVE' contains notes made by FitzGibbon, presumably from the *Time* material, though not used by him in his book. It mentions events on four days: 28 and 31 October and 2 and 4 November.

from the night just passed, of taking a dislike to a woman who was with him in a taxi, and of throwing her into the street. Nothing further about the incident came to light; Miss Reitell wondered later if it was a confused version of what had happened a week earlier, when she left the taxi to go home by herself. It was probably during this weekend that Thomas said he saw a mouse at Howard Moss's apartment. On Sunday night, at the same apartment, he is unreliably reported to have scratched his eyeball on a rose-thorn.

At the Chelsea on Monday morning, Ruthven Todd found him in bed, unwell but making lugubriously comic remarks about his condition. Todd noted that he was drinking beer, and that an unopened bottle of Old Grandad, his favourite American whisky, was on the dressing table. During the day he was out and about with Liz. They were invited to dinner at the Colony Restaurant. Thomas behaved normally except that he was not wearing socks.

On Tuesday, 3 November, Thomas was again in bed at the Chelsea, alternately drinking with friends who looked in, and sleeping. Todd was there when Thomas offered a drink to the maid who arrived to clean the room. She accepted a whisky from the bottle of Old Grandad, which was opened for the purpose. Brinnin says that one of the callers was a lecture agent, and that Thomas signed a contract guaranteeing him a thousand dollars a week. Later in the day, complaining that he was exhausted, he went out with Liz to keep two appointments for drinks, but returned to the Chelsea in mid-evening. In the bedroom he seemed to break down entirely, weeping, telling Liz that he wanted to die and 'go to the garden of Eden', that he couldn't bear the thought that he would never see Colm again, that there was 'an illumination' about Caitlin. At two o'clock in the morning he got out of bed, declaring that he must have a drink. Liz failed to dissuade him. He was absent for an hour or an hour and a half. When he returned, he spoke the words that were quickly embedded in the legend: 'I've had eighteen straight whiskies. I think that's the record.' Then he told Miss Reitell, 'I love you, but I'm alone,' and fell asleep.

It is not a satisfactory story. In the first place, why did he go out at all when there was whisky in the room? Ruthven Todd and other friends tried to establish how much whisky he had drunk that night. The bottle of Old Grandad was found to have only the one drink missing. The friends went to the White Horse, where Thomas had apparently been seen. The proprietor concluded, on the evidence of his stocks, that he could not have drunk more than six whiskies, or eight if two regulars who usually took Old Grandad as a nightcap had changed their brand. No one had noticed anything excessive about Thomas's drinking. Liz, on the other hand, thinks that he used a bar closer to the Chelsea. But Todd was convinced that Thomas had been exaggerating. This was only to be expected. In a manuscript of *Adventures in the Skin Trade*, a character was made to say, 'I remember once I drank twenty-nine Guinnesses straight off'. Then Thomas had second thoughts and altered it to read 'forty-nine Guinnesses'. In Cornwall in 1937 he boasted that he had drunk forty pints of beer, an unlikely feat.

If Thomas did, in fact, drink eighteen U.S. measures of whisky (equivalent to at least twice that number of British 'singles'), he had taken a dangerous amount of alcohol. Death could result from direct brain damage; or a lack of oxygen if breathing was depressed by the effect on the brain of alcohol. Even a dozen double whiskies, British measure, drunk over a short period, may be fatal. The phrase that came to be used of Thomas's collapse, that he had suffered 'a severe insult to the brain',[3] is a colourful way of describing direct alcoholic poisoning.

But in that case, events should have followed a different course. In all probability he would have collapsed within a few hours. Instead, he slept until the middle of the morning – it was now 4 November – when he woke saying that he was suf-

3. Brinnin quoted an unnamed doctor – 'we learned that it was now established that Dylan had sustained "a severe insult to the brain" and that this was due to direct alcoholic poisoning of brain cells and brain tissue'. But as the post-mortem makes clear, 'direct alcoholic poisoning' was never established. FitzGibbon went further and said the post-mortem gave the cause of death as 'insult to the brain'. No such phrase appears in the report.

focating and must have some air. Miss Reitell walked with him to the White Horse, at least half a mile away, where he had 'two glasses of beer' before returning unwell to the Chelsea. Feltenstein was sent for. Brinnin said he gave Thomas 'medications that would relieve his sufferings, temporarily at least', after which Thomas slept fitfully through the afternoon. By this time most of his blood-alcohol would have been eliminated; although if his nocturnal drinking had been very heavy, he could still have been drunk to some degree, with the lunchtime beers adding marginally to the effect. But he was suffering severe discomfort. Gastritis, which had troubled him for years, was causing him pain and making him vomit; the attack could have been brought on by drinking spirits on an empty stomach. Liz Reitell remembers 'ghastly racking spasms'. He also had pain from his gout. Feltenstein was summoned again, and gave Thomas an injection of ACTH. When he had left, Thomas promised her that he would begin a new regime, as the doctor insisted. During the evening he slept for 'a couple of hours', vomited again, and presently told her that he was seeing things – 'not animals ... abstractions'. She thought she recognized delirium tremens, and for the third time Feltenstein came to the hotel.

What happened then has been debated ever since, although the answer has been on record all along in the office of the Chief Medical Examiner for New York City. Brinnin wrote, 'As Dylan, raving now, begged to be put out, the doctor gave him a sedative.' At the time it was rumoured that this sedative was morphine. Howard Moss, who was friendly with Feltenstein, asked him if it was true. Feltenstein replied, 'He was in pain.' But to assert publicly and positively that a doctor gave morphine to a patient in Thomas's condition was more than any third party cared to do. Feltenstein refused to answer letters on the subject, a wise course. What he had done was to inject Thomas with half a grain of morphine sulphate, the form in which the drug is commonly given. Even without any special reason for avoiding morphine, it is too powerful and addictive to be administered merely for discomfort and malaise. The medical consensus is that under no circumstances would it be given for gout or gastritis. Liz Reitell has described Feltenstein as 'rather a wild doctor who thought injections would cure anything'. Whatever his logic, his motives were still unexplained when he died in 1974.[4]

He not only gave Thomas morphine, he gave him what is, in medical terms, a large amount. A normal dose to relieve acute pain is one-sixth of a grain. Thomas received three times as much. In the absence of other factors it is well below a lethal dose. But other factors were present. The 'breathlessness' from which Thomas had suffered in Wales was probably the result of asthma and smoking, which impaired the function of his lungs. Conceivably there was still sufficient alcohol in his blood to depress his breathing. It is possible that the pneumonia which soon developed had begun already; it could have been caused by inhaling a particle of vomit. If Thomas was suffering from any difficulty in breathing, the effect of half a grain of morphine could be catastrophic.

In any event, the injection was given, and once more Liz was left alone with him. According to Brinnin, Feltenstein suggested that someone should stay with her, in case 'delirium tremens might make Dylan uncontrollable'. She telephoned a painter, Jack Heliker, who arrived within a few minutes.[5] Between dozes, Thomas said that he still had 'the horrors', and spoke of 'abstractions, triangles and squares and circles', echoing his words to Pamela long ago, when, neurotic and sleepless, he told her how he lay in the dark and thought of 'God and Death and Triangles'. Thomas's life was marked with these ghostly echoes. Liz and Heliker sat, talked and waited. Making conversation, she mentioned that a friend of hers with D.T.s saw white mice and roses. Thomas, playing with words, said,

4. Dr B. W. Murphy suggests it may not have been incompetence on Feltenstein's part, but an unconscious desire to rid himself of an 'insufferable client'. Murphy – who later studied the case and discussed it with the neurologist in charge, Dr C. G. de Gutierrez-Mahoney – argues that Feltenstein's failure to see that Thomas was gravely ill with an 'acute confusional psychosis', and to have him admitted to hospital earlier, was even more culpable than his use of morphine.

5. Perhaps there were other visitors that night. The detective was prowling; a bare entry in FitzGibbon's 'TIME DETECTIVE' notebook refers to a 'get-together' at the Chelsea, then says: 'Reitell. Friends left.'

'Roses plural or Rose's roses with an apostrophe?' She was lying on the bed beside him, fully dressed. Heliker was in the room. His recollection is that Liz Reitell telephoned him at about 11 p.m. When he arrived at the hotel, he 'understood that Dylan had been given a sedative shortly before. When I came into the room, Liz said, "This is Jack," and Dylan sat up in bed and said, "Hello, Jack." He wanted a drink very badly, but she wouldn't give him one.' Heliker thinks he sat in the bedroom for about an hour. On a desk or table near the bed were some of Thomas's papers, and Heliker remembers reading a line that 'went something like, "He cried for death in his mother's breast" '. This must have been from the unfinished 'Elegy', which has the line, 'Above all he longed for his mother's breast'. According to Heliker, Thomas's last words were: 'After thirty-nine years, this is all I've done.'

Liz says she thought he was falling asleep. Then she heard him breathing with 'a terrible sound'. He was unconscious. Feltenstein came again and sent for an ambulance. Thomas was admitted to St Vincent's, a private Roman Catholic hospital, at two minutes before two a.m.[6]

It was Thursday, 5 November. In Laugharne that day, his radio talk about the town, recorded before he left, was included in the live broadcast from the school hall. For four and a half days, Thomas lay in a coma, under intensive care. According to Brinnin's account, and that of Dr Murphy, who later saw some of the clinical material, the hospital excluded possible diagnoses of brain haemorrhage, brain injury as the result of a fall, and diabetic shock. The opinion of Dr James Smith, an alcoholic specialist from Bellevue Hospital (now dead), and Dr Gutierrez-

6. The medical notes, as summarized by the hospital for the New York Medical Examiner's Office after Thomas's death, said: 'Patient brought into hospital in coma at 1.58 a.m. [5 November 1953]. Remained in coma during hospital stay. History of heavy alcoholic intake. Received ½ grain of M.S. shortly before admission . . . Impression on admission was acute alcoholic encephalopathy, for which patient was treated without response.' The 'acute alcoholic encephalopathy' would have been the 'insult to the brain'. A second document, the 'Notice of Death', said: 'History: (1) Heavy alcoholism (2) ½ grain morphine administered by a private doctor. Treated in hospital for toxic encephalopathy but diagnosis unconfirmed.'

Mahoney, the neurologist (who is untraceable), was apparently that Thomas had acute alcoholic poisoning; it may have been the neurologist who spoke of an 'insult to the brain'. What part, if any, was played by the morphine, which may have caused the breathing difficulties, thus starving the brain of oxygen and setting in train the fatal process, is speculative. The hospital's detailed case-notes are not available, ostensibly on the grounds that under New York law, information about a patient which would 'tend to disgrace the memory of the decedent' is privileged. But the possible effects of half a grain of morphine can hardly have been ignored at St Vincent's.[7]

A conversation that David Lougée had with the Bellevue specialist suggests what was being said in private. Lougée, a young admirer who became friendly with both Dylan and Caitlin, remembers the specialist telling him that 'the morphine shot could have been the trigger that led into the coma'. The specialist added that the cerebral oedema – virtually 'water on the brain' – which was established at the post-mortem as the immediate cause of death, was so extensive that 'it was going to happen anyway – it was just there, waiting to be triggered off'. Lougée wondered at the time if this last remark was made in order to protect Feltenstein. He was told at the hospital that Feltenstein was 'not allowed near the case'.

While Thomas lay unconscious, and the doctors debated, streams of friends, acquaintances and hangers-on came and went at St Vincent's. Factions developed; sinister accusations were whispered. It was rumoured that he had been given barbiturates as well as morphine in those last hours at the hotel;

7. Dr Graham Curtis Jenkins, of London, a doctor of medicine who first met Feltenstein when the latter was in Britain during the war, heard the story of Thomas's death from Feltenstein in New York in the early 1960s. Thomas is said to have been drunk, violent and 'in acute liver failure', a condition that was likely to prove fatal whatever happened. Curtis Jenkins, who defends Feltenstein as 'a careful, gentle physician of the highest integrity', thinks that for someone in Thomas's allegedly desperate condition, with a liver that may have been unable to cope with more conventional drugs, morphine was a reasonable sedative to use. But it's worth noting that Feltenstein himself didn't mention morphine to the British doctor.

that the doctors at St Vincent's had found it difficult to obtain a proper medical history; that Caitlin was being discouraged from coming to New York. Immediately after Thomas's death, Edith Sitwell, who was visiting America, found herself bombarded with telephone calls from strangers, denouncing one another to her. (She concluded loftily that 'he did know the most awful people'.) These antagonisms were to last a lifetime. Dylan the clown and good companion was regarded as common property by too many people for comfort when they all crowded to the deathbed.

Caitlin arrived at the weekend, driven from the airport to the city with an escort of police motor-cycles, and was looked after by Rose Slivka. At the hospital she made violent scenes on Sunday, while Brinnin's party tried to make sure that she didn't catch sight of Miss Reitell (according to Mrs Slivka, she did). Perhaps by arriving with a flourish and storming angrily to the bedside, she hoped that somehow she would generate the power to awaken him; this was how the faithful Mrs Slivka interpreted Caitlin's mixture of grief and rage. 'I was possessed of ten thousand ravaging demons,' wrote Caitlin. 'My madness: an untutored broken heart.' She smashed a crucifix and a statue of the Virgin, and attacked various people, including Brinnin, while Rose Slivka screamed, 'Go for the jugular, baby!' Both Caitlin and Rose were put in straitjackets, and Caitlin was taken to a private clinic on Long Island. Lougée says that before they sedated her at the clinic, they lied to her that Dylan was already dead.

In Wales, Vernon Watkins had been telephoned by the London *Times* and asked to provide an obituary at short notice. It took him most of Sunday at Pennard. 'Innocence is always a paradox,' he wrote, 'and Dylan Thomas presents, in retrospect, the greatest paradox of our time.' Thomas lived through one more night. He died when a nurse was washing him at lunchtime on Monday, 9 November. The post-mortem found the primary cause of death to be pneumonia, with 'pial oedema', the pressure on the brain, as the 'immediate cause', and a fatty liver, the sign of a heavy drinker, as an 'antecedent'. There were other signs associated with alcoholism, and the death was classified under two headings, 'Acute and chronic ethylism', which means the same as alcoholism, and 'Hypostatic bronchopneumonia'. As far as the pathologist was concerned, Thomas died of drink.

Among the effects that came back to Wales were fragments of Thomas's last poem to his father, 'Elegy', and a copy of his radio script, 'Return Journey'; letters from the Savage Club, Stravinsky, Philip Burton, Caitlin, 'Jean', Stephen Spender and his bank-manager; the *Sunday Pictorial* Diet Sheet; an inhaler, a tube of pills and a prescription from Dr Milton D. Feltenstein; a fountain-pen, a box of cigars, four suits, four shirts, two vests, two hot-water bottles, an empty cheque-book with blank stubs, and a few pounds in cash. He died intestate, as befitted a poet, and a nominal value of a hundred pounds was put on his possessions. It was a little time before the income from his books, records and play began to flood in, the public's homage to a poet who thoughtfully died young, or young enough for tears, in bizarre circumstances, having kept up his performance or caricature to the last.

In Laugharne, twenty-odd years after his death, they seemed to have stopped selling scraps of cloth to tourists and pretending they were true relics from the Boat House, which now had a curator and a visitors' book. His younger son, visiting Wales in 1975 from the other side of the world, where he had made his home, wrote in the book, 'It used to be a good house to live in', and signed it with his full name, Colm Garan Dylan Thomas. The herons still ruled the estuary. In Swansea, Americans still called occasionally at 5, Cwmdonkin Drive, and asked to see the bedroom by the boiler. Or they walked down the steep side of Cwmdonkin Park to examine the stone memorial that bears the last three lines of 'Fern Hill', incised in letters already succumbing to the Welsh weather.

POSTSCRIPT

# *Dylan Thomas as an Industry*

AFTER Thomas's death, there was no shortage of events to nourish the legend. New York buzzed with rumours about how he had died. He was said to have fallen at a party and struck his head. The morphine story circulated in whispers. In one account he was a diabetic. Some people (including Edith Sitwell) pretended to believe the story that he had scratched his eyeball on a rose-thorn a day or two before he collapsed, and that this was mysteriously connected with his death. But Rayner Heppenstall saw Thomas with a bloodshot eye in London years before, and was told then that a rose-thorn was to blame. As Heppenstall wrote sarcastically, 'A very suitable misadventure for a poet'.

While Thomas's body was being embalmed and prepared for its return to Britain, friends and hangers-on squabbled about whether he had been properly looked after. Brinnin was quick to record his version of events, which was essentially the version that he gave in his book two years later. Writing to John Davenport on 15 November, he said that Thomas had spoken of suicide in his last days, and that his final collapse followed a drinking bout; delirium tremens, said Brinnin, led to 'a comatose condition'. Drugs were not mentioned. Davenport heard a different version from George Reavey, who said morphine was involved and that the facts of Thomas's death were not emerging. Reavey quoted an unnamed doctor at St Vincent's as saying there had been difficulty in obtaining a case history because 'everyone was too emotional'.

The funeral was at Laugharne on 24 November. This produced its own crop of stories, the best of them still libellous of the living. The coffin had been taken to the Pelican; neighbours who called to pay their respects were allowed to raise the lid and view the body, dressed in a new suit supplied by the New York undertaker. Caitlin, with a sour eye for Welsh mourners, described the event as a 'mingling of the original black beetles, raffish Londoners, and Swansea boys in their best provincial suits'. John Davenport wrote that 'as his coffin was carried through the lych gate of the village church a cock began crowing redly'. Louis MacNeice, passing the grave with a bunch of flowers, was said to have dropped a packet of sandwiches by mistake. Nicolette Devas said it was 'a passionate day of sorrow and drinking ... a time of dignity and farce'. The pubs were open till all hours. While the drinking went on, the literary robbers were already at work. At least two signed copies of books by Thomas were stolen before the day was out. Two years later Caitlin sought permission to remove her husband's remains from the graveyard and have them re-interred in the garden of the Boat House, 'facing the water'. The Home Office gave provisional approval, but the matter was not pursued.

In 1953, Caitlin was left with three children, a house that didn't belong to her, and a backlog of debts against her husband's apparently non-existent estate. Funds in Britain and America raised substantial sums, which were held in trust. Current income, which at first seemed likely to be small, was in the hands of a trust to administer Thomas's copyrights that was set up, with Caitlin's agreement, five or six weeks after the funeral. The original trustees were David Higham, Thomas's literary agent; Stuart Thomas, his Swansea solicitor; and Daniel Jones, who resigned in 1955 and was replaced by Wynford Vaughan-Thomas. At first the trustees spent much of their time finding people who had been owed money by Thomas, and paying them off. Thomas cheques that had bounced were re-presented by creditors who had given up hope of seeing their money again. Debts in Laugharne had to be met. The milkman, owed for nine months' milk, asked that five pounds be deducted from his bill and given to the family. Months after Thomas's death, the trustees were still calculating prudently that over the next six or seven years his writings and recordings might with luck earn three thousand pounds. In the event, by 1955 far more than this was being earned in a single year, and the amounts rose steadily until the Trustees for the Copyrights of Dylan Thomas were administering an annual income believed to be well over twenty thousand pounds. The income has remained much larger than anything Dylan Thomas dreamt of in his lifetime. Half goes to Caitlin; the other half is divided between the children.

*Collected Poems* was a best-seller. So was the text of *Under Milk Wood*, the British edition of which sold twenty-five thousand copies within six months of Thomas's death. A year later, in May 1955, the book was in its seventh British impression. Earnings from America were still more surprising to those conditioned to equate Thomas with poverty. The copyrights of the Caedmon records and tapes became the most lucrative of all the properties. Material from Thomas's two formal sessions in 1952 and 1953 was supplemented by poems and prose recorded at the Poetry Centre and elsewhere, the first stage production of *Milk Wood*, and a number of B.B.C. recordings. Thomas made rich women of Barbara Holdridge and Marianne Mantell.

By the modest standards of modern poetry, Thomas came to be recognized as a star name throughout the world. He seemed to fill a need – whether as rebel against machine society, or romantic figure that all could recognize – in Japan and Italy (for example), as in Britain and America. No modern poet of any country has generated such a quantity of gossip, reminiscence and criticism, with America in the lead. Since his death, full-length critical studies in English have appeared at the rate of rather more than one a year. But the only major biography has been FitzGibbon's *The Life of Dylan Thomas* (1965). John Ackerman's *Dylan Thomas: His Life and Works* (1964) was written without access to the papers. *The Days of Dylan Thomas* (1964) by Bill Read was a short illustrated book (many of the photographs by Rollie McKenna) which failed to do justice to Read's extensive research; he was not allowed to quote from Thomas's letters and other papers. John Brinnin's *Dylan Thomas in America* (1955) was an enthralling, emotive account, with an introductory 'statement' by Caitlin Thomas. Andrew Sinclair's *Dylan Thomas: Poet of His People* (1975) was an unexceptional text, handsomely illustrated. *My Friend Dylan Thomas* (1977) by Daniel Jones was a slim volume of reminiscence, long awaited. Other friends who have written at length about Thomas in the course of books of memoirs are cited in the Notes. A play by Sidney Michaels, *Dylan*, had a successful run in New York in 1964. A novel by John Summers, also called *Dylan*, appeared in Britain in 1970. Hundreds of articles about Thomas and his poetry have been written. At least forty academic theses, mainly by American scholars, can be listed. Kent Thompson's 'Dylan Thomas in Swansea' is the most useful to a biographer.

Most of Thomas's writing for radio, and many of his performances, are mentioned in the text or the Notes. No one has yet attempted a full bibliography of his broadcasts. A complete edition of Dylan Thomas would presumably include all the material in the B.B.C. Archives and script libraries. Books by Thomas have continued to appear. *Quite Early One Morning* (1954) and *A Prospect of the Sea* (1955) collected a number of radio scripts and early stories. Four film scripts have been published posthumously: *The Beach at Falesa, 20 Years A-Growing* (both 1964), *Me and My Bike*, *Rebecca's Daughters* (both 1965). The satire written jointly with John Davenport, *The Death of the King's Canary*, appeared in 1976. Various selections of poems and prose have been made. Some of Thomas's critical articles, esoteric stories and juvenilia were collected in *Dylan Thomas: Early Prose Writings*, edited by Walford Davies (1971). *Letters to Vernon Watkins*, edited by Watkins (1957), and *Selected Letters*, edited by FitzGibbon (1966), between them contain fewer than half the letters extant, though a larger proportion of the important letters. Whoever edits a collected edition will have to correct many minor errors in transcription, some of which (where letters have been taken from FitzGibbon or other printed, and not manuscript, sources) are no doubt repeated here.

In *Poet in the Making: The Notebooks of Dylan Thomas* (1967), Ralph Maud transcribed and annotated the contents of the four poetry notebooks at Buffalo. In 1971 Daniel Jones edited *Dylan Thomas: The Poems*; this contains everything that is in *Collected Poems* and more than a hundred other poems, mostly taken from the notebooks. It is thus a mixture of poems that Thomas wanted to keep in print and poems in which, presumably, he had no lasting interest. The only accessible verse by Thomas that has escaped publication in one form or another is in the Texas manuscripts. Most of it is doggerel, but there is a manuscript of an unfinished poem of about 1936, 'For as long as forever is', which is mentioned by Watkins; this (together with one of the juvenile poems, several of which are in unpublished manuscripts at Texas) is printed as an Appendix.

Caitlin Thomas has contributed two books of her own. *Leftover Life to Kill* (1957) and *Not Quite Posthumous Letters to My Daughter* (1963) express her grief, while dealing savagely with life and people in general. For many years Mrs Thomas has lived in Italy, and has perhaps found a kind of peace at last. In 1977 she wrote to me: 'There was no one highlight in my life with Dylan, it was all highlights and rock bottoms. It still rankles with me that he obtained both fame and escape, his two most desired ends, in one fell swoop – leaving me holding his babies. But the best things, in fact, that he left me were his babies, now of course grown-up children, who are a constant reminder to me, with their funny looks and his brains, of *who* it was who, *miraculously* – because they could so easily have been somebody else's, but God, not me, saw to it that they weren't – fathered them. So that, in each one of my three children separately, I can see and love a different aspect of Dylan. So that for me Dylan, in one shape or another, is always with me. This is the greatest gift that Dylan has given to me. Never mind the poetry which I am not clever enough to read. Never mind the money either which has caused more ill-feeling than good, which does not mean nevertheless that I do not need it body and soul. But that is a long-drawn-out argument that I am not going into now. I will spare you that pain. Pain is a more or less constant state of being, sometimes dulled, sometimes accentuated into acute distress. Work is the best antidote to it ...'

Thomas's letters and papers of all kinds have been sought by collectors for a quarter of a century. There are unprintable allegations concerning some of the items and how they passed into circulation. No doubt most of them have been sold in a straightforward way by their owners. Bert Trick sold his important five Thomas letters to an American dealer for $1,500 in 1965. Douglas Cleverdon sold his manuscript of *Under Milk Wood* to the Times Book Company for £2,000 in 1961; it is said to have changed hands later for five times as much. The records of Sothebys, who have handled much of the material that has gone through the London market, show the kind of prices paid for smaller items: a short letter thanking T. S. Eliot for his cheque, £110 (1966); two sheets of drafts for 'A Story', £150 (1966); three pages of drafts for 'Elegy', £150 (1966); one-page letter to Nigel Henderson, £220 (1970); one-page letter to Cordelia Locke (about renting her cottage at South Leigh), £100 (1972); three letters to Robert Byron, author, and one to Edith Sitwell, £300 (1972); a notebook with eighteen pages of notes about the Llangollen Eisteddfod and a press ticket, £550 (1973). Any scrap of paper with Thomas's handwriting on it – a copied-out poem by someone else, a galley-proof with a couple of corrections – has found a market. The Texas collection includes a betting slip, a tax-exemption certificate and a restaurant bill. A duplicated copy of the script of a radio documentary about Thomas (dozens of which would have been run off by the B.B.C.), inscribed by a friend of Thomas, has been catalogued in London at £80. A London dealer, in correspondence with a seller of Thomas manuscripts who wished the transactions to be kept strictly private, has even added the letters requesting privacy to the items in question that he bought and then resold. Thus the vendor's letters, one asking for 'especially vigorous' secrecy and another explaining that he doesn't want his wife to know, can now be read in one of the American collections.

In Britain, the most important public collection is in the British Museum, which has the letters to Vernon Watkins and a few other items. The National Library of Wales at Aberystwyth has acquired some letters, and was given manuscript drafts of parts of 'A Story' and 'Elegy' by Emlyn Williams in 1976 (he had been given them by Florence Thomas after his stage appearance as Dylan Thomas). Swansea University College has copies of Kent Thompson's thesis and his interview notes. West Glamorgan County Library, Swansea, has a collection of articles and books about Thomas.

The bulk of the manuscripts have gone to America. Texas has by far the largest collection. Buffalo has the notebooks and much other material, including letters to Trevor Hughes and Pamela Hansford Johnson, and Miss Johnson's diaries. Other material is at Harvard, Indiana and Ohio universities, and the New York Public Library. The list is not exhaustive. I have read most of the available material during the research for this book. But the labour of describing and listing the Thomas Papers in their entirety, including the items still in private hands, awaits a research student with some years to spare, supported by a university wealthy enough to pay.

APPENDIX

# *Two Unpublished Poems by Dylan Thomas*

## *La Danseuse*

(written as a child; see Note to p. 38)

She moved like silence swathed in light,
Like mist in moonshine clear;
A music that enamoured sight
Yet did elude the ear.

A rapture and a spirit clad
In motion soft as sleep;
The epitome of all things glad,
The sum of all that weep.

Her form was like a poet's mind,
By all sensations sought.
She seemed the substance of the wind,
One shape of lyric thought;

A being 'mid terrestrial things
Transcendently forlorn;
Through time bound far on gleaming wings
For some diviner bourn.

The rhythms of the swooning heart
Swayed to her sweet control;
Life in her keeping all was art,
And all of body soul.

Faint-shimmering in the roseate air
She seemed to ebb and flow
Like memories perilously fair,
And pale from long ago.

She stooped to grief's remembered tears,
Yearned to undawned delight.
Ah, beauty – passionate from the years!
Oh, body – wise and white!

She vanished like an evening cloud,
A sunset's radiant gleam.
She vanished. Life awhile endowed
The darkness with a dream.

## *For as long as forever is*

(unfinished, circa 1936 – see *Letters to Vernon Watkins*, pp. 47–8). Thomas abandoned the poem because the opening line was 'completely out of place'. Later he used it as the last line of the poem 'Twenty-four years'. (See also Note to p. 147.)

For as long as forever is
And the fast sky quakes in the web, as the fox in the wave,
With heels of birds & the plumed eyes,
Shakes in its stride the partridge fence and the sea-duck rows,
And a flame in a wheel jumps the nave,
As a dozen winds drop the dark by the one moonrise,
And a stag through a trap grave,
Forever the hunted world at a snail's gallop goes.

Over the packed nests now, the snare & the she-bear's floes,
Through the cats' mountain & the cave
By the market & feather street near the townspires,
Narrowly time's slow riders shave . . .

# *Notes*

Where an informant is named but no context given for the information, it can be assumed it was in an interview with the author. Similarly, unless otherwise stated, 'in a letter' means in a letter to the author.

The following abbreviations are used:

*Papers:*

| | |
|---|---|
| Texas mss | Humanities Research Centre, the University of Texas at Austin. |
| Buffalo mss | Lockwood Memorial Library, State University of New York at Buffalo. |
| Harvard mss | The Houghton Library, Harvard University. |
| Berg mss | The Berg Collection, New York Public Library. |
| Indiana mss | The Lilly Library, the Universities Libraries, Indiana University. |
| Wales mss | National Library of Wales. |
| BM mss | British Museum. |
| D.H.A. | Papers seen at David Higham Associates. |

*Books and magazines* (book page-references to English hard-cover edition unless stated):

| | |
|---|---|
| *The Poems* | *Dylan Thomas: The Poems* (ed. Daniel Jones). |
| *T.F.F.* | *Two Flamboyant Fathers* (Nicolette Devas). |
| *A.W.R.* | *Anglo-Welsh Review.* |
| *S.L.* | *Selected Letters of Dylan Thomas* (ed. Constantine FitzGibbon). |
| *C.P.* | *Dylan Thomas. Collected Poems 1934–1952.* |

| | |
|---|---|
| *E.P.W.* | *Dylan Thomas: Early Prose Writings* (ed. Walford Davies). |
| *Q.E.O.M.* | *Quite Early One Morning* (ed. Aneirin Talfan Davies). |
| Tedlock | *Dylan Thomas: the Legend and the Poet* (ed. E. W. Tedlock). |
| *L.V.W.* | *Dylan Thomas: Letters to Vernon Watkins* (ed. Watkins). |
| *Leftover* | *Leftover Life to Kill* (Caitlin Thomas). |
| *Prospect* | *A Prospect of the Sea* (ed. Daniel Jones). |
| Brinnin (with page-reference) | *Dylan Thomas in America* (John Malcolm Brinnin), Ace Books (paperback), 1957. |
| FitzGibbon (with page-reference) | *The Life of Dylan Thomas* (Constantine FitzGibbon). |
| *Not Quite* | *Not Quite Posthumous Letters to My Daughter* (Caitlin Thomas). |
| *Skin Trade* | *Adventures in the Skin Trade.* |

*Introduction*

p. xvii. Interviews:

A few of Thomas's contemporaries in Swansea still grow tight-lipped when asked to reminisce, but this may be irritation with two and a half decades of interviewers. One former B.B.C. person in London bellowed 'Bugger off' down the telephone when I approached him. Fortunately this didn't happen often.

1. *Names from the Past*

p. 1. 'Silly ravens': Thomas to Vernon Watkins, 20 December 1938.

p. 2. Six poems at Laugharne:

'Over Sir John's hill', 'In the white giant's thigh', 'Lament', 'Do not go gentle', 'Poem on his birthday', 'Prologue'.

p. 3. Rehashing his adolescence:

Caitlin to Oscar and Gene Williams, 9 February 1952, error for 1953. Harvard mss.

pp. 8–11. Information about the Thomas family in the nineteenth century:

(*a*) *Dictionary of Welsh Biography;* (*b*) W. Greville-Griffiths, whose grandmother was one of D. J. Thomas's sisters; (*c*) Mrs Rachael Evans (a cousin of D. J. Thomas), Miss Mary Davies (with whom Florence Thomas lived temporarily towards the end of her life) and A. E. Savage (who knew D. J. Thomas in his youth), all three interviewed in Carmarthen in December 1963 by Kent Thompson. Thompson, an American post-graduate student at Swansea University College, later wrote his Ph.D. thesis on 'Dylan Thomas in Swansea' (1965). He interviewed many local people.

p. 10. 'Elegy' notes: photocopy in Texas mss.

pp. 12–17. The Williams family, and Florence's marriage to D. J. Thomas:

(*a*) interviews, including (in Carmarthenshire) Mrs Mary Ann Williams, Llwyn Gwyn; Mrs Annie Lewis, Lletyrneadd; Alderman J. Davies, Llanybri. 'Dr Dan' was recalled at both Llwyn Gwyn and Lletyrneadd. (In Swansea) Mrs Addie Elliott, Miss Ethel Ross and Mrs Irene Howell, whose grandmother was a sister of Anna Williams; (in Cardiff) Mrs Theodosia Legg, daughter of Florence's brother, John. (*b*) Kent Thompson's ms. The gravestones at Capel Newydd, Llanybri, were also useful.

p. 12. 'Undeniably mad peasantry': Thomas to Oscar Williams, 30 July 1945. *S.L.*

p. 15. 'I hate you':

Gwen Watkins. She heard the line from Vernon Watkins, who remembered Thomas reading it to him.

pp. 16–17. Florence and D.J.:

Ethel Ross kept a diary in which she noted these and other statements by Mrs Thomas.

p. 18. The midwife was Mrs Gillian Williams, quoted by Ethel Ross, 'We Had Evidence and No Doubt', *Gower*, No. 16, 1964. Miss Ross, with Mrs Williams as her source, says that Florence 'lost her first child'. (FitzGibbon (p. 22) says it was her *second* child that died.)

p. 18. D. J. at Blaen Cwm: Mrs Hettie Owen (see Note, p. 34).

p. 18. etc. D. J. as schoolmaster, etc.:

Interviews with Wynford Vaughan-Thomas, Stuart Thomas, Charles McKelvie, John Prichard, Waldo Clarke (who were all more or less contemporary with Dylan Thomas at the Grammar School); Gwevril Dawkins, Nancy's friend; J. Morgan Williams, former master at the school. Letter from E. G. Lewis, former master. Charles Fisher, *Herald of Wales*, 12 March 1938. *Swansea Grammar*

*School Magazine*, March 1937, article on D. J. Thomas's retirement.

p. 19. The journalist was C. Gordon Glover. See pp. 235–7.

p. 19. Caitlin on D.J.:

Copy of a fragment in Caitlin's hand. Texas mss.

p. 20. D.J. teaching Welsh:

Interview with Florence Thomas, 24 May 1955. I interviewed Mrs Thomas for an article that I wrote for *Everybody's*, 'Go and Write, Boy', 21 April 1956. Much of her information was not used, but the original notes survived.

p. 20. etc. Paying the tradesmen, and other household information:

Mrs Elliott, who as 'Addie' was the maid at 5, Cwmdonkin Drive.

pp. 22–3. Difficulties over name:

Florence Thomas, 1955 interview. FitzGibbon suggests that 'D.J. cannot fail to have been reminded of the name Dylan in the year of his son's birth. In July of 1914 an opera was staged at Covent Garden with the title *Dylan, Son of the Wave*. The music was by Josef Holbrook, the libretto by T. E. Ellis, which was the pseudonym of Lord Howard de Walden. This opera, of which D.J. must have heard from Dr Vaughan Thomas, the composer, whom he was seeing at the time, was part of an attempted "Welsh Revival" ...'

p. 23. 'Dillan' or 'Dullan':

Dr Daniel Jones, Thomas's friend, has argued in *Dylan Thomas: The Poems*, p. 259, that even in Welsh, the pronunciation should be 'Dillan', on the ground that in the *Mabinogion* 'the name occurs with a circumflex over the "y"'. When Thomas became a regular broadcaster, he asked the B.B.C. to stop using the orthodox Welsh pronunciation of 'Dullan'. The Cardiff *Western Mail* of 4 March 1954 quoted a letter written by a B.B.C. official which said, 'We originally used the Welsh pronunciation of the name Dylan, but changed this in May 1946 to the anglicized form of Dill-an at the request of Mr Dylan Thomas himself.'

## 2. *His Father's Son*

p. 25. Pocock:

In a B.B.C. radio documentary about Dylan Thomas that was hurriedly put together by Marguerite Scott, following his death in November 1953. Home Service, 11 December.

p. 26. Ruthven Todd:

B.B.C. radio talk, reprinted in the *Listener*, 17 December 1959.

p. 26. Locked in in Hampshire: Thomas to Charles Fisher, 11 February 1938. *S.L.*

p. 26. Feather bed: Nicolette Devas, *Two Flamboyant Fathers*, p. 207.

p. 26 fn. Lord Marley: in an interview.

p. 27 fn. Murphy: *Br. J. med. Psychol.* (1968), *41*, 149.

pp. 27–8. The *Struwwelpeter* theory:

Michael Neill's 'Dylan Thomas's "Tailor Age"', *Notes and Queries*, February 1970, p. 59. *Dylan and the Scissor-men*, Christopher Page, *Anglo-Welsh Review*, Summer 1974, and Murphy, op. cit. Thomas mentions the book in his radio feature, 'Return Journey': 'In the afternoons, when the children were good, they read aloud from *Struwwelpeter*.'

p. 28. Thomas to Treece: 31 December 1938. *S.L.*

p. 28. 'That fearful D.J.':

Later, Pamela Hansford Johnson was on good terms with both Jack and Florence Thomas.

p. 29. Ruthven Todd: unpublished ms, Texas mss.

p. 29. Answers to a student:

The replies, to five questions, were reprinted in *Texas Quarterly*, Winter 1961, and in *Dylan Thomas: Early Prose Writings*, as 'Poetic Manifesto'; they were given in 1951 to a research student in Wales who was writing a short thesis. The original consists of nine ms pages.

p. 30. Dylan in church: Mrs Gwen Nobbs.

p. 32. Jim Jones borrowing money: Mary Ann Williams, Llfyn Gwyn.

p. 32. The ms notes about Fernhill also say:

'I made that story "The Peaches" out of a number of tiny incidents that occurred that happened [*sic*] one summer holiday when I was a child; "The Peaches" was based on a true incident; but what made the story were many other tiny incidents, and memories, of many other holidays. I worked them in all together to make one story.' Texas mss.

p. 32. Idris Jones died in 1959.

p. 33. The hangman, who was to appear in early poems, is recalled in local gossip as a real person, and Fernhill as 'the hangman's house'. A local resident says it had the reputation of being an unlucky house. The owner of Fernhill in 1975, Mr Ken Davies, says he has researched the hangman story and established that the man was Robert Ricketts Evans, assistant to the Carmarthen hangman.

Evans's daughter, who had money of her own that Evans wanted to get hold of, is supposed to have run off with a German. One story goes that her father locked her up in Fernhill to keep her away from her lover – the windows were said to have been barred – but that she escaped and walked to Carmarthen in her nightgown. Ken Davies, who claims to have seen a woman's ghost at Fernhill, gives the year of Evans's death as 1901. Dylan Thomas's ms notes about Fernhill include the following: 'Very lonely. The hangman used to live there, though not in my time. I remember the bars he'd put across the window: I suppose to keep out the incensed relations of his involuntary customers, or even the customers themselves. He committed suicide: of course with his rope. It was a lovely farm.' The former Carmarthenshire County Archivist, Major Francis Jones, says Fernhill is a nineteenth-century house of no historical significance, and adds that he has seen 'no documentary proof or other reputable evidence' to support the hangman story and its romantic embellishments.

p. 33. The acquaintance who met Mrs Bassett was Gwevril Dawkins.

p. 34. D. J. Thomas's brothers:

Mrs Hettie Owen, who (with her husband Ken) lived at Blaen Cwm during the war and knew the Thomas family well. Mrs Owen came from Port Talbot, on Swansea Bay, and in the 1930s Arthur Thomas moved from nearby Aberavon and lodged with her family. Mrs Owen remembers Arthur as 'a kind-hearted man who liked his pint, an ordinary sort of man, not educated'.

p. 34. etc. Dylan, school and health: Florence Thomas, the 1955 interview.

p. 35. Mrs Hole's school:

Evelyn Burman Jones; Kent Thompson, interviewing Mrs Dorothy de Mattos (now dead), Mrs Hole's daughter, in 1963.

p. 35. Jerseys, etc.: Evelyn Jones.

p. 36. Dylan as the colonel: Mrs de Mattos.

p. 36. 'Reminiscences of Childhood' was written in two versions. The extract is from the second.

p. 38. Thomas to Watkins:

N.d., probably August 1940. *Letters to Vernon Watkins*, p. 100. The originals of this correspondence are in B.M. mss. Watkins's edited version is scrupulous, but he deleted a number of passages and names to avoid offence.

p. 38. Walking in August:

The radio talk was 'The Crumbs of One Man's Year', 27 December 1946, B.B.C. Home Service, reprinted in *Quite Early One Morning*.

p. 38. Juvenilia:

Hettie Owen was helping Florence Thomas clear out cupboards at Blaen Cwm after Dylan's death, when Mrs Thomas found the poems and asked her friend to burn them. Mrs Owen got her permission to keep the poems. They are now in the Texas mss. There were seven: 'The Maniac', 'Inspirations', 'Decision', 'The Mishap', 'My Party', 'Little Dreams' and 'La Danseuse'.

p. 38. Mrs Thomas on juvenilia: 1955 interview.

## 3. *A Sort of Schoolboy*

p. 40. D.J. and the chair of English:

This persistent local story is doubted by Professor Cecil Price of Swansea University College. But E. Glyn Lewis, former senior English master at the Grammar School (where his career briefly overlapped that of D. J. Thomas) is 'convinced from all that I have heard and from my own inferences that the university chair story is true'. Glyn Lewis adds (in a letter): 'The Grammar School of my time had only two fine teachers – D. J. Thomas and W. S. Davies – both of a kind and both close friends so far as they could be friends with anybody.'

p. 40. D.J. and T. J. Rees: Gwevril Dawkins.

p. 40 etc. D.J. as master:

Much of the information is from J. Morgan Williams.

p. 41. 'His Requiem':

The *Sunday Telegraph* printed it on 30 May 1971. Its follow-up story a week later reported the observant reader, Mr Richard Parker of London. Thomas's changes included dropping two words to give two of the lines an iambic beat, and replacing 'the cortège grim' with 'the coffin grim'.

p. 42. School magazine:

Thomas contributed to the issues of December 1925, December 1926, March 1927, July 1927; to all three of each year's issues for 1928, 1929 and 1930; to those of April 1931 and July 1931, his last term at school. After he left he had a signed poem in the July 1933 issue. December 1933 and July 1934 each carries a story signed 'Old Boy', probably Thomas. *Dylan Thomas in Print*, pp. 45–7.

p. 43. '. . . self-deprecating writers':

10 pp. of undated ms notes, beginning 'I'm going to read some modern poems tonight'. Most of the passage quoted has been lightly crossed through. Probably in Texas mss; I saw a copy elsewhere. In the last few years of his life, Thomas's lecture notes, and some of his radio talks and other pieces, cannibalize one another for phrases and sometimes long passages. The 10 pp. of lecture notes echo or are echoed by the 1951 'Poetic Manifesto' (see note to p. 29).

p. 45. 'A bad boy':

P. E. S.[mart], 'Under Milk Wood and a reminiscence of school-days' in *Spread Eagle*, published by Barclays Bank, April 1954.

p. 45. Bad language:

Guido Heller, a contemporary, quoted by Kent Thompson.

p. 45. Florence's Welsh: 1955 interview.

p. 46. 'Old Smalley': Raymond Mitchell.

p. 46. School sports:

The photograph was in the *Cambria Daily Leader*, 23 June 1926; the caption said he was aged twelve, but he was eleven. This may have been the 'yellowed newspaper clipping' of a photograph that Thomas kept in his wallet and showed John Brinnin in New York in 1950. Brinnin says it reported a 220-yard race.

p. 46. Childhood accidents:

Florence Thomas, 1955; Kent Thompson; Gwevril Dawkins; Professor Armel Diverres, then a neighbour; Raymond Mitchell.

p. 47. Running at Rhossili:

John Bennett says in a letter, 'I remember [Dylan] saying to me, "Can't understand why you people pick your feet up so much" – his running style was most unorthodox – he seemed to raise his feet a little and glide over the ground.'

p. 47. Daniel Jones, at work on his own reminiscences for some years, was not anxious to help.

p. 48. Joint plays:

An exercise-book has a draft of 'Bismuth'. The characters include Arnold, an impotent architect; Patricia, his wife; Derek, a homosexual; Phoebe, also homosexual, and Arthur, 'of doubtful parentage, sex and inclination'. Texas mss.

p. 48. 'Bram':

This is a rather formal way of saying 'fart' in Welsh. Perhaps Thomas and Jones were also thinking of Bram Stoker, author of *Dracula*.

p. 48. Jones on joint poems:

*The Legend and the Poet* (ed. Tedlock), pp. 16–17.

p. 50. Warmley Broadcasting ms: Texas mss.

p. 51. Thomas to Jones:

From 'Glen Lough, Meenacross, nr. Glencolumkille, Lifford, Co. Donegal, Irish Free State. Tuesday, 14 August 1935. Addressed, unavoidably, to Fred [Janes].' Texas mss.

p. 54–5. McInerny: to Kent Thompson, and in letters.

p. 54. Obscurity:

McInerny heard Thomas defend an obscure line in another poem in discussion with a master. He remembers the line (apparently never published) as 'They toil, powdered with a white music'. Thomas said it had 'come into his head', and was the best thing he had ever written. McInerny wrote an anonymous poem in the school magazine, protesting at obscurity in modern verse, which caught Thomas's attention. Another of McInerny's anonymous poems, 'The Sun', was later unearthed by a German researcher in Swansea and attributed to Thomas.

p. 54. 'The Elm': *The Poems*, p. 226.

p. 57. Models for writing: 'Poetic Manifesto'.

p. 58. Disastrous results: Armel Diverres.

p. 58. Haemorrhage: the Colin Edwards interview (see p. 23, fn.).

p. 58. Breakdown: 1955 interview.

p. 59. Charles Fisher: in a letter.

p. 59. 'Little Dogs' ms: Texas mss.

p. 60. Dates and notebook poems:

No doubt most of the dates appended to poems are close to the date of composition. But none of the original drafts of these notebook poems survives, and time may have elapsed between draft and fair copy. For example: a notebook poem dated July 1931, beginning 'Sever from what I trust', appears in a slightly different form as a pencilled draft, itself probably a copy, at the back of a book of Osbert Sitwell's poems, *Argonaut and Juggernaut* (published 1927) and dated 29 April 1931, which is in the Texas mss.

## 4. *Reporter, Actor, Poet*

p. 63. 'A good opening': 1955 interview.

p. 63. The reader: Trevor Ogborn, in the 1953 radio documentary.

pp. 63–4 fn. Nellie Wallace interview:

Thomas presumably went to see her while he was still a copyholder; or even before he left school. The article was unsigned and headed: 'Nellie Wallace's Mimicry – Marie Dressler Her Favourite

Star – Harder Work.' It described how 'Last night, in her dressing-room, Miss Wallace gave a *Daily Post* reporter just one example of her art of mimicry – with a perfect impersonation of Marie Dressler, whose latest films are the only ones that she has found interesting, for she is very interested in films as a whole. On the subject of talkies, however, she said that she felt that they were not gaining ground ...' W.V.-T.'s account: the *Listener*, 16 January 1958, reprinting an Overseas Service talk.

p. 64. An older colleague:

Eric Hughes, another Grammar School boy who went to the *Post.*

p. 64. Thomas to Treece: 31 December 1938. *S.L.*

p. 64. The matron: 1955 interview.

p. 65. J. D. Williams on Dylan:

In his review of *Twenty-five Poems* ('Some of His Joyous Adventures in a Newspaper Office'), *Herald of Wales*, 19 September 1936. Reprinted in *Dylan Thomas in Print*, pp. 58–60.

p. 65. American newshound: Charles Fisher, in a letter.

p. 66. 'Three Lamps':

Thomas wrote in 'Old Garbo' that his father was 'visiting Uncle A. in Aberavon', the nearest he ever came to writing about D.J.'s brothers.

p. 70. D.J.'s appearance: Hettie Owen.

p. 71. Affluent Taylor:

Local gossip remembers him as more affluent still, earning '£2,000 a year as a quantity surveyor'. He went to Swansea as a travelling salesman in asbestos bricks. But in later life he was a prosperous businessman.

p. 71. *Evening Post* paragraph: 9 September 1932, identified by Haydn Taylor.

p. 71. Nancy's letters are in the possession of Haydn Taylor, who made the extracts.

p. 74. 'End of a Great Ministry':

5 November 1932. It is just possible that Thomas's dutiful response to the retirement of this unfavourite uncle was the starting-point for a poem about (among other things) hypocrisy, 'I have longed to move away'. In the notebook this is dated 1 March 1933. The published version has 'the old lie burning on the ground'. The longer notebook version makes it clear that Thomas was thinking of fireworks ('like some sulphurous reminder of November'). 5 November is fireworks night, when, conceivably, the poem or the mood that led to it was germinating.

p. 76. Jones: *The Poems*, p. 271.

p. 76. Trevor Hughes:

Biographical details in 'A Friend who Lives on in a Dylan Thomas Story', by Bernard Lloyd, *A.W.R.*, Autumn 1971. 'Trevor Tregaskis Hughes of Harrow, who had been on the British Railways staff at Euston for ten years, died in November 1966 at the age of sixty-two ... Hughes had been taught by Dylan's father at the Grammar School. "I first met Dylan," Hughes wrote later, "when he was sixteen and about to leave school. I called at his home in Cwmdonkin Drive. His sister and he were listening to a gramophone record of a Negro spiritual ... On those first evenings which we spent together, he would sit on the settee and read aloud. He was pushing out his immature poems, watching his listener's face" ... Hughes [whose family moved to London] also helped Dylan to accustom himself to London on his first visits there. About the end of 1931 he accompanied Dylan to the British Museum, where Dylan is said to have mistaken a meteorite for a piece of abstract sculpture ... Sometime in 1935, however, the close friendship cooled – perhaps because Dylan thought an article Hughes wrote about his *18 Poems* was "exaggerated praise". Also Dylan did not like Hughes's story "A Cobbler's Vane" in which Hughes portrayed Dylan as an eighteenth-century cobbler – "he told his tales until the variety of drinks confused him and Caleb's rhymes lost their reason".' Possibly Hughes knew from Thomas that his great-uncle Gwilym Marles had been a cobbler.

p. 77. Undated letter: *S.L.*, p. 6, where FitzGibbon dates it 'December 1932?'.

p. 77. Early February letter:

*S.L.*, p. 9, where FitzGibbon dates it January. Thomas says his mother has gone to Carmarthen to be at Aunt Ann's deathbed. Ann Jones died 7 February.

p. 78. 'Out of the sighs':

The lines quoted are from the notebook, and differ slightly from the published version.

p. 78. Thomas to Hughes: *S.L.*, p. 9.

p. 79. 'Was there a time':

The notebook version, which begins 'Hold on whatever slips beyond the edge/To hope', is more than twice as long. Maggots on 'my' track had become a single maggot on 'their', i.e. children's, track, by the time the poem was revised for publication.

p. 79. Bert Trick:

His ms account of 'The Young Dylan Thomas' is in Texas mss. Kent Thompson interviewed him.

p. 81. Informal group:

Among the names Trick recalled for Kent Thompson were Tom Warner, Leonard Morris (later a musician), Fred Janes and 'sometimes, although rarely, Dan Jones'. Their cosy private gatherings are faintly reflected in the *Portrait* story, 'Where Tawe Flows', in which 'young Mr Thomas' and three older friends meet to plan a novel.

p. 81. 'What colour is glory':

Thomas first used it in the notebook version of 'Why east wind chills' ('What colour is glory? the children ask'), 1 July 1933; the phrase disappeared when the poem was revised.

p. 81. Naming the child: Nell, Bert Trick's widow.

pp. 82–3. Trick told Kent Thompson the story of 'And death shall have no dominion'.

p. 82. Sleeping badly:

'Last night I slept for the first time this month ... Minute by minute through the eight hours of the dark I lay and looked up into the empty corners of this room ... soon my lips would speak sentences aloud, and I listen to them ...' Thomas to Pamela, n.d., probably 11 November 1933, *S.L.* p. 58.

pp. 84–5. Poems to the end of August 1933:

The twelve already written that were close to or strongly suggestive of their final form were: 'The spire cranes', 'The Hunchback in the Park', 'Out of the sighs', 'Was there a time', 'I have longed to move away', 'And death shall have no dominion', 'Why east wind chills', 'Here in this spring', 'Find meat on bones', 'Ears in the turrets hear', 'Shall gods be said', 'The hand that signed the paper'. The eleven poems that were more substantially revised (in some cases losing all but a few phrases) became 'How shall my animal', 'Today, this insect', 'After the funeral', 'On no work of words', 'On the marriage of a virgin', 'O make me a mask', 'Not from this anger', 'We lying by seasand', 'Incarnate devil', 'The tombstone told when she died', 'Grief thief of time'. It is likely that missing notebooks contained early versions of other published poems.

p. 85. *18 Poems* written later:

Ralph Maud was probably the first to draw attention to the order in which Thomas wrote his poems, in 'Dylan Thomas' *Collected Poems*: Chronology of Composition', *Publications of the Modern Language Association of America*, June 1961.

## 5. *A Case of Cancer*

p. 86. First visit:

FitzGibbon cites Hughes and Reavey, but thinks they were wrong. Florence Thomas said Dylan first went to London 'the year Nancy got married', i.e. 1933, according to a recording she made at Carmarthen in 1957 for Ethel Ross. The recording has much family detail. Transcript published in the *Arts Festival Magazine* of the Swansea College of Education, 1966; copy in West Glamorgan County Library, Swansea, D.T. 2964.

p. 87. Connolly:

Reviewing *New Verse: An Anthology*, *New Statesman*, 16 September, 1939.

p. 87. Thomas to Grigson: *S.L.*, p. 18.

p. 88. Jones at Steyning:

He mentions his visit in *The Poems*, p. 258, but doesn't say why he was there.

p. 88. 'That sanity be kept':

Stephen Spender thinks it was this poem which led him to write to Thomas. But a letter from Thomas to Spender in *S.L.*, March 1934, suggests their first contact followed 'Light breaks' in the *Listener*. See p. 102.

p. 88. D.J.'s cancer:

It was possible to trace details of this distant episode because Gwevril Dawkins remembered that when D.J. was admitted to hospital in London, a junior doctor called Thurgar, a former pupil at the Grammar School, examined him. John Thurgar, F.R.C.S., turned out to be a surgeon living in Scotland. He remembered the case and was able to produce the clinical notes.

p. 89. Thomas to Hughes: 12 January 1934, *S.L.*

p. 90. Thomas upset: Eric Hughes.

p. 90–91. 'The force' . . . :

William Empson in the *New Statesman*, 15 May 1954, said that 'what hit the town of London was the child Dylan publishing "The force that through the green fuse" as a prize poem in the *Sunday Referee*, and from that day he was a famous poet; I think the incident does some credit to the town, making it look less clumsy than you would think.' There are small variations between the *Referee* version and the version of *18 Poems* and later. The notebook version is inscribed 'To E.P.', possibly Evelyn Phillips, an attractive girl in the group that included Thomas. She says there is no special reason why the poem should have been dedicated to her.

p. 91. 'Beat-pounding rhythms':

'On Reading One's Own Poems', B.B.C. Third Programme, 24 September 1949; reprinted in *Q.E.O.M.* A Texas ms, probably written for a Third Programme broadcast in 1947, 'The Poet and His Critic', has more to say about early poems:

> A house where you once lived and where you were happy and sad, in love, in peace or at war . . . may, when you visit it again, raise only doubt and ghostly curiosity. Why did I live there? and did I, really, at all? Then suddenly, on a stone of the house, you see a little meaningless mark scraped with a nail. And you remember the nail itself, and the day you scraped with it on the stone, and the time of the day, and the weather, and exactly how you felt when you did it, and why. That alone of the house makes memories move in you. For the rest: the house is for other people. Re-reading an early poem, the poet may see, perhaps in one rearing line or one clumsy word, the nail-mark of the past, all that is left to him alone of the original reason for the poem . . .

p. 91. Three poems in November:

The other two were 'When once the twilight locks no longer' and 'I fellowed sleep'.

p. 91. Thomas to Fisher: February 1935. *S.L.*, p. 151.

p. 92. Sex at fifteen:

The fact that Thomas talked about it is reported in FitzGibbon's 'Time detective' notebook. Texas mss. See p. 333.

p. 92. Thomas's lecture:

Ms fragment, probably written for an American audience, beginning 'Looking back, from an eminence which I have little hope, or ambition, of ever achieving . . .' Texas mss.

pp. 92–3. Girls:

Kent Thompson says that 'On one occasion [Thomas] and his friends were chased away from the Strand . . . because they were too well dressed. One of them [Raymond Mitchell] recalls their horror when an aged prostitute addressed them with "I only want a pint, boys, and I ain't got disease." But Dylan went back, dressed for the occasion, and presumably made a habit of this.' Perhaps he only *said* he went back.

p. 95. Letters to Pamela:

At one time Lady Snow thought she had about a hundred letters from Thomas; but she is positive that the twenty-five or so that she has deposited at Buffalo are all that now exist. Many of the letters are undated. Some are only fragments. The arrangement in *Selected Letters* is sometime arbitrary, and in at least one instance (see note to pp. 104–6), elements of two letters have been wrongly assembled. As FitzGibbon indicates in his notes between the letters, some passages have been cut. Kent Thompson makes the valid comment that 'the letters are more like a journal – written, like a personal memoir, to impress and elucidate – than they are like a personal correspondence'.

When the correspondence began is not certain. Lady Snow has always said that she first wrote after she read 'That sanity be kept' on 3 September. But in an early letter to her (Buffalo lists it as the first; *S.L.* as the second), Thomas wrote: 'I, too, should like to meet you. This possibly can be arranged, but not before the beginning of September when I am going to see my sister near Chertsey.' This suggests they were already corresponding in August. Some of the early letters have certainly disappeared. Lady Snow says (in a letter to the author) that 'I met Dan Jones at Steyning before I met Dylan. Dylan wrote, "I have met a man who has met you and doesn't like you!"' This remark doesn't seem to be in an existing Thomas letter.

pp. 99–100. Lady Snow's diaries are in Buffalo mss. There are copies of sections in Texas mss.

p. 100 etc. Lady Snow on Thomas:

From an interview and correspondence with her; in the Dylan Thomas Memorial Number of *Adam*, 1953; *Important to Me* (1974), where she devotes a chapter to 'the story of Dylan, as much as I care to say'.

p. 102. The *Listener* row:

Janet Adam Smith, then on the staff of the magazine.

p. 102. Letters from Eliot, etc.:

Mentioned in a letter to Pamela, ascribed to 28 March 1934. *S.L.*

p. 102. Miss Sitwell's comments were in *Aspects of Modern Poetry*. She quoted at length but didn't name Dylan Thomas. In an undated letter to Glyn Jones, probably December 1934 (*S.L.*, p. 149), he refers to 'Edith Sitwell's latest piece of virgin dung' and calls her 'a poisonous thing of a woman, lying, concealing, flipping, plagiarizing, misquoting . . .'

p. 103. 'The hole in space':

See p. 242, where a dream about falling inside a hill (related by

Thomas in 1949) echoes a passage about 'holes in hills' in a draft of his unfinished novel, *Adventures in the Skin Trade*. This occurs in a fragment in the Texas mss (the published version is different): 'Joseph Bennet in common striped pyjamas too short for him with his dog-brown hair disturbed from the dented, womanly pillow, and his eyes still heavy from a dream of untouchable city women and falling down the holes in hills, opened the living-room door and peered uneasily around him.' In 'The Fight', 'The school had vanished, leaving on Mount Pleasant hill a deep hole that smelt of cloakrooms and locker mice . . .' In a notebook poem (15 September 1933), 'A hole in space shall keep the shape of thought.' In a letter to Oscar Williams, 30 July 1945, 'Over the hill, the hoarse noise of a train carrying holes to Hugh's Castle.' *S.L.*

p. 103. Thomas to Glyn Jones: undated, probably mid-March 1934. *S.L.*

pp. 104–7. Letters to Pamela of 9 May and at Whitsun:

*S.L.* confuses them. The 'long, neurotic letter' of 9 May begins in *S.L.* on p. 120 but is broken off on p. 124. It should continue (following a short passage that FitzGibbon omits) with the side-heading 'Morning. Sunday 13', which is at *S.L.*, p. 129. This continuation of the 9 May letter is shown in *S.L.* as belonging to a different letter, beginning on p. 125, headed 'May 11, 1934. Laugharne'. The 'May 11' letter should be dated on or about Whit Monday, 21 May; the original ms is headed simply 'May. Laugharne', and the date, '11th', is FitzGibbon's addition. The correction moves the incident, where Thomas is cornered by three youths in a deserted seaside pub, from Laugharne to Swansea, which makes it more probable.

p. 104. Caitlin:

Elisabeth Lutyens in *A Goldfish Bowl* (p. 154) recalls Caitlin at the Lutyens' house in London, knocking on bedroom doors at night 'to borrow some matches with which to burn Dylan's handkerchiefs, saying they were so bourgeois',

p.105. Thomas to Treece: 16 May 1938. *S.L.*

p. 105. Glyn Jones: *The Dragon Has Two Tongues*, p. 199.

p. 107. 'Evil oozing': Glyn Jones, ibid., p. 193.

p. 108. The critic: Raymond Stephens, *Dylan Thomas: New Critical Essays*, p. 42.

p. 108. 'Huddled': Glyn Jones, op. cit., p. 194.

p. 108. Experiment: Peter McKellar, *Imagination and Thinking*, p. 106.

p. 109. Clare review: *Adelphi*, June 1935; reprinted in *E.P.W*.

p. 109. Dried eyes: Gwen Watkins.

p. 109. Oswell Blakeston:

In an interview and a typescript headed 'Dylan at Wimbledon and after'.

p. 109. Grigson and Glyn Jones on the drawings: in interviews.

p. 110. 'This horrifying skin': R. B. Marriott, *Adam* Memorial Number.

p. 110. 'That creature . . .':

The 10 pp. of ms cited in the note to p. 43.

p. 110. Confession:

The 'friend of mine' may have been a former reporter on the *Evening Post*, two or three years older than Thomas, the 'Ted Williams' (a pseudonym) of 'Old Garbo' who 'dreamed of Fleet Street'. He died in 1975. The girl with the 'loose red mouth' does not appear elsewhere in this book.

p. 111. Thomas to Hughes:

The ms is at Buffalo. I have seen only the version as published in *Twelve More Letters by Dylan Thomas* (1969).

p. 112. Thomas to *Swansea Guardian*: 3 August 1934.

p. 112. Trick on the Mosley meeting:

Ms draft of a letter from Trick to 'My dear Bill Read', owned by Nell Trick.

p. 113. Thomas to Grigson: 'Summer 1934' in *S.L.*, p. 140.

p. 113. *New Verse* poems:

'Our eunuch dreams', 'When once the twilight locks no longer', 'I see the boys of summer in their ruin', 'If I were tickled by the rub of love'.

p. 114. The answers to *New Verse* were reprinted in *E.P.W.* as 'Answers to an enquiry'.

p. 114. Glyn Jones on Thomas: *The Dragon Has Two Tongues* and an interview.

p. 114. Caradoc Evans:

Writing to Pamela (n.d.; *S.L.*, p. 141), Thomas described how he and Evans 'made a tour of the pubs in the evening, drinking to the soon-to-be-hoped-for destruction of the Tin Bethels', and didn't mention Glyn Jones. But Jones thinks he may have been describing a second visit to Aberystwyth.

p. 115. Thomas to Treece: 1 June 1938. *S.L.*

p. 115. Thomas to Spender: 9 December 1952. *S.L.*

p. 115. Spender's review: *Spectator*, 5 December 1952.

p. 116. What Watkins failed to notice:

His Introduction to *Letters to Vernon Watkins*, p. 15.

p. 116. Thomas to his publisher: to E. F. Bozman at Dent, 10 September 1952. *S.L.*

p. 116. Letter to an editor:

To 'Dear Mr Miles', perhaps Hamish Miles of Cape, the publishers, and drafted in a 'Walter Bram' exercise-book where joint Thomas–Jones poems are entered. On adjoining pages are draft lines and working notes for the opening of 'I dreamed my genesis', which show that it was altered from its original form to make it a 'syllable-count' poem. In the notebook it has straightforward iambic stresses, like most of Thomas's poems at the time. The first four lines read:

> I dreamed your genesis in sweat of sleep
> Breaking the dark and the rotating shell,
> From limbs that had the worm upon the shuffle
> Let off the creaking flesh. Since first I sucked ...

But in the published version (and presumably in the version sent to Miles) the poem had an extra word tacked on to three out of four iambic lines:

> I dreamed my genesis in sweat of sleep, breaking
> Through the rotating shell, strong
> As motor muscle on the drill, driving
> Through vision and the girdered nerve...

This pattern of 12, 7, 10, and 8 syllables is then repeated, with minor divergences, through six stanzas. Texas mss.

p. 117. Trick's account:

'The Young Dylan Thomas.' Texas mss. Thomas's letter: Buffalo mss, but seen only in *Twelve More Letters.*

6. *London*

p. 118. Thomas to Trick:

Both quotations from an undated letter, probably written December 1934. *S.L.*, p. 147.

p. 118. Collapsing bed, etc.: Florence Thomas, recorded by Ethel Ross.

p. 119. 'Apples carved in oil':

'Swansea and the Arts', a scripted radio discussion in which Thomas took part, B.B.C. Welsh Home Service, 24 October 1949. Extract in *Q.E.O.M.*

p. 120. Publication of *18 Poems*:

In a letter to Pamela, 2 July 1934, Thomas wrote: 'I'm glad, too, that [Neuberg] hasn't been able as yet to get my book published, for I want to cut some of the poems out & substitute some of the later ones.' Buffalo mss. This is part of a passage omitted from *S.L.* Other details: Runia Sheila Macleod, Neuberg's assistant, in 'The Dylan I Knew', *Adam* Memorial Number; Miss Macleod wrote that 'for history's sake, one should add that the initial thirty pounds for the printing were supplied by Mr Mark Goulden, on behalf of the *Sunday Referee*, and that David Archer contributed the rest – twenty pounds'. Mark Goulden says it is 'not true' that he paid only part: 'I defrayed the costs, whatever they were.'

p. 121. Kardomah: Mervyn Levy

p. 121. Henry Treece: *Dylan Thomas: 'Dog among the Fairies'*, pp. 96–7.

p. 122. *Referee* interview:

30 December 1934 – 'Our Literary "Gangsters" – Young Poet Attacks Modern Writers.'

p. 122. *Swansea Guardian* review: 11 January 1935.

p. 122. *Time & Tide* review: 9 February 1935.

p. 122. *Listener* review: 27 February 1935.

p. 123. Anthony Powell was reviewing FitzGibbon in the *Daily Telegraph*, 14 October 1965.

p. 123. Thomas to Trick: Buffalo mss, seen in *Twelve More Letters*.

p. 124. Thomas to Glyn Jones: *S.L.*

p. 125. *Herald of Wales* poem:

The notebook version, which is longer, says 'Poem completed March 31, '33'. Its title for publication on 8 June 1935 was 'Poet, 1935'. In the first version of his radio talk 'Reminiscences of Childhood' (*Q.E.O.M.*) Thomas quoted eight lines of it, disparagingly; he said it was 'a poem never to be published'.

pp. 125–6. Vernon Watkins and Thomas:

Watkins wrote about their relationship in *L.V.W.* and a 19-p. typescript, 'Notes on Dylan Thomas', owned by Gwen Watkins. Watkins's mental illness was first noted in a monograph about him by Roland Mathias in the *Writers of Wales* series (1974). Other details from Gwen Watkins.

p. 125. 'Oh, what a bore' etc.: Caitlin, interviwed for B.B.C. Wales, 1977.

p. 126. Barking at Antonia White: Ian Henderson.

p. 127. A religious poet:

Watkins told Jane McCormick shortly before his death, 'Yes, I still believe Dylan to be a religious poet, but he was not a religious man, and certainly not a Christian. I mean, if you're a Christian, it changes your life, doesn't it? Dylan certainly never changed. If he had had half the respect for his life that he had for his poetry, he would have been a good man – and alive today.' 'Sorry, Old Christian,' *A.W.R.*, February 1970.

p. 127. Cameron on Thomas: Geoffrey Grigson.

p. 128. Cutting a poor figure:

In the Texas mss, attached to an undated letter, Thomas to Grigson, is a typewritten poem, on the back of which Grigson has written 'DYLAN, MY GOD'. (*S.L.* has the letter, pp. 145–6, but not the poem.) Grigson says (in a letter) that the poem was a version by Thomas of some verses by Wilhelm Busch, the 'German Edward Lear'. Grigson and Cameron were fond of his poems. Thomas saw them in one or the other's flat, and 'said he would make some English versions if we gave him a literal crib (he knew no German). I gave him such a crib of Busch's elephant poem & that's what he did with it, my God. He should have known better & we should have known better; though there was something in common between Busch's verbal extravaganza & Dylan's (conversational) verbal form.' The poem consists of twelve couplets, beginning

The Elephant one sees afar
Goes for a walk in Africa

He goes with nosey airs and graces
To drink a lot at the oasis

A Blackamoor for spite and fun
Pops at the Jumbo with his gun

Then round turns Jumbo bumpeting
And follows Nigger trumpeting

The bad Moor sprints! no use! he's here!
The Elephant nabs him by the ear . . .

p. 128. Caitlin: *Leftover Life to Kill.*

p. 129. Burton's review: *New York Herald Tribune* (European edition) 26 October 1965.

p. 130. Thomas to Blakeston:

*S.L.* differs slightly from the version printed here, taken from *Ambit*, 1966, No. 27.

p. 130. Connolly: in a recording, transcript in Indiana mss.

p. 131. Stories and poems:

A notebook revision of 'Grief thief of time' has the note: 'Written and copied in later, August 1935. Glen Lough. Donegal.'

p. 132. Thomas to Trick: undated, 'July? 1935' in *S.L.*, p. 155.

p. 132. 'I wouldn't be at home':

Thomas is probably echoing a phrase from the journal of John Clare, the Northampton poet who went mad, when he had escaped from the asylum and was looking in vain for his childhood sweetheart – 'so here I am, homeless at home and half gratified to feel that I can be happy anywhere'. He had reviewed Clare's poems for the *Adelphi* in June.

p. 132. Estrangement:

Grigson says (in a letter), 'After Ireland I saw less and less of him. No "break", but a slide away. Both Norman Cameron and I found him less engaging, and more interested in arse-licking the eminent; and there was the business of welshing . . . in Donegal.'

p. 133. 'Should lanterns shine' is not in a notebook, so can't be dated.

pp. 133–4. Church and Thomas:

Church gave some details when he reviewed *A Prospect of the Sea* in *Country Life*, 18 August 1955; and *L.V.W.*, *Truth*, 15 November 1957.

p. 133. Poems to Church:

Thomas's letter is dated 6 October 1935 – 'Here, anyway, are most of the manuscripts. I haven't titled any of them . . .' Ms: Dent.

p. 134. Church's reply: 26 November 1935. Copy typescript at Dent.

p. 134. Thomas to Church: *S.L.*

pp. 134–5. Watkins: 'Notes on Dylan Thomas'.

p. 135. Poems to choose from:

Between 1933 and 1936, Thomas published in journals eight poems that were not re-published in book form: 'Greek Play in a Garden' (*Herald of Wales*, 15 July 1933); 'That sanity be kept' (*S. Referee*, 3 September 1933); 'No man believes' (*Adelphi*, September 1933); 'Love me, not as the dreaming nurses' (*S. Referee*, 7 January 1934); 'Out of the pit' (*New English Weekly*, 25 January 1934); 'The Woman Speaks' (*Adelphi*, March 1934); 'Poet, 1935' (*Herald of Wales,* 8 June 1935); 'Before we mothernaked fall' (*New English Weekly*, 30 July 1936).

p. 135. Thomas to Nancy and Haydn: ms, Haydn Taylor.

p. 136. Thomas to Grigson:

Texas mss. Grigson is 'almost sure' it was written in June 1935, 'certainly before we went to Donegal'. If so, and if the letter is about gonorrhoea, this may be the reason Thomas's friends packed him off to Ireland for the summer. But he was ill later in the year. His letter to Church of 6 October says that 'this wretched illness of mine keeps me indoors'.

p. 137. Telling her cronies:

Kent Thompson, interview with Mrs Gwilym Morgan, family friend.

p. 137. Thomas to Sitwell:

Berg mss. He was nineteen, not eighteen, when he wrote the poem.

p. 138. Miss Sitwell's advice:

Another Thomas letter in the Berg mss, dated 24 January 1936, says, 'You must have listened to a great deal of the woes of young poets. And to take a regular job is the most sensible suggestion in the world. I would willingly and gladly, but have, apart from the little writing, reviewing, hack journalism, and odd-jobbery I've done, hardly any qualifications.'

p.139. Heppenstall: *Four Absentees*, p. 95.

p. 139. Limericks:

Rayner Heppenstall says there was a sequence of three. 'The second of the cycle was not composed. The third, which is not so good as the first, went:

Now, Joe was the kind of a bloke
Who looked for his bit of a poke
  And when he found Mary
  'd been fucked by a fairy
He didn't think much of the joke.'

A friend remembers walking with Dylan one night on Townhill, overlooking Swansea, when he produced the following:

I wish I was a baby
I'd look up Mummy's clothes

And see the Cockett Tunnel
Where Daddy's engine goes.

(Cockett, a suburb of Swansea, has a railway tunnel.)

p. 140. Playing at dogs:

Tillyard, letter to *Times Literary Supplement*, 27 April 1962. He said that Thomas, 'the new adolescent prodigy', was aged sixteen or seventeen; but he was probably several years older.

p. 141. Howard Moss: *New Yorker*, 7 October 1967.

p. 142. Glyn Jones: *The Dragon Has Two Tongues*, p. 185.

p. 142. Cordelia Locke: in an interview

p. 142. G. S. Fraser: Tedlock, p. 82.

p. 143. Glyn Jones: op. cit., p. 197.

p. 144. Thomas to Wyn Henderson: 9 March 1936. *S.L.*

p. 144. Thomas to Church: 17 March 1936. *S.L.*

p. 145. Thomas to Watkins: *L.V.W.*

p. 145. Church's letter: 28 April, copy typescript at Dent.

p. 146. Thomas to Church:

1 July. Ms Dent, which also has the letter sending the final batch of poems, on 22 June: 'Do forgive me for being so long in sending them. I haven't, actually, been at all well . . .'

p. 146. The letter to Church was the one of 22 June.

p. 146. *T.L.S.* review: 19 September 1936.

p. 146. *Spectator* review: 11 December 1936.

p. 146. *New Statesman* review: 3 October 1936.

p. 147. Poems in 1936:

'We lying by seasand' was revised from a notebook version and published in *Poetry* (Chicago), January 1937 (later in *Map of Love.* In the U.S., the poem is included in the 1957 New Directions edition of *Collection Poems*). 'It is the sinners' dust-tongued bell' appeared in *Twentieth Century Verse*, January 1937 (later in *Map of Love*). In 'Notes on Dylan Thomas', Watkins wrote of this poem: 'I remember [Dylan] coming to my house one day in a state of excitement. He had been given his next poem by a particularly dull thriller in which his eye had suddenly fallen on the sentence: "The shadow is dark directly under the candle." The poem he projected from this statement is the poem about churches . . .' An unpublished poem, written about this time, is 'For as long as forever is'; see Appendix. In the Texas mss, this poem is written on the reverse of a sheet which has part of 'It is the sinners' dust-tongued bell', with small variants from the published form

p. 148. Book earnings: D.H.A.

7. *Caitlin*

p. 149. etc. The Macnamaras:

*T.F.F.*, and interview with Nicolette Devas; Yvonne Macnamara, written answers to questions from Bill Read (the 'American author' of my p. 150), in Texas mss.

p. 150. Caitlin dancing: *Leftover*, p. 52.

p. 151. The newspaper article: *Sunday Graphic*, 19 February 1956.

p. 151. Dancing at Fryern Court:

Nicolette Devas. T. S. Eliot was observed by Rupert Shephard.

p. 151. Caitlin's account: interviewed for B.B.C. Wales, 1977.

p. 152. Caitlin's denial: quoted in *Augustus John*, Vol. 2, *The Years of Experience*, p. 231.

p. 152. Caitlin at Laugharne, etc.:

ibid., p. 154. John always said he didn't strike Thomas, but is not generally believed. The paintings at Fishguard, including some by John, were part of an Arts and Crafts section being prepared for the following month's National Eisteddfod.

p. 152. The start of the affair:

A conversation with Thomas reported by Brinnin (*Dylan Thomas in America*, p. 159) suggests Laugharne is where they became involved. 'They first saw one another at a party in London . . . [afterwards] Dylan found he had either neglected to record Caitlin's address, or had lost it . . . [Hughes invited him to Laugharne] . . . Augustus John drove up to the house [with Caitlin] . . . Dylan had found Caitlin again, and was not going to let her move out of his sight. They stayed on as Hughes's guests for days and did not leave until they had decided to be married.' Without taking this version (any more than the others) as gospel, it has an air of probability.

p. 152. Thomas's postcard:

Texas mss. It was published in *McCall's* February 1966, 'Love Letters from a Poet to His Wife'. The rest of the letters to Caitlin were in Mrs Thomas's possession, but copies have been made at different times. FitzGibbon used parts of several letters to her in his biography, but omitted them entirely from *S.L.* In all, five letters from Thomas to Caitlin were printed (with minor omissions) in *McCall's*.

p. 154. Caitlin at Blashford: Rupert Shephard.

p. 154. Falls Hotel: Nicolette Devas, Rupert Shephard.

p. 154. 'Thwarted bombast': Caitlin's ms – see 'Caitlin' note to p. 19.

p. 152. B.B.C. contract:

'Cardiff Registry' file at B.B.C. Written Archives Centre, Caversham, Reading. Previously one or two Thomas poems had been broadcast, read by others: 'The Romantic Isle' (pp. 81, 84), of which there is no trace in B.B.C. Archives; and 'Especially when the October wind' – a B.B.C. letter to Thomas, 21 January 1937, says that 'it is possible we may wish to include' the poem in a reading on 6 February, and offers a fee of fifteen shillings. George Barker presented a selection of poems in the Regional Programme on 6 February, and Thomas's may have been among them.

p. 155. Plaintive requests: B B.C. Archives.

p. 155. Thomas to Caitlin:

This is the letter that FitzGibbon places in 1936. His account (pp. 217–18) describes how Thomas contracted gonorrhoea from a girl at the 1936 Surrealist Exhibition; was treated in a nursing home; and decided to go back to Swansea to recuperate. 'It was in these inauspicious circumstances that he wrote his first love-letter to Caitlin that has survived, perhaps the first of all.' FitzGibbon then quotes the opening of the letter. But the letter, the third and not the first, was written nearly a year after the exhibition.

p. 156. Mrs Emlyn Davies, who has lived at 5, Cwmdonkin Drive since 1938, says the Thomases left in April 1937.

p. 156. D.J.'s retirement: J. Morgan Williams.

p. 156. D. J. Thomas to Taylor: ms, Haydn Taylor.

p. 156. Dylan Thomas to his parents: ms, Haydn Taylor, who was sent it by D. J. Thomas as part of his campaign to stop the marriage.

p. 157. fn. Bert Trick: 'The Young Dylan Thomas', Texas mss.

p. 158. Florence: to Ethel Ross.

p. 158. Taylor and Caitlin's mother: *T.F.F.*, p. 193. Taylor says he has no memory of phoning her.

pp. 158–9. D. J. Thomas to Taylor: ms, Haydn Taylor.

p. 159. Dylan Thomas to Taylor: ms, Haydn Taylor.

p. 161. Heppenstall: *Four Absentees*, p. 139.

p. 161. 'Somebody's boring me': ibid.

p. 161. 'A warring absence':

Thomas wrote a much-quoted exegesis of the poem in a letter to Hermann Peschmann, 1 February 1938, in *S.L.* As with other glosses by Thomas, the explanation itself seems to need explaining.

'Nearly a year to write' – Watkins, *L.V.W.*, p. 30; Thomas to Watkins, n.d., *L.V.W.*, p. 32

p. 162. Thomas to Watkins:

*L.V.W.*, p. 28. 'Bluebell Wood' and 'Cuckoo Hill' were names invented by the Macnamara children. Nicolette Devas.

p. 162. Caitlin on marriage: *Leftover*, p. 55.

p. 162. Nicolette Devas: *T.F.F.*, p. 197

p. 162. Caitlin on fighting: interviewed for B.B.C. Wales, 1977.

pp. 162–3. Thomas as reviewer:

Over the years he dealt with poems, novels and thrillers. A book that impressed him deeply when he reviewed it for *Light and Dark* (March 1937) was the fantastical *Nightwood* by Djuna Barnes. Distant echoes can be heard in the *Portrait* stories.

p. 163. Writing for *Janus*: Royston Morley.

p. 163. Thomas to Watkins: *L.V.W.*

p. 163. Four notebook poems:

The other three were 'O make me a mask', 'Not from this anger' and 'How shall my animal'. All can be dated by references in letters to Watkins, to whom they were sent.

p. 164. 'Warm slippers . . .' B.B.C. interview, op. cit.

p. 164. Empson: *New Statesman*, 29 October 1965.

p. 164. Thomas to Fisher: 16 March 1938. Texas mss.

p. 164. Money in advance:

Thomas wrote to the B.B.C., 'My fare, I am afraid, will have to be paid from Laugharne to Manchester, and not from Swansea. Also, owing to my circumstances, I find it necessary to have to be given the rail fare and subsistence allowance *before* I travel.' B.B.C. Archives.

p. 165. 'Four rooms . . .': Thomas to Treece, 16 June 1938. *S.L.*

p. 165. Thomas to Treece: ibid.

p. 165. Cockles underfoot, etc.: John Davenport, *Vogue*, August 1955.

p. 166. Davenport: ibid.

p. 166. Caitlin: *Not Quite*, p. 27.

p. 167. Thomas to Reavey: 16 June 1938. Harvard mss.

p. 167. Thomas to Davenport: Texas mss.

p. 167. Dent's objections:

Thomas to Watkins, n.d., about 20 March 1939, *L.V.W.*

p. 168. T. S. Eliot backwards: Alan Brien, *Sunday Times*, 25 March 1973.

p. 168. Llanmadog backwards: Sybil Walters.

p. 168. Church's proposal:

Letter to Thomas, 28 April 1936. Copy typescript at Dent.

p. 168. 'A Visit to Grandpa's':

Published *New English Weekly*, 10 March 1938.

p. 168. 'Illuminated reporting': Watkins, 'Notes on Dylan Thomas'.

p. 168. 'Most potboilers': Thomas to Trick, 27 October 1939. *S.L.*

p. 169. *Patricia* . . . ms: Buffalo mss.

p. 169. 'Dead youth . . .': 'Old Garbo', p. 195.

p. 169 fn. 'Flippant title': Thomas to Watkins, n.d. about 30 January 1940. *L.V.W.*

p. 169. Thomas to Treece, on Church: n.d., probably February 1938. Texas mss.

p. 169. 'Brawling hypocrite':

Thomas to Tambimuttu, 9 June 1941 Texas mss: the *S.L.* version is cut.

p. 170. Thomas to Treece, on poverty with dignity: 23 March 1938, *S.L.*

p. 170. Thomas to Treece, on cruel Laugharne: 16 June 1938, *S.L.*

p. 170. 'Straight poems' written first:

Thomas to Treece, 6 or 7 July 1938. *S.L.* Treece seems either to have forgotten or to have ignored this information, which no one else had at the time, when he published his critical study of Thomas, '*Dog among the Fairies*', in 1949.

p. 170. Thomas to Treece, on poetry:

23 March 1938. *S.L.*, where a section of text has been transposed, making nonsense of the crucial passage. On p. 191, line 2, from 'other two together', to line 32, 'images were left' should be inserted in p. 190 between the words 'the' and 'dangling'. There are also minor errors of transcription.

p. 170. Thomas to Treece, taking poems literally: 16 May 1938, *S.L.*

p. 170. Thomas to Treece on Edith Sitwell:

1 June 1938, *S.L.* Thomas is concerned with her 'interesting misreadings or, rather, half-readings' of lines in 'A grief ago' and the first of the 'Altarwise by owl-light' sonnets, in the *Sunday Times.*

p. 170. Thomas on beast and angel: 16 May 1938, *S.L.*

p. 170. Thomas to Treece, 'cut out that remark': probably May 1939, *S.L.*, p. 230.

p. 171. Thomas to Treece, on poets:

23 March 1938, Buffalo mss – the passage is omitted from *S.L.*

p. 171. Thomas to Treece, 'putting little trust': 23 March 1938, *S.L.*

p. 171. Society for Welsh authors:

Thomas to W. T. (Pennar) Davies, four letters n.d. or with dates in summer 1939. Wales mss. The letter quoted is undated.

p. 171. Five poems:

The other three were 'On no work of words', a notebook revision dated 'Laugharne. September 1938'; 'The tombstone told when she died', another revision, similarly dated; and the four-line 'I, the first named', published only in the magazine *Seven*, October 1938, in Thomas's lifetime.

p. 171. Thomas to Watkins:

(Ascribed to) 14 October 1938. *L.V.W.* p. 44. 'A saint about to fall' was provisionally titled 'In September'.

p. 172. 'Boom boom boom': Thomas to Davenport, 23 June 1939. Texas mss.

p. 172. Radio anthology: Thomas to T. Rowland Hughes, B.B.C. Cardiff, 2? October 1938. B.B.C. Archives.

p. 172. 'Man under the sea': Thomas to T. Rowland Hughes, 1 November 1938. B.B.C. Archives.

p. 172. 'In a rush': Watkins, quoting Thomas, *L.V.W.* p. 57.

p. 173. Thomas to Laughlin: 28 March 1938. *S.L.*

p. 173. A few pounds:

Thomas to Davenport, 24 August 1938: '[Laughlin] gave me, when I was broke and hungry, eight pounds, which I regarded foolishly as a present. Later, he sent me a contract to sign that said the eight pounds was an advance on royalties . . .' Texas mss. Laughlin says (in a letter) that small payments would have been for material in a *New Directions in Poetry and Prose* anthology, where a number of Thomas poems and stories appeared in 1938 and 1939. Laughlin thinks it was Edith Sitwell who told him about Thomas.

p. 173. Book earnings: D.H.A.

pp. 173–4. Thomas to Davenport: 14 October 1938. Texas mss.

p. 174. 'Our saint or monster': Thomas to Davenport, 24 August 1938. Texas mss.

p. 174. Thomas to Higham: 24 November 1938. Texas mss.

p. 174. Thomas to Watkins: 20 December 1938. *L.V.W.*

p. 175. New poems at Blashford:

Others were (*a*) 'Once it was the colour of saying', sent to Watkins about 8 January 1939 (*L.V.W.* p. 53). In 'Notes on Dylan Thomas' Watkins said it was 'about the room in the house in Cwmdonkin Drive where he wrote many poems. Its wide windows looked across the road to a sloping field where girls used to play hockey'. (In fact, the room was the best bedroom.) Watkins saw it as a key poem, anticipating a change of style by Thomas to a more straightforward manner, 'in the direction of the living voice' (*L.V.W.*, pp. 20–21). But it sounds as if it may have originated much earlier in a notebook, now missing.

(*b*) ' "If my head hurt a hair's foot" ', sent to Watkins with letter of 3 March 1939 – 'I've got to do the proofs of my new book of poems [*The Map of Love*] this week, & I'm thinking of putting in this poem just finished.' *L.V.W.*

p. 175. Poem from a dream: 'Notes on Dylan Thomas'.

p. 175. Miller, Durrell, 'nightmare London': Thomas to Watkins, about 8 January 1939. *L.V.W.*

p. 175. Thomas to Trick: probably March 1939. *S.L.*, p. 227.

p. 176. Money from Dent:

Thomas to Higham, n.d., probably July 1939. Texas mss.

p. 176. Five-shilling plan:

Thomas to Davenport, 11 May 1939, *S.L.*; 23 June 1939, and n.d., Texas mss.

p. 176. 'No dank debtors' walls': Thomas to Davenport, n.d. Texas mss.

p. 176. Thomas to Watkins: n.d., about 25 August 1939, *L.V.W.*, p. 70.

p. 176. Thomas to his father: 29 August 1939, *S.L.*

p. 177. Thomas to Treece:

6 or 7 July 1938, and n.d., probably July 1939, both *S.L.*

p. 177. Thomas to Trick: 29 September 1939. *S.L.*

p. 177. Thomas to D. S. Savage: 27 October 1939. *S.L.*

pp. 177–8. Connolly review: 16 September 1939.

p. 177 fn. B.B.C. memo: B.B.C. Archives

p. 177 fn. Thomas to Rhys: n.d. Texas mss.

p. 178. 'Map of Love' earnings etc.: D.H.A.

p. 178. Tribunal: Keidrych Rhys, interview; Vernon Watkins, 'Notes on D.T.'.

p. 179. Gwynfor Evans:

Letter from Evans (later a Welsh Nationalist Member of Parliament).

p. 179. 'Punctured lungs': Ethel Ross, quoting Florence Thomas.

p. 179. 'Scarred lungs':

Vernon Watkins, quoted at second hand in Bill Read's papers. Texas mss.

p. 179. Thomas to Spender: Harvard mss.

p. 179. Thomas to Pollinger: Texas mss.

p. 179 fn. Thomas to Spender: 13 May 1940. *S.L.*

p. 180. Bed: Thomas to Watkins, 6 March 1940. *L.V.W.*

p. 180. 'TA for the pound': n.d., pres. 1940. *L.V.W.*, p. 90.

p. 180. Appeal to Spender: 13 May 1940. *S.L.*

p. 180. Thomas to Spender: 4 June 1940. Ms: Stephen Spender.

p. 180. 'Agonizing hours': *Not Quite*, p. 17.

pp. 180–82. At Marshfield: interviews with Antonia White and Ian Henderson.

p. 181. *Canary*:

A galley-proof of 'The Parachutist' is in Texas mss, with a note signed Cyril Connolly to say it was 'set up by *Horizon* . . . but not published owing to lack of space'. 'Request to Leda' appeared in the July 1942 issue.

p. 181. 'Talked itself away': Thomas to Davenport, 8 January 1941. *S.L.*

p. 182. Raids on Swansea: Thomas to Watkins, n.d., *L.V.W.* p. 98.

p. 182. Thomas to Watkins: ibid.

p. 182. In London:

B.B.C. internal memo, 12 December 1940, asking that Thomas be sent a cheque immediately 'if humanly possible . . . He came in to see me today, in an exceedingly nervous state, having been bombed. He is terribly anxious to leave London and is unable to do so as he has no money till this cheque reaches him.' B.B.C. Archives.

p. 182. Train to Wales: Thomas to Davenport, 8 January 1941. *S.L.*

p. 182. Alec Waugh: Thomas to Davenport, 27 January 1941. Texas mss.

p. 182. 'Long-legged Bait':

A letter to Davenport, probably of April 1941 (*S.L.*, p .252) says: 'I've just finished my ballad. Too late, unfortunately, for the May *Horizon*. It's about 220 lines long, a tremendous effort for me . . .' Watkins wrote in 'Notes on D.T.':

> I saw Dylan a great deal when he was writing the 'Ballad of the Long-legged Bait', and I saw this poem grow from its first fifteen lines through all the stages of its composition. He wrote the four-lined verses in pairs. The poem is full of visual imagery. It was so much a visual poem that he made a coloured picture for it which he pinned on the wall of his room, a picture of a woman lying at

the bottom of the sea. She was a new Loreley revealing the pitfalls of destruction awaiting those who attempted to put off the flesh.

p. 182. Connolly: 'Dylan Thomas', B.B.C. radio documentary, 9 November 1963.

p. 183. Scripts:

B.B.C. Archives. The letter to the producer (Royston Morley) is n.d. and begins: 'Is this kind of propoganda [*sic*] too sticky?' In a letter to another official (6 May 1941), Thomas thanks him for sending on documents about the Czech Legion to be used in a script, but adds:

> I am afraid I found them pretty useless: just dry accounts, with no personal detail to speak of, of the taking of towns and military positions. 'Then we took Omsk and Tomsk and Bomsk. We lost forty wagons and three men. This was in April' . . . The Czech officers who so very kindly wrote their reminiscences have apparently so little dramatic feeling that they could make their reminiscences of Dunkirk as uneventful as a meeting of the Coke Board. I hope the script is not too unsatisfactory . . .

p. 183. Thomas to Clement Davenport: 2 April (1941). Texas mss.

p. 183. Meeting with Trick: 'The Young D.T.'. Texas mss.

p. 184. D.J. on Polly, and other Blaen Cwm details: Hettie Owen.

p. 184. Bus conductor: Haydn Taylor.

p. 184. Thomas to Watkins: 22 May 1941. *L.V.W*.

pp. 184–5. Thomas to Clement Davenport: 2 April 1941. Texas mss.

p. 185. FitzGibbon on Keats: p. 281.

p. 185. 'Happy while it lasted':

Dated 1 July 1932; later part of the poem that was published as 'Out of the sighs'.

p. 185. Sale to Buffalo: *Poet in the Making*, pp. 273–4.

p. 185. Thomas to Fisher: 15 July 1941. *S.L.*

p. 185. 'Squeeze another drop': Thomas to Watkins, n.d., *L.V.W.*, p. 104.

p. 186. Pollinger to Thomas: D.H.A.

p. 186. *Skin Trade* first mentioned:

N.d., probably August 1940, *L.V.W.*, p. 100. Watkins wrote in his Foreword to the posthumously published edition that 'in Dylan's first plan, as far as I can remember it, there were to be seven skins.

At the end of the story the character would be naked at last. It would be in one way a journey through the Inferno of London, but it would also be a comedy.' Perhaps the recollection of a 'journey through the Inferno' owed more to Watkins's than to Thomas's ideas.

p. 186. 'My prosebook': Thomas to Watkins, 22 May 1941, *L.V.W.*

p. 186. 'My novel blathers on':

ibid., n.d., p. 104; a reference to the sinking of the battlecruiser *Hood* dates it to May 1941.

p. 186. 'The Rimbaud of Cwmdonkin Drive':

In a 1950 radio discussion which included Roy Campbell, Thomas said, 'I won't forgive you for the Swansea's Rimbaud, because you called me that first, Roy, I remember'. 'Poetic Licence', B.B.C. Home Service, 13 December 1950. B.B.C. Archives.

p. 186. Dent's £25: reported by Laurence Pollinger to Thomas, 3 June 1941. D.H.A.

p. 186. Hadfield to Pollinger: 10 July 1941. Texas mss.

p. 187. Staying with Thomas:

Reported by Watkins in his Foreword to *Skin Trade*, op. cit., p. 9.

p. 187. Profitable *Skin Trade*:

A magazine, John Lehmann's *Folios of New Writings V*, published the first part as 'A Fine Beginning' in autumn 1941. Later the ms passed through the hands of other London publishers. Graham Greene read it in 1947 for Eyre & Spottiswoode and was interested (Thomas to David Higham, 8 October and 12 November 1947. Texas mss. Higham to Thomas, 24 November 1947, D.H.A.). So were Dent again, briefly. Everyone thought Thomas was sure to finish it sooner or later. In the U.S.A. the New American Library paid a $397 advance for the first two chapters in 1952 and published them in a *New World Writing* selection (New American Library to Thomas, 9 May 1952. Indiana mss). N.A.L. later published the third chapter as 'Four Lost Souls'. Since Thomas's death the unfinished book has been published in several editions in Britain and the U.S.A.

p. 187. 'Dawn Raid':

Sent to Watkins with undated letter, probably 1941. *L.V.W.*, p. 108. First published *Life and Letters Today*, August 1941.

p. 187. 'Friendless London': Thomas to Watkins, 28 August 1941. *L.V.W.*

p. 187. 'Late in 1941':

The date is disputed. Donald Taylor (now dead) told Bill Read he hired Thomas on a fine summer's evening in 1940 (letter of 15 November 1963, Texas mss). FitzGibbon, presumably using the same source, also says 1940 (pp. 277–8). But until the end of August 1941, Thomas was based in Laugharne, writing poverty-stricken letters. There seem to be no extant Thomas letters between 28 August 1941 and 20 May 1942; this would agree with a move to London. Thomas's first credit on a film was in May 1942, 'This is Colour' (*Dylan Thomas in Print*, p. 135). Ivan Moffat says (in a letter) that the 'summer of '41 sounds reasonable', although he may have introduced Thomas and Taylor the previous year.

p. 188. £10 a week: Taylor to Read, 15 November 1963. Texas mss.

8. *War and 'Fern Hill'*

p. 189. Ten films:

*Dylan Thomas in Print* (pp. 135–41) identifies eight; FitzGibbon (p. 401) the other two.

p. 189. Taylor: letter to Read, op. cit.

p. 189 etc. Moffat quoted: in letters, unless otherwise indicated.

p. 189 etc. Maclaren-Ross: *Memoirs of the Forties*. 'The Pole-star Neighbour'.

p. 190. 'These Are the Men': Jack Lindsay has a draft typescript.

p. 191. 'Green Mountain, Black Mountain':

Lindsay's typescript. Prints of these two films are at the Imperial War Museum. 'Green Mountain' runs for about twelve minutes. It uses two narrators and has the inevitable Welsh singing in the background. Prints of some other Thomas films are at the British Film Institute.

p. 192. M.O.I. in Wales: Arthur Calder-Marshall, in an interview.

p. 192. 'Our Country':

The passage quoted is from an untitled script in Thomas's hand, in Texas mss, which can be identified from the synopsis in *Dylan Thomas in Print*, p. 139.

pp. 192–3. Corruption: Lindsay, *Meetings with Poets*, pp. 6–7.

p. 193. The Thomases at the Herberts': FitzGibbon, p. 288.

p. 193. Thomas to Earp: *S.L.*

p. 193 fn. Mss at Laugharne: Elisabeth Lutyens, *A Goldfish Bowl*, pp. 205–6.

p. 194. Manresa Road: *T.F.F.*, pp. 199–200. FitzGibbon, pp. 289–90.

p. 194. Thomas to Caitlin: Unpublished Copies, Texas mss.

p. 195. Maclaren-Ross: op. cit., p. 132

p. 195. Lindsay's story: op. cit., p. 11.

pp. 195–6. Ruth Wynn Owen: in an interview.

p. 195. Thomas to Ruth:

N.d., probably May 1942. Ms: Ruth Wynn Owen.

pp. 195–6. Thomas to Ruth: Ms: Ruth Wynn Owen.

p. 196. Ms of a poem:

Thomas seems to have written this out for her benefit, heading it 'For Ruth'. Perhaps it was conceived with her in mind. But as Ruth Wynn Owen observes, 'Most young poets carry some half- or even completely-formed piece that they can dash off spontaneously and give to someone.' The poem was published in *Poetry* (*London*), April 1944, as 'Last night I dived my beggar arm'; it is one of the few poems known to have been written after the 1930s that does not appear in *C.P.* The version in Ruth Wynn Owen's possession has variants throughout, and two pairs of alternative words:

Last night he / I } dived my beggar arm
Into her breast that wore no heart
For me / her } alone only the deep drum
Telling her hurt heart

That her luminous, tumbled limbs
Will plunge his betrayal through the sky
So the betrayed will read in the sunbeams
Of a death in another country.

The *Poetry* (*London*) version is in *The Poems*, p. 175.

p. 196. One further letter:

Thomas to Ruth, 19 September 1943. '. . . I 've been in Wales for some weeks now, and have had time and a rinsed head enough to be able to write what I want. In London, I mean to write you every day, but the laziness, the horror and selfpity, that London drizzles down on me stop everything but the ghost of a hope that perhaps you will ring . . .' Ms: Ruth Wynn Owen.

p. 196. Ties and the dachshund: Donald Taylor, letters to Bill Read. Texas mss.

p. 196. Stealing the silver: Rupert Shephard.

p. 197. Elisabeth Lutyens: in an interview.

p. 197. Ivan Moffat:

'Dylan Thomas', the 1963 radio documentary.

p. 197. Davenport on Thomas: ibid., and in unused B.B.C. recordings.

p. 197. Hugh Porteus: *Spectator*, 2 September 1950. 'Nights Out in the Thirties'.

p. 197. William Saroyan:

*Books and Bookmen*, July 1964, 'The Wild Boy'. One of the other writers was Ivan Moffat. His account (in a letter) is not at all like Saroyan's. 'Dylan would sometimes start the morning off with a couple of double Pimms, but this would usually be when travelling, or before some non-working occasion on a weekend (as on the morning I brought him and William Saroyan together at the Café Royal early in '44, during which Saroyan uttered a thousand sentences and Dylan one, though he poked his face about pretty expressively – a face much stretched and flushed with Pimms)...'

p.198. Gwen Watkins:

*A.W.R.*, Winter 1972. 'A Newly-Discovered Letter: Dylan Thomas to Vernon Watkins'.

p. 198. At the Devases: *T.F.F.*, pp. 238–9.

p. 199. 'To correct the imbalance':

Ivan Moffat, in a letter.

p. 199. Jack Lindsay: *Meetings with Poets*, pp. 20–25.

p. 199 fn. Thomas to Taylor and Tennant: *S.L.*

p. 200. Margaret Taylor: in an interview.

p. 200. Caitlin on TV:

'Tonight', B.B.C. 1, 3 December 1975. She was in Rome, interviewed from London, shortly before her husband's letters to her were put up for auction.

p. 200. Thomas to Watkins:

27 July 1944, from the Blaen Cwm cottage. *L.V.W.* This letter also contains the remarks about Llangain; the place-name is deleted from the published letter, but is in the B.M. mss.

p. 201. Bungalow: Mrs Evans, Lampeter, widow of the doctor who owned it.

p. 201. 'Ceremony After a Fire Raid':

First published *Our Time*, May 1944.

p. 201. 'Holy Spring':

Sent to Watkins with a letter in November 1944 – 'a poem ...

which I started a long time ago but finished very recently, after a lot of work'. *L.V.W.*, p. 123.

p. 201. 'Vision and Prayer':

Sent to Watkins 26 August 1944. from Blaen Cwm, with 'Poem in October' – 'I've just finished two poems, one over 200 lines, and I'm excited by it'.

p. 201. Christian position:

Aneirin Talfan Davies, the most persistent advocate of Thomas as religious poet (and crypto-Roman Catholic), believes that 'the turning point in his poetic career came in the patterned poem, "Vision and Prayer", in the style of George Herbert, one of Dylan's favourites ... It is a poem about birth and re-birth, and twice in crucial sections of the poem, he speaks of being "found".' Lecture to Dylan Thomas Summer School, Swansea University College, 1974.

p. 202. Watkins on 'Poem in October': 'Notes on Dylan Thomas'.

p. 202. Grigson: *New Statesman*, 8 December 1964, 'Dylan and the Dragon'.

p. 203. Watkins: Foreword to *Skin Trade*, pp. 15–16.

p. 203. 'Catllewdylaer':

Thomas to Watkins, 30 August 1944. 'On Monday, 4 September, we are moving into a new house ...' *L.V.W.*

p. 203. Thomas to T. W. Earp: post-marked 21 September 1944. *S.L.*

p. 203. At Majoda: Mrs Evans.

p. 204. Cousin: the late Mrs Theodosia Legg, of Cardiff, in an interview.

p. 204. Thomas to Taylor: 28 October 1944. *S.L.*

p. 204. *Twenty Years A-Growing*: Bill Read, *The Days of Dylan Thomas*, p. 106.

p. 204. Burke and Hare:

Thomas to Taylor, 19? September 1944. 'I hope you're not quite so penniless, & in debt, as I am, but, anyway, the dough from B & H will be, I'm sure, welcome. And oh the difference to me!' Photocopy in Texas mss.

p. 204. 'A Book of Streets':

Wales mss, which has the synopsis and a file of publisher's correspondence.

p. 205. 'ON NOT TURNING UP':

Sent with letter to Watkins, 28 October 1944. *L.V.W.*

p. 205. Gwen Watkins on 'fake letter': *A.W.R.*, Winter 1972.

p. 206. Café Royal: Gwen Watkins, ibid.

p. 206. Thomas to Watkins:

26 February 1945. Facsimile published *A.W.R.*, above. B.M. mss. Misspellings include 'occassion', 'expells', 'dissapations' and 'acheived'.

p. 207. 'Book of Streets' letters: Wales mss.

p. 208–9. The shooting incident:

Interviews with the former Commando and his wife; *Welsh Gazette*, 12 April 1945 (reprinted *Dylan Thomas in Print*, p. 72) and 28 June 1945; *News of the World* 24 June 1945. Donald Taylor wrote an account in a letter to Bill Read, in Texas mss. The incident is often recalled in garbled form. One version, which I heard in a long and detailed account in 1976 from an acquaintance of Thomas, was set in the West of England. Thomas was supposed to have been pursued by a vengeful American Army officer. The officer had a machine-gun, and chased the poet down lanes and through fields. Trouble over a woman was given as the reason. No doubt Thomas himself was the source of this stirring tale.

p. 208. A Thomas brawl: Nicolette Devas, *T.F.F.*, p. 242.

p. 209. Thomas to Watkins:

28 March 1945. *L.V.W.* The first part of the letter has been heavily cut to remove details of the assailant.

p. 210. *Deaths and Entrances*:

Laurence Pollinger to Thomas, 15 November 1944, says Dent would like to publish in 1945, and are offering an advance of £50. D.H.A.

p. 210. Thomas to Laughlin:

10 February 1945. Copy typescript, Dylan Thomas Trustees.

p. 211. 'A little ladleful': 28 March 1945. *S.L.*

p. 211. Thomas to Williams, 30 July:

*S.L.* Glyn Jones says Thomas always wrote 'Revelations' for 'Revelation'.

p. 212. 'Vegetable background': *Leftover*, p. 35.

p. 212. Thomas to Williams: 30 July, above.

p. 213. Thomas to Caitlin: Unpublished. Copy, Texas mss.

p. 213. London not impressed, etc.:

Memo from G. R. Barnes, Director of Talks in London, to Aneirin Talfan Davies, 6 January 1945. 'I should have thought the wit would have been much better appreciated if it had been read caustically, or, at least, dryly . . .' B.B.C. Archives.

p. 214. Thomas to Dent: Ms: Dent.

p. 214. Worksheets: Brinnin, p. 95.

9. *A Voice on the Radio*

p. 216. Moving to London:

A letter from Thomas at Blaen Cwm to 'Dear Francis' is headed 'Friday 21, 45.' 21 September 1945 was a Friday. The letter concerns arrangements for a return to London: 'Caitlin and I are sending up some things to London–a trunk or two and a single bed among them – which we want temporarily put among our other things in the studio ... we might be in London before [Wednesday the 26th] staying temporarily with Toni ...' Ms: Eric Barton.

p. 216. Visa:

Thomas to Oscar Williams, 5 December 1945, from 39, Markham Square, Chelsea. Photocopy, Dylan Thomas Trustees.

p. 216. Thomas in hospital: FitzGibbon, p. 313.

p. 216. Thomas to Watkins: *L.V.W.*

p. 216. Jack Lindsay: *Meeting with Poets*, pp. 21–2

p. 217. Holywell Ford: Margaret Taylor, in interviews.

p. 217. Jack Lindsay: op. cit., pp. 18–19.

p. 218. *Deaths and Entrances*:

3,000 copies, *Dylan Thomas in Print*. Other printing details: Thomas to Higham, 25 March 1946. Texas mss.

p. 218. Titles for stories: ibid.

p. 218. Freelance date:

Leslie Andrews (accountant) to David Higham, 7 April 1948. D.H.A.

p. 218. John Arlott: 'Dylan Thomas and Radio', *Adelphi*, February 1954.

p. 219. With James Stephens:

18 June 1946, in a series called 'Books and Writers'. Extracts are in *Q.E.O.M.*, titled 'On Poetry'. Fuller text, *Encounter*, November 1954.

p. 219. With Edward Shanks:

'What Has Happened to English Poetry', in a series called 'Freedom Forum', recorded 11 October 1946, for transmission later that month. The B.B.C. Archives transcript doesn't indicate who is speaking, and not all the remarks can be safely ascribed. But it must have been Thomas who described the Georgian revival as 'a revival of rather tepid poets, sitting in deck chairs outside public houses in the country: or inns, I'm sorry. Sitting outside inns and writing poems about how lovely it was to see a cow or a bull or even an obscure bird for perhaps the third time.'

p. 219. 'The Londoner':

Recorded 15 July 1946, for transmission later that month to Africa and North America.

p. 219. Gilliam:

Letter to Thomas, 18 July 1946, praising 'a most sensitive and successful piece of radio'. B.B.C. Archives.

p. 219. Margate programme: 'Margate – Past and Present' recorded 22 September 1946.

p. 219. Elisabeth Lutyens: in an interview.

p. 219. Oxford by car: FitzGibbon, p. 317.

p. 220. Campbell:

'Memories of Dylan Thomas at the B.B.C.', *Poetry* (Chicago), November 1955.

p. 220 fn. Richard Burton: *Book Week*, 24 October 1965.

p. 221. Third Programme memo: 10 December 1951, from the Controller, Third Programme to the Head of Copyright. B.B.C. Archives.

p. 221. Margaret Taylor: in an interview.

p. 221. The perfect contract: Elisabeth Lutyens, *A Goldfish Bowl*, p. 155.

p. 221. Seeking employment: memo from Controller, Third Programme, to Controller, Talks, 18 August 1950.

p. 221. Trip to Ireland:

FitzGibbon, p. 324. A letter to John Ormond (Thomas), then on the staff of *Picture Post*, 6 March 1948, promises 'no repetition of the disastrous Puck Fair visit!' Texas mss.

pp. 221–2. Thomas to Mrs Taylor: 29 August 1946. Texas mss.

p. 222. Thomas to Laughlin: copy typescript, Dylan Thomas Trustees.

p. 222. Edith Sitwell to John Lehmann: *Edith Sitwell. Selected Letters*.

p. 222. Edith Sitwell pulls strings, etc.:

ibid., to Lehmann, 11 December 1946, and Ronald Bottrall, 25 February 1947.

p. 223. £150: FitzGibbon, p. 325.

p. 223. Thomas to Durrell: ? December 1938. *S.L.*, p. 210.

p. 223. 'Return Journey':

After some internal politicking by the Welsh Region of the B.B.C., the programme was presently handed over to them, and made in Cardiff; the producer was P. H. Burton, Richard Burton's legal guardian. The notebook, in Texas mss, also contains notes on

Oxford eccentrics, headed 'Eccentric figures'. 'Return Journey' was first broadcast 14 June 1947, Home Service.

p. 223. Swansea friend: Cecil Price, *Adam* Memorial Number.

pp. 223–4. Mrs Ferguson and Mrs Hole: Thomas to Margaret Taylor, 11 July 1947.

p. 224. Who went to Italy:

Thomas to Charles Fisher, 1 March 1947. Copy typescript, Texas mss.

p. 224. Thomas to Fisher: ibid.

p. 224. Lost luggage:

Thomas to parents, 11 April 1947; Thomas to Margaret Taylor, 12 April 1947. *S.L.*

p. 224. 'The slowest in the world':

Thomas to Margaret Taylor, 4 June 1947. Texas mss.

p. 224. Thomas to Davenport: 29 May 1947. *S.L.*

p. 224. Thomas to T. W. Earp: 11 July 1947. *S.L.*

p. 225. Thomas to Margaret Taylor, 20 June and 11 July: Texas mss.

p. 225. Gazing into space:

Mario Luizi, *Adam* Memorial Number. 'Entering the *Giubbe Rosse* late of an evening, he was to be found entrenched behind a small forest of bottles, a full glass in his hand, and one wondered whether those large pale blue eyes [they were brown] were gazing upon something ineffable or merely into vacancy.'

p. 225. In the wardrobe: Gwen Watkins.

p. 225. Thomas to Margaret Taylor: 12 April 1947. *S.L.*

p. 225. Manor House details: Thomas to parents, 5 June 1947. *S.L.*

p. 225–6. Thomas to Margaret Taylor (thanking her): 4 June 1947. Texas mss.

p. 226. Thomas to Margaret Taylor, 11 July: Texas mss.

p. 226. William York Tindall: *A Reader's Guide to Dylan Thomas*, p. 285.

p. 226. Woman admirer:

Helen Bevington, who described the conversation in *When Found, Make a Verse Of*. She met Thomas at Duke University, May 1953.

p. 227. Reporter:

Mary Ellin Barrett, *The Reporter*, 27 April 1954. She met Thomas in New York, 21 February 1952.

p. 227. American student:

Alastair Reid, then at Sarah Lawrence College, New York.

p. 227. Thomas to Margaret Taylor: 3 August 1947. *S.L.*

p. 227. Broken arm: FitzGibbon, p. 333.

p. 227 etc. Thomases at South Leigh:

Cordelia Locke in an interview, and in letters to Bill Read and a manuscript about the period. Texas mss.

p. 229. Taylor to Higham: D.H.A.

p. 230. Payments to Thomas: Higham to Thomas, 10 October 1947, and D.H.A.

p. 230. Thomas and British National:

Sydney Box, letters to Bill Read, Texas mss; Cordelia Locke; memo, 11 September 1947, D.H.A.

p. 230. Thomas at Gainsborough:

Letters from Box to Bill Read, Texas mss; Jan Read, former script editor at Gainsborough, in an interview.

p. 231. Thomas's earnings: D.H.A.

p. 231. Thomas to Higham: Texas mss.

p. 232. Doctors' bills: Thomas to Graham Greene, 11 January 1947. *S.L.*

p. 232. Rome creditor:

Letter to Thomas from J.T., 10 March 1950, with Oscar Williams papers. Indiana mss.

p. 233. 'Grand opera': Thomas to parents, 12 January 1947, *S.L.*

p. 233. Michael Ayrton: B.B.C. Radio 3, 18 October 1975, 'Man of Action'.

p. 233. Thomas to lady producer: 11 January 1947. B.B.C. Archives.

p. 234. Irritable memorandum:

To Director of Schools Broadcasting, 13 May 1947. B.B.C. Archives.

p. 234. 'Poems,1934–1947': Thomas to Higham, 7 October 1947. Texas mss.

p.234. *Skin Trade*:

Thomas to Higham, 12 November 1947. Texas mss.

p. 234. Thomas to Caitlin: part in FitzGibbon, p. 334. Copy at Texas.

p. 235. Thomas to Caitlin (his father, etc): Unpublished. Copy in Texas mss.

p. 235. Thomas to Davenport: Texas mss.

pp. 235–7. Thomas to Glover: Texas mss.

p. 237. Thomas to Frances Hughes: 10 October 1948. *S.L.*

p. 237. Radio talk:

'Living in Wales', Scottish Home Service, 23 June 1949. FitzGibbon prints it (pp. 338–42). A B.B.C. memo from London (where the talk was recorded) to the Scottish Region said: 'Dylan Thomas's piece for you is first-class rococo. He makes an exuberant attack on British Railways buffet cars, and Oxford residents, and paints a pretty dreary picture of Wales; the only country not attacked is fortunately Scotland. We shall record at three o'clock today, but wish to warn you that a solemn railway official might take treble umbrage. Please return discs here: I shall recommend it to Third.' B.B.C. Archives.

p. 237. Speaking at Edinburgh:

The talk went on, 'Caradoc Evans, by the way, had his portrait painted some years ago by Evan Walters of Swansea, who offered it, free, to Swansea Art Gallery. I was a newspaper reporter at the time, devoting myself to critical reviews of performances, in Ystradgynlais, by girls' schools' dramatic societies of the *Mikado*, and inquests on drinkers of methylated spirits . . . And as a reporter I attended, sucking a glove, the Art Gallery meeting in which the offer of the portrait of Caradoc Evans was discussed.

'The chairman of the Art Gallery Committee was Sir Dai Davies, the proprietor of the newspaper for which I doodled. "About this picture of Caradoc Evans, now," he said. "Caradoc Evans is a liar. He says that Welshmen are narrow-minded hypocrites. I throw that lie in his teeth. We are not hypocrites. We are not narrow-minded. We'll show him. I refuse to have his portrait hung in our gallery . . .' *Voice of Scotland*, December 1948. A dialect poem, presumably by Thomas, is appended.

p. 238. The Old Rectory: Ethel Ross.

p. 238. *Picture Post* letter: to John Ormond (Thomas), 6 March 1948. Texas mss.

p. 238. Mrs Taylor and Gosport: from interviews in Laugharne.

p. 238. Richard Hughes's house: Thomas to Frances Hughes, 10 October 1948. *S.L.*

p. 238. Thomas to Watkins: *L.V.W.*

p. 238. Bicycle accident: Thomas to Higham, 21 December 1948. Texas mss.

p. 239. Thomas in Prague:

Jack Lindsay, *Meetings with Poets*, pp. 36–7; FitzGibbon, pp. 343–7.

p. 239. Thomas to Margaret Taylor: n.d. *S.L.* p. 325.

10. *Laugharne and America*

pp. 240–41. Shed and house are described in 'Poet in the Boat House', Mimi Josephson, *John O'London's*, 7 August 1953; *T.F.F.*, pp. 204–5 etc.; Glyn Jones, *The Dragon Has Two Tongues*, p. 197.

p. 241. Mains water:

This, and converting the garage into the work-shed, cost about £150.

p. 241. Elisabeth Lutyens: in an interview.

p. 241. Caitlin: *Leftover*, p. 36.

p. 241. Brown ale: Margaret Taylor, in an interview.

p. 241. 'In country heaven' design:

Radio talk and reading, B.B.C. Third Programme, 25 September 1950; reprinted as 'Three Poems' in *Q.E.O.M*. (Dent edition only).

p. 242. Florence Thomas:

Tape-recorded interview with Colin Edwards; Glyn Jones has a copy of the tape.

p. 242. Vernon Watkins:

In a recording made for the B.B.C radio documentary, 'Dylan Thomas', 1963.

p. 242. Caitlin: *Leftover*, p. 69.

p. 242. Leo Abse: in an interview.

p. 242 fn. Dannie Abse:

In a B.B.C. television programme about Thomas, 9 April 1976. 'Once just after the war Dylan Thomas told my elder brother Leo of a dream he'd had recently. Of how in his dream he had floated into a large unlit cavern and there saw Job smitten by boils sitting with his three false comforters. That cavern led into another, and that one into yet another, and back and back in time Dylan wandered in his dream, seeing one Biblical scene after another . . . Until he wandered right back to the darkest cave of all, the very first one, and there saw a man and a woman hand in hand. I doubt if this was a real dream but it does illustrate the direction of Dylan Thomas's imagination. A journey back to Paradise . . .'

p. 243. Brinnin on subscriptions: in an interview.

p. 243. Brinnin's invitation:

He was appointed director of the Poetry Centre on 4 April 1949. and wrote to Thomas on 14 April (from a letter).

p. 243. Thomas to Brinnin: *S.L.*

p. 243. Thomas to Laughlin: 13 October 1949. *S.L.*

p. 243. *The Plain Dealer*:

A letter from David Higham Associates to Thomas, 10 February 1945, says the B.B.C. will not pay more than seventy-five guineas for the script. But he was offered a further twenty-five guineas for acting in it. B.B.C. Archives.

p. 244. *The Trojan Women*:

B.B.C. memo from Royston Morley, 29 September 1947: 'Special acting version of Euripides *The Trojan Women* by Dylan Thomas. I have been in touch with Dylan Thomas about the above, and he is interested.' B.B.C. Archives.

p. 244. Auden approached: Royston Morley, in an interview.

p. 244. 'A favourite play':

Thomas to Robert McDermott, head of television drama, 6 January 1949. McDermott had written on 20 December, 'How allergic are you to Peer Gynt? I ask because we want to do a full-scale television production of it . . .' B.B.C. Archives.

p. 244. Thomas to his agent: 9 July 1949. Texas mss.

p. 245. 'Awful', 'wretched' script: Thomas to Davenport, 11 October 1949; to Margaret Taylor, 28 November 1949. Texas mss.

p. 245. Thomas to Davenport: Texas mss.

p. 245. Thomas to Margaret Taylor: Texas mss.

p. 245 fn. Thomas the clubman:

Letter from Mervyn Levy to Bill Read says Thomas was elected to the Savage on 10 March 1949; and was a member of the National Liberal Club from January 1947 to February 1949. Texas mss. Thomas to Davenport, 26 August 1948: 'And thank you very much for putting me up, with Parry as seconder, for the Savage. In a year, then, unless I am blackballed . . . I can give up the National Lavatory and be bad in worse company.' Texas mss.

p. 246. Swansea broadcast:

'Swansea and the Arts', B.B.C. Welsh Home Service, 24 October 1949. 'We speak from the Grove of Swansea. But if anyone in the deep damp caverns of the rustic dead, in some Welsh tenebrous regional, should have seen this programme announced in the Radio Tombs, turned on his badger's set, tuned in on a long-forgotten gravelength and caught that opening statement, let me hasten to tell him that he, alas, would hardly recognize the Grove at all . . .' B.B.C. Archives. A brief extract is in *Q.E.O.M.* as 'Wales and the Artist'.

p. 246. Thomas to Laughlin: 23 November 1949. *S.L.*

p. 246. The opening line: Watkins. 'Notes on Dylan Thomas'.

p. 246. 'White giant's thigh' worksheet:

Indiana mss. In the 'Three Poems' broadcast, 25 September 1950, Thomas said the poem was 'just written'.

p. 246. Marguerite Caetani:

The London meeting and £100 advance are mentioned in Thomas's letter to her, 2 November 1949. *S.L.*

p. 246. The finished letter: Thomas to Marguerite Caetani, 24 November 1949. *S.L.*

pp. 246–7. Thomas to Brinnin: 23 November 1949. *S.L.* Draft in Indiana mss.

p. 247. Thomas to Davenport: *S.L.*

p. 247. B.M.A. letter: Thomas to Mr Cellan-Jones, 10 January 1950. *S.L.*

pp. 247–8. The car-journey:

Mervyn Levy and Bernard Gutteridge, in interviews; Dan Davin, *Closing Times*, pp. 135–8.

p. 248. Brinnin as agent:

Brinnin (p. 52) says: 'As agent for Dylan's first tour, I retained ten per cent of his payments. Actually, this amounted only to a token payment' (because of his outgoings on Thomas's behalf). Writing to David Higham on 1 December 1949, Thomas said:

> John Malcolm Brinnin has written to me at length, suggesting that he, as a wellknown lecturer, literary journalist, etc., in the States, and as Director of the Poetry Centre ... should become my secretary and agent for my stay there ... He said that the Lecture Agencies, which prefer novelists anyway, have nowhere near his own acquaintanceship with the institutions, etc., which like poets, and would take, for their services, anything up to forty per cent. He, although he would do it for friendship, as a fellow poet (dear God!), cannot afford to do so, & would have to ask [a percentage] of what I make on my appearances as a reader and lecturer. I cabled back & agreed ... believing that Brinnin will really do a good job for me. (I hear extremely well of him from Laughlin) ...

Texas mss. The *S.L.* version (p. 340) has been more heavily cut.

p. 248. Thomas to Brinnin: 23 November 1949. *S.L.*

p. 249. Thomas to Laughlin: 23 November 1949. *S.L.*

p. 249. Thomas to Margaret Taylor: Texas mss.

p. 249. Glyn Jones: *The Dragon Has Two Tongues*, p. 197.

p. 249. The telegram: B.B.C. Archives.

p. 249. Thomas to Davenport: 30 January 1949 (error for 1950), Texas mss.

p. 250. A posh dentist:

In an undated (and unpublished) letter from the Savage Club, Thomas told Caitlin that his visa and the bank were taken care of; said he was to visit a 'posh dentist'; and asked her to collect and send him his suit from the cleaners so that he could be in a Picasso play. The play was *Desire Caught by the Tail*. Thomas appeared in it at the Rudolf Steiner Hall, Baker Street, in a 'theatrical evening' organized by the Institute of Contemporary Arts. Reviewed by Alan Dent, *News Chronicle*, 18 February 1950.

p. 250. Radio talk:

'A Visit to America', recorded in Swansea, 5 October 1953, broadcast posthumously (B.B.C. Welsh Home Service) 30 March 1954. Printed in *Q.E.O.M*. A duplicated B.B.C. typescript, privately owned, has variants, in the form of corrections and additions in Thomas's hand; e.g. the sentence, 'And there shiver and teeter also, meek and driven, those British authors' etc. (*Q.E.O.M*., p. 65) inserts between 'driven' and 'those' the words 'their little eyes lost and rabbit-scared behind bi-focal glasses steamed over by the smoke of countless cocktail parties'.

p. 250 etc. Thomas in New York:

Unless otherwise stated, the chronology and basic information are Brinnin's.

p. 251. The 'Ballad' interpreted:

William York Tindall, *A Reader's Guide to Dylan Thomas*. Presumably what Thomas said was 'fuck', but Tindall used a dash instead, and now cannot remember what it signified. Tindall wrote (p. 302) that Thomas 'looked like, and acted the part of, an amorous Volkswagen, driven by Harpo Marx. Chasing the girls round the room, he blew down their dickies. Everyone, wives and husbands alike, took this in good part, except John Malcolm Brinnin, who sat frowning in a corner. Thomas was a poet, after all, and we were academic bourgeoisie, except John Malcolm Brinnin. It was plain, moreover, that the harmless poet, doing his best, was doing what he thought expected of him or else was hiding shyness under what he thought its opposite.'

p. 251. 'Out of the mists':

Reel 12 of Dylan Thomas tapes at the Poetry Centre. These tapes consist of fragments apparently arbitrarily linked, and with no index or check-list. Some items, including this one, can be dated by internal evidence.

p. 251 fn. Thomas at Llanelli:

*Llanelli Star*, 13 December 1952, 'Wales, by Dylan Thomas. In an address to Llanelli Little Theatre at the British Legion buildings, Vauxhall, last week'. The newspaper printed a verbatim report of Thomas's opening remarks, presumably taken down in shorthand.

p. 252. Thomas to parents: 26 February 1950. *S.L.*

p. 252. Thomas to Caitlin:

25 February 1950. FitzGibbon (pp. 355–7) prints most of it.

p. 252. *Reuben, Reuben*:

De Vries's Thomas-figure was Gowan Glamorgan McGland, with Irish and Scots blood, but mainly Welsh. 'How' (speculates a character) 'could a man who mumbled so in conversation read with such ethereal magic on the public platform and into phonograph mikes?' And, 'He was a rogue and we both knew that.'

pp. 252–3. At the Hymans': Brinnin, pp. 30–31.

p. 253. Gill's account:

*Here at the New Yorker*, p. 248. Gill defends it (in a letter): 'My account came directly from Stanley Hyman, very soon after the event. Stanley was amused that it was the floor-plan of the old house they were living in at the time that made the pursuit of Shirley possible – a circular steeplechase. Three less Grecian-urn-like people it would be hard to imagine.'

p. 253. Further details from Brinnin: in an interview.

p. 253. Brinnin on Yale: pp. 32–3.

p. 253–4. Norman Pearson: in an interview.

p. 254. Diary:

About five inches by seven, bound in tartan cloth. Texas mss. It was presumably provided by Brinnin; the only entries in Thomas's hand are phone numbers, addresses and occasional reminders of appointments.

p. 254. Telegram: Mt Holyoke files.

pp. 254–7. Thomas at Mt Holyoke:

Interviews with Joseph McG. Bottkol, Ben Reid, Marianne Brock, Peter Viereck.

p. 255. University of California recording:

Issued by Caedmon Records as part of 'An Evening with Dylan Thomas', CDL 51157. Apart from Thomas's two formal recording sessions for Caedmon, in 1952 and 1953, Caedmon's material is drawn from local recordings of Thomas talking and reading, and from the B.B.C.

pp. 255–6. Brinnin on Mt Holyoke: pp. 34–5.

p. 256. Holyoke story challenged:

'A Poet's Corpse: or, 'Me and Dylan', by Dorothy Van Ghent, *Centaur*, Spring 1956.

p. 256. Gray Burr: in an interview.

pp. 257–8. Thomas at Amherst: Armour Craig, in an interview.

p. 258. Caitlin: *Leftover*, p. 53.

p. 258. Brinnin's cable: Mt Holyoke files.

pp. 258–9. Introductory remarks: See note to p. 43.

p. 259. Thomas to Margaret Taylor: 18 June 1950. Texas mss.

p. 259 fn. List of poets: Thomas to Margaret Taylor: 18 June 1950.

p. 260. Introducing Hardy: Caedmon CDL 51157, op. cit.

p. 260. At the Poetry Centre: Reel 10 of Centre's tapes.

p. 260. 'No tepid don':

Caedmon CDL 53006 (2c), part of the 'Complete recorded stories and humorous essays' series, 'A Few Words of a Kind', recorded at M.I.T., Cambridge, Mass., by a local radio station, WGBH.

p. 260. 'Don't ask me any questions', etc.: ibid.

p. 260. Thomas to Margaret Taylor: 18 June 1950. Texas mss.

p. 261. Dartmouth College magazine: *The Dartmouth*, 14 May 1952.

p. 262. Bryn Mawr fee: College files.

p. 262–3. At Cornell:

David Daiches, in the *Adam* Memorial Number, and an interview.

p. 263–4. Thomas to Caitlin:

Extracts from letters in FitzGibbon, pp. 357–8.

p. 264. Thomas's itinerary:

Louise Baughan Murdy's thesis (later a book), *Sound and Sense in Dylan Thomas's Poetry*, contains a detailed itinerary of Thomas's four visits to the U.S.A.; it has a few omissions and minor errors. FitzGibbon prints it as an Appendix.

p. 264. Ray West:

'Dylan Thomas in Iowa 1951' (error for 1950), *San Francisco Fault*, October 1972.

p. 264. Teeth:

Thomas knew they were unsightly; Glyn Jones (my p. 249) saw him cover his mouth. In Peter de Vries's *Reuben, Reuben*, his Thomas-figure, McGland, suffers 'the agonies of hell' worrying about his teeth, and commits suicide when he hears he must have them all out. This is an odd fancy to get from nowhere. De Vries says (in a letter): 'An interview with Dylan Thomas, I think in the [New York] *Sunday Times Book Review*, in which he said something like, "Say I'm balding and toothlessing", put me on the track of his probably acute dental problems. He was ostensibly satirizing American journalese which makes verbs of nouns and adjectives, but publicly betraying an actual private obsession – so I surmise. It was only a step, or leap, of the imagination to make me suspect what a horror terminal tooth loss might be to a chronic womanizer, something tantamount to emasculation . . We've all suffered enough in a dentist's chair to know that dental can become mental, and hindsight makes me seriously suspect clairvoyance in my divination of Dylan's teeth woes and anxieties vis-à-vis McGland's.'

p. 265. Howard Moss: in an interview.

p. 265. Radio producer: Thomas to E. J. King Bull, 26 December 1946. Texas mss.

p. 265. Davin: *Closing Times*, p. 133.

p. 267. Thomas to Caitlin, after Berkeley:

5 April 1950. FitzGibbon prints some of it, p. 358.

p. 267. Thomas to Caitlin, from Vancouver:

7 April 1950. FitzGibbon quotes briefly, p. 359. Published in *McCall's*, February 1966.

p. 268. Moffat: letters to the author.

p. 269. Thomas to Ruth Witt-Diamant: 10 October 1951. Berg mss.

p. 269. Thomas at Pomona College: Ernest A. Strathmann of the college, in a letter.

p. 269. Thomas at Berkeley: Mrs B. J. Connors, in a letter.

pp. 269–70. The Berkeley appointment:

Professor Garff B. Wilson, who was the member of the committee, in a letter.

p. 270. Thomas at Vassar:

Interview with the secretary of Vassar, May 1975; *Vassar Chronicle*, 13 May 1950.

p. 270. Vernon Venable: in an interview.

p. 271. Thomas to Caitlin: Most was published in *McCall's*, op. cit.

p. 271 fn. *Picture Post* essay:

A Swansea friend who worked for the magazine, John Ormond (Thomas), says he asked Thomas to write something about Christmas; they had met by chance at Waterloo Station, and caught the same train. Thomas refused at first, saying he had written too much about Christmas, but accepted before the journey was over, for a fee of £50.

p. 271. John Gruen: *The Party's Over Now*, pp. 27–30.

p. 271. 'Liquid, libidinous': Thomas to Mr and Mrs Nims, 17 July, 1950. *S.L.*

p. 272. Thomas to Margaret Taylor: 18 June 1950. Texas mss.

p. 273. In love with 'Sarah', etc.: quoted by Brinnin, p. 71.

## 11. *No Money, Few Poems*

p. 274. Florence Thomas:

In the 1963 radio documentary, 'Dylan Thomas'.

p. 274. Earnings in America:

D.H.A. In a letter to Higham (21 July 1952. *S.L.*) Thomas mentions a figure of £1,907 earned in the U.S. in 1950. This was presumably after business expenses had been agreed; the file suggests these were about £1,000. Brinnin implies (p. 53) that tax was paid in the U.S., but now says (in a letter) that he does not think this happened. D.H.A. files suggest that only U.K. tax was paid.

p. 274. $800 for Caitlin: Brinnin, p. 64.

p. 274. Thomas to Margaret Taylor: Texas mss.

p. 275. Unwritten script:

A B.B.C. memo, 28 August 1950, refers to a thirty-minute feature, 'Letter to America', for which Thomas would have received fifty guineas. B.B.C. Archives.

p. 275. Seeking B.B.C. post:

Memo from Grisewood to the Head of Features, 18 August 1950. It is marked, 'After discussion with H.F. decided not to proceed'. B.B.C. Archives.

p. 275. Thomas to Caitlin: (1) 18 April 1950 (2) 7 May 1950. Copies at Texas.

p. 275. TV interview: B.B.C., 3 December 1975, op. cit.

p. 276. Thomas to friends: Mr and Mrs Nims; 17 July. *S.L.*

p. 276. Caitlin on Laugharne: *Leftover*, p. 15.

p. 276. Margaret Taylor: in an interview.

p. 276. Dressing for market: *Leftover*, p. 57.

p. 276. Davenport:

'Patterns of Friendship', B.B.C. radio, Home Service, 12 December 1961. B.B.C. Archives.

pp. 276–7. Fighting: Caitlin, B.B.C. televisoin, 3 December 1975.

p. 277. 'It seems extraordinary'; *Leftover*, pp. 60–61.

p. 277. 'Physical act': interviewed for B.B.C. Wales, 1977.

p. 277. 'Neither of us . . .' etc.: letter to the author.

p. 277. 'Weaknesses . . . no curbs': B.B.C.-TV, op. cit.

p. 277. 'I always danced . . .' B.B.C. Wales, op. cit.

p. 278. 'Did all I could . . .': *Leftover*, p. 35.

p. 278. Brinnin on Thomas, and 'Sarah's' visit: pp. 65–71.

p. 278. Heppenstall: *Four Absentees*, p. 180.

p. 279. Letters intercepted: Brinnin, pp. 72–3.

p. 279. At an hotel:

A B.B.C. producer's letter to Thomas, 3 November 1950, says, 'We learn that you've moved to the Cadogan Hotel.' B.B.C. Archives.

p. 279. 'Mad with rage', and Thomas on 'Sarah': B.B.C. Wales interview, op. cit.

p. 279. Thomas to Davenport: written from '*You know where*', signed '*You know who*'. Texas mss.

p. 279. 'In country heaven':

A version based on material in Texas mss was assembled by Vernon Watkins, and published in the *Weekend Telegraph* magazine, 16 December 1968, with an article by Douglas Cleverdon. Daniel Jones prints a slightly different version in *The Poems*. By Thomas's 25 September 1950 broadcast (reprinted in *Q.E.O.M.*), certain phrases from the draft poem had already been written (e.g. 'Bushes and owls blow out like candles'). One of the worksheets has a draft letter to 'Dear Sir' (probably a bank manager) dated 8 December 1950, on verso. Caedmon CDL 51281, '"In country heaven". The Evolution of a Poem', includes a reminiscence by Humphrey Searle – 'He told me he had two long poems in mind, one of which was about the shepherds on the moon watching the earth after it had been destroyed in an atomic war. And I asked him when he hoped to be able to finish the poem, but he said he didn't think he could finish it, which was very sad. He was feeling at this time rather depressed about his work.'

p. 280. Cleverdon to Thomas: 20 October 1950. B.B.C. Archives.

p. 280. The original *Milk Wood* plot:

Douglas Cleverdon, *The Growth of Milk Wood*, pp. 4–6; some of Cleverdon's information came from Gwen Watkins. The book gives a detailed history of the play, and includes much information about Thomas's relationship with the B.B.C.

p. 280. Cleverdon to Thomas, 5 December:

'. . . Sorry to keep on pestering you, but I am frightfully anxious to get the programme on the air. Moreover, I can get the whole thing paid for immediately the script is approved . . .' B.B.C. Archives.

p. 280. Thomas to Cleverdon: B.B.C. Archives. The 39-p. ms is assumed to be lost.

p. 281. The Iranian film:

Ronald Tritton, formerly head of B.P. information. The B.P. file has disappeared.

p. 281. Thomas to Caitlin: FitzGibbon, p. 363.

p. 281. 'Made me want to die':

Thomas to Caitlin, n.d FitzGibbon prints part, p. 365.

p. 281. Thomas to 'Sarah':

A typescript of the letter, which is apparently an extract only, is with FitzGibbon's copies of letters at Texas. *S.L.*, p. 351, headed 'To an American friend'.

p. 282. Thomas to Oscar Williams: 25 March 1951. *S.L.*

p. 282. 'Persian Oil':

Home Service, 17 April 1951, in a series called 'Report to the People'. B.B.C. Archives.

p. 282. Rose gardens: Margaret Taylor.

p. 282. Thomas to Princess Caetani:

*S.L.* 'Lament' was first published in November 1951, in her *Botteghe Oscure*.

p. 282. 'The Miner's Lament': Texas mss.

p. 282. One critic:

Michael Neill in *Notes and Queries*, February 1970. Another critic, David Holbrook, sees 'Lament' as 'mad with abandon to the joys of hate'. However interpreted, it has a streak of desperation.

p. 282 fn. Memo about proposed script:

Douglas Cleverdon to Maurice Brown, 13 March 1951. B.B.C. Archives.

p. 283. Thomas to Princess Caetani: *S.L.*

pp. 283–4. The acquaintance: Cecil Price, in the *Adam* Memorial Number.

p. 284. Kingsley Amis's account:

'An evening with Dylan Thomas', *Spectator*, 29 November 1957. Geoffrey Nicholson: *Sunday Times* Magazine, 29 January 1967. A draft of a talk (probably this one, because it refers to 'Ralph's', a Swansea second-hand bookshop), is in Texas mss. It begins: 'If only I hadn't scribbled this, with invisible ink, on pieces of wet wallpaper, & then left them in the sun, maybe I could understand them better.'

p. 285. Thomas to Eliot: Texas mss.

p. 285. Thomas to Gilliam: B.B.C. Archives.

p. 285. Anxious letters:

For example, an undated draft in Texas mss, probably of the period 1951–3:

Dear Sir, I am applying for a Grant because I most urgently need financial help so that I can go on working and be able to make enough money to keep myself and my family.

I am extremely badly in debt; these debts are pressing, and daily and horribly becoming more so; and it seems that I cannot think of anything else at all.

Surrounded by these debts, hurt and worried to despair in the very middle of them, and seeing and hearing my home crumble because of them, I cannot write, they come between me and everything else I do. And, as I can't write, I can't make any money, and so new day-by-day debts arise; and I can't see any good end to this, and I would be insane if I could.

Less and less do I seem able to concentrate on anything except these worries and despairs – (the writing of this letter is a kind of torture, my mind keeps jerking painfully away to the thoughts of writs and tradesmen's bills) – and more and more important grow these beastly little griefs to me . . . (the fragment ends).

p. 286. Thomas to Brinnin: 12 April 1951. *S.L.*

p. 286. Billy Williams:

His account of the outing is in *Laugharne and Dylan Thomas*, by Min Lewis, pp. 93–4. *Cf.* Brinnin's account, pp. 80–84.

p. 286. 'No strength of character . . .': Caitlin interviewed for B.B.C. Wales, 1977.

p. 286. Thomas to Williams: 28 May 1951. *S.L.*

pp. 286–7. Thomas to Caitlin: Unpublished letter. Copy in Texas mss.

p. 287. 'Happy' poems: Brinnin, pp. 96–7.

p. 288. Synopsis of 'Poem on his birthday':

Bill Read printed it, thinly disguised as a paraphrase, in *The Days of Dylan Thomas* (p. 149). It was also copied at second hand by Patricia Leong for her thesis written at Mt Holyoke, 'Dylan Thomas: the Creative Process'.

p. 288. 'Poem on his birthday' worksheets: Texas mss.

p. 288 fn. Dating 'Poem on his birthday':

Thomas sent it to Oscar Williams, in New York, with an undated letter (see p. 292) that must be ascribed to the autumn of 1951. He described the enclosure as 'a long new poem'. But if the poem *was* begun in 1949, when he was aged thirty-five, as in the synopsis, this would explain a remark in a letter to Margaret Taylor of 28 November 1949 (Texas mss.) that 'my poem is now eighty lines long'. The only poem of this length written in his last years was *P.O.H.B.*, with 108 lines. Further evidence in this direction is in a letter from Daniel Jones to a collector, now in the Texas mss, which refers to rough workings of the poem in Jones's possession. According to Jones's letter, Thomas stayed with him in Swansea in the autumn of 1949, when he was writing 'Poem on his birthday', and completed it during the visit, taking away a fair copy and leaving the worksheets with Jones. From this, one might conclude that the poem was written before the end of 1949; put aside because Thomas was dissatisfied with it; and rewritten in 1951. But in editing *The Poems*, Jones says unequivocally that a reference in the poem to a thirty-fifth birthday is 'misleading', and that it was 'written after Thomas's return from Persia, when he spent the summer [1951] in Laugharne'; he cites FitzGibbon as his authority. Jones has no comment to make on the discrepancy between this account and the one he gave to the collector.

p. 289. The notebook: Texas mss.

p. 289 fn. Holbrook:

'The Code of Night', in *Dylan Thomas: New Critical Essays*, pp. 182–9.

p. 291. Marged Howard-Stepney's son:

Mark S. Murray Threipland, who says (in a letter) that 'I only met Dylan Thomas on one occasion when, aged seventeen and having just passed my driving test, I drove my mother from Cilymaenllwyd [the family house at Llanelli] to Laugharne, where we met Thomas in the pub. I can remember being very disapproving about the evening, as Thomas had had a lot to drink, and my mother was not far behind him. I sat at a table sipping orange squash while they sat at the bar, and my mother borrowed money from me to pay for the drinks. I know that on another occasion Thomas came to Cilymaen-llwyd and read poetry to all the members of the staff, and everyone else my mother could gather . . . My mother was extremely generous to a number of people, one of them being Dylan Thomas. I suspect that she gave him quite a lot of money and that this would have been in cash and therefore unrecorded.'

p. 291. 'Dear Marged': Texas mss.

p. 292. Income details: D.H.A.

p. 292. Williams's sales: Indiana mss.

p. 292. Thomas to Williams: Indiana mss.

p. 292. Weeks to Williams: Indiana mss.

p. 293. Thomas to Ruth Witt-Diamant:

Berg mss. This is the letter already quoted from in Ch. 10.

p. 293. Thomas to Margaret Taylor:

N.d., but there are references to Elisabeth Lutyens's visit and Delancey Street. Texas mss.

p. 294. Elisabeth Lutyens at Laugharne:

In an interview, and *A Goldfish Bowl*, pp. 202–6.

p. 294. Thomas to Marguerite Caetani: *S.L.*, p. 363.

p. 294. Thomas to Brinnin: *S.L.*

p. 294. 'Say the Word':

A D.H.A. memo, 13 November 1951, says Thomas would like to do more quiz programmes.

p. 295. 'Floe's Tusks':

The title, and perhaps the idea for a story, seem to have originated in an obsessive play on two words that occur in a number of 'Poems on his birthday' worksheets, 'floes' (presumably ice floes) and 'tusks', e.g. the published line, 'On skull and scar where his loves lie wrecked', read at one stage, 'On scars and floes where his loves lie wrecked'. On another sheet are 'Flo's tusks' and 'floes' tusks'; the published poem has: 'And the tusked, ramshackling sea exults'. In the notebook, a second version of the notes for the story emphasizes the connection with Thomas's past life – Samuel Bennet, in a bed-sitting room 'near the Fulham Road, brushed off the Woodbine ash from the first scrawled page of "Love and the Sea, A Sonnet Sequence", and wrote down firmly, in violet ink, Flo's Tusks'.

p. 295. 'Such Things Do Happen': Texas mss.

## 12. *The Knot*

p. 296. Thomas to Brinnin: 3 December 1951. *S.L.*

p. 296. Student at Sarah Lawrence: in an interview.

p. 296. Caitlin quoted: *Leftover*, pp. 59; 62–3.

p. 297. 'Stuffed shirts': Brinnin, p. 107.

p. 297. Nelson Algren to Ellen Borden Stevenson:

Texas mss. A later account of the evening by Algren, when he reviewed Brinnin in the *Chicago Sun-Times* ('An Intimate Look at Dylan Thomas', 1 January 1956), gave a different emphasis:

> 'Anyhow,' I told him, 'I once knew a man named Champaign who drank nothing but beer.'

'I knew a man named Beers who drank nothing but champagne,' Thomas assured me.

I decided I liked him whatever his trade, and we went forth in search of either beer or champagne. We found both.

I never saw Thomas after that night. But I began listening to his recordings that I had not till then heard. Before he died it was at last borne in upon me that I had been greatly privileged. I had been with a great man, the only great man I had ever known.

I had also been with a babyish self-indulgent fellow carrying too much weight for his size. . . .

p. 297. Professor Alfred: in an interview.

p. 297. Oscar Williams and Caitlin's poems:

There are references in correspondence between them. Harvard mss.

pp. 297–8. Rose Slivka: in an interview.

p. 298. 'A feebler Soho': Thomas to Caitlin, 25 February 1950.

pp. 298–9. The *Time* interview:

Mrs Barrett, now a novelist, is Irving Berlin's daughter. She says (in an interview) that Thomas told her to put away her notebook, so she had to rely on memory and frequent trips to the cloakroom where she could make hurried notes. Her account was published in *The Reporter*, 27 April 1954.

p. 300 etc. Holdridge and Mantell:

In interviews; Barbara Holdridge, 'Dylan as He Was', *New York*, the Sunday *Herald Tribune* magazine, 12 January 1966.

p. 300. 'Blue thunder', *Leftover*, p. 59.

p. 301. Caedmon recording: CDL 51002.

p. 301. University of Vermont:

Samuel N. Bogorad, 'I Remember Dylan Thomas', *Centaur* (University of Vermont), Spring 1956.

p. 301. Skidmore College: from an interview.

p. 301. University of California: *Occident*, student magazine, Spring 1952.

p.302. University of Utah:

A student who was present, Marjorie Adix, reported the session from memory without notes, and her account has been widely reprinted (including Tedlock, pp. 60–66). Like so many recollections of Thomas, it has an odd discrepancy. Thomas is made to declare that his father 'went blind and was very ill before he died'. But in April 1952, D. J. Thomas was still alive. Marjorie Adix says (letter to the author) she is 'astonished to find his father had not died by then. I can only suggest that maybe, for Thomas, he had.'

p. 302. Engagements book:

This is a 'year book' in a red binding, supplied with dates but not the days of the week. Like the 1950 diary, it seems to have been used only for engagements and addresses. But Thomas continued to use it, intermittently, for brief entries when he returned to Britain. Texas mss.

p. 302. Penniless in Arizona: Brinnin, p. 123.

p. 302. Thomas to Jones: *S.L.*

p. 302. Llewelyn's fees:

Thomas to Brinnin from San Francisco, 4 April 1952. *S.L.* At the back of the engagements book Thomas has written: '£100 unpaid for two previous terms. £50 for present term. And I must pay another term (£50) *at least* before Ll. will be taken back after this holiday *which is coming very soon*. Minimum = £200. But £250 wd. be better.'

p. 303. Rose Slivka, Alastair Reid: in interviews.

p. 303. Poetry Centre tape:

Reel 7. No date is shown, but it can only have been 1952. On the 1950 trip, the last Poetry Centre reading was more than two weeks before he left America. On the April–June 1953 trip, Thomas read at the Centre ten days before he left, by air.

p. 304. 'Poems 1934–1950': D.H.A. memo, September 1951.

p. 304. £100 for Preface: D.H.A.

p. 304. Dent 'howling': Higham to Thomas, 2 May 1952. D.H.A.

p. 304. Party at Margaret Taylor's: the engagements book. Texas mss.

p. 304. Thomas to Higham: 28 June 1952. *S.L.*

p. 305. How *Prologue* began:

Brinnin's account, pp. 94–5, places the conversation at Laugharne in the summer of 1951. This seems more than a year too soon. They met in London in September 1952. But Brinnin dismisses this date. He says (in a letter) that 'I may have been shown an early version of the poem, because I definitely did not discuss it anywhere else with Dylan but in the confines of his little shack. It's possible that my account may be coloured by thoughts on later readings of the poem, but my memory of the poem itself – on long, legal-sized pages held together by a straight pin – remains clear.'

p. 305. Thomas to Williams: 3 March 1953. Indiana mss.

p. 305. Cat and mouse: B.M. mss.

p. 305. Thomas to Bozman: *S.L.*

p. 305. Thomas to Fry: 16 February 1953. *S.L.*

p. 305. Davenport: *Vogue*, August 1955.

p. 305. 'Llareggub':

Thomas to Marguerite Caetani, (about) October 1951. *S.L.* p. 363.

p. 305. Thomas to Caetani: ibid.

p. 306. 'Spoon River Anthology': correspondence in B.B.C. Archives.

p. 306. The five-guinea scheme:

B.B.C. memo from Head of Copyright, 2 September 1952. Thomas proposed it in a letter to Cleverdon, 23 or 24 August 1952: '... If the B.B.C. could pay me a weekly sum (not less than £10 a week) for the period of six weeks [which he said he needed to complete the play], I could shove all other small jobs aside and work on "Llareggub" only ... I could devote my time, with the greatest enjoyment, to writing imaginative full-length things for the radio if I could be paid a weekly wage. Otherwise, it's bits and pieces for me all the time ...' Cleverdon told the B.B.C. management that 'I have sufficient confidence in [Thomas] to guarantee the Corporation (by deduction from my salary) against any loss that may be incurred' B.B.C. Archives. B.B.C. memos show Thomas in a weak position when it came to negotiating fees. The B.B.C. already had the first half of the play. They decided they could use this even if no more script was forthcoming, and pay him forty-five guineas. But all they would pay him on account of this first half was fifteen guineas.

p. 306 fn. 'Paper and Sticks':

Thomas to E. F. Bozman, 10 September 1952 – 'Proofreading the Collected Poems, I have the horrors of "Paper & Sticks" on page 116.' *S.L.* Corrected proofs of *C.P.*: Texas mss.

p. 307. W. R. Rodgers: reviewing FitzGibbon in the *Sunday Times*, 17 October 1965.

p. 307. Philip Toynbee: 'A Great Poet', 11 November 1952.

p. 307. Cyril Connolly: 'The Boyhood of Merlin', 11 November 1952.

p. 307. G. S. Fraser: 'Craft and Sullen Art', 29 November 1952.

p. 307. William Empson: 'Books in General', *New Statesman*, 15 May 1954.

p. 307. Thomas to Spender: 9 December 1952. *S.L.*

p. 308. Llanelli interview:

'Poet likes Llanelli', *Llanelli Star*, 13 December 1952. 'Mr Thomas is a friendly man, with the pride and humility of a real poet.'

p. 308. Thomas to Marguerite Caetani: 6 November 1952. *S.L.*

p. 308. Appeal to Spender: letter from Thomas, 22 November 1952. *S.L.*

p. 308. Marged's difficulties: interview with her former solicitor.

p. 309. Caitlin to Oscar Williams: 9 February 1952, error for 1953. Harvard mss.

p. 309. Thomas to Ellen: Texas mss.

p. 309. The affectionate doggerel has not been published. Copy, Texas mss.

p. 309. Nancy's illness: Gwevril Dawkins.

p. 309. D.J.'s illness:

Thomas to 'Mr Evans', about a dinner he cannot attend, 3 December 1952: 'My father, who lives in the same village, has been blind and very ill for a long time; but, in the last few days, his condition has grown desperate . . .' Wales mss.

pp. 309–10. Aneirin Talfan Davies:

At the Dylan Thomas Summer School, Swansea University College, 1974.

p. 310. D.J.'s failing sight:

Thomas's statement (to Mrs Evans and others) that his father was blind seems to have been exaggeration. The doctor who attended D.J. says his sight failed only at the end.

p. 310. Thomas to Fred Janes: 5 January 1953. *S.L.*

p. 310. Thomas to Watkins: *L.V.W.*

p. 310. Thomas to Williams: *S.L.*

p. 310. Higham to Thomas: 8 January 1953. D.H.A.

p. 310. Marged's death:

Reports in *Llanelli Star*, 24 January, 31 January and 7 February 1953; interview with Margaret Taylor.

pp. 310–11. Boat House purchase:

Margaret Taylor says that contracts for Marged's purchase of the Boat House were ready to be exchanged when she died, and that the deal might have already gone through had it not been for delays in Laugharne.

Under the borough's ancient charter, all property in the town must be offered to the Corporation. It is only a formality, but Laugharne is fond of its formalities. Mrs Taylor believes that the Boat House was not offered, and that this held up the transaction. If so, Thomas was the victim of an episode worthy of *Milk Wood*. But Marged's former solicitor insists there was 'hardly any negotiation'.

p. 310. In New York:

One of his hearers was the house-manager at the Poetry Centre. Later her husband was Mark, Marged Howard-Stepney's son. Mrs Murray Threipland says in a letter, 'We were all sorry for [Dylan] as the house obviously meant a lot to him. Seven years later I married the "bloody woman's" son and met the "bastards".'

p. 311. Nancy's husband: Thomas to Brinnin, 18 March 1953. *S.L.*

p. 311. Rationalizing Thomas's affairs:

A D.H.A. memo of 23 February 1953, says, '... D.H. intends to try to put his affairs on an even keel. [Dylan] is to let us have a list of his debts – he says that his local debts amount to about £200 now. Outside of local debts he says he has only one, of £100 he borrowed ... He is anxious that some provision should be made ahead for the schooling of his two elder children. The eldest's fees are £150 a year and the other one's will be the same probably. His other large debt is the income tax one, and some provision would have to be made to pay this off and keep enough to pay regularly in future. When Dylan sends the information, we'll see what can be devised ...'

p. 311. Collected stories: Thomas to Bozman, 31 March 1953. *S.L.*

p. 311. 'Too raw': Thomas to Higham, 6 April 1953. Texas mss.

p. 311. Fairy tales:

A contract, with £50 on signature, was signed in February 1953. D.H.A.

p. 311. Thomas's earnings: D.H.A.

p. 311. *Skin Trade* payment:

New American Library to Thomas, 9 May 1952. Indiana mss.

p. 311. 'Prologue' worksheets:

Thomas to Williams, 27 February 1953. *S.L.*; 3 March 1953, Indiana mss.

p. 311. 'P.O.H.B.' worksheets: receipt in Indiana mss.

p. 312. Davenport: the 1963 radio documentary, 'Dylan Thomas'

p. 312. Thomas to Fry: *S.L.*

p. 314. America: D.H.A. memo, 23 February: 'He isn't going to America.'

p. 314. Making arrangements: Thomas to Brinnin, 18 March 1953. *S.L.*

## 13. *Running Faster*

p. 315. Thomas's mother: to Colin Edwards.

p. 315. Thomas to Williams: Indiana mss.

p. 315. 'Fell like a stone': Min Lewis, *Laugharne and Dylan Thomas*, p. 94.

p. 316. Thomas to Brinnin: *S.L.*

p. 316. Thomas to Caitlin: 20 April 1953. Unpublished. Copy at Texas.

p. 316 fn. Ingenious critic: J. S. Dugdale, Brodie's *Notes on Under Milk Wood*, p. 52.

p. 317. Mrs Gardner Cox: in an interview.

p. 317. *Milk Wood* reading: Brinnin, pp. 150–51.

p. 317. Recording *Milk Wood*:

The Caedmon tapes are CDL 52005 (1c and 2c). Caedmon's programme note says that 'it owes its existence to the chance thought someone had just before curtain time of setting up the little tape recorder that was at hand and laying a microphone on the floor at the centre of the stage'. Brinnin says (in a letter) it was definitely not an afterthought.

p. 317. *Milk Wood* and the B.B.C.:

The play was first broadcast on 25 January 1954, on the Third Programme. Behind the scenes there was much agonizing over whether parts of it were fit to be heard. Cleverdon fought fiercely against censorship, arguing that the play 'should be acceptable in uncut form to any reasonable Third Programme listener. The humour is broad but never dirty; and the whole work is on a plane of poetic imagination which would entitle it to disregard the pettifogging hypocrisies of those who never listen to the Third, but whose hostility would be encouraged rather than placated by timidity on our part . . . To leave Dylan's script untouched, as the work of a major poet of our time, is a defensible position; but to cut half a dozen sentences leaves us open to attack for not cutting two dozen or more.' Among the phrases that were threatened but which survived were 'Parlez-vous jig-jig' and 'let me shipwreck in your thighs'. Apparently the only cuts that were finally made were: 'wriggle her roly poly bum' (Dent edition, p. 43); 'strip her to the nipples and the bees' (p. 60), and 'draws circles of lipstick round her nipples' (p. 78). These were referred to ever afterwards at Broadcasting House as the 'two tits and a bum'. Third Programme reception in Wales was poor at that time, and the programme was barely audible in Laugharne. A senior B.B.C. official in Wales wrote to London that it was 'not a programme for the Welsh Home Service', or indeed for any 'family or home listening'. But the Controller of the Third told

Cleverdon it was 'the best radio production I have ever heard'. B.B.C. Archives.

p. 317 etc. Liz Reitell: in an interview (1975); letters to Bill Read, Texas mss.

p. 319. Thomas to Caitlin: FitzGibbon, p. 387.

pp. 319–20. Opera proposal:

Telegram from Sara Caldwell, director of the Opera Workshop, to Thomas. Texas mss.

p. 320. Thomas to Llewelyn: 23 June 1953. Texas mss.

p. 321. Recording session: Issued by Caedmon, CDL 51018.

p. 321. 'Miles of orange peel': Thomas to Oscar Williams, 22 June 1953. *S.L.*

p. 322. *John O'London's* article: 'Poet in the Boat House', 7 August 1953.

p. 322. Draft of letter: Texas mss.

p. 322. *Milk Wood* revisions: Texas mss, which have many worksheets.

p. 322. Llangollen:

The radio talk was broadcast 5 June 1951, Welsh Home Service; reprinted *Q.E.O.M.* Some of Thomas's notes are in Texas mss, mixed up with *Milk Wood* worksheets.

p. 322. Stravinsky to Thomas: 22 June 1953. Texas mss.

p. 322 and fn. 'Speaking Personally':

Later reprinted as 'A Story' in *Prospect* (in the U.S.: 'The True Story' in *Skin Trade*). A few worksheets are in Texas mss; more in Wales mss. The producer, D. J. Thomas, was previously a master at Swansea Grammar School, and a colleague of D. J. Thomas, Thomas's father. The memos: B.B.C. Archives.

p. 323. Caitlin at Brown's:

Rollie McKenna, who was staying at Laugharne, in an interview.

pp. 323–4. 'Elegy' worksheets and other notes: Texas mss.

p. 323. Thomas to Jones: *S.L.*

p. 325. Stravinsky to Thomas: 26 August 1953. Texas mss.

p. 325. Brinnin quoted: p. 172.

p. 326. 'A Visit to America':

This, and the Laugharne talk, are in *Q.E.O.M.*

p. 326. At the cinema:

Florence Thomas, the 1955 interview; the family doctor, in an interview.

p. 327. Leaving Laugharne:

Mrs Thomas, quoted by Ethel Ross, *Gower*, No. 16, 1964.

p. 327. Plane ticket: Brinnin, pp. 184–5.

p. 327. FitzGibbon: pp. 390–91.

p. 327. Philip Burton: *Adam* Memorial Number.

p. 327 fn. Richard Burton: *Richard Burton . . . A Biography*, pp. 174–5.

p. 328. Margaret Taylor: in an interview.

p. 328. The lost script:

Cleverdon's *The Growth of Milk Wood*, p. 35; *Bookseller*, 12 and 19 March 1966. Caitlin contended in the High Court that the script (which Cleverdon sold to the Times Book Company in 1961) belonged to her husband's estate. The action failed.

p. 328. At the air terminal: Cordelia Locke.

## 14. *Alcohol and Morphia*

p. 329. Caitlin: B.B.C. television, 3 December 1975.

pp. 332–3. 'Poetry and the Film':

Part of the transcript was published by Gotham Book Mart, 1972. Arthur Miller was on the panel. The account in Brinnin (p. 198) flatters Thomas, if the transcript is a fair guide.

p. 333. At City College: Professor Samuel Middlebrook.

p. 335. *Skin Trade* ms: Harvard mss.

p. 335. In Cornwall: Wyn Henderson.

p. 337. 'Death and Triangles': Thomas to Pamela, 9 May 1934. *S.L.*

p. 337 fn. Murphy: letter to the author.

p. 339. David Lougée: in an interview.

p. 340. Edith Sitwell:

Letter to Sir Maurice Bowra, 25 November 1953. *Edith Sitwell. Selected Letters.*

p. 340. Caitlin: *Leftover*, pp. 79, 80.

p. 340. Obituary: *The Times*, 10 November 1953.

p. 341. Thomas's effects: papers at D.H.A.

## *Postscript*

p. 342. Edith Sitwell: quoted in *Time*, 30 May 1955.

p. 342. Heppenstall: *Four Absentees*, p. 170.

p. 342. Brinnin to Davenport: copy typescript from Arthur Calder-Marshall.

p. 342. Reavey to Davenport: ibid.

p. 343. Caitlin: *Leftover*, p. 50.

p. 343. Davenport: *Vogue*, August 1955.

p. 343. Mrs Devas: *T.F.F.*, p. 274.

p. 343. Three children:

Llewelyn (b. 1939) went to Harvard and then joined J. Walter Thompson, the advertising agency, in London, where he became a successful copywriter. Later he worked for the same company in Australia; he married and had a child. Colm (b. 1949) was at an Australian university, and, like his brother, has settled in that country; he is in Government service, and married in 1976. Aeronwy (b. 1943) lives in a London suburb and is married to a Welsh social worker. She met him in America, when he was on tour with a Welsh choir and she was reading her father's poetry in public. A book of her poems, *Later than Laugharne*, was published in 1976, under her married name of Aeronwy Thomas-Ellis. Her first child was born in 1975, and named Huw Dylan.

# *Bibliography*

Only the books I have read and used are listed here. The standard bibliographies are J. Alexander Rolph, *Dylan Thomas. A Bibliography* (Dent, 1956) and Ralph Maud, *Dylan Thomas in Print: A Bibliographical History* (Dent, 1970).


Thomas, Dylan, *Collected Poems 1934–1952* (Dent, 1952).

*18 Poems* (*Sunday Referee* and Parton Bookshop, 1934).

*Twenty-five Poems* (Dent, 1936).

*The Map of Love* (Dent, 1939).

*Portrait of the Artist as a Young Dog* (Dent, 1940).

*Deaths and Entrances* (Dent, 1946).

*The Doctor and the Devils* (Dent, 1953).

*Adventures in the Skin Trade* (Aldine Paperback, 1955).

*Under Milk Wood* (Dent, 1954).

*Quite Early One Morning* (Dent, 1954).

*A Prospect of the Sea* (Dent, 1955).

*Letters to Vernon Watkins* (Dent and Faber, 1957).

*The Beach at Falesa* (Cape, 1964).

*Twenty Years A-Growing* (Dent, 1964).

*Rebecca's Daughters* (Triton, 1965).

*Me and My Bike* (Triton, 1965).

*Selected Letters of Dylan Thomas* (ed. Constantine FitzGibbon) (Dent, 1966).

*Poet in the Making. The Notebooks of Dylan Thomas* (Dent, 1968.)

*Twelve More Letters by Dylan Thomas* (Turret Books, 1970).

*Dylan Thomas: The Poems* (ed. Daniel Jones) (Dent, 1971).

*Dylan Thomas: Early Prose Writings* (ed. Walford Davies) (Dent, 1971).

*The Death of the King's Canary* (with John Davenport) (Hutchinson, 1976).

(Date is that of first English edition, unless stated.)

Ackerman, John, *Dylan Thomas: His Life and Work* (O.U.P., 1964).

Barnes, Djuna, *Nightwood* (Faber, 1936).

Bevington, Helen, *When Found, Make a Verse of* (Simon and Schuster, 1961). U.S.A.

Brinnin, John Malcolm, *Dylan Thomas in America* (Dent, 1956).

Cleverdon, Douglas, *The Growth of Milk Wood* (Dent, 1969).

Cottrell, John and Cashin, Fergus, *Richard Burton . . . A Biography* (Arthur Barker, 1971).

Davies, Aneirin Talfan, *Dylan: Druid of the Broken Body* (Dent, 1964).

Davies, Walford (ed.), *Dylan Thomas: Early Prose Writings* (Dent, 1971).

Davin, Dan, *Closing Times* (O.U.P., 1975).

Devas, Nicolette, *Two Flamboyant Fathers* (Collins, 1966).

Dugdale, J .S., *Dylan Thomas. Under Milk Wood* (Notes on chosen English texts) (James Brodie, 1964).

Emery, Clark, *The World of Dylan Thomas* (Dent, 1971).

FitzGibbon, Constantine, *The Life of Dylan Thomas* (Dent, 1965).

Fuller, Jean Overton, *The Magical Dilemma of Victor Neuberg* (W. H. Allen, 1965).

Gill, Brendan, *Here at the New Yorker* (Random House, 1976). U.S.A.

Grigson, Geoffrey, *The Crest on the Silver* (Cresset Press, 1950).

Gruen, John, *The Party's Over Now. Reminiscences of the Fifties* (Viking Press). U.S.A.

Heppenstall, Rayner, *Four Absentees* (Barrie & Rockliff, 1960).

Holbrook, David, *Llareggub Revisited: Dylan Thomas and the State of Modern Poetry* (Bowes & Bowes, 1962).

Holroyd, Michael, *Augustus John.* Vol. II, *The Years of Experience* (Heinemann, 1975).

Johnson, Pamela Hansford, *Important to me. Personalia* (Macmillan, 1974).

Jones, Daniel (ed.), *Dylan Thomas: The Poems* (Dent, 1971).

*My Friend Dylan Thomas* (Dent, 1977).

Jones, Glyn, *The Dragon Has Two Tongues* (Dent, 1968).

Lewis, Min, *Laugharne and Dylan Thomas* (Dennis Dobson, 1967).

Lindsay, Jack, *Meetings with Poets* (Muller, 1968).

Lutyens, Elisabeth, *A Goldfish Bowl* (Cassell, 1972).

Maclaren-Ross, J., *Memoirs of the Forties* (Alan Ross, 1965).

Marland, Michael, *Dylan Thomas* (The Times Authors No. 3) (Times Newspapers, 1970).

Mathias, Roland, *Vernon Watkins* (University of Wales Press, 1974).

Maud, Ralph, *Entrances to Dylan Thomas' Poetry* (Scorpion Press, 1963).

(ed.) *Poet in the Making. The Notebooks of Dylan Thomas* (Dent, 1968).

McKellar, Peter, *Imagination and Thinking. A Psychological Analysis* (Cohen & West, 1957).

Parkin, Michael, *Fitzrovia and the Road to the York Minster* (Catalogue of an exhibition at the Parkin Gallery) (Michael Parkin Fine Art).

Ray, Paul C., *The Surrealist Movement in England* (Cornell University Press, 1971).

Read, Bill, *The Days of Dylan Thomas* (Weidenfeld, 1964).

Sitwell, Edith, *Selected Letters* (Macmillan, 1970).

Symons, Julian, *The Thirties. A Dream Revolved* (Cresset Press, 1960).

Tedlock, E. W. (ed.), *Dylan Thomas: The Legend and the Poet* (Heinemann, 1960).

Thomas, Caitlin, *Leftover Life to Kill* (Putnam, 1957).

*Not Quite Posthumous Letters to My Daughter* (Putnam, 1963).

Tindall, William York, *A Reader's Guide to Dylan Thomas* (Thames & Hudson, 1962).

Treece, Henry, *Dylan Thomas: 'Dog among the Fairies'* (Lindsay Drummond, 1949).

Welsh Arts Council, *Welsh Dylan*, 'Catalogue of an exhibition tc mark the twentieth anniversary of the poet's death' (1973).

# Index

*Note:* (P) = Poetry; (S) = Story